—————

COUNSELING AND THERAPY
FOR COUPLES

COUNSELING AND THERAPY FOR COUPLES

SECOND EDITION

LYNN L. LONG

Stetson University

MARK E. YOUNG

University of Central Florida

BROOKS/COLE
CENGAGE Learning

Australia • Brazil • Japan • Korea • Mexico • Singapore • Spain • United Kingdom • United States

BROOKS/COLE
CENGAGE Learning

**Counseling and Therapy for Couples,
Second Edition**

Lynn L. Long, Mark E. Young

Editor in Chief: Marcus Boggs

Senior Acquisitions Editor: Marquita
Flemming

Assistant Editor: Jennifer Walsh

Editorial Assistant: Samantha Shook

Technology Project Manager: Inna
Fedoseyeva

Marketing Manager: Caroline Concilla

Senior Marketing Communications Manager:
Tami Strang

Project Manager, Editorial Production:
Christy Krueger

Creative Director: Rob Hugel

Art Director: Vernon Boes

Print Buyer: Linda Hsu

Permissions Editor: Roberta Broyer

Production Service: Matrix Productions, Inc.

Production Editor: Aaron Downey

Copy Editor: Betty Duncan

Cover Designer: William Stanton

Cover Image: © Tamara Lischka/Images.com

Compositor: International Typesetting
and Composition

For product information and technology assistance, contact us at
Cengage Learning Customer & Sales Support, 1-800-354-9706

For permission to use material from this text or product,
submit all requests online **www.cengage.com/permissions**
Further permissions questions can be emailed to
permissionrequest@cengage.com

Library of Congress Control Number: 2006923925

ISBN-13: 978-0-495-00595-7

ISBN-10: 0-495-00595-9

Brooks/Cole
20 Davis Drive
Belmont, CA 94002
USA

Cengage Learning is a leading provider of customized learning solutions with
office locations around the globe, including Singapore, the United Kingdom,
Australia, Mexico, Brazil, and Japan. Locate your local office at
www.cengage.com/global

Cengage Learning products are represented in Canada by
Nelson Education, Ltd.

To learn more about Wadsworth, visit **www.cengage.com/brookscole**

Purchase any of our products at your local college store or at our preferred
online store **www.cengagebrain.com**

Printed in the United States of America

Prii 7 8 9 10 11   18 17 16 15 14

———

To Stan,
My husband and my heart's inspiration; and to Andrew Landis and Evan Landis,
my children and the joy of my life.
L. LONG

To Jora Defalco Young,
Far together.
M. YOUNG

CONTENTS

PREFACE

Although there are a growing number of unmarried couples in the United States, most of us are married. Despite the popularity of marriage, however, the divorce rate is high. There are about half as many divorces each year as there are marriages, and odds are only about 50/50 that a marriage will stay intact. As many as 1 in 7 marriages are considered "unhappy," and marital troubles are the precipitating factor in nearly 50% of admissions to mental hospitals. A troubled marriage is a significant factor in many homicides and violent relationships. Marital or couple discord can trigger or exacerbate severe emotional and behavioral problems of children. In fact, marital difficulties may be the most common problem that clients present when they seek any kind of therapy.

Despite the awareness of the prevalence of marital difficulties and the financial and emotional hardships that are created by divorce, the mental health community has not focused strongly on the couple relationship. Until recently, professionals have been affected by our culture's preoccupation with the individual, and training has focused almost entirely on working with a single client. There is, however, burgeoning interest in couples dynamics and couples counseling fueled by research from leading experts such as John Gottman and an awakening of a marriage movement in this country. Insurance companies often thwart a focus on couples relationships by failing to reimburse clinicians when the diagnosis is a pathological relationship (Kaslow, 1996). However, even when finances are not a factor, it has traditionally been much more difficult to bring both members of a couple to the therapy session. Usually, the wife called with a concern, and the husband, if he attended, participated with reluctance. Thus, a "gender barrier" has existed in couples therapy.

Another set of hurdles for couples counseling is cultural. Therapy of any kind carries a stigma—an implicit admission that you cannot handle your own problems. The intimacies of a couple relationship are some of the last things that people want to discuss, and these issues are magnified when it comes to couples from minority cultures. Therapists have not yet found an effective way to get minority couples to consider therapy when they experience problems. Part of the difficulty, of course, comes from language barriers, religious differences, and lack of faith in agencies and institutions. But there is also something else: The way that therapy is delivered and therapists themselves are geared to the majority culture. As more minority therapists are trained and the American population becomes more diverse, couples therapy must change to become more accessible to those who have traditionally been outside the mainstream. As we look around, though, we see reason for hope: Values are shifting, professionals are flocking to receive training in couples and family therapy, and professional literature is focusing more on couples therapy as a separate specialty. More programs include multicultural training as part of the curriculum, and more undergraduate and graduate courses address couples issues.

In the community at large, marriage and relationships are still valued institutions—after divorce, more than 80% remarry. Men and women have committed to be good partners and parents. More people are attending marriage encounter weekends, and more communication training and psychoeducational programs are being offered. The specialty of couples counseling will certainly continue to grow.

An Integrative Model

Research suggests that all mental health professionals are moving toward a more eclectic, or integrative, view of practice, with less adherence to particular schools (Long, Burnett, & Thomas, 2006; Young, 1992, Young, 2005). *Counseling and Therapy for Couples* proposes a single structure to bring together the major theoretical viewpoints for couples therapy. Because it is a synthesis, the integrative model of couples therapy is nothing new, nor is it intended to be followed slavishly. Rather, it is a structured way of learning couples therapy that will be especially helpful to those who are new to this work, whether they are just beginning as therapists or have been practicing for many years. The model has been extensively tested with graduate students in marriage and family therapy and with practicing clinicians. They tell us that it is easy to apply in actual therapy sessions and gives them a reference point so that they can develop plans for the next step. It encourages the therapist to identify workable goals and lead couples to agreement rather than spending time analyzing the personality of each individual in the couple. The model is a useful starting point or framework for anyone who is struggling or needs direction.

So that the reader will not think that this integrative approach is too extreme, let's take a look at the training of group therapists as an example. Although there are still group therapists who call themselves rational–emotive therapists or psychodynamic therapists, group work, for the most part, is currently practiced in an integrative, eclectic way, bringing in skills and knowledge from many realms. The theoretical base for group work includes the findings of small-group dynamics and group development. It also involves recognition of common curative factors (Young, 2005). In practice, nearly all group therapists use Rogerian listening skills, help groups break through developmental impasses, and encourage cohesion (a curative factor). These are important foundations regardless of the practitioner's theoretical learning.

In the same way, this integrative approach recognizes that couples therapy as a therapeutic modality has many different roots. For example, couples therapists who are interested in the specific critical incidents across the life span turn to theory and research from developmental psychology. Couples therapists also deal with crises caused by such stressors as infidelity, chemical dependency, sexual incompatibility, and domestic violence. Research and theory in these areas come from medicine, sociology, linguistics, and even religion. Our viewpoint is that, in the absence of a universally agreed-on paradigm, the integrative position gives therapists the best opportunity to recognize and use contributions from many fields and techniques from various theoretical positions.

Some Notes on Terminology

Use of the terms *counseling* and *therapy* have often been divisive issues in the mental health community. *Counseling* is often perceived as focusing on a relatively "normal" population; *therapy,* as focusing on more disturbed people. In reality, all counselors and therapists see both people with serious problems and people who are doing well but want to grow.

Therapists and counselors are not very different from each other. Until a few years ago, the American Association for Marriage and Family Therapy (AAMFT) was known as the American Association for Marriage and Family Counseling. Many members of the International Association of Marriage and Family Counselors (IAMFC) are also clinical members of AAMFT. We do not wish to enter into a political debate over these terms or endorse one organization over another. Therefore, we use the term *therapy* throughout this text.

The old standby term, *marriage counseling,* is fast fading from the therapist's lexicon because, today, many people who are in couples are not legally married. Commitment and marriage are no longer synonymous; many couples stay together for years and have long, intimate relationships without marriage. And many seek therapy to improve their relationship, even though neither may be contemplating a ceremony. For same-sex couples, marriage is not yet a legal alternative, but these couples can also benefit from therapy. For these reasons, we generally use the term *couple* instead of *marital* or *marriage.*

Goals and Organization of the Book

When we began this book, we had the following goals in mind:

1. To help readers recognize that the couple is a unique and distinct system different from the family, the individual, or the group and requires specific methods of assessment and treatment
2. To offer readers a simple, practical way of working with couples that does not force them to accept any single theoretical orientation but allows them to choose strategies based on a simple, understandable model
3. To include wide coverage of topics in couples therapy so that readers are exposed to the key issues and the varieties of couples with whom they will be working
4. To provide active learning opportunities in the text through case examples and role-play scenarios for either reflection or classroom work
5. To examine the theoretical basis behind various therapy strategies and to make readers aware of the sociological forces affecting couples today

With these goals, we decided to write a book that would consist of three parts offering extensive coverage of virtually every aspect of principles, evaluation, treatment strategies and special challenges. Part One, "Principles, Evaluation, and Planning," deals with the knotty problem of how to draw from theoretical bases of practice and develop a treatment plan using our integrative model of couples therapy. Chapter 1 looks at the couple as a unique focus in therapy and the developmental processes that must be considered. Chapters 2 and 3 provide an overview of the foundational schools of thought in marriage and family therapy and illustrate the key systems concepts.

We explain the integrative model in Chapter 4 as one alternative for solving the dilemma of overemphasizing technique versus becoming locked into a single theory's viewpoint. Although the integrative model allows for the use of a range of therapeutic techniques drawn from the various schools of family therapy, we help readers select the methods and techniques that they will find the most effective for working with specific clients. For pedagogical reasons, the model identifies five stages in the therapy process with couples. Although the model is more circular than steplike, students and therapists can use the model to determine where they are in the process with a particular couple and what needs to be done next.

Chapters 5 and 6 are linked. Chapter 5 examines various assessment methods, including paper-and-pencil tests. Chapter 6 takes aim at the difficult issue of identifying key goals and planning treatment for couples using the integrative model.

Part Two, "Common Issues in the Life of the Couple," takes a close-up look at the major issues that couples face. Chapter 7 provides in-depth practical information on creating and implementing effective treatment strategies, both verbal and nonverbal. Much emphasis is given to the creative arts as methods of treatment for a wide variety of presenting issues. In Chapter 8, we address the important issue of couples communication—why it becomes so confused and how it can be fixed. Also, we focus on psychoeducational training. Next, problems in sexuality and intimacy are covered in Chapter 9. In Chapter 10, we examine identifying and healing conflict within the relationship, from arguments to domestic violence. Chapter 11 focuses on the issues associated with divorcing and how couples can learn to navigate this passage. In Chapter 12, we describe various types of extramarital affairs and the means for treating them.

Part Three, "Special Challenges," examines particular types of couples who are facing long-term strains and living alternative lifestyles. These include couples with alcohol problems (Chapter 13), couples in blending or stepfamilies (Chapter 14), and same-sex couples (Chapter 15).

Acknowledgments

Writing together is a special kind of relationship. This book is a true collaboration, with each of us providing an equal amount of ideas and sweat. We wish to extend our thanks to our students and our clients who have been our greatest teachers. Our students in the marital, couple, and family counseling/therapy department at Stetson University and students in the Counselor Education program at the University of Central Florida have provided critical feedback on the model. We also want to thank clinicians and experts who used and evaluated the integrative model, especially Joanne Vogel, director of the Stronger Marriages, Stronger Families Program at the University of Central Florida and faculty member; and Andrew Daire who cowrote the initial federal grant that provides couples with free counseling services in the Community Counseling Clinic at UCF. Special thanks go to Jacqui Williams and Donna Schick of Stetson University for helping prepare the manuscript. Also, we are fortunate to have the expertise of Brigid Noonan, Elizabeth O'Brien, and Joanne Vogel who cowrote three of the chapters in this book. Judith Burnett and Valorie Thomas helped refine many of the interventions that we discussed in the sexuality chapter.

We wish to thank Lynne Batten Puder, Alice Wells Burden, Pamela Northrup Shaw, and Suzanne Richard Thomas and their spouses for their valuable input on relationships and the ability to celebrate life and play together as couples.

Many experts reviewed this manuscript including Montserrat Casado, University of Central Florida; Don Hebbard, Oklahoma Christian University; Susan S. Hendrick, Texas Tech University; Nina Spadero, West Virginia University; and David Spruill, Louisiana State University. We thank them for their valuable comments.

Finally, we want to mention our spouses, Stan Long and Jora DeFalco Young, who loved us and supported us through this process.

Lynn Long
Mark Young

ONE

PRINCIPLES, EVALUATION, AND PLANNING

1

The Couple as a Unique System

KEY CONCEPTS

- A couple is a unique dyad, separate from the individual and family but interacting with both of these systems.
- Couples pose special challenges for the counselor because of their history, of the possibility of antagonism, that they do not have an individual bond with the therapist, and that they are significantly caught in recurring negative communication cycles. Finally, couples are frequently quite distressed and near breaking up when they arrive in counseling.
- Couples face vertical stressors or issues that come from within the individual, such as a history of abuse. Couples are also influenced by their partners' similar or different cultural backgrounds and each individual's personality.
- Couples also face horizontal stressors coming from predictable and unpredictable life events, such as the birth of a child, the parenting of adolescents, and the death of family members.
- Couples face systems-level stressors, too. These are due to political, social, and other changes in the environment. Among these are increased life span, altered status of women, changes in options for birth control, and economic realities.
- The large number of cohabiting couples, the marriage movement, and the fight for gay marriage are three current social trends that influence the values of couples and couples' counselors.
- Couples must also deal with dynamic elements of the relationship such as boundaries, couple needs versus individual needs, family-of-origin expectations, dealing with conflicting roles and children, intimacy, and power.
- Couples must establish boundaries to ensure the integrity of the relationship. Boundaries are imaginary lines drawn around relationships that keep others at a distance. Some boundaries are rigid, others are porous, and still others are weak.
- One way of conceptualizing a couple's development is its ability to confront and master psychological tasks through the life span. This chapter presents

Wallerstein's seven tasks of marriage as a way of conceptualizing these challenges.

• Besides stressors and tasks, couples can also be understood in terms of their strengths. Healthy couple behaviors include the abilities to communicate, solve problems, avoid blaming, and share tasks equally.

• Healthy couples can see the other person's reality, have a positive philosophy about their relationship, and engage in relationship-promoting activities. More research is needed in this arena.

The concept of two people living together for 25 years without a serious dispute suggests a lack of spirit only to be admired in sheep.
    A. P. Herbert

A couple is a unique relationship. In a couple, one can find the deepest experience of intimacy in life, of friendship, and of comfort, as well as betrayal and the greatest possible hurt. Being a member of a couple can lead to astounding personal growth and self-awareness, and its failure can cause wounds that take years to heal. Few other relationships have as much power to challenge us and cause such anguish. James Framo says that compared to all other relationships, marriage is "real" (1993). What he meant is that the one person who knows you best is your partner. They typically see beyond the face that we prepare for others. They know the worst and the best of us. What makes the couple relationship (married or committed) different from a friendship or family bond more "real" than other relationships? Bubenzer and West (1992) identify the following characteristics that set couples apart:

1. A couple relationship is voluntary, and both parties realize that they do not have to be together. Recognizing that a relationship is a choice can make a couple work harder to keep it going. At the same time, its voluntary nature makes it easier to justify an exit.

2. A couple relationship contains a balance of stability and growth. For a relationship to remain healthy, there must be a sense of not only predictability and stability but also some novelty and flexibility. This is not true in friendships or other family relationships. Although they may want you to be a reliable friend, parent, or child, they usually do not require that you constantly spice up the relationship or continually seek to improve yourself.

3. A couple relationship has a past, a present, and a future. Couples are connected through their past histories and their future plans. Couples cannot rely on their memories alone; they must keep their relationship fresh in the present and develop future goals. Again, compare this with a friendship. Friends may have a goal to vacation together sometime, but they do not ordinarily set goals about how they will be with each other in the future or prepare together for the aging process.

4. Becoming a couple means merging two perspectives and histories, including different values and worldviews. A couple relationship is one

in which everything has to be negotiated. We recently treated a couple in which the Brazilian wife and the American husband nearly broke up over his talking to a woman at a party. He talked with her for 30 minutes because he knew no one else there. His Brazilian wife became enraged at his disrespectful behavior because this was tantamount to an affair in her mind. Whether the culture or past histories were to blame, the differing meanings associated were enough to threaten their union. It is not merely jealousy that makes a couple relationship unique; it is the fact that a couple is forced to confront differences so that they can live together. Unlike roommates who can have separate sides of the refrigerator, a couple is constantly negotiating the question, "What aspects of my behavior affect you?"

5. A couple relationship requires that each person maintain a separate identity and individuality but also have the ability to put that identity aside, at times, for the good of the couple. It means thinking of the other person's needs as just as important and valuable as one's own. The relationship must be reciprocal, with both partners giving and receiving or resentment can emerge. Because giving and receiving support is a two-way street, it is here that a couple relationship most resembles a friendship except that a great deal more is required. In a couple relationship, problems with the spouse's job have a special meaning and impact that a friend's work situation does not possess. It is not merely the financial consequences, but also the partner's happiness on the job that affects the other on a daily basis. The intertwining of lives means that giving support and listening to the other person's problems is constantly required.

Given these unique aspects and the many practical issues involved in being roommates for life, becoming a couple is one of the most difficult and complex tasks of adulthood. Surprisingly, this milestone is frequently portrayed as the easiest and most romantic stage in the life cycle. Rather than viewing marriage or joining as a couple as the solution to one's loneliness and one's personal and family problems, we should acknowledge it as a time of transition to a new life stage, requiring the formation of goals, rules, and a different family structure (Carter & McGoldrick, 1980). This is where premarital education may be able to help. If couples can confront developmental hurdles, mythologies, differences, and prejudices together, there is a chance that the uniqueness of the relationship can be understood and appreciated.

COUPLES COUNSELING POSES UNIQUE CHALLENGES FOR THE COUNSELOR

Therapists who enter the world of couples counseling realize that changing a couple system is one of the most challenging tasks ever contemplated. It requires special skills, knowledge, and attitudes. Our clinical experience has shown us that couples counseling presents at least five special challenges when compared with other forms of therapy. First, counseling couples is a challenge because many couples wait to receive counseling until their problems are severe. This has led some writers to conclude that most relationships are dead on arrival at the first session. Like two weary boxers, couples enter a condition called "stonewalling" in which they retreat to their individual corner, afraid to engage each other at all (Gottman, 2002). Even worse, they come to counseling in the middle of a crisis because of an affair, a legal problem, a financial distress, or a change in the family situation, such as illness. These issues require crisis intervention. When the crisis is over, the couple may disappear until the next issue explodes. Thus, the couples counselor must be a proficient crisis intervener as well as able to think about the larger issues.

A second challenge is that many couples have a long history of problems, which affects their current relationship. The therapist arrives in the middle of the third act, not knowing that the past is prologue. For example, one partner's infidelity may be retaliation to the other's affair. In short, there are hidden reasons for many actions that clients do not want to divulge. In the same way, couples seem to fight about apparently insignificant topics but which are really about deeper issues. The therapist enters this world of secret meanings and often remains confused for some time.

Third, couples develop destructive patterns of behavior in which both people collude. These patterns are resistant to change because they keep the relationship functioning and balanced. For example, one member of the couple bullies the other, and that person caves in to obtain peace. The peace-loving member gets tranquility temporarily and for a price. The bully gets control but loses intimacy and partnership. It takes experience to know how to both stop the bullying and help the peace lover become more assertive. Couples have a unique regulatory way of functioning. They may initially resist change to their arrangement because the alternative—chaos—seems worse. Barry Dym (1995) in his book, *Readiness and Change in Couples Therapy*, compares these couples to a 400-pound sumo wrestler who is hunkered down to resist your push. The competent couples therapist must be patient, persistent, and not take these rebuffs personally.

Fourth, couples counseling is qualitatively different and challenging compared to individual therapy because couples bicker. Disagreements may occur in group therapy, but it is a relatively short-lived phenomenon because these members do not have enough background and are pressured by the group to resolve issues. Not so with couples. They have an almost limitless supply of stories and examples of the other person's misdeeds over many years. Some couples make little or no progress in counseling because they address negative comments to each other throughout the entire therapy process. They see the therapy session as either a continuation of the disagreements at home or a safe place to argue. Either way, it is unproductive (except for assessment purposes). Couples generally do not make progress toward their goals while they are tearing each other apart because defensiveness and blame means that neither person is listening. One of the challenges this presents to the couple is that the therapist must be like a lion tamer, holding one person back while letting the other person talk. The therapist must be much, much more active and willing to structure the session or risk allowing the session to deteriorate into a screaming match.

Finally, couples do not have a special individual bond with the therapist that keeps them involved. They are too busy responding to their partner. The therapist tries to support both individuals to keep them engaged but is much more a facilitator than a close confidant. For this reason, couples are more likely to drop out, feel blamed, or believe that the counselor and his or her partner are "ganging up." Of course, the therapist cannot remain totally neutral. Sometimes it is important to take sides when one member of the couple is hurting the other or hindering the process of reconciliation. It takes a great deal of restraint not to be too heavy handed when one partner is clearly off base.

After discussing these special difficulties and recognizing that many couples seem bent on separating or continuing their unhappiness, why should we try to improve their relationships and keep them together? The answer is simple. If we can help heal the breach in a couple's relationship and help it function properly, we can improve their happiness as individuals and potentially bring peace to a wider group—their children and families. A functioning primary couple relationship in a family and in a community of friends is a blessing to everyone. A happy couple can support each other and those around them as they pass through the trials of life and through the work of childrearing. The humorist Paul Reiser, in his book *Couplehood* (1994), says that he feels sorry for those who are not part of a couple. They order only one meal in a restaurant, and they cannot divide labor by letting one person park the car while the other gets the theater tickets. But to further our point, when a couple can function as a team, they can create a wonderful synergy and a friendship that has great value in itself. What "hooks" a couples counselor is the experience of seeing that bond reawaken and the net amount of love in the world increase.

In the next sections, we look at couples from a variety of perspectives:

1. In terms of the types of stressors that couples face. One of the systems level stressors is the changing attitudes in society about the nature of marriage itself. In the section "Couples, Marriage, and Unmarriage, in the New Millennium," we examine these new trends.
2. The internal dynamics of the couple system including boundaries, roles, and power
3. Psychological tasks that couples face as their relationship develops
4. Characteristics of healthy couples

STRESSORS AND THE COUPLE

Carter and McGoldrick (1980) recognized that couples are affected by stressors coming from within and from without. By *stressors* we mean any force that creates conflict in the couple. These include such differing influences as economic trends and relationship issues stemming from childhood. Carter and McGoldrick categorize potential stressors as either vertical, horizontal, or systems level (Figure 1.1). Putting stressors in this category has several implications. First, some stressors are normal because they are coming from societal demands or are due to the normal stages of life. Other people are addressing them. There may be

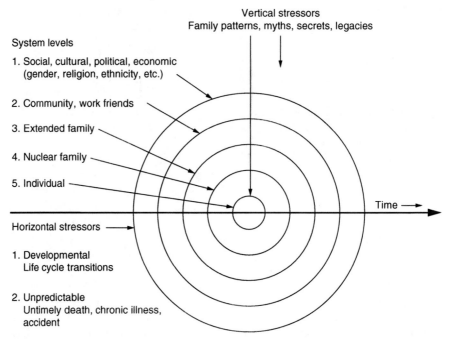

Figure 1.1   Vertical, horizontal, and systems-level stressors
Source: From *The Family Life Cycle: A Framework for Family Therapy*, by E. Carter and M. McGoldrick, p.10. Copyright © 1980 by Allyn and Bacon. Reprinted by permission of the publisher.

help, support, and education for dealing with these. Second, thinking about these as stressors rather than problems tends to "externalize" the problems that a couple is facing. Instead of blaming each other, it may be possible to recognize them as threats that are best solved by teamwork. For the counselor, taking stock of the stressors can help in the assessment process. When a wide variety of stressors are considered, we can identify the ones that are exerting the most pressure and are pulling the couple apart.

Vertical Stressors

Vertical stressors include the internal perceptions that each individual brings to the relationship from their family of origin. *Vertical* refers to the fact that these influences come down to us from the higher branches, or earlier generations, of our family trees. Memories, behavioral patterns, myths about becoming a couple, family secrets, and legacies from these past generations—all shape new couples, whether or not they are overtly aware of these influences. For example, our most prominent model of a relationship is that of our parents. We may desperately want to have that same kind of marriage, or we may vow to never live like that. These expectations will clash. A couples counselor must be aware of each person's background, culture, and secrets.

Horizontal Stressors

Horizontal stressors are the predictable life-cycle transitions such as birth of a child, the parenting of adolescent children, and syndromes like "the empty nest" that occur in the normal course of couple development. Horizontal stressors also include unpredictable life events such as an unexpected death, accident, or chronic illness. These stressors are identified as horizontal, as if a couple's relationship were a time line running left to right on the page. They can be conceived of as marks on a continuum, starting with the couple's first meeting and proceeding until the end of the relationship through death or divorce. Predictable and unpredictable events are high and low points on the couple's lifeline. For example, when a couple sends their only child to college, the couples counselor can view this as a transition in the couple's relationship. When a couple experiences difficulty at this point, the couples counselor's knowledge about these developmental changes can help them normalize their reactions.

Systems-Level Stressors

Systems-level stressors include social, cultural, political, religious, and economic influences. In addition to the impact of extended family, this group of stressors includes pressures from obligations to the nuclear family, work groups, organizations, and friends with whom the couple interacts during their life together. Some of the more common social stressors for couples include in-laws and extended family members, religion, economics, career, leisure-time opportunities, friends, higher education, political beliefs, financial opportunities, and pressure to have children.

COUPLES, MARRIAGE, AND UNMARRIAGE IN THE NEW MILLENNIUM

One of the systems-level stressors on couples that bears closer examination is changes in the way that society views the couple. For example, the institution of marriage has changed considerably over the past few generations. The traditional marriage contained culturally defined and prescribed roles and duties to be performed by each partner. In the 20th century, men's traditional roles included husband, father, breadwinner, sexual aggressor, financial planner, and household mechanic. Traditional female roles were wife, mother, homemaker, sexual recipient, child-care provider, and housemaid (Sperry & Carlson, 2005). The agenda for these marriages usually centered on the development of a family and the acquisition of property. Role definition was rather narrowly defined and was based on gender; each partner's contributions to the family goals were based on the traditional male and female role models.

Although divorce was unusual in the United States in past generations, life expectancy for both sexes was shorter than it is today. "'Till death do us part" was not as big a commitment in early 1900s as it is today. As life expectancy increased and societal expectations shifted, a new model of marriage emerged based on intimacy, companionship, and cooperation, rather than solely on duty and responsibility (Sperry & Carlson, 2005). Equality and choice are central tenets of modern marriage; with the freedom of choice in mate selection, friendship, love, and passion emerged as powerful ingredients in couple formation. This change reflects a basic change in society over the century. The women's movement, economic stress, childbearing at a later age, and increased career opportunities have influenced people's choices about when and how to become a couple (Furstenberg, 2005; Lamanna & Reidmann, 1991).

The language about being a couple has also changed. Perhaps one of the reasons for this is that the "M word" has become politically charged. Today even some married people refer to each other as "partners," a business term, because for them "husband and wife" implies a male-dominant relationship. Conversely, many same-sex couples are also looking for the economic and legal advantages of marriage, and they are hoping for society's approval of their bond. Meanwhile, *unmarriage* (cohabiting couples) is on the increase with more than 11 million unmarried partners cohabiting (Taylor, 2002). Now, a new "marriage movement" has sprung up, in some part, a reaction to gay marriage, the high divorce rate, and the number of couples living together without marriage. The marriage movement believes in marriage education and in changing public policy about marriage.

In the paragraphs that follow, we go into a little more depth on these three current trends in order to place the field of couples counseling in a cultural context.

The Unmarried and the Cohabiting

Not everyone wants to be married. It is estimated that nearly 5 million U.S. citizens are cohabiting (National Marriage Project, 2005). Still, it is argued that de facto marriage does not have all the legal protections that it needs. Such couples do not routinely put their assets into joint ownership, and when a breakup occurs, one member of the couple can lose significantly more than the other. Sometimes cohabiting couples are not religious or object to the notion of marriage because of its societal implications and paternalistic connotations. This unmarriage movement (Alternatives to Marriage Project, 2005) is really asking for legal equality for cohabiting couples whether they be straight or homosexual. Thus, domestic partner benefits and legal equality solves the problem (Taylor, 2002). Many now see cohabitation not as a prelude to marriage but as an alternative. Nearly 40% of cohabiting couples have children (Bumpass & Lu, 2000).

In the last 40 years, cohabitation has increased 1100%. It is thought that about 25% of young people are living with a partner and another 25% have lived with someone. More than 50% of first marriages begin by living together. Cohabitation prior to marriage was unheard of 50 years ago (Bumpass & Lu, 2000). It has been widely reported that living together before marriage increases the chance of divorce later. But these statistics are murky because of the selection effect. It may not be the experience of living together that predicts divorce but those who live together prior to marriage are considerably different from those who do not (Teachman, 2003). For example, they are less religious, less educated, and have a higher incidence of disruption in their families of origin (Bumpass & Lu, 2000). What we can say is that those who cohabit do not have stronger marriages than those who do not live together before marriage (Popenoe & Whitehead, 2002; Smock, 2000). There are also real concerns for children of cohabiting parents (Brown, 2004). We can also say that the couples counselor can expect that a large percentage of the clients who arrive at the counseling office will be unmarried and may have lived together for many years.

Same-Sex Marriage

As we write this text, there is a flurry of activity in many states where municipalities have recognized same-sex marriage and have granted marriage licenses. State legislatures have in some cases intervened and overturned marriages allowed by cities. At this moment, only Massachusetts allows same-sex marriage, and efforts are underway to outlaw it by amending the state constitution. Groups against gay marriage are forming, and the Southern Baptist Church has made this a legislative priority. Some politicians support a constitutional amendment defining marriage as between a man and a woman.

We ask, "Why do gays and lesbians want marriage?" Beyond the usual reasons that people give when they get married, each state offers special protections and benefits to married partners. Here are some of them, based on the State of Wisconsin's current laws: assuming a deceased spouse's pension, automatic housing lease transfer, automatic inheritance, bereavement leave, burial determination, child custody, divorce protections, domestic violence protections, exemption from property tax on partner's death, family leave to care for a sick partner, foster-care custody, immunity from testifying against spouse, insurance reductions, joint adoption, joint bankruptcy, medical decision-making rights for the partner, property rights, reduced rate or family memberships, Social Security benefits from a deceased spouse, spousal immigration rights, and tax advantages (Action Wisconsin, 2005). The crux of the fight over same-sex marriage is both a religious and a legal one. Some religious groups feel that they should prevent gay marriage because it is a religious duty, and yet there is a strong incentive for gays and lesbians to seek marriage because of its protections.

The Marriage Movement

The marriage movement, a loosely held together coalition of grassroots groups with slightly different agendas, is gaining momentum. It is an educational movement supporting premarital and marital education through programmed marriage education programs. There is also a divorce law reform movement aimed at the laws that make it too easy to get divorces. In addition, governors and state governments are promoting marriage because having committed fathers in the home improves the lives of children and decreases spending on assistance programs. Finally, there is a Christian marriage movement aimed at bringing biblical principles about marriage to education and law. This coalition has been held together by some general principles:

1. Marriage should be supported.
2. The special status of marriage should be respected.
3. Marriage and childbearing should be connected.
4. Interdependence of marriage partners should not be discouraged.
5. The ideal of permanent marriage and marriage improvement should be supported (Coalition for Marriage and Family and Couples Education, 2000).

Although these ideals are noble, they have been criticized as sexist, for promoting Christianity, and being antigay (Peterson, 2004). For example, "interdependence" (item 4) may mean that gender roles should be maintained. Though not openly antigay, conferences and writings focus on male–female marriages. For example, the Coalition for Marriage, Family and Couples Education is the largest organization of educators, laypersons, and clergy promoting premarital and marriage education. The Coalition is an extensive resource of promarriage activities through its annual Smart Marriages conference and through its website. The Coalition makes no mention of same-sex marriage but does not rail against it either (see www.smartmarriages.com). Nonetheless, the marriage movement is a reaction to the trends of cohabitation and same-sex marriage and is both political and educational in its aims. On the one hand, it wants to improve marriage through premarital and marriage education like Smart Marriages. At the same time, it wants government support to eliminate marriage penalties and promote laws that support marriage.

One of the pillars of the marriage movement is divorce reform. In short, some groups believe that marriages end because it is too easy to get married and too easy to get divorced. The main success of divorce-reform activities has been the establishment of the *covenant marriage*. The notion of a covenant has religious overtones and implies a permanent sanctified relationship. Several states (primarily in the southern United States) have enacted legislation allowing couples to choose a covenant marriage, which makes getting a no-fault divorce a little more difficult and requires premarital counseling or marriage education before getting married or divorced. Statistics on the longevity of such marriages will be difficult to analyze because religious individuals are more likely to choose a covenant marriage. Religious people divorce less.

Although evangelical and antigay sentiments exist in the marriage movement, it cannot be pigeonholed as a Christian conservative movement because many researchers, therapists, and social activists agree that marriage is in trouble (Furstenberg, 2005). The divorce rate is between 50 and 65% and is even higher for remarriages. It is clear from research that separation and divorce, in general, have negative effects on the mental health of both members of the couple. There is increased risk for automobile accidents, suicide, violence, homicide, and physical illness including suppression of the immune system. Children, whose parents' marriages are disrupted, are more likely to experience poor health, school problems, social skills deficits, and depression (Gottman, 1998).

The marriage movement has brought a spotlight to the state of our unions and has encouraged research in couple relationships. It has not, however, universally supported couples counseling. It is probably true that, in the past, counselors and therapists have not held promarriage values. There are still suspicions in the marriage movement that therapists are still primarily supportive of the individual. Hopefully, the future will bring reconciliation between marriage education and couples counseling. Although marriage education is popular and useful, it cannot be the only tool in our armamentarium.

DYNAMICS OF THE COUPLE SYSTEM

In the preceding discussion, we examined couples from the perspective of stressors in three broad categories, vertical, horizontal and systemic. In this section, we look at couple dynamics as a way of understanding conflicts that couples face. **Dynamics** refers to both structures and forces within a system. Just as Freud felt that an individual is dealing with structures such as id, ego, and superego and with forces such as libido in the intrapsychic system, similar elements are at work in the couple system. Among these are boundaries, individual needs, expectations and myths about the couple relationship, roles, intimacy, and power.

Boundaries and Boundary Violations

Minuchin (1974) describes the couple hierarchically as a separate system that must be maintained intact to remain healthy. This means that couples must form a boundary, or a sort of invisible protective shield, around their relationship to ensure protection, privacy, and intimacy in their relationship. If a relationship is to have integrity, then family, children, work, and friends cannot be allowed to interfere with its functioning, no matter how stressful or complicated life becomes. In traditional wedding vows, the rather severe phrase "forsaking all others" was used to remind couples of the need for such boundaries.

To maintain their distinctiveness as a couple, partners must create a boundary by letting others know the limits. Couples who do not create a boundary around their relationship are drawn into their families of origin or into previous friendships and then remain part of those systems, sometimes to the detriment of their relationships with their partners. This boundary drawing is particularly difficult when there is unfinished business from childhood or when other family members live with the couple. Families normally recognize when an adolescent needs some space to become his or her own person. But they sometimes forget that a couple needs to carve out its own identity, too, and they frequently violate the boundaries by trying to influence their offspring to act in the family's interests rather than in the couple's interests. It is a fact of couplehood that boundary violations will occur.

A boundary violation can occur when a third party interferes with a couple's functioning, creating the so-called eternal triangle. For a newly married couple, a typical boundary violation might happen like this: Selena and Marco have been living together for 4 months, and they are planning a big wedding in the near future. During the weeks leading up to the wedding, Selena spends every Saturday night with her mother, shopping, running errands, and preparing for the big event. The relationship between mother and daughter has always been close, but it appears to have intensified, based on the time they spend together arranging this important event. Selena now sees her mother every weekend and talks to her on the phone for about an hour every night. Marco is a little annoyed but tells himself that this will change after the wedding. Marco, on the other hand, spends quite a bit of time deep-sea fishing with his buddies because, according to Marco, Selena is not available. Both express disappointment in the other for not spending enough time together as a couple. Although they have been cohabiting for only a short time, both are worried about the future of the relationship if their allegiances to other relationships are stronger than the couple bond. The appearance of this kind of pattern does not mean that Selena and Marco will have serious problems; more likely it is a normal part of the couple's development as they begin to decide how their need to relate to others fits with their commitment to each other.

Couple Needs Versus Individual Needs

Some people choose marital partners to make up for some flaw they see in themselves. For them, at least initially, the couple relationship provides an avenue to wholeness and security. For others who have been fiercely independent or self-centered, thinking of someone else's needs and negotiating all phases of life is like being imprisoned. Even if the couple is not at one of these polar extremes, a committed relationship can become a challenge to one's sense of self. Even the smallest daily activities such as loading the dishwasher, watching television, or inviting friends to the house can affect the other person enormously.

Friendship is a good example because our friends form part of our self-definition. When two people become a couple, other relationships normally take second place, and part of who we are is lost. For example, we saw a couple who had been married for 18 months and were expecting their first child. The major problem for the 21-year-old father-to-be was the fact that he had no personal life because his wife was no longer interested in continuing their "party" lifestyle. He was on the brink of leaving the marriage because his wife asked him to choose between her (and baby) and his friends. It is easy to write off this young father's dilemma as one based on simple immaturity. But it exemplifies the tension between one's individuality and being immersed in the couple that must be dealt with throughout life. This is to some extent a values issue. How much individual time should be allowed?

Families of Origin Shape Expectations and Influence the Couple System

It is sometimes difficult for families to adjust to relating to the new couple as a separate unit rather than to the individual to whom they are tied by genetics or choices. The new couple also faces changes because each partner must now relate to his or her parents from the standpoint of being part of a couple, as well as relating as individual children. Parents may feel jealous toward the interloper who now has more influence than they do, while the couple believes that parents are interfering. This is the boundaries issue that we discussed earlier. However, the expectations based on family history also come from each partner. To become a couple requires that two individuals who have been accustomed to one set of expectations and values in their own families of origin must renegotiate with their partners to accommodate each other and define a new set of expectations. The new expectations provide a blueprint for their lifestyle as a couple.

Let's take a somewhat typical example of a newly married couple, Craig and Stacy, who are deciding how to celebrate a special occasion. As Craig grew up, he spent most of his birthdays fishing with his friends. It was more or less a family tradition to let the birthday person have the day to do with as he or she wished. In Stacy's family, however, birthdays were times for the family to get together; perhaps going out to dinner or having a family party. During the first year of marriage, the couple had difficulty comprehending these conflicting traditions when each person's birthday arrived. Stacy was hurt that Craig did not plan a party; Craig felt criticized as being selfish when he went golfing with some friends and came home too late for a celebration.

Stacy and Craig's problem may appear to be a minor one, but it illustrates the unanticipated ways in which family backgrounds, traditions, and expectations collide when two people join their lives. Other issues to be defined as two people become a couple include everyday decisions about eating, sleeping, working, and playing, as well as more complex issues such as money management, influences of extended family, gender roles, career choice, conflict resolution, and expressions of love and intimacy. Another way of explaining this dynamic is to say that couples have myths about their partners, about marriage in general, and about what makes a good relationship. These myths need to be confronted whether they have been learned in families of origin, from society, or from the media. Nearly every marriage education and marriage preparation program asks couples to discuss these expectations or myths that play such a vital role in the couple's happiness. Table 1.1 illustrates a number of common myths of couples. Couples who confront the myths early in their relationship may have a better chance of

Table 1.1   Myths of Couple Relationships

1. If we love each other, we should be happy at all times.
2. We should always be completely honest with the other person regardless of the impact on him or her.
3. We should want to be together all the time and be unselfish with our leisure hours.
4. We should agree on every issue in order to support each other.
5. If we have a problem, we must decide who is to blame.
6. We know what the other is thinking and what the other person likes, so we don't need to communicate.
7. Good relationships just happen and do not need to be worked on or renegotiated.
8. If we create joint activities, we will be close forever.
9. We do not need friends or family as long as we have each other.

renegotiating the ingrained influences of family and society. As couples explore unrealistic messages, they are able to create new, shared beliefs and traditions for their relationship.

Dealing With Conflicting Roles: Husband/Father and Wife/Mother

Another common boundary issue involves the complex shift that couples must negotiate when they become parents. Consider the situation of Jim and Valerie, who are in conflict over their needs as a couple and messages from their family of origin: Jim and Valerie have been married for 5 years. Their daughter, Emily, is just 2 years old. The spouses have frequent disagreements about how they should spend their time with Emily and about how much time is appropriate. Valerie was raised in a family where children rarely went out unaccompanied by their parents, nor did the parents often leave their children with babysitters. Jim grew up in a family of five children, and his parents often went together to movies, to dinner, and to visit friends. The children made popcorn with their babysitter and had a party of their own on these occasions. Jim is angry with Valerie because she refuses to get a babysitter for Emily; Valerie believes that Jim is not involved enough as a parent and is trying to get her to neglect their daughter as well.

This distinction between roles as spouse and parent may seem simple, but it is very difficult for many couples to achieve. Roles can easily become blurred. Sometimes even counselors confuse the two roles and will talk about the roles of mom/dad and husband/wife as if they are interchangeable. Spouses may even refer to each other as "Mom" and "Dad." The challenge is to keep these two functions separate so that the couple relationship is not erased in the development of a new family. Couples who relate to each other only in their roles as parents (a role filled with anxiety and responsibility) will find that their ability to become intimate is diminished as their role as a separate couple is neglected. Because parenting requires less time as children grow older, couples who relate only as parents may eventually find themselves staring across the breakfast table at someone with whom they have little in common.

Couples Need Intimacy

Intimacy is thought to be a hallmark of a couple relationship, a kind of closeness defined by mutual self-disclosure and an understanding of the other person. In a partnership of equals, even if the relationship was "made in heaven," it is clear that maintenance work must be done if intimacy is to be kept alive. Even if the couple is not troubled by boundary violations by family members, the pressures of work and children now assail both members of the couple much more than when only one partner worked and the other tended the home. Time for each other is at a premium, and so is intimacy.

Intimacy involves the degree of closeness and caring that each partner feels and expresses (see Laurenceau, Barrett, & Rovine, 2005). The way that couples express closeness is strongly influenced by needs and expectations that both partners have developed in their respective families of origin. Other factors affecting their expression of intimacy include their individual personality styles, the relationship style they have developed together, and the developmental stage of the relationship (Sperry & Carlson, 2005). In many cases, one partner has grown up in a family with minimal physical contact and little overt communication of love and affection between parents or toward the children. Expressions of affection may have been in the form of food, money, or other tangible items. Conversely, the other partner may have been raised by parents who spent a significant amount of time communicating with each other and with the children, as well as demonstrating physical affection for family members. Such differences set the stage for varying expectations about intimacy. The lack of communication about intimacy can lead to relationship stress and can contribute to the termination of the relationship if partners do not address the issue together and create a positive resolution on which they both agree.

Couples Must Deal With Power

Power differentials are determined by identifying whether one partner has more influence in making decisions or whether the couple shares power in the decision-making process. The degree of competition for power between the two people determines whether or not solutions that the couple generates are mutual and cooperative or are made by solely one partner (Sperry & Carlson, 2005). Typical issues of competition and power surface when decisions are made about who will primarily handle the money, whose career will take precedence, how the division of duties at home will be divided, and who will be in charge of planning social activities with family and friends.

Consider the situation of Marti and Eugene, who have been married for 5 years. They have two children, ages 2 and 4. Marti has given up her career as a social worker to take a part-time position in a day-care center so that she can spend more time with the children. Eugene has been offered a promotion and a significant raise in salary in his career as a systems analyst. The change will necessitate moving several states away. Marti is unhappy and believes that Eugene should turn down the promotion to stay in their current community. Marti asserts that she has given up her career to assume more child-care responsibility and has developed a strong support system of family and friends. She is happy with her work in the day-care center and believes that Eugene should consider the sacrifices she made early in their relationship. Eugene is angry and claims that he is the primary breadwinner and that the family should go where he has the greatest opportunity to advance his career. In this case, both are competing for their "rights" to either stay in the same location or move to advance Eugene's career. Marti believes that she has made changes whereas her husband has not. She wants Eugene to place her desires first. Eugene sees the situation differently. He views increased income potential as a sufficient reason to move. Once again, the issue is not "who is right and who is wrong" but how these two people negotiate the issue in the relationship.

WHAT A COUPLE GOES THROUGH: PSYCHOLOGICAL TASKS

Wallerstein (1993) extends the concept of the psychological task developed by Erikson (1950) as a useful way of describing the life cycle of healthy couples. This model may be more useful than older ideas because previous conceptualizations about couple development have been based on the premise that couples marry between the ages of 18 and 22 years and remain together forever. Divorce and remarriage are now as common as an intact marriage. People are marrying and having children later, and many choose not to have children at all. Thus, Wallerstein proposes to look at how couples handle psychological tasks rather than by observing them from a typical life-cycle perspective. These tasks are not bound by time limitations or by traditional notions of the intact couple over the life span. Thus, you can judge the health of a couple—or at least identify the current hurdle—by looking at how well the couple has handled the psychological task before them. The tasks that Wallerstein (1993) has outlined represent both the early and the enduring stages of marriage and can be considered regardless of the ages of the couple or a history of prior relationships by one or both partners. The tasks are as follows.

Task 1: Consolidating psychological separation and establishing new connections with the family of origin   This task is the passport required to travel through life together, separate from one's original family and yet maintaining healthy contact. For young people in their 20s, this task is to learn to listen to the advice of their parents without rebelliousness and discover their own solutions without harming the relationship with the older generation. They must learn to spend time with their families of origin but not neglect their own relationship. Although this is particularly important for young adults, older adults who have been divorced or widowed for a period of time face the same challenges. They must negotiate a new role as part of a couple after being single and maintain contact with adult children. Role confusion is characteristic in this stage because there are competing loyalties and expectations.

Sometimes these new roles create a change in identity even if the couple has lived together prior to marriage or if there have been former spouses. Expectations may change when the relationship is formalized by a legal commitment. Often, at this stage, the couple matures but feels overwhelmed with the dramatic changes. There may have been a sense of fun and freedom living as two separate adults orbiting each other's lives. The sense of responsibility to each other and competing loyalties after becoming a couple may cast a sobering shadow.

Task 2: Building the marital identity for the couple and for the individuals— togetherness versus autonomy   This multifaceted task involves creating a "we-ness." This means a shift from the self centered "I" to thinking of "I" as a part of "we." When a person in a couple even temporarily abandons self interests and addresses the concepts of "good" and "fair" in the relationship, the capacity for intimacy and friendship blossoms. Closeness requires that each has access to the other and that each confronts and sets aside the narcissistic element to develop the "we" identity. Throughout the cycle of a relationship, there is a push-pull between these two poles of protecting one's individuality and setting it aside for the good of the couple.

Task 3: Establishing the sexual identity of the couple   Sexual identity refers to the frequency, intensity, and accessibility for the sexual expression of affection between partners. This task promotes a sense of connection and openness to the "we" part of the relationship. It means arranging a safe haven (time and place) from the stressors of life. The sexual relationship still requires negotiation after marriage or commitment even if the couple has engaged in a prior sexual relationship. Couples must find a balance between the differing needs for sex and intimacy.

Task 4: Establishing the marriage as a zone of safety and nurturing   The relationship provides a place to address individual and couple failures, struggles, successes, and fears in a supportive, caring atmosphere. Each partner should be comfortable enough to turn to the other in times of stress. This task is particularly important because individuals who do not meet their needs for safety and nurturing may be prone to go outside the relationship by engaging in extramarital affairs or by devoting a large amount of time to work, friendships, extended family, or leisure activities that do not include the spouse.

Task 5: Parenthood   For couples who choose to have children, there is an expansion of the marital relationship to include psychological room for a child while safeguarding the relationship of the spouses. There is also a need to examine the flexibility of roles in the relationship because they will require modification with the addition of children. What expectations about child care and parenting does each partner bring into the mix? To what extent will the child be allowed to subsume time spent as a couple?

For remarrying couples, children may already be a part of the package. Immediate negotiation of roles as stepparent, parent, and spouse is required. This can get complicated when there have been multiple marriages with stepchildren and biological children from prior relationships. The task of the couple is to preserve its ability to function and not be compromised and divided by other loyalties.

Task 6: Building a relationship that is fun and interesting   A priority of marriage is to keep it alive with new and interesting experiences with a balance of spontaneity and tradition. A "good" marriage is not a constant but requires continual work to infuse excitement and passion into the relationship. These experiences become part of the shared memories for the couple and are part of the maintenance of the relationship in times of acute stress or illness because the couple can reminisce about the "fun" times.

Task 7: Maintaining a dual vision of one's partner that combines early idealization with reality perception   Keeping love alive means that each partner stays in touch with the passion that they initially felt for the other and yet is aware of how that passion has grown into a realistic friendship over the years. It is also important for each partner to remember the characteristics that drew them to each other and continue to view them as special and as unique qualities. These characteristics should be considered as strengths of the individual and part of the gift that each provides for the long-term maintenance and enhancement of the relationship.

CHARACTERISTICS OF HEALTHY COUPLES

The final perspective that we want to touch on is looking at the positive or healthy aspects of couples' functioning. Much has been written about unhealthy and dysfunctional relationships. It is not uncommon to hear people discuss their spouses or families as "dysfunctional"; even therapists are guilty of this. They may speak of the relationship as unhealthy or use the term *interlocking pathologies* to refer to a "sick" couple. We believe that it is important that therapists also keep the focus on healthy behaviors and strengths in the relationship to facilitate positive change, rather than focus solely on weaknesses and limitations. Because couples come to counseling with a clear idea about what is wrong, it may be difficult to get them to examine their strengths. Yet this can be one of the strongest measures that a counselor can take against demoralization and helping couples gain perspective. Frequently, a couple is focusing solely on what is wrong, when it may also be useful to identify what is right with the relationship and how that can be used to get through the current problem.

We believe that characteristics of healthy couples could give us insight into how to help those that are distressed, but few researchers have tackled this topic (Young, 2004). In the literature, there is a distinction between *marital stability* and *marital quality*. Just because a relationship is stable (divorce is not imminent), it does not mean that it is healthy or happy (quality). It is difficult to look at the literature and definitively identify what healthy couples look like because most of the studies have focused on stable couples, not necessarily happy couples (Fennell, 1993). For example, listening and disclosing skills may not be necessary for stability (Carrere & Gottman, 1999), but they may be important for happiness (Eckstein & Goldman, 2001). Because the approach of this book is strength based, we include here some of the healthy patterns or strengths that Olson and Olson (2000), Beavers (1985), Fennell (1993), and Sperry and Carlson (2005) have identified and which we have added to and adapted:

1. *A belief in relative rather than absolute truth.* In any relationship, one's version of the truth must make room for another person's perspective. In a couple relationship, "My taste in furniture is good, and yours is bad" is an example of believing in absolute truth. Healthy couples allow for differences in taste and accept different points of view. A corollary of this statement is that healthy couples understand that two people can have a different view of the same situation. When couples have this perspective, partners are not always trying to change the other person to take their viewpoint but instead are attempting to listen and understand.

2. *My spouse is my friend.* Intimacy, disclosure, and feeling close to the spouse are part of friendship. It also means generally expecting that the other person's motives are good. They do not assume that the other person is the enemy or that the other person's annoying habits are directed at them. Healthy couples talk about "respect."

3. *Able to deal with conflict.* Healthy couples are masters of disasters. Not only can they handle conflict without running away but they also have confidence that differences will be resolved. They also recognize that some arguments will not be resolved and that there will be ongoing discussion and negotiation.

4. *A belief in something larger.* The writer Antoine de Saint-Exupery said that love is not looking into each other's eyes; it is looking in the same direction. Healthy couples often share a belief or mission that is larger than themselves. It may be religious, political, or a family orientation. When spirituality is shared, it can be a couple strength (Fennell, 1993; Olson & Olson, 2000).

CONCLUSION

There is a burgeoning interest in the couple and in couples counseling fueled by research from leading experts such as John Gottman and the awakening of a marriage movement in this country. Although the promarriage voices are strong, many couples remain unmarried, and the divorce rate is relatively unchanged. In this context, we have presented a few ideas to organize your introduction to couples counseling. First, the couple relationship is unique, and it demands special expertise and a different viewpoint compared to other counseling modalities such as individual, family, and group counseling. We also have presented a holistic view of the kinds of stressors that couples face. They deal with internal needs and conflicts and developmental changes such as childrearing; the larger systems such as the social changes that we alluded to also affect them.

All couples encounter some predictable issues or dynamics. They include dealing with boundary violations, conflicts between individual and couple needs, expectations from family of origin, other roles such as being a parent or a worker; maintaining intimacy in the face of competing relationships; and determining who has the power in the relationship. We also used Wallerstein's seven developmental tasks as a way of conceptualizing normal issues that couples face across the life span. We ended with a discussion of healthy couple functioning. All these issues are important background for the theories and the skills that you will learn later in this text. Each couple can be described in terms of their cultural background, the stressors they are dealing with, the dynamics operating in their relationship, their developmental level, and the healthy behaviors they already possess. These are the "big-picture" issues that will serve as a guide when you collect information about a unique couple.

2

Theories of Couples Therapy: Part One

KEY CONCEPTS

- Theories of couples therapy have been developed from theories of individual and family therapy.
- Previously, behavior therapy with couples focused mainly on changing reinforcement and improving communication.
- Now, behavior theory applied to couples includes learning new skills including negotiation, communication, and assertiveness; increasing positive reinforcement; and identifying and modifying cognitive errors.
- John Gottman's research has spawned an integrative approach that includes skill training along with cognitive and affective elements to reduce divorce proneness and increase satisfaction.
- Psychodynamic therapy previously treated individuals in the couple separately. The most popular form of psychodynamic work is now object-relations therapy, which most often sees the couple together.
- Multigenerational psychodynamic theories focus on the "unfinished business" that couples bring to their relationship from their families of origin.
- Object-relations theory originated when psychodynamic thinkers proposed that object seeking, or the need to be in a relationship, was a primary drive.
- Object-relations therapists help couples look at how their needs are projected upon their partners and how to develop realistic relationships.
- The Bowen theory shares many concepts with psychodynamic thinkers. Bowen highlighted the importance of differentiation, or emotional autonomy, as a goal for each person. People who are differentiated can balance intimacy and autonomy.

Theories are like different human languages. Although most . . . do an equally good job as representational systems, some languages are better than others for solving

a specific problem. Street language may be better in a hostage negotiation situation, while proper English would be more useful for a scientific presentation. However, it makes no sense to say one language is closer to the truth or reality than another.
      Segal, 1991, p. 184

In this chapter and the next, we look at five theoretical groups and their offshoots: (1) behavior therapy, (2) multigenerational therapy approaches, (3) structural and strategic therapy, (4) solution-focused therapy, and (5) narrative therapy and emotionally focused therapy. Such an overview is helpful for historical purposes, but more important it helps us identify the common curative factors that theorists have independently identified. For example, in this chapter, you will see that most of the schools of therapy indicate that couples tend to engage in repetitive patterns of unproductive behavior. Nearly all would agree that a primary task of any therapist is to identify these patterns and disrupt or end them. After looking at all six theory groups, we then present our own integrative model, which draws many of its premises from the perspectives presented in these chapters.

Although we call Chapters 2 and 3 "Theories of Couples Therapy," it would be more accurate to say that we look at theories of therapy that have been *applied* to couples because all the theoretical groups we describe originated mainly as individual or family approaches. Couples therapy has been "a technique in search of a theory" because its practice preceded theory development. The need for therapy with couples appeared before it was investigated as an entity separate from individual therapy, and the family therapy "boom" of the 1980s left couples therapy behind. Most of the emphasis has been on working with whole families, including children and other extended family members. For one reason, the reorganization of child welfare systems and their focus on family reintegration has encouraged training and practice of the whole family. In the last few years, things have changed and couples therapy finds itself in the limelight (Gurman, 2003).

Like group therapy, couples therapy has been integrative, or eclectic, from its outset, borrowing from the systemic theories of family therapy, psychodynamic therapy, behaviorism, and the study of communication. But perhaps couples therapy is no different than individual therapy at this point in history. This is a time of integration and technique, rather than theory and thought. It is a practical time, and eclecticism and integration hold center stage (Gurman, 2003; Norcross & Goldfried, 2003; Young 2005).

In the past, chapters like this tended to compare and contrast different points of view with dimensions on which each theory might be evaluated. But is that really fair? As the quote at the beginning of this chapter indicates, theories are like different languages, and they lose something in the translation. In keeping with the integrative spirit of the book, we don't discuss the merits of each therapy as they are presented. We also don't present a lengthy history, detailing the lives of major contributors, nor do we spend much time on minor points of theory. Also, we don't say much about differing ideas about etiology (the causes of problems) unless they relate directly to treatment. What we do in this chapter is identify key terms, recognize specific couple problem areas discovered by each theory, and indicate some key therapeutic techniques.

We have selected the theories that are most used by couples therapists today, and we have tried to identify the important techniques. We don't discuss several influential family therapy methodologies, such as the Milan or systemic school, because they have focused very little on couples and have centered their efforts on families with children. Instead, we include theoretical positions that we believe are contributing most to the understanding and treatment of couples. The techniques from each approach are only outlined in these chapters to give you a feel for the therapies that the theories have spawned. Elsewhere in the text, you will find many of the methods from various theories. They are separated from their "theory of origin," and we describe how you can put them directly into practice using an eclectic, or integrative, philosophy.

Although each viewpoint is separate, therapists from different persuasions still agree about some of the necessities. Most would agree that thorough assessment is important, as is developing a good working relationship with the couple. Most agree that couples need to work together rather than separately and must find ways to change together. This is what we mean by *common factors*. Later, we try to pull together some of these threads that underpin our brief integrative approach.

As you read, you may find yourself more attracted to one theory or another, so we have included key references for further reading. Some educators believe that it is important for a counselor or therapist to be trained in a single school of thought so that the student develops a coherent framework in the beginning. This approach has merit because you feel more confident working within one school of thought. Alternately, during your study or review of the theories, you might see truth in many or all of them, and you may want to use techniques from more than one school. Integrative theorists try to help students develop a coherent and systematic approach that combines findings from a number of theories. We believe that this is a difficult and arduous task because it requires that you have a great deal of understanding about the full range of theoretical perspectives and perhaps requires you to become proficient with a wider range of techniques.

In Chapter 4, we describe our integrative model of couples therapy. The purpose of that model is to combine what is best from a number of theories. The approach is based on our combined 20 years of working with this model with hundreds of couples in a variety of settings and training scores of clinicians in our approach. The model is a tool, not the only truth. You will need to make your own decisions about your own theoretical direction. Our aim is to help develop a "reflective practitioner," who can in this information age provide a systematic therapy while remaining open to new ideas from the ever-expanding field of couples therapy.

BEHAVIOR THERAPY APPLIED TO COUPLES

What Is Behavior Therapy?

In this chapter, we include cognitive–behavioral approaches under the heading of behavior therapy. We examine ways that counselors modify thoughts and behaviors of couples using learning. Behavior therapy is the application of learning principles to the task of changing human behavior. You may think of learning as only an internal, mental process, but try to think of learning as a transaction with the environment. In other words, consider how we are changed by the experiences that we have. Behavior therapy is concerned with how people learn and unlearn dysfunctional behavior and how human behavior is maintained by rewards and punishments from the external world and from other people.

Many counselors think that behavior therapy is very mechanical and looks at people as machines. Some of us have a negative attitude about behavior therapy because of its history in the 1960s, when it was associated with delivering electric shock to modify behavior. But modern behavior therapy is neither electric shocks nor rats in boxes. Modern behaviorists recognize the complexities of human behavior, the cognitive (or thinking) component, the necessity for a therapeutic relationship, and the need to avoid blame when identifying the causes of couple problems (Bornstein & Bornstein, 1986; Gurman & Fraenkel, 2002; Spiegler & Guevremont, 1993). Therapists who reject behavioral methods entirely will be "throwing the baby out with the bath water." Behaviorally oriented therapists are developing many creative formats for working with couples and are strengthening their findings with good research.

Originally, behavior therapy dealing with couples had three major thrusts: (1) helping couples increase positive reinforcement (Stuart, 1969), (2) teaching new skills, such as communication training or assertiveness (Jacobson & Margolin, 1979), and (3) using cognitive therapy to alter destructive individual thinking patterns (Baucom & Epstein, 1990). Since 1990, a new trend has emerged, which Gurman (2003, p. 490) calls "integrative behavioral couple therapy." Integration was deemed necessary because researchers were disappointed in the outcomes of traditional behavior therapy approaches. They concluded that many couples were not dealing with skill deficits in communication as much as with sharp differences in personality, values, and lifestyle. This approach includes the pioneering work of John Gottman (1999) who has developed an integrative approach to helping couples deal with these "perpetual problems" while still trying to help couples develop some skills and lower emotional arousal during conflicts. One of Gottman's main contributions is his discovery of the role of negative affect in the satisfaction of couples. For example, Gottman and his colleagues have been able to predict divorce in newly married couples based on the frequency of their negative and positive emotional reactions (Carrere & Gottman, 1999; Gottman, Coan, Carrere, & Swanson, 1998). Gottman's treatment approach will be described more fully in Chapter 8 where we discuss communication training and couples education.

Definitions of Key Terms

Following are some of the important terms used in behavior therapies for couples:

contingency Withholding reinforcement until a behavior is exhibited. This makes the reward *contingent* on the behavior.

contingency contracting Making an agreement regarding the circumstances in which one person will reinforce another's behavior. In couples counseling, contracts are used to increase the amount of positive reinforcers in a relationship. "If you do X, then I will do Y" is the algorithm of such a contract. In this case, X is something rewarding to one party, and Y is rewarding to the other.

functional analysis Looking at behavior patterns and the situations that maintain them (reinforcers) in order to select interventions that will disrupt these patterns. It involves analyzing the situations, times, and conditions in which the problem behaviors occur and eliminating these triggers. For example, a functional analysis might reveal that a couple tends to argue most right after work. An intervention might be devised to delay discussions to a time when the couple feels less tired and frustrated.

modeling An educational/therapeutic procedure based on Bandura's social learning theory. Bandura (1969) found that children who observed violence were more likely to reproduce it in their own interactions. Similarly, positive models can teach positive, or prosocial, behaviors. In therapy we try to expose clients to situations in which they can observe someone else exhibiting a new behavior. Couples group therapy and relationship enhancement seminars can use this kind of learning because clients can observe other participants. Seeing modeling by a counselor or observing someone in a film can also prompt a new behavior, motivate clients, and reduce anxiety about the novel behavior.

negative reinforcement (often confused with punishment) Anything that when removed acts as a reinforcer. For example, if one member of a couple agrees not to play country music when the other is home, the absence of country music operates as a reward (removing a negative).

positive reinforcement Presenting something rewarding to a person as a way of strengthening a certain behavior. For example, if one member of the couple has agreed to keep dirty laundry off the bedroom floor, such behavior is positively reinforced when the other member notices when things are cleaned and delivers a compliment or other sign of appreciation.

punishment An aversive stimulus; anything that decreases the likelihood that a behavior will be exhibited in the future. For example, if one member of a couple is criticized by the other when he or she expresses an opinion, the criticism (for most people, a moderately strong punishment) decreases the likelihood that the person criticized will express opinions in the future.

reinforcer or reinforcement Anything that increases the likelihood that a behavior will be exhibited in the future. Reinforcement is a reward or the reduction of something negative.

successive approximation Rewarding each successive step in a new behavior. When a behavior is complex or when it is first being learned, sometimes it is useful to break the behavior into smaller steps and reward each successive step, rather than wait for the full manifestation of the behavior. For example, if one partner is learning to cook for the household, it would be useful to notice the positives during each attempt rather than wait for the perfect meal. Cooking dinner is a complex behavior, which takes practice in proper preparation and timing.

Some Premises of Behavior Theory

Some key theoretical tenets of the behavioral approach, as it is applied to couples, are as follows:

1. The principles of human learning discovered by Pavlov, Skinner, Thorndike, and Bandura explain how couples have developed maladaptive patterns of interaction. Human beings have histories of past reinforcement patterns, have conditioned reflexes, and can be shaped and changed through modeling and vicarious learning processes.
2. Relationship skills are learned, and treatment normally involves an educational or relearning process.
3. We should strive for precision in identifying a problem and use quantitative measures to validate change via a *functional analysis*. Success should be objectively measurable.
4. The history of the relationship and of one's family of origin is not usually relevant. Covert behavior (not observable), such as thinking about the past, might have an influence on the present, and it might be important to change one's thinking about one's family of origin.
5. When we change rewarding and punishing behaviors of couples, we change their relationship.
6. Modeling positive behaviors is an important way for couples to learn better interaction.
7. Reinforcement is generally a more effective tool in learning new behaviors than is punishment. Punishment tells us what not to do. Modeling and rewarding successful behaviors tell us what to do. Maladaptive behaviors tend to drop off when they are not rewarded.
8. Couples can learn to reinforce healthy behavior in their partners and ignore maladaptive behaviors when possible.
9. Negative and positive emotions are powerful reinforcers that affect a person's willingness to engage the partner.

Problems That Couples Experience

Maladaptive Communication Patterns

Stuart (1969) was among the first to identify the ways that couples engage in specific types of ineffective and potentially damaging communication exchanges when they experience a conflict. The following are a number of specific patterns in which couples find themselves enmeshed.

Figure 2.1   Example of a coercive exchange cycle in a married couple

Coercive exchange   In coercive exchange, one member employs negative reinforcement in return for a positive reinforcement from the other partner. For example, a husband criticizes and argues with his wife until she gives in and lets him win. He is rewarded by getting what he wants (positive reinforcement); she is reinforced by the fact that he stops criticizing and abusing (negative reinforcement). But remember, negative reinforcement increases the likelihood of the behaviors recurring in the future. Therefore, in this cycle the couple is rewarding the husband's abusing behavior (see Figure 2.1).

Withdrawal   This is a cycle of negative reinforcement in which arguing over a conflict is so aversive that one or both members of the couple withdraw from the conflict because the negative reinforcement of removing the arguing is so powerful. This action may be a result of the individuals' reinforcement histories. If one grew up in a household where arguing was a constant and destructive pattern and withdrawal was the common coping mechanism, this previous learning may be brought forward into the couple's relationship. In addition, a withdrawing individual has no expectancy that arguing will be rewarded. Such a person needs encouragement because he or she may never have experienced the satisfaction of expressing feelings to another and coming to a joint solution of problems. Gottman (1999) uses the term *stonewalling* to refer to a behavior by one member of the couple who withdraws from the conversation by looking away and down. This member reduces talking and conveys the impression of a stonewall.

Retaliatory exchange   Research shows that couples who are distressed engage in rapid retaliatory exchanges (Jacobson & Margolin, 1979). Each partner tends to give back negative responses to the other immediately after receiving a negative comment from the partner. Both become so conditioned to respond that often they perceive punishment from the partner when it is not intended. This is what is sometimes called *differential relational currencies* (Villard & Whipple, 1976). Edward Albee's play *Who's Afraid of Virginia Woolf?*

(1962/1991, pp. 154–155) demonstrates the retaliatory exchanges of the fictional couple, George and Martha, who have spent the evening humiliating each other.

> *Martha:* Before I'm through with you you'll wish you'd died in that automobile, you bastard.
> *George:* And you'll wish you'd never mentioned our son!
> *Martha:* You . . .
> *George:* Now, I said I warned you.
> *Martha:* I'm impressed.
> *George:* I warned you not to go too far.
> *Martha:* I'm just beginning.

George and Martha's interaction is sadly quite common. One hallmark of the pattern is the ongoing nature of the fight. It can be picked up just where it left off, seemingly without interruption, as Martha says, "I'm just beginning." This brief dialogue (and the entire play) shows how two intelligent people become engaged in a game of revenge from which both emerge as losers. The film *War of the Roses* is another example that shows a couple who simultaneously destroy their marriage and the house that they built.

How do people end up in such tragic situations? Punishing remarks to another person can be rewarding temporarily because they put one in a superior position, increasing feelings of self-esteem. Punishing provides a distance from which the initiator can escape from feelings of dependency. Such exchanges may be intellectually stimulating or may be maintained by the fun and sex of making up after the quarrel. All these motives are at work in Albee's play.

Cross-complaining   In cross-complaining, the partners take turns exchanging different complaints without ever validating the other's concerns. Each complaint is designed to cancel out the other's. The underlying process is one of blaming the partner, and this kind of interaction is typical in couples communication even when it is not severe, as in the following example.

> *He:* Boy, what a day! I am exhausted.
> *She:* Well so am I. I worked hard, too.
> *He:* Not like I did. You sit down all day.
> *She:* But then I have to come home and work here all evening.

This kind of interaction does not lead to clear communication because her response to him is based on a hidden agenda. She may be feeling angry that he does not share in the household responsibilities; therefore, she is afraid to validate his tiredness.

Repairs   Consider this alternative to the couple interaction above:

> *He:* Boy, what a day! I am exhausted.
> *She:* You even sound tired.
> *He:* I am. What's for dinner?
> *She:* I haven't thought about it. Any ideas?

This interaction does not lead to discussing how they are going to deal with housework, which might be saved for a better time. On the other hand, her response "You even sound tired" is a direct answer to his statement. When she acknowledges it, he can move on to the next topic. She then asks a question rather than cross-complaining. This interaction is not maladaptive but is called a *repair.* Repairs are John Gottman's (1999) way of explaining what couples counselors have been noticing for years: Couples also have ways of maintaining conversations even when they are zinged by their partner.

Summarizing Self Syndrome (SSS)   Similar to cross complaining, the SSS exchange (Gottman, Notarius, Gonso, & Markman, 1976) is something like this:

He: I feel good about this investment plan.
She: That agent has been unreliable in the past.
He: There are a number of good things about the plan that I really like.
She: Did you know that he did some work for Bonnie and she lost money?
He: The plan allows us to take money out of our savings when we need to without interest. Not like our present plan.

Like ships passing in the night, each person's message does not affect the other. He promotes the plan; she is uncertain about the agent's trustworthiness. Neither is hearing the important ideas or feelings that the other has to offer. Such patterns lead to win–lose struggles in which one person comes out on top temporarily.

Low Rates of Positive Reinforcement
or High Rates of Punishment

Research supports the fact that troubled couples are nicer to other people than to their spouses (Birchler, Weiss, & Vincent, 1975). It is not just that couples punish each other or get involved in communication loops; they also have very few positive exchanges (Wills, Weiss, & Patterson, 1974). Thibaut and Kelley (1959) indicate that people tend to stay in relationships as long as they are satisfying in terms of both rewards and costs. In other words, how much does it cost me to stay in this relationship compared to the rewards that I get out of it? Costs include the amount of time, energy, and money required to sustain the bond. People want a high-rewarding relationship but at the lowest personal cost. It may sound cold blooded, but the decision to remain in a relationship is very much like buying a car; we want the most for the least cost. Sometimes the relationship gives too few rewards; sometimes the cost is too great. Interestingly, it appears that people weigh the rewards and costs in a relationship and compare it with other relationships that they might have. That is how they make the decision to stay or leave a relationship.

It is also interesting to note that research indicates that positive and negative events are thought to be independent of each other. Increasing the rewards in the relationship will have relatively little effect on the unpleasant aspects of the alliance. Reducing a negative like name-calling will not necessarily make the partner feel that the relationship is very positive. Gottman (1999) claims that it takes 5 positive interactions to compensate for 1 negative interaction. When the ratio exceeds this—say, 3/1—the couple's relationship becomes unstable.

Often couples come to therapy indicating that they have either too few positives or too many negatives: "We are stuck, in neutral. We don't fight but we don't have much fun together either." This statement exemplifies a couple with few negatives but not enough positives. Over time, many relationships undergo *reinforcement erosion,* meaning that things that used to be satisfying in the relationship are not so exciting anymore. In behavioral terms, we say we *habituate* to our partner. On the negative side, a counselor might hear this kind of statement: "We enjoy each other's company, and we can really communicate most of the time, but when we get into a fight, we create a lot of damage for weeks to come." Some distressed couples have both low rates of positive reinforcement and high rates of negative or punishing interactions.

Distorted Thinking About the Partner and the Relationship

Cognitive therapy and cognitive–behavioral therapy are two names for the branch of therapy that focuses on the role of bad thinking as the cause of emotional and behavioral problems. Cognitive therapy also proposes that if one's negative or distorted thinking patterns can be corrected, then behavior will change. Cognitive therapy for couples is aimed at attacking distorted thinking about the other person and about the relationship (McKay, Fanning, & Paleg, 1994). Albert Ellis (1977) identifies *self-talk,* or the irrational sentences that people say to themselves. These thoughts, which can cause emotional disturbance in individuals, are often "nutty" ideas about relationships.

Ellis is known for his A-B-C theory of emotional disturbance. An event at "A" is perceived by the individual, and the individual's beliefs at "B" cause an emotional consequence, "C." If someone brought a black cat into the room (A) and we felt afraid (C), it would be because of the beliefs (B) we have about black cats causing bad luck. So it is not things that disturb us but what we make of these events. In looking at how illogical people are in relationships, Ellis (1985) identifies a number of irrational beliefs:

1. I must have love or approval from everyone who is significant to me, especially the one I love.
2. I must be completely competent, adequate, and achieving, and the one I love must know this.
3. When people (including my partner) treat me unfairly or badly, they are to blame, and I must see them as bad, wicked, or rotten.
4. When I am rejected or treated unfairly by the person I love, it is the end of the world, a catastrophe.
5. My unhappiness and emotional turmoil is the result of the way people and life treat me, and I have little control to change my feelings.
6. If something appears dangerous (such as the loss of my partner), I should worry about it and make myself anxious.

7. My history of bad relationships caused my present problems, and my history cannot be escaped. This has crippled me, and I am unlovable and unable to have a good relationship.
8. Life should turn out better than it often does. People should be kinder and should treat me lovingly at all times. If the people I love treat me badly, it is awful and I will never be able to deal with life's grim realities.

Instead of addressing specific thoughts, several writers have examined general errors in thinking rather than internal sentences that Ellis describes. Aaron Beck (1988) distinguishes several *categories* of distorted perceptions, which he identifies as the source of depression. Beck found that depression consists of a negative view of the self, of others, and of the future (the cognitive triad). Unfortunately, negative and distorted thinking patterns are "automatic." One does not have to ruminate; they are immediate reactions. For example, Epstein (1986) gives the example of a spouse who automatically thinks, "He always interrupts me." This automatic thought is not a description of fact; it carries the distortion *always*. This is called *overgeneralization* in Beck's terminology of cognitive distortions. If the spouse then concludes "He thinks we have nothing of value to say to each other anymore," a new distortion would be detected, *arbitrary inference*. When individuals engage in these distorted thinking patterns, they create anger, depression, and arguments with their partners. By stopping automatic thoughts and introducing more reasonable interpretations of reality, clients rid themselves of negative emotions.

Therapy Methods and Techniques

Gurman (2003) indicates that there are three normal treatment goals of behavioral marital therapists. They are (1) improving skills, (2) changing cognitions, or (3) increasing acceptance of one's partner. Listed below are some general guidelines about using behavioral techniques with a couple:

1. *Increase positives in the relationship first.* Try to bind the couple together by increasing the good feelings about the relationship so that each partner begins to see it as a source of satisfaction.
2. *Collect objective evidence about the problem.* By focusing on the data, the counselor can get a better feel about the severity of problems. A behavioral counselor will collect data on the intensity, duration, and frequency of marital arguments. In addition, the therapist might watch and count the number of repairs or negative interactions.
3. *Have the couple make a public commitment to change.* By making an agreement with each other and with the counselor, the partners increase their commitment to the goals.
4. *Both parties are involved in a behavioral cycle, so both need to change together.* This is consistent with a nonblaming atmosphere in counseling and in the relationship in general.
5. *Ask clients to keep track of their own progress.* In so doing, they are learning self-control and learning something about the gradual, steplike nature of change.

Improving Skills

Treating communication problems   Communication training may take place with the couple in the counselor's office or in a larger seminar setting with a group of couples. In the office, the counselor can adjust to each couple, whereas in the seminar general principles of communication are taught. Typically, communication training focuses on learning very specific skills such as respect, reflective listening, negotiation, timely discussion of problems, problem solving, marital manners, overcoming mind reading, and nonverbal communication. Regardless of the setting or the skills taught, most trainers employ some general procedures; they begin with simple skills and build to the more complex in the following sequence. (We go into greater depth on this topic later in this book.)

1. *Modeling.* Social learning theory, as described by Bandura, suggests that one of the primary ways that we learn is by observing others. We learned negative communication patterns primarily from our families of origin; we can also learn better communication skills by watching them being modeled. For this reason, couples are asked to watch films or listen to tapes of couples communicating effectively. During a therapy session, the counselor may model appropriate communication by role playing with one member of the couple while the other observes and then practices what the counselor has demonstrated.

2. *Rehearsal.* A key part of learning any new skill is rehearsing, or practicing. In communication training, couples can rehearse in the actual therapy session under the counselor's supervision. In a couples psychoeducational group, several couples may either rehearse simultaneously or rehearse in front of the whole group and receive feedback.

3. *Reinforcement and feedback.* The therapist reinforces positive communications practices after the couple rehearses by pointing out the couple's progress and complimenting each member on specific behaviors that were demonstrated. Then the therapist points out areas for improvement. Using what was learned from the coaching, the couple rehearses again and receives a second round of reinforcement and feedback.

4. *Homework.* Homework is specifically geared to the couple working in the clinical setting. In the communications seminar, general homework is assigned to the class and is related to the skill being discussed that week. The first item on the agenda the following week is to report on homework assignments.

Changing Reinforcement Patterns

Changing reinforcement patterns means trying to influence the low rate of positive reinforcement and high rate of punishment that often occurs in distressed couples. In couples behavior therapy, this begins with the counselor immediately insisting on the need for reciprocal change (both partners must change) and a commitment to a nonblaming attitude. In general, the strategy is to increase positives in the relationship first, which helps give the couple faith in the process at the onset. Behaviorally oriented counselors suggest that couples should begin by choosing several relatively high payoff, low-cost exchanges. For example, it might be very important for Barry if Linda would remember to kiss him good-bye before going to work in the morning, and it would require relatively little effort from Linda. The "Caring Days" technique is a behavioral technique whereby couples agree to publicly commit to increasing the positives in their relationship. They post the rewards that they will give to each other and objectively document their completion. The chart helps encourage the couple because both members see real evidence of behavioral differences.

Although increasing the positives in the relationship is important, decreasing negative interactions is also vital to treating the couple from a behavioral standpoint. Most punishing responses in couples therapy are verbal "arrows" fired in anger, and communication training is the basic method that most behavior therapy counselors use to treat this problem. Couples learn to give compliments and reduce degrading or punishing comments. Many people are surprised to find that their common expressions are taken very negatively by their spouses, despite good intentions.

Correcting Cognitive Errors

Couples tend to commit cognitive errors in their thinking about each other and in their ideas about the relationship. They tend to misinterpret and jump to conclusions about their partner's behavior. They see the tiniest flicker of a smile as outright mockery; they hear the refrigerator slam as a slap in the face. In individual counseling, distortions are treated by helping each individual identify his or her own errors and substitute more constructive thinking patterns. Dattilio and Padesky (1990) have written about the application of cognitive therapy to couples following Beck's lead. They suggest that couples cognitive therapy should examine beliefs about relationships in general and beliefs or cognitions about the partner specifically. Several specific beliefs may be tied together by a common theme. For example, "I have always chosen the wrong person," "Everything turns out wrong," and "I always allow myself to be used" may be three common thoughts of an individual. When we look a little deeper, we see that they all suggest an underlying view of the self as ineffective. Most cognitive therapists would try to help the individual challenge the more general thinking pattern, whether it shows up in the relationship with the partner or in one with the boss. Following Beck's ideas, McKay and colleagues (1994) identified the following eight basic fallacies, or cognitive distortions, that most frequently operate in the couple situation.

1. *Tunnel vision fallacy.* This is the tendency to see only the negative aspect of the relationship or the other person's problem behaviors and to ignore the positive aspects.
2. *Assumed intent fallacy.* Especially when couples have been together for some time, they think they know what the other is thinking or intending. On the basis of only a few words or gestures, they guess their partner's intentions. Once, during a therapy session, I asked a husband to tell me what he liked about his wife. He complimented her sense of style and dress. She reacted angrily and at length to this compliment, taking it as a veiled criticism of her tendency to spend money on clothing.

3. *Magnification fallacy.* This is the human tendency to make mountains out of molehills. Albert Ellis refers to this distortion as catastrophizing. Couples may describe their wedding as "a disaster" when in fact there were both high spots and bad moments.

4. *Global labeling fallacy.* In global labeling, one member of the couple labels the other one—for example, "She is irresponsible," or "He is a pathological liar." This fallacy takes an example of the person's behavior and uses it to sum up his or her whole personality. When a birthday is forgotten, this turns into the global label of "thoughtless."

5. *Good–bad dichotomizing fallacy.* This is the tendency to see reality and the partner in black-and-white terms as in these communications: "While you were away, everything was peaceful; now it's chaos." "You were wrong not to consult with me, and you won't admit it."

6. *Fractured logic fallacy.* Fractured logic can be detected in client statements like this: "He obviously doesn't want to work on the marriage because he was so mean to my mother." "She loves her work so much that she will probably find someone there she likes more." Fractured logic is not often expressed directly, but the implications are there in the argument. Fractured logic consists of a premise and a conclusion that are independent of each other. The therapist may point out the client's argument and identify the fracture so that the client can examine his or her faulty thinking.

7. *Control fallacies.* Control fallacies can exist on both ends of a continuum. On one end, a person thinks that he or she is totally responsible for all that happens in a relationship or at the other extreme can believe that he or she is powerless and out of control. For example, "He is emotionally distant. There is no way I can have an intimate marriage," or "I can't make him happy anymore."

8. *Letting it out fallacy.* This fallacy involves the belief that when your partner is wrong, he or she deserves to be punished and it is all right to unleash your wrath upon him or her. A corollary of this idea is that screaming and emotional violence is necessary and a justifiable way to get the partner's attention.

Let's take an example of cognitive therapy in the realm of couples therapy: Patricia and Richard have been in conflict about how to deal with the misbehavior of Patricia's adolescent son, who lives with them. Patricia's ex-husband is very much involved in the situation; he is concerned and talks with Patricia at length about the problem. Table 2.1 lists some events as they occurred and each person's thoughts about the situations. This homework assignment was given to the couple as an assessment tool for the therapist and to increase the couple's awareness of their thinking patterns. The partners were asked to write down upsetting events during the week, their thoughts about the events, and their resultant emotions. In the counseling session, the therapist may help the couple identify the cognitive errors. See if you can identify some of the eight fallacies in the recorded thoughts of the couple.

Table 2.1   Thoughts and Emotions Recorded by Each Member of a Couple

Event	Thoughts	Emotions
Richard		
Patricia is talking to her ex again.	I bet they are thinking about reuniting.	Hurt, jealous
I come home and find Brian's books and papers in the living room.	The kid is lazy; he'll never amount to anything.	Angry
Patricia comes home from work, talks to Brian, but doesn't ask me about my day.	(She babies him.) She cares more about everyone else; I'm not important.	Hurt, angry
Patricia		
I come home, Richard is in our room, and Brian in his. They do not talk to each other over dinner.	I'm a failure as a wife and mother.	Sad
Richard asks Brian about his homework.	He's just hoping that Brian hasn't done it so that he can put him down.	Angry
I yell at Richard when he complains to me about Brian's laziness.	He was wrong. I needed to release. Maybe now, he'll let up.	Angry

You might infer from the dialogue between Richard and Patricia that this approach appears to be a treatment of individuals. Cognitive therapists do help each member of the couple discover his or her nonconstructive thinking and encourage that person to change thinking patterns. But cognitive therapists also try to help couples sort out their distortions when they are seen conjointly (together). The counselor challenges both partners to examine the rationality or irrationality of their own thoughts and to identify the errors in their thinking. In addition, the astute cognitive therapist will look at how beliefs and thoughts of the members interact in a unique way. For example, perhaps Patricia's low opinion of herself is activated by Richard's criticism. The counselor can examine this through homework or by stopping the action during the therapy session and asking the clients to report their automatic thoughts that occur when the other person is speaking.

MULTIGENERATIONAL APPROACHES TO COUPLES THERAPY: OBJECT RELATIONS AND THE BOWEN THEORY

No one who has any experience of the rifts which so divide a family will, if he is an analyst, be surprised to find that the patient's closest relatives sometimes betray less interest in his recovering than in his remaining as he is.
Freud, 1917/1963, p. 459

Four family therapy approaches have as a central premise that one's family of origin is the most important experience that affects one's current relationships. They are the Bowen theory (Bowen, 1978), experiential family therapy (Whitaker & Bumberry, 1988), contextual therapy (Boszormenyi-Nagy & Ulrich, 1981), and object-relations theory (Slipp, 1991). The two most relevant to couples work are Bowen's theory and object relations, so, we examine these in more detail. These schools of thought are bound together by their origin in psychodynamic concepts. Many of the roots are found in the writings of Frenczi, Sullivan, Horney, Klein, Kernberg, and Kohut. For both, there is a belief in the importance of history and in the centrality of early experiences with caregivers. But the two approaches have significant differences. As the name implies, the multigenerational (or sometimes *transgenerational*) theories are most concerned with the transmission of family patterns through the generations whereas object-relations therapy focuses more on the interactions of two individuals' projections.

Object-Relations Theory

The object-relations approach is not a single school of thought (Finkelstein, 1987; Kilpatrick & Kilpatrick, 1991; Scharff & Scharff, 1991; St. Clair, 2003), but we try in this section to find some common elements to avoid too much detail because the theory is difficult to grasp. In general, object-relations theories beginning with Dicks (1967) have tried to bridge the gap between the strictly intrapersonal theory of Freud and the growing awareness that relationships and the social context are also critical to mental health. Instead of sex, seeking connection and nurturance (mothering) is considered to be a primary drive. The source of problems is that each member projects his or her unmet needs on the other and the other person accepts this projection.

The definition of an internal object is crucial to understanding object-relations theory. Let's say that an *internal object* is the mental representation that one has of self or others. Figure 2.2 shows how an individual represents the self and parents as internal objects. For example, a child may have had both strong positive and negative experiences with the mother; at one moment she is nurturing, the next rejecting. The child's idea or image of the mother (internal object) contains contradictory experiences, which creates cognitive dissonance and anxiety. To deal with anxiety, the child splits internal objects into their good and bad parts, making them into separate fantasy objects. Contradiction is reduced and equilibrium is achieved. In this case, the child splits the mother into the good mother and the bad mother representations. Because this splitting reduces anxiety, the child learns to apply this same mechanism to discrepant experiences of the self. Unacceptable (bad) and idealized (good) parts of the self become detached and projected onto others. According to the theory, many of the things that we do not like about others are actually our own negative attributes, split off and projected onto those around us.

When a child reaches adulthood and becomes involved in intimate relationships outside the family, the other member of the couple is a prime target for

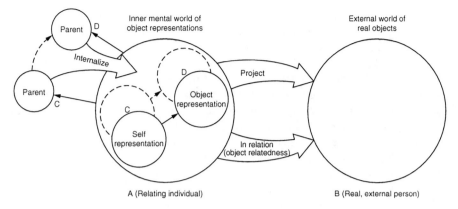

Figure 2.2   Internal and external objects
Source: From *Object Relations and Self-Psychology: An Introduction* (4th ed.), by M. St. Clair.
Copyright 2003 by Brooks/Cole Publishing Company, a part of Cengage Learning.

projection because any intense relationship brings back feelings from earlier connections and catalyzes a defensive reaction. Instead of responding to our partner, we respond to our internal object (for example, mother), projecting these same feelings onto the partner. The other member's response to this projection may be affected by his or her own unique background and upbringing. According to the theory, the interaction of these mutual projections creates most of the problems that couples experience. In other words, the partners are dealing not with their real issues but with projections of themselves and images of previous relationships. Connected to the object-relations view of couples is the notion of *interlocking pathologies*. This means that, in very disturbed relationships, each member intensely needs the other person and that their internal objects have found a match. For example, she needs him to be the father she never had; and he needs her to be weak so that he can feel strong.

Definitions of Key Terms

Following are some of the key terms associated with object relations.

   object   A person (not a thing) toward whom desires and behaviors are focused. An object may be represented internally (internal object) or may be an actual person.

   object seeking   Humans' motivation to search for and maintain contact with others. Human beings are looking for intimacy and nurturing. The object-relations approach's biggest departure from Freud was Fairbairn's substitution of "object seeking" as the major motivation for human behavior, replacing the concept of libidinal drive.

   projective identification   Also referred to as *collusion*, a defense mechanism first explicated by Melanie Klein, whereby unacceptable parts of the self are attributed to another person and the other person is invited or induced to play a certain role (Siegel, 1991). The domineering husband and nonassertive wife is a common example; he projects his unacceptable need for nurturing onto her, and she accepts the role. The husband then feels smothered by the role he has induced her to play. According to Kilpatrick and Kilpatrick (1991), the Freudian concept of transference, the idea of scapegoating in family therapy, Framo's notion of irrational role assignments, Mahler's term *symbiosis,* and Bowen's family projective process are all different ways of describing projective identification.

self-representation The internal image of the developing self. An infant begins at birth to differentiate the self from surrounding objects and, by contrast, forms an internal representation of the self.

splitting A psychological mechanism that divides a contradictory object into two or more parts. A child parcels a parent who is nurturing and occasionally rejecting into a two-part object, one "good father" and one "rejecting father." Splitting can serve an important defensive function, but it can also be unhealthy. When projective identification takes place, the individual is not dealing with reality but with a mental construction.

symbiosis The relationship between two or more people who cannot function without the other(s), as opposed to the concept of differentiation; this is basically an unhealthy state.

Some Premises of Object-Relations Theory

1. Object seeking/attachment is a primary motivational force. We are all seeking interpersonal fulfillment.
2. Maturity means more than autonomy; it includes the capacity of becoming intimate and interdependent. In other words, growing up means allowing for appropriate dependency without loss of self-respect.
3. Human beings develop from symbiotic to dependent to interdependent, or *individuated,* people.
4. Couples counselors who use the object-relations approach will help each member of the couple develop a better capacity for connectedness, attachment, and commitment (Finkelstein, 1987).
5. Sexual problems in marriage primarily reflect relationship problems as well as individual inhibitions and anxieties.
6. Conflicts about autonomy, attachment, and commitment are ongoing in a couple's relationship because they relate to the conflicting human needs to feel connected and autonomous.
7. Childhood relationships with parents determine an individual's ability to function in an intimate couple relationship and deal with the issues of autonomy, attachment, and commitment.
8. Intimacy is a major motivation for becoming a couple, but intimacy brings about fears of dependency and lack of autonomy.
9. Everyone has idealistic ideas about the intimate relationship, hoping to fulfill unmet needs from the childhood relationship with parents.

10. Intrapsychic conflicts arise from experiences in the original family. The individual shapes the present relationship to mirror the family of origin as a way of trying to resolve the past.
11. By reviewing the past in individual, family, or couples counseling, the individual can gain insight into his or her original conflicts and begin treating the partner as a present reality rather than as a reflection of the past.
12. Mates select each other to recover lost aspects of their primary object relations. They reexperience these aspects in the partner through projective identification (Dicks, 1967).

Problems That Couples Experience

Complementary neurotic patterns based on projections and wishes   *Neurotic* is a psychodynamic term that refers to the individual's tendency to operate on the basis of projections, wishes, and defense mechanisms rather than rationality and reality. Other theorists often refer to neurotic behavior as self-defeating behavior. These patterns are complementary and promote stability but probably stifle an individual's movement toward individuation (mental health). Strean (1985) identifies several such couple patterns based on psychodynamic thinking:

1. *The partner as superego.* This is the couples arrangement in which one partner plays the parent and the other plays the child. The "child" cannot approve of anything that he or she does without the partner's approval. The "parent" in the relationship needs the partner to play the id; the "child" helps the "parent" experience id impulses. One is "stable," the other is "wild."

2. *The partner as a devaluated self-image.* In this pattern, everything bad about the self can be projected onto the partner. Claiming that "she has no head for money" is a way of not taking responsibility for financial problems.

3. *The partner as ego ideal.* "My better half" is one way of expressing the tendency to idealize one's mate. One member achieves a rather fragile self-esteem by idealizing the mate or becoming a satellite to the partner's success. Because no one can live up to fantasies of perfection, the "ideal person" eventually falls off the pedestal, bringing disappointment and conflict; the other partner may not develop his or her full potential.

4. *The dominant–submissive dyad.* In this arrangement, one member is described as sadistic or aggressive and humiliates the partner. The partner is submissive, dependent, and a martyr. From a psychodynamic perspective, the sadistic behavior is a defense against dependent feelings. The dominant member controls the self by controlling the other person.

5. *The detached–demanding dyad.* This cycle is similar to the classic pursuer–distancer relationship in which one member chases and the other withdraws. Here, the demanding partner is seen as dependent, and the detached one fears his or her own dependency needs.

6. *Romantic–rational partnership.* Sager (1976) identifies several types of pathological relationships based on unmet needs. Among these is the

romantic–rational partnership in which one member is extremely logical and devoid of emotion and the other is prone to living in a fantasy world. Perhaps this is why engineers seem to marry artists. The rational one provides grounding for the romantic, and the romantic one provides excitement for the rational. This may stifle the growth of each.

7. *The partner as parent.* Sager (1976) recognizes parent–child combinations in marriage as one of the most common pathological problems; one partner assumes control, and the other is allowed to be irresponsible and dependent. Both are meeting needs because the responsible partner needs to gain a sense of control, be viewed as "in charge," feel nurturing, or be seen as a martyr. The "child" enjoys being taken care of. In transactional analysis, this combination with a male "parent" and female "child" has been called the Big Daddy–Cinderella partnership. Again, the price paid is that one is forced to be joyless, and the other remains a child.

8. *The "love-sick" wife and the "cold-sick" husband.* Psychodynamic thinkers Martin and Bird (1959) identify this pattern as a classic pairing of "obsessive husbands" and "hysterical wives." Today, we think of this as a rather sexist understanding of the couple's relationship, not to mention an extremely pathological portrayal. In the pattern, as originally described, the woman complains that her husband is cold and unable to love, and she describes her own symptoms as "anxiety." The wife suffers from low self-esteem and requires attention from her spouse to feel worthwhile. The husband is described as emotionless with a strong ego and a tyrannical superego. In short, the husbands were thought to be rigid and the wives unstable. The reversal of this common entanglement was the "hysterical husband and the obsessional wife." This pattern was thought to be the result of the husband searching for a "mother"—that is, someone to take care of him. Psychodynamic theorists found this pattern to be specific evidence of *interlocking pathologies,* meaning that certain personality patterns seek out others to meet needs and to achieve stability.

Therapy Methods and Techniques

Following are some guidelines for object-relations techniques with couples. It should be noted that because object relations bridges the individual and family therapy realms, the therapist might see members individually and conjointly.

1. Slipp (1991) contends that one of the most important measures a counselor can take is to develop a safe "holding environment" with empathy. The counselor extends this protection to the couple in re-creating a nurturing, "maternal" environment (Seinfeld, 1993). Facilitating trust lowers defensiveness and allows the couple to deal safely with aggression and pent-up frustration.

2. The major method in object-relations therapy is to explore the past. The counselor ordinarily works one on one with each person, exploring childhood experiences and developmental history (Finkelstein, 1987). When both the relationship with the parents and the parents' own marital relationship is explored, the individual may gain insight into his or her own behavior in the present relationship. Fairbairn (1952) thought this exploration would help clients realize

that everyone is basically striving to be taken care of in their couple relationship. We seek the couple relationship as a way of fulfilling unmet dependency needs from childhood. When this dynamic is interpreted in counseling, the client gains insight through which he or she is supposed to learn to accept a "normal" amount of dependency without hostility.

3. The counselor uses interpretation to help clients understand the roots of their problems. *Interpretation* is the counselor's reformulation of the clients' current dilemma in terms of its psychological meaning. For example, after examining the couple's background, a counselor might interpret the projective identification process brought forward from families of origin. Rather than interpreting the husband's behavior as "domineering," the therapist will point out that, to achieve self-worth, the husband's history taught him that it was important for him to see himself as "in charge." The therapist might then help the wife see how she colludes with her husband's projection by being submissive. By identifying the origin and describing its current manifestation, the couple can see that there may be more productive ways to meet their needs.

4. The dynamically oriented counselor helps couples understand their individual families of origin and how they interact. The genogram is a popular technique for this activity. A *genogram* is a family tree that is drawn to describe relationships between people from the past and present (see Chapter 5). Whether a genogram is used or not, special emphasis will be placed on personal perspectives, or "representations," of parents and on the client's view of the parents' relationship, which serves as an internal model for the client's present relationships.

Is Transactional Analysis Object Relations?

Transactional analysis, or TA (Berne, 1964), is a form of therapy whose popularity has waned in recent years (Young, 1992). One of the reasons for its decline may be the popular, "cutesy" language used to describe its various components, such as "warm fuzzies." But TA, as promoted by its founder Eric Berne, was one of the most easily understandable ways to explain object relations. Berne believed that parents pass on "implants" to their children. These messages come in the form of "scripts," "tapes," and "injunctions." These implants were expectations and ideas about the world and the self that continued to unconsciously affect a person's behavior. Berne understood that in husband–wife interactions, "the parent" in one person was sometimes speaking to "the child" in the other. Berne's *Sex in Human Loving* (1970) and *Games People Play* (1964) point out the reasons that people, and especially couples, become involved in elaborate game-playing behavior. According to Berne, they are fulfilling childhood versions of reality or trying to receive "strokes" and other payoffs based on early learning.

The Bowen Theory

Murray Bowen (1978), a pioneer and major theorist in the field of family therapy, developed the Bowen family systems theory. Bowen's preferred method for working with families was to see the marital couple either individually or conjointly even if the issue to be dealt with was dealing with one of the children. Bowen felt that the couple had the power and motivation to make the changes. Bowen's theory is a systems theory, so change in one part of the system shows up in other parts of the system. Bowen sees marital or couples conflict as a symptom of a problem within the system, and it is the system that must be treated. Symptoms may also show up in illness, emotional distancing by one partner, or an "acting out" of a child.

All of Bowen's concepts are based on the premise that life for all species is accompanied by a chronic anxiety. The level of this anxiety is influenced by the amount of differentiation one gained from one's original family members and within oneself. Individuals still operating out of their original family relationships (fusion) are not truly healthy. The cure and the preventive medicine for anxiety is differentiation for each member of the couple. To be truly differentiated, a person must be able to separate the feeling process and the thinking process within himself or herself. One must (1) let the thinking rule while understanding that emotions are important and (2) be independent of one's early conditioning by the family of origin. If one can act autonomously and intimately and function interdependently with one's relatives, he or she could be said to have achieved differentiation. In other words, if one cannot operate independently, one can never achieve intimacy. Intimacy would be confused with dependence and fusion. Couples problems occur when anxiety rises in one individual or the couple, and they must reach out and involve other members of their family to achieve stability (triangulation).

Definitions of Key Terms

Some of the key terms in the Bowen theory are as follows:

differentiation The process of becoming emotionally independent. Differentiation involves the ability to express one's own opinions and feelings while listening to others and remaining emotionally connected. It also includes decisions based on nonanxious thinking rather than by simply reacting. For example, a couple with a low-level differentiation will frequently argue because both are reacting to each other in an anxious and emotionally reactive way rather than focusing on the problem and thinking it through.

emotional triangles Involve any three parts of an emotional system, usually composed of three people, with the dyad bringing in (triangulating) a third person to diffuse the anxiety of the two-person system. For example, in marital conflict, spouses may triangulate a child by focusing on the child's problem and thus diffuse the anxiety of their conflict (Bowen, 1978).

genogram A format for drawing a family tree that records information about family members and their relationships, spanning at least three generations (McGoldrick, Gerson, & Shellenberger, 1999). This visual aid quickly points out the patterns and multigenerational transmissions of the family system. It is generally drawn during the first counseling session, and their additions are made during counseling. Genograms are most often associated with Bowen's therapy but are also used by counselors of other orientations. (Genograms are described in detail in Chapter 5 of this book.)

individuality versus togetherness forces Two natural forces constantly at work in individuals and in relationships. People want togetherness and separateness, communion and agency. If one partner feels too close, he or she will create distance, and the other, feeling this distance, may experience a need for more togetherness and pursue the partner. Such patterns are frequently presenting problems for couples.

intellectual versus emotional functioning People are capable of making choices by using either their objective intellectual system or their subjective emotional system. To make a real choice, people must be able to distinguish between these two systems within themselves. The more anxious a person is, the greater will be the possibility of fusion between the two systems and fusion with the emotions of others. For example, if partners can remain calm in problem solving, they can think fairly clearly and objectively. However, if too much emotionality over a long period occurs, the emotions run the system, and problems do not get solved.

multigenerational transmission The passing down of typical ways of responding to emotions from generation to generation, both in the nature and the degree of intensity. What happens in one generation often happens in the next. Bowen believes that people are attracted to partners who are operating at the same level of differentiation.

Some Premises of Bowenian Theory

Following are basic tenets of Bowen's theory as they relate to couples counseling:

1. Couples are attracted to and marry or committed to someone at their own level of differentiation.
2. Couples repeat the behaviors of their families of origin and extended families, so the counselor must collect a history of at least three generations.
3. Couples conflicts or a dysfunctional partner point to problems in the family system, and thus the system must be treated.
4. The goal of all therapy with couples is the same: to raise the level of differentiation in both partners to the highest level possible. Couples are coached to take back the energy invested in changing their partners and concentrate on changing themselves.
5. A couple's levels of differentiation can grow no higher than the level of the therapist, so Bowenian therapists must have high levels of differentiation.

Problems That Couples Experience

Chronic conflict   When high levels of chronic anxiety and low levels of differentiation are present in couples relationships, the partners will react emotionally rather than using rational thinking to solve problems. Severe conflict between the two partners is one of the most frequent symptoms in the family system.

Differences in levels of differentiation   Sometimes one partner will raise his or her own level of differentiation through education or counseling, but the other does not. Bowen felt that if the difference is significant there may be little remaining commonality in lifestyles.

Distancer–pursuer pattern   Sometimes one partner in the relationship will distance emotionally, and the other will pursue. This is often done through blaming or accusing and results in conflict. This revolving conflict does not settle the issue of the need to be together and separate.

Problems due to dissimilar family-of-origin messages   Couples often have very different family-of-origin messages about issues such as gender roles, how to handle money, how to raise children, and sexual issues. Each partner will fight to make the new family like his or her family of origin.

Triangulation   When anxiety is high in a couple's relationship, another person or habit may be triangulated by the couple to ease pressure but may become problems themselves. Examples of triangulation include extramarital affairs, alcoholism, children's behavioral problems, and in-laws.

Overfunctioning/underfunctioning pattern   An overfunctioning/underfunctioning pattern may emerge. A clear example is when one partner is a substance abuser and the other overfunctions as a codependent.

Unresolved family-of-origin issues   One or both partners may have left the family of origin with unresolved emotional issues involving parents. According to Bowen, we seek partners similar to that parent with whom we have unfinished business.

Therapy Methods and Techniques

A discussion of Bowenian therapy with couples must start with the description of the counselor because a mature counselor is considered the main tool in promoting differentiation. Bowenian therapists have worked on and continue to address their own issues with their families of origin and have experienced growth in their own levels of differentiation. Supervision involves self-examination and personal growth through examining one's own family background.

A Bowenian counselor is a coach and a teacher with four main functions: (1) defining and clarifying the relationship between the spouses, (2) keeping oneself "detriangulated" from the family emotional system, (3) teaching the couple how emotional systems work, and (4) demonstrating differentiation by taking "I" position stands during the course of the therapy (Bowen, 1978). (An "I" position is letting the couple know where the therapist stands on an issue even if it goes against the grain.) It is a model for couples to be more honest and to gain the courage to differentiate.

In Bowenian therapy, couples are normally seen together. If the relationship is too filled with conflict or if only one partner wants to change the relationship, work must first be done with the highest functioning and most differentiated partner.

The Work of James Framo

I am half inclined to think we are all ghosts, Mr. Manders. It is not only what we have inherited from our fathers and mothers that exists again in us, but all sorts of old dead ideas and all kinds of old dead beliefs and things of that kind. They are not actually alive in us; but there they are dormant, all the same, and we can never be rid of them. Whenever I take up a newspaper and read it, I fancy I see ghosts creeping between the lines. There must be ghosts all over the world. They must be as countless as the grains of the sands, it seems to me. And we are so miserably afraid of the light, all of us. (Ibsen, 1911, pp.105–106)

James Framo impressed those who knew him as a psychodynamic Carl Rogers. His easy-going manner, gentle personality, sense of humor, and shrewd insights made him a popular speaker and respected teacher. His ability to disarm difficult clients by his caring was impressive. His recent passing was a tremendous loss to the field of family therapy. In essence, Framo saw present relationship problems as reflections of family-of-origin issues; we cannot see our partners clearly, and we project on them because "old ghosts stand in the way" (Framo, 1990, p. 49). Framo believed in helping individuals within the couple to face their old ghosts by addressing the living members of their families of origin.

Framo's work is truly multigenerational and borrows from the object-relations theories, but it also blends with some ideas of Boszromenyi-Nagy and Bowen (see Framo, 1970, 1976). I (Mark Young) once asked Dr. Framo, "What is the difference between you and Murray Bowen?" He replied, "About 30 pounds." I think he was humbly recognizing Bowen's contribution to the beginnings of multigenerational family therapy, but Framo made his own mark on couples work and family therapy. In a demonstration filmed by the American Therapy Association, Framo (1993) demonstrated his approach with a real couple experiencing problems in their marriage. Framo's attention turned immediately to both partners' families of origin. Both husband and wife admitted to having severely troubled relationships with their fathers, which Framo suggested they address. Framo referred to their relationships with their fathers as a "shared object," implying that both are left with similar unfinished business. He encouraged the husband and wife to meet separately with their parents and voice some of the unexpressed issues from the past in a nonblameful way to promote a stronger parent–child relationship. Framo seemed to suggest that the partners were initially drawn to each other because of similar family-of-origin problems and problems persist because of unresolved issues in those core relationships. Framo's multigenerational work went beyond seeing couples. He frequently met with an individual and the members of his or her family of origin (without the spouse) to deal with historical family issues. Framo's text *Family-of-Origin Therapy: An Intergenerational Approach* (1992) explains this unique method.

As one partner gains a higher level of differentiation, the other is expected to reciprocate with more maturity. Once this is settled, the counselor takes a thorough family history of at least three generations using a genogram. The therapist presents this to the couple as a research project. They are told that by getting to know more about their families of origin they will be able to see what each has brought to the table. Partners are given homework assignments to increase differentiation. The therapist may ask them to visit their families of origin for more information, insight, and practice in taking "I" positions.

Questions and coaching are the counselor's main techniques, and the counselor takes primary control of the sessions. The atmosphere is calm and cerebral, with one partner responding directly to the counselor's questions and the other partner listening. The listening partner is then asked to report thoughts that arose as he or she heard his or her partner speak. The counselor clarifies for the couple and insists that both partners stay focused and take responsibility for their own parts of the problem. The counselor asks questions to point out the problems and uses words like *opinions, thoughts,* and *ideas* when asking for comments. Feelings or other subjective responses are avoided. Bowen thought that the magic of couples counseling was that it allowed each member a chance to externalize their thoughts while the other overhears them. This helps them differentiate because it draws the distinction between the two individuals.

Stages of Bowenian Couples Therapy

In the beginning stage of high anxiety, the main work of counseling is to deal with the emotionality of the couple and neutralize it. The therapist must keep detriangulated, repeatedly confirming neutrality. As the anxiety decreases through calm questioning and genogram work, one partner will move toward individuation by focusing on self-responsibility in the relationship and by beginning to accept blame for his or her own discomfort or unhappiness. The other partner will then see the need for personal change and give up trying to change the other. Differentiation is a stress on the family system. As one partner becomes more of an individual, the other may pursue, feeling that they are losing their means of gaining closeness. Eventually, the couple adjusts to a more differentiated system as each person grows.

CONCLUSION

This chapter presented two rather opposing views of couples therapy, the behavioral and psychodynamic/multigenerational viewpoints. It also looked at the multigenerational theories focusing on the work of Murray Bowen. The unique approach of James Framo, which blends object relations and multigenerational work, is also touched upon.

The most important new trends in couples counseling have emerged from the research of Gottman and his associates who have been studying couple communication problems and have concluded that perpetual problems that clients face must be dealt with in addition to merely teaching skills to clients. This integrative behavioral approach has gained wide acceptance in the therapeutic community. By contrast, psychodynamic and multigenerational approaches have waned. Part of this is merely that research has not turned in this direction and that such approaches are not compatible with new constructivist ideas and the pressure of managed care. In Chapter 3, we take up the structural and strategic points of view, along with newer and emerging therapies. At the end of Chapter 3, we make a case for the integrative model proposed by this book.

3

Theories of Couples Therapy: Part Two

KEY CONCEPTS

- Structural therapy and strategic therapy have been major forces in the history of family therapy. There are many similarities theoretically, but they are different in technique.
- Structural therapy begins by joining the therapist with the couple. The therapist may then make changes in the couple's boundaries, power rules, or the coalitions that may exist in the family and that prevent a good couple relationship.
- Strategic therapy is aimed at "rocking the boat." Anything that can disrupt couple patterns or changes their interactions is healthy. Strategic therapy is action oriented and often uses methods that are not rational.
- The Brief Family Therapy Center approach is called solution-focused therapy. It is a brief, historical method that is future oriented, focusing on future possibilities rather than past problems.
- Solution-focused therapy has been applied to couple work because it focuses the couples on those aspects of the relationship that are working and have worked in the past. It is now a well-established couples therapy.
- Two newer approaches to couples work are gaining ground: narrative therapy and emotionally focused therapy, which are briefly described in the last part of the chapter.
- Narrative therapy is based on constructivism and focuses on the stories that the couple tells about their relationship. Some of these stories are empowering, and others are tragic. The narrative therapist gets the couple to see the problem as something outside of themselves and encourages them to engage in conversations about the positive and changeable aspects of the story.

- Emotionally focused therapy adds an emphasis on affect that appears to be missing in many methods. Rather than stifling emotional expression, the therapist encourages it, validates it, and helps the couple to meet each other's need for comfort and attachment.

In this chapter, we continue with our exploration of the various theories of therapy begun in Chapter 2. In that chapter, we described several traditional approaches to couples work. Here, we begin by examining structural and strategic therapies because they represent a transition from traditional theories to brief and constructivist approaches. Chief among these is solution-focused therapy because it has established itself as a clear approach for dealing with couples. Two newer therapies, narrative therapy and emotionally focused therapy, also deserve some attention, and we give you the major terminology and premises. Emotionally focused therapy draws from several major theoretical positions including attachment theory and gestalt therapy. Understanding this theory will pave the way for understanding and using other integrative approaches such as the model proposed by this book.

STRUCTURAL THERAPY AND STRATEGIC THERAPY APPLIED TO COUPLES

The major conflicts in a marriage center in the problem of who is to tell whom what to do under what circumstances.
Haley, 1963, p. 227

The structural and strategic schools of family therapy are distinct theoretical positions, but they contain many similarities when applied. For that reason, they have frequently been linked and are often discussed together (Friesen, 1985; Keim & Lappin, 2002; Stanton, 1980; Todd, 1984, 1986). Not everyone agrees that they should be integrated (Fish & Piercy, 1987) because considerable differences exist in the two approaches. In this section, we look at them both individually and as separate systems.

Salvador Minuchin (1974) is the person most often associated with structural family therapy, and Jay Haley (1976) is a key theorist in strategic therapy. For more information on how to apply a structural approach to couples, see Aponte and DiCesare's (2000) chapter. For more on brief strategic therapy with couples, see Shoham and Rohrbaugh (2002).

Definitions of Key Terms

alliance (coalition) When two or more people in a family form an alliance to achieve a goal or to relate to a third party as a team. Alliances are made for mutual protection, to keep secrets and maintain homeostasis.

boundary An imaginary line that separates systems from each other and subsystems from the larger family. For example, the marital couple is distinct from the children. The degree to which this is made known and enforced shows the strength of the generational boundary. Boundaries are like membranes around a family, a couple, or a subsystem. Sometimes they are too permeable, allowing other people to interfere in the system; sometimes they are too rigid, creating too small a world for the members. Ideally, boundaries allow the couple (feeling like a couple) or family system (feeling like a family) to have an identifiable life while allowing individuals to have some degree of autonomy.

disengaged A high degree of autonomy in each member of the family but also a lack of intimacy, self-disclosure, and belongingness. *Disengaged* is at the opposite end of the continuum from *enmeshed*.

enmeshment An excessive amount of connection and cohesion among family members. In its extreme form, there is little privacy or sense of self for individual members. Enmeshment is dysfunctional when families are overinvolved in each other's lives and when families do not allow individuals to be themselves. Another way of describing enmeshment is to say that external boundaries of the family may be strong but boundaries between individuals within the family are blurred.

hierarchy The way a family is organized from top to bottom in terms of love, authority, and caretaking (Keim & Lappin, 2002). There may also be a hierarchy in the couple relationship.

homeostasis A medical term applied metaphorically to families; the tendency of a family to seek a lower level of anxiety or stability. Homeostasis is a self-regulating function, a state of balance or relative quietude during which the unit can perform some of its functions and support some of the members. Homeostasis is not necessarily a healthy state for all members.

joining Both an attitude and an activity of the therapist. It means becoming a part of the family while developing a supportive and therapeutic relationship; it is the attitude of being "on their side." At certain times, the therapist may shift and "join" with an individual or a subsystem of the family when required.

scapegoating The tendency for a family to blame its problems on one member, who is then the "identified patient" or "symptom bearer." Scapegoating appears to relieve pressure on the overall system and helps the family achieve homeostasis.

subsystem A group of family members that join to perform specific tasks or functions. For example, there may be a parent subsystem.

triangle A family configuration formed when a dyad is under stress and a third member is recruited to reduce pressure. For example, a mother may seek intimacy from her daughter that she is not receiving in the couple relationship.

Some Premises of the Theories

Following are some basic premises of structural and strategic therapies.

Structural Therapy

1. Couples relationships have three basic dimensions: *boundaries, power,* and *alignment.*

2. Boundary problems are described as enmeshment or disengagement (see definitions above). Couples need to have boundaries that allow them to experience themselves as a couple and as individuals.
3. Problems with power are due to a dysfunctional set of basic agreements about the hierarchy of the family unit, leaving some members less powerful and the others more powerful.
4. Unhealthy alliances between family members are a major source of problems. For example, some couple problems are the result of a cross-generational alliance with a child. Such an alliance may be unhealthy when it empowers the child at the expense of one member of the couple or when a child becomes "parentified," requiring adult or spouselike responsibilities as a part of the child's family role.
5. Healthy families have clearly defined generational boundaries, with parents aligning together as the executives especially on important issues.
6. Healthy couples have clear rules related to power. They have a workable system for making decisions.
7. Changing boundaries, alignments, and redistributing power (family structure) leads to change. Insight alone is not sufficient for change. Structural change in the family leads to change in individuals.
8. It is crucial that the counselor join with the couple or family in order to treat them. Only by joining can the counselor become influential in making the structural changes in the family. Sometimes it is said that the role of the counselor is "joining and kicking." This means that first the counselor joins the couple and then begins changing boundaries, alignments, and redistributing power.
9. Normal and expected milestones in a couple's life can create problems. Family organizational structure needs to change in response to developmental events, and new rules need to be made.
10. A couple's problems develop and are maintained in the context of family relationships. The whole family needs to be considered when dealing with a couple's problems.
11. The focus is on the here and now. The past is relevant only as it is enacted in the present.

Strategic Therapy

1. Causality is circular and problem behaviors are part of a recursive sequence of events. It makes little sense to try to track down the culprit in a couple because both are cocreating the situation.
2. Therapist and clients are constantly influencing each other. Because therapists cannot remain neutral, the therapist's influence should be planned.
3. The therapist is a change agent. Even maladaptive behaviors maintain homeostatic balance, and changing them means "upsetting the apple cart."

4. A symptom is a communication, and the therapist's job is to help decode the message behind the behavior. When one member of the couple barricades himself or herself in the study most nights, the therapist hypothesizes that this is not just a way of avoiding the other person; it is also a message of revenge or hurt sent through this particular channel.

5. Couples form repeating patterns of responding to stress. Simply disrupting dysfunctional patterns may lead to more adaptive interactions. Insight alone is insufficient for change.

6. A person's view of his or her partner and the problem are subjective and unique. Therefore, the therapist must understand the client's particular view of reality and must adapt methods to fit that construction.

7. Therapists should be action oriented and pragmatic; do what works.

Premises Common to Both Theories

1. The family is a system. As described earlier, this means that all the parts of the family influence each other reciprocally. Identifying one member as the cause of family problems is inconsistent with the idea of the family system. Thus, in the couple situation, the couple as a whole is the focus of treatment.

2. Symptoms keep the family system functional. For example, a symptom such as arguing over the discipline of a child may keep the parents occupied so that they do not deal with their sexual problems. This action maintains homeostasis.

3. Symptoms are maintained by the system. When the counselor attempts to eliminate a symptom, he or she may find that the family seems to collude in keeping the symptom going. Symptoms serve functions such as reducing aversive fights.

4. Couples engage in repetitive patterns of behavior that can be destructive and keep the unit from achieving its goals. When dysfunctional patterns are interrupted, the pattern does not continue.

5. All couples (because they are families) proceed through developmental sequences through life that involve the completion of specific tasks. When tasks for a specific stage are not completed, development is retarded. For example, a couple at the "launching stage" of development is sending its children out on their own. If children are not allowed to grow up, the family will deal with intergenerational conflict until more firm lines are drawn.

6. The couple's current context (the present) is more important than its history.

7. Therapy is brief and problem focused, and the therapist (a) is goal oriented, (b) assigns tasks, and (c) is active and directive.

8. Change is more important than insight.

Problems That Couples Face

Communication Problems

According to structural/strategic thinking, couples communication can be of two types: symmetrical or asymmetrical. *Symmetrical* means that both people do the same thing alternately; *asymmetrical* means that they take complementary roles. If both members of the couple withdraw in a fight, they are acting symmetrically. If one blames and the other placates, they are acting asymmetrically. Asymmetrical pairings lead to more conflict but are not necessarily more functional.

Couples tend to balance each other (Minuchin & Nichols, 1993). If one is frugal, the other often spends too much. Sometimes partners can influence each other to more moderate positions. The "compulsive house cleaner" may ease up and the "sloppy" partner may get organized. Partners in conflict tend to polarize and become more extreme in response to each other. If one is too indulgent with the children, the other becomes overly strict. Sullaway and Christensen (1983) have identified the following asymmetrical pairings that are often seen as presenting problems in couples therapy:

- introvert/extrovert
- flirtatious/jealous
- assertive/nonassertive
- more involved/less involved
- repress/express emotions
- less/more devoted to partner
- dependent/independent
- relationship/work-oriented
- emotional/rational
- demand/withdraw
- leader/follower
- cautious/committed

Game Playing

Friesen (1985), a structural/strategic therapist, suggests that couple patterns could be described as games similar to those defined by the transactional analysts (Berne, 1964). He identifies seven games or repetitive patterns, four of which are examined next.

"This Is War!"   In this game of revenge, both try to hurt the other person more than they were hurt the last time. The strategy is to find and attack the other's weak points, including family, job, and other things that are important. Never give a compliment. This game is a dangerous one because it requires "upping the ante" each time it is played.

"I've Got the Debit, and You've Got the Credit!"   In this pattern, it seems that each member of the couple keeps a balance sheet, always making sure that the other person is doing his or her share. Anything done for the other person must be repaid. Early on in relationships, especially when there are young children or many responsibilities, this kind of pattern can easily emerge and is sometimes called "I changed the diaper last time."

"I Don't Want to Discuss It!"   This is a game of one-upmanship. When a fight emerges, one member of the couple disengages and remains cool, refusing to lower him- or herself to the emotional level of the other person. One member feels put down and out of control emotionally; the other feels superior and withdraws.

"Where Would You Be Without Me?"   In transactional analysis, this game is called "If it weren't for you." In that version, one player constantly complains that life would be perfect if not for the partner, who is like a millstone around the neck. As Friesen describes this pattern, a relationship often develops between someone who is competent and someone who is incompetent, ill, uneducated, or from a lower social class. The silent message behind this game is, "Because I have rescued you from your fate, I have the right to make continuing demands on you. I will remind you of my benevolence by occasionally accompanying you on visits to your dysfunctional family of origin."

Becoming Disengaged or Polarized

One common couple problem, according to the structural strategic point of view, is that of the *disengagement*. The relationship is symmetrical and stable, but there is little satisfaction. This may result from a change in family development, such as when a couple with two or three young children finds that the stress of the life stage saps all the energy from the marriage. Because the two have not kept their relationship vital, they are more vulnerable to alliances with children and others who may provide them with nurturing.

Another symmetrical couple type could be called "the Bickersons," or the *polarized* couple (Todd, 1984). This is the couple who argues about everything (a symmetrical pattern; both attack). Ironically, just as disengaging does by avoiding fighting, so arguing in polarized couples prevents intimacy and prevents the couple from functioning as a unit.

Therapy Methods and Techniques

Table 3.1 shows a portion of the results of Fish and Piercy's (1987) Delphi study of structural and strategic therapy. A Delphi study is a compilation of the views of invited experts. In this case, the experts were nationally known authorities in family therapy who were asked to identify the core concepts and techniques of structural and strategic therapies. Their lists indicate several of the most representative or commonly used techniques in each of the two approaches. We describe several of the techniques in this list in greater detail here along with a few others.

The list in Table 3.1 suggests that although many of the theoretical notions are similar there are significant differences in technique. Strategic therapists are more problem focused and are more likely to use a variety of methods to unbalance the interactional sequence. Structural therapists are more concerned with changing

Table 3.1   Experts' List of Major Techniques and Interventions of Structural and Strategic Therapies

Structural	*Strategic*
Joining	Reframing
Boundary marking/making	Obtaining an identifiable problem
Restructuring	Prescribing the symptom
Tracking	Use of client language and position
Enactment	Determining the interactional sequence and interrupting it in some way.

the family structure—that is, boundaries, alignments, and rules—as a way of promoting long-term change. Keim and Lappin (2002) indicate that structural/strategic therapists use two very general techniques that might be described as attitudes: clinical optimism and clinical endurance. *Optimism* means that the therapist maintains a belief that the couple has strengths that can be awakened in therapy. *Endurance* means that the therapist maintains the relationship (joining) despite the countervailing forces and setbacks. Other methods include the following.

Enactment   Enactment is both an assessment tool and a therapeutic intervention. It consists of allowing or encouraging a couple to engage in the dysfunctional behavior in the counseling setting. By observing and making the couple aware of the pattern, the problem comes out into the open. Finally, the therapist encourages the development of new transactions or patterns to replace the dysfunctional ones.

Reframing   Reframing is a central technique in couples therapy. It means gently asking the couple to view the situation in a positive way. Reframing, or relabeling, is similar to the cognitive therapy technique called *cognitive restructuring*. One version of reframing developed by the Milan school of family therapy is called *positive connotation*. Positive connotation involves attributing good intentions to a partner's behavior as a way of seeing the problem differently.

The directive   A directive is an instruction that the therapist gives to the couple or family to get them to behave differently (Schilson, 1991). Sometimes the clients themselves are the inspiration for these directives (Keim & Lappin, 2002). For example, when a couple finds a new way to spend time together, the therapist makes it a directive. Jay Haley (1989) developed a number of directives in strategic therapy that are designed simply to break up rigid patterns of behavior. Some directives are straightforward, whereas others are paradoxical and absurd. Some examples include the following:

1. *Tell the couple directly what you want them to do.* Assign a task that is absurd such as "I want the two of you to drive seventeen point two miles from your home, stop the car, and find a reason for being there."

2. *Use the "devil's pact."* Here, the couple is told that the counselor has a solution to the problem, but it is difficult and arduous and the couple must agree to do it before it is disclosed to them. Normally, the couple is given time to think this over and decide whether or not they really want to solve the problem.

3. *Give the couple an "ordeal."* An ordeal is a task that is just about as difficult as the symptom and is good for the couple as well. The presenting problem becomes more difficult to maintain because of the added ordeal, and therefore the couple abandons the presenting problem. Child therapist Haim Ginott (1965) described an ordeal that he used when his children argued and wanted him to serve as judge. He would ask them each to write a 100-word essay on his or her point of view and then he would settle the "case." Of course, the kids wandered away and found another way to settle their differences. For a couple, the ordeal may be something arduous that they have to do together, such as exercising.

4. *Assign penance or some action that will make up for guilt feelings.*

5. *Give the couple metaphorical tasks.* Here, the partners are assigned a task that symbolically relates to their problem. For example, a couple might be given the job of discussing in detail how an orchestra might be run with two conductors when each is slightly different in style and in the music they like (Becvar & Becvar, 1988).

Paradoxical techniques   A variety of paradoxical techniques in strategic and structural therapy can be used when more obvious directives and suggestions do not work. One of these is called *restraining change*. In this technique, a couple who is progressing very rapidly in therapy (perhaps too quickly) is given the suggestion that both should slow down the process because sudden change can be harmful (Stanton, Todd, & Associates, 1982). Such an intervention probably works to reinforce the reality of the change process and allows the couple to recognize that they have the power to change their relationship.

Structural moves, or restructuring   Healthy families establish boundaries between the couple and the children. Healthy couples allow each person to actualize their talents and experience a degree of autonomy. Similarly, children have the freedom to be individuals but are also part of the family, and they may be part of a sibling subsystem as well. Boundaries should be permeable enough to allow access to individuals and information outside the family but should also enclose the family and each subsystem enough to give them a sense of unity and identity. Figure 3.1 shows these boundaries in a diagram of a healthy family structure.

Sometimes couples therapists form coalitions with the partners' parents to support the couple's relationship when other alliances, coalitions, or third parties threaten it. Figure 3.2 is a diagram of a situation in which the mother of one partner has aligned herself with her son in order to gain power in the family. This triangle is considered to be unhealthy for the couple, and it places the son "in the middle." If the therapist decides to make a change in such a family, it would be a change in structure, or a structural move. The therapist might choose to support

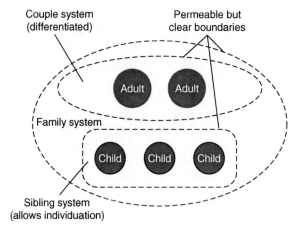

Figure 3.1   Healthy family structure

the couple's relationship by asking the mother not to confide in the son. This creates a boundary between the generations and takes pressure off the son; but on the other hand, the wife or mother may feel unsupported. The therapist must then negotiate a redistribution of authority. One way that the therapist can do this is to join with the wife to balance the system. System homeostasis can be maintained without supporting the current symptom pattern. Power, boundaries, and alignments can be redistributed to achieve equilibrium and equity.

Joining   Joining was mentioned several times earlier in this chapter, but it is actually a complex method, not easily explained in a few sentences. Joining refers to the technique of providing support and a sense of being connected to the couple. Joining, though, is a two-way street; it means being accepted by the couple as a leader or guide (Colapinto, 1991; Nichols & Schwartz, 2006). Although the

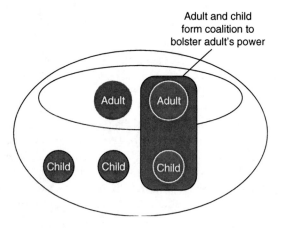

Figure 3.2   Cross-generational alliance, an unhealthy structure

therapist initially joins with both members of the couple, the therapist may shift and provide more support for the member who is less motivated or more in need of nurturance.

Prescribing the symptom   Prescribing the symptom is a classic paradoxical technique designed to produce the opposite effect. For example, a couple who argues a great deal is given the assignment to argue (nonviolently) twice daily at assigned times using the dysfunctional behaviors that they most often employ. Both members are instructed to respond without listening, talk at the same time, or engage in any of the usual ways that they have found to be nonproductive. Arguing decreases as the couple gains control of the behavior by practicing it as prescribed by the counselor.

Pretending   This paradoxical method, designed by Chloe Madanes (1981), is intended to break a pattern by introducing absurdity. One member of the couple is to pretend to have the problem, and the other is to try to determine when the partner is truly exhibiting the symptom and when the partner is pretending. For example, if one partner is accused of not really listening when the other talks to him, he is given the assignment to "pretend" not to listen and his partner is to try to guess when he is pretending and when he is not. The purpose is to disrupt their fighting pattern and heighten their awareness of the problem.

Tracking and use of client language and position   In structural therapy, *tracking* refers to the therapist's activity of closely listening and following the family's idioms, speech, and worldview. By traveling on this track, the therapist learns the family's peculiar "way of being." When the therapist issues a directive or makes an intervention, it will then be phrased in a way that brings out special meanings because the therapist is using the clients' own frame of reference (Colapinto, 1991). As we will see, this aspect of the therapy shares similarities with the narrative approach.

In strategic therapy, the use of client language and position is similar to the structural idea of tracking. *Position* refers to the verbal and nonverbal ways that a person communicates his or her idiosyncratic way of viewing the world. A couple has many shared ways of looking at things, and the strategic therapist identifies the clients' position (the couple's worldview) and uses it when developing interventions. Either way, there is respect for the clients' unique way of being.

SOLUTION-FOCUSED THERAPY

Constructivism

An underlying philosophy of both solution-focused and narrative therapies (which we describe next) is constructivism. Constructivism is initially difficult to grasp, giving rise to the joke: "What happens when you cross a constructivist with the Godfather? An offer you can't understand." In a few words, *constructivism* is a belief about beliefs. It proposes that we each see the world through different spectacles. Constructivism maintains that truth is socially constructed and that no one has the real truth (Anderson, 1990). We do not have a "god's-eye view" of reality but only multiple versions, like the different perspectives of so many witnesses to a traffic accident.

To bring this concept down to a more concrete level, constructivism affects therapy in that everyone in a family will have a different interpretation of an event. Although all might agree that Father cried at the dinner table, the meaning of the event differs from person to person (see Cade & O'Hanlon, 1993). Thus, therapists are not searching to identify the "real problem" but are trying to help clients construe the problems they have in a way that is solvable. This contrasts with rational–emotive therapy (RET) that contends that problems will be alleviated when people become more realistic and scientific (closer to reality). According to RET, there is a right way and a wrong way of thinking, and the counselor's job is to seduce, induce, and persuade the client to accept the premises of the theory. Similarly, in the psychodynamic realm, analysts believe that remnants of the past are the sole causes of present problems and that clients' ideas about these problems are defense mechanisms preventing them from seeing reality. This fundamental nature about how we see reality is what separates the constructivist thinkers from the rest of the pack. Specifically, it means that the client's version of reality is the one we try to work with rather than fitting the client into our therapeutic mold.

Overview

If therapy is to end properly, it must begin properly; by negotiating a solvable problem. The act of therapy begins with the way the problem is examined.
Haley, 1976, p. 9

Solution-focused therapy has its roots in the work of the Mental Research Institute, strategic therapy, and the techniques of Milton Erickson. All these approaches might fall under the rubric of *brief therapy*. Brief therapy has gained considerable popularity since 1990 because of its goal-oriented, direct, active, and creative techniques. It has also been encouraged by insurance companies and agencies where working faster saves money. Because of this sudden acceptance and the "managed-care revolution," a number of theoretical orientations have joined in the "rush to be brief" (Lipchik, 1994). Rational–emotive therapy, psychodynamic therapy, emotionally focused therapy, solution-focused therapy, structural therapy, strategic therapy (Shoham & Rohrbaugh, 2002), and cognitive–behavioral therapy all can now be applied as brief therapy (see Budman, 1992).

One brief approach that has maintained its status as a major methodology for couples therapists is solution-focused therapy that originated in Milwaukee by Steve de Shazer, Insoo Kim Berg, and colleagues at the Brief Family Therapy Center (BFTC) (de Shazer, Berg, Nunnally, et al., 1986). The therapy generally takes four to seven sessions (de Shazer, 1991). It works by focusing on what is working and emphasizes the use of language as a way of helping clients construct solutions (Hoyt, 2002). When it comes to couples therapy, solution-focused therapy asserts that too much time is spent searching for weaknesses rather than building on a couple's strengths and abilities (Hoyt, 2002). Sometimes couples have forgotten to use what they know. They often have the resources and experiences in their own relationship to achieve a solution, but they are using the most recent ways of interacting and have forgotten about more distant experiences of success. Counselors with a solution-focused orientation remind couples of ways that they solved the problem successfully in the past.

Solution-focused therapy is becoming more popular in therapy in general and has also been extended to couples groups (Pichot & Dolan, 2003) and premarital counseling (Murray & Murray, 2004). Michelle Weiner-Davis and William O'Hanlon (O'Hanlon & Weiner-Davis, 1989) have written extensively about their work with de Shazer and have done the most popular writing on couples work using this approach. Weiner-Davis's *Divorce Busting* (1992) and her newest book, *The Divorce Remedy* (2002), outline the basic ideas of the BFTC and help readers apply them in their own setting.

Definitions of Key Terms

exceptions One of the most important concepts in solution-focused brief therapy is helping clients find exceptions, or times when the symptom is not present. When clients are able to identify those times, they are asked to determine how they created those exceptional events and then are directed to find a way to produce more of these exceptions. For example, when a couple says that they cannot communicate, the solution-focused therapist might respond, "Tell me about the times when you do communicate or have communicated well in the past." The couple is then asked to indicate what was different about those times compared to present circumstances.

miracle question When applied to couples, the miracle question goes something like this. "Let's pretend that when you go to sleep tonight a miracle occurs and the problem that brought you into therapy was solved. Because you were asleep though, you were not aware that the problem was solved, so the next day when you awaken and proceed with you daily activities, you find that things are different. But remember, you don't know that the miracle has occurred. What are the first things that you notice that give you a clue that the miracle has occurred? What would you notice that your partner is doing differently? What would your partner see you doing differently?"

scaling question This is a question designed to investigate the clients' individual perspectives on the situation. For example, in a couples session, the therapist might ask, "On a scale of one to ten, how hopeful do each of you feel about the possibility of resolving this problem?" To each person, the therapist might respond by asking them what it would take to move from that number to a more hopeful number. For example, "What do you think it would take to move from a three to a four? How would you know you were there?"

skeleton key question This is a question that focuses the couple on the exceptions and is not specific to the problem. For example, the therapist might say, "Between now and when we meet again, I want the two of you to notice and observe what is happening in the relationship that you would like to continue to have happen. I want you to report the results of your observation at our next meeting." Although it is not really a question, the directive gets clients to focus on the positive and they are identifying exceptions.

solution The solution is "what works." The solution is different for each couple, and there is no ideal of good couple functioning. Inquiring about exceptions may discover solutions.

visitors, complainants, and customers De Shazer (1988) has identified several levels of motivation, differentiating between visitors, complainants, and customers. Visitors are not really committed to the therapy process and may be ambivalent about the need for help. They are unsure whether a problem exists and may be coming to soothe another person. Complainants are experiencing some discomfort but are not yet willing to take action. Customers are ready, willing, and able to take action to change their situation. [Compare this proposal to Prochaska and DiClemente's work on the stages of change in the book *Changing for Good* (Prochaska, Norcross, & DiClemente, 1994).] The implication for therapists is that we often make the mistake of treating everyone as a customer. When someone is a visitor, our best treatment may be education, bibliotherapy, or referral to attend a lecture or an Alcoholics Anonymous meeting. Inducing clients who do not wish to commit to a demanding form of treatment reflects a misunderstanding of their current state of readiness.

Some Premises of Solution-Focused Theory

1. If it "ain't" broke, don't fix it. The therapist tries to take the clients at their word and accepts what the clients say is the problem and what the clients feel is *not* the problem. The presenting complaint is the problem, not a symptom of something deeper. One solution-focused therapist is said to have remarked that the reason why psychodynamic therapists do not treat symptoms is that "they don't know how." This notion of a deeper "disease" is deeply ingrained in our culture and in the dynamic paradigm that most mental health professionals have learned. Thus, our first inclination is to search for original causes of problems, rather than to deal with the client's present circumstances. Clients may be able to locate what caused their problem but cannot see either how it is being maintained in the present or how to unravel it.

2. When something is working, do more of it. When a therapist spots an exception, the client is encouraged to do more of it. For example, if a couple finds that when they discuss money problems in the morning they are better able to agree, the therapist would encourage them to continue this meeting.

3. If it is not working, do something different. Clients frequently do not succeed at homework or even fail to complete outside assignments given by the therapist. In either case, the therapist is flexible and encourages the client to do something different rather than continuing something that is not effective.

4. Changing one member of the family or couple can change the other people in the system. Segal (1991) describes working with wives of men who had had heart attacks but who refused to alter their high-risk behaviors, such as smoking and overeating. Rather than continuing to cajole and struggle with their husbands, the wives were trained to disengage by doing estate and insurance planning with their husbands, as if preparing for their husbands' demise. In some cases, this was enough to reinvolve the husbands in preventive and wellness behaviors. This is what Michele Weiner-Davis (1992) calls "doing a 180."

5. Solution-focused therapy can help people at various degrees of readiness. Therapy is over when there is a behavioral or perceptual change that reduces the client's pain to the extent that therapy is no longer desired. The therapy is an ongoing process of getting the client to define success (Hoyt, 2002). Sometimes a small change is enough to begin a chain of events that leads to the resolution of other problems—the "snowball effect." As Milton Erickson said, sometimes it is enough to tip over the first domino (Rossi, 1980a). Bill O'Hanlon (1999) emphasizes this point in his book, *Do One Thing Different*.

6. Goals should be formulated as positives rather than the absence of something. A poorly formulated goal, according to this idea, would be "to eliminate arguing." A better goal might be stated as "the ability to resolve a problem through open discussion."

7. Marital therapy is identical to family therapy except that, normally, the therapist is dealing with a relationship between two people of the same generation (de Shazer et al., 1986).

8. Clients have resources and strengths to resolve complaints, and when time is limited, it is best to rely on the knowledge that they already have. For example, if a corporate executive is having trouble solving a problem with her husband, the counselor might ask her how she would deal with such a conflict at work, using the management training and negotiation skills, which she has already mastered.

Problems That Couples Face

The constructivist philosophy that underlies solution-focused theory suggests that each couple's problems are unique. Thus, assessment is minimal and history taking is meager. What is important is how the problems are perceived and construed by those who are in the relationship rather than the diagnostic formulation of the therapist. It usually is not necessary to know a great deal about the history or cause of a complaint in order to resolve it (O'Hanlon & Weiner-Davis, 1989), so little effort has to be made to identify standard patterns of interaction. Also, solution-focused therapists are more interested in identifying patterns that work than in identifying those that are causing the problems.

Therapy Methods and Techniques

Solution focused-therapy sessions tend to follow a prescribed order (de Shazer & Berg, 1997):
- The therapist spends a few minutes joining and "schmoozing" with the client.

- The therapist asks the miracle question (usually in the first session).
- The therapist uses scaling questions or other questions to build goals, identify exceptions, empower the clients, increase hope and motivation and to recognize progress, endurance, and effort.
- The therapist takes a break sometime during the session to reflect or consult with a team. The couple may be asked to consider homework.
- After the break, the therapist gives the client compliments and usually a homework assignment.

Linguistic Changes

The constructivist viewpoint behind brief therapy suggests that we can persuade clients to change their viewing of a problem in a more useful way. By so doing, we are not fooling clients into denying a problem when it exists; we are simply working from the premise that there is not one correct perspective. We are asking clients to question the meaning that they have placed on the event and see whether an alternative point of view makes the problem more accessible to change. Table 3.2 shows suggestions for a new therapist who wants to develop a solution-focused vocabulary. For each word in the "Problem Language" column, there is a corresponding word in the "Solution Language" column." Therapists new to solution-focused therapy will find it useful to think about and practice this relabeling or reframing of pathologizing terms.

Changing the Viewing

Using the language of the future   Because the way we see ourselves is affected by the language we use, the therapist should use hopeful communications such as "When the two of you are getting along better, what effect will that have on your children?" This "embedded question" has an underlying assumption of hope; the assumption is that eventually the two will be getting along better. Milton Erickson said that therapists "ought to expect to find solutions rather than passively

Table 3.2   Developing a Solution-Focused Vocabulary

Problem Language	Solution Language
Never	Not yet, not enough
Always	Most of the time but there are exceptions
Limitation	Possibility
Treat	Facilitate
Reduce	Increase or add
Symptoms	Assets
Pathology	Health or wellness
Talking about the past	Talking about the future
Absent	Latent or hidden
Conflicts	Options

accepting a decree of 'uncurable' [sic]. Such an attitude of expectancy is far more conducive to our task of exploration, discovery and healing" (Rossi, 1980b, p. 202). The solution-focused approach suggests that even if some things are unchangeable, let therapy focus on what is possible and changeable rather than on what is impossible and intractable (O'Hanlon & Weiner-Davis, 1989).

Finding exceptions   Identifying exceptions not only brings hope, but it is also effective in helping couples immediately reduce the scope of a problem that might have seemed overwhelming. When the situation is framed as "We never get along," it is immediately improved when reconstrued as "We get along best when we have spent some leisure time together." Exceptions also demonstrate to a couple that people can change. By changing how the problem is viewed, couples are not looking for the flaws in each other but for the times when the other person is trying.

Following are two leads that counselors use to help couples find exceptions (Weiner-Davis, 1992).

Example 1: "Pay attention to the times when the two of you are getting along. What is different about those times?"

Example 2: "If you can't think of any exceptions recently, recall times in the past when you and your spouse were more satisfied. What were you doing differently?"

Changing the doing   Exceptions help couples change the viewing of a complaint, but there are also methods that they use to change the "doing" of it. Action strategies usually take place during homework assignments. These methods are sometimes called *complaint pattern interventions* and are similar to many strategic therapy interventions. Habitual and rigid patterns maintain themselves, and when the routine is broken, the strength of the pattern weakens. The main idea is to interrupt the pattern by manipulating the frequency, rate, the timing, duration, or location of the problem. Couples are directed to add a new element or change the sequence. For example, an arguing couple may be asked to change the time of day that they argue, where they argue, and how long they argue.

Giving homework assignments to change the viewing or doing   It is important to recognize that the exact choice of a homework assignment depends on a number of client factors such as whether the clients are visitors, complainants, or customers: whether they are able to identify exceptions; and whether they can set clear goals (DeJong & Berg, 1998). Space does not allow us to explore how a solution-focused therapist would analyze each of these conditions and choose a specific task, but we are including two examples of homework assignments:

Assignment 1: Before we meet again, pay close attention to what is happening in your relationship that tells you that this problem is solvable (changing the viewing).

Assignment 2: At the next session, I want the two of you to have done something different. The two of you can decide what it is going to be, but when the problem occurs, do something different (changing the doing).

NARRATIVE THERAPY AND EMOTIONALLY FOCUSED COUPLE THERAPY

We have now given an overview of some of the major established methods that address couple problems. Two relative newcomers are narrative therapy (White & Epston, 1990) and emotionally focused therapy (Johnson & Greenberg, 1994). We address them here briefly, but they both play key parts in the integrative approach, which we describe in Chapter 4. The notions of externalizing the problem and the importance of emotion in couples work are important contributions that have had a major impact on the field of couples work. Along with definitions of major terms, we present the basic tenets of the theories as an introduction while recognizing that becoming familiar with these methods requires further study.

Narrative Therapy

Narrative therapy involves getting clients to tell their stories and then helping them develop alternative stories that they prefer or which work better for them. Like the solution-focused approach, narrative therapy takes a constructivist view. This means that the therapist is not looking for the right solution to the couple's problems but to find one that works for them.

This approach assumes that engaging the client in the problem-saturated story will not be of much help, but instead the couple must find new ways of making meaning, have conversations about contentious issues, and develop new stories that are more productive.

Narrative therapy owes its foundation to Gregory Bateson (1972), the anthropologist who was associated with the Mental Research Institute, although the theory was actually developed by Michael White and David Epston (1990). Since that time, it has grown into a very popular therapy and has been applied to individual, family, and group psychotherapy. There is a value of social justice that pervades narrative therapy. Compared to other approaches, narrative therapists are interested in helping couples discuss gender, power, and violence in their lives; in this way, narrative theory comes close to feminist theory. Narrative therapy's work with couples is relatively new and in its infancy (Freedman & Combs, 2002).

Because narrative therapy arose not from psychology but from anthropology, learning about this postmodern approach means learning a new language and different words for similar concepts. You may find it confusing because the terms are new and because narrative writers do not like to take stands on "the right way of doing things." So, rather than introducing the therapy any further, let's first look at the key terms so that the tenets of the theory will make sense.

Definitions of Key Terms

deconstruction Taking stories apart so that the taken-for-granted aspects of the story emerge. By deconstructing the story, we can see what effect these hidden assumptions and gaps have.

externalizing conversations Getting clients to focus on the problem, not on the person. A narrative therapist would initiate conversations around the problem instead of the usual story, which is that someone has a personality disorder or that someone is to blame. Externalizing conversations are about the problem and how it is maintained, instead of a construction that is someone's fault.

narrative A story that a person tells. Most stories reflect a person's worldview, or they are cultural stories that have been adopted to form our version of reality. Thus, a person's view of reality is gained from what he or she has learned from others (social construction).

normal or **healthy functioning** Narrative therapists try and discourage people from comparing their functioning to society's norms. Thus, the terms *normal* and *healthy* have no meaning.

project Narrative therapists like clients to name their problems in order to begin the process of externalization. Projects are what clients want to achieve or "prefer." You could not call them *goals,* but you could say they are *directions.* Sometimes both partners share problems and projects, and often they have separate ones (Freedman & Combs, 2002).

reflecting teams Reflecting teams is a technique that is compatible with narrative therapy (see Andersen, 1991). Reflecting teams are normally groups of therapists who observe a therapy session and then switch places with the clients. At that point, the clients watch the therapists discuss their situation in a special way. Reflecting team members wonder aloud about the client's issues and give strength to alternative stories. Finally, the two groups exchange places again, and the clients reflect on what has been heard.

unique outcomes Traces of an alternative story that show up in client narratives. For example, a couple might say, "Once in a while, we just laugh about that issue but usually, it brings about a fight." Narrative therapists are interested in expanding conversations about these alternative counterplots.

Some Premises of Narrative Theory

1. A client's worldview or version of reality is contained in the stories that he or she tells. The therapist listens curiously and respectfully to the story while noting what is left out or incongruent, which parts are empowering, and which parts are disempowering.
2. Talking about alternative stories (more positive views) strengthens them. Therapy is largely encouraging conversation about these alternate stories (thickening the plot).
3. The therapist tries to externalize the problem to take it out of the realm of blame and to help the couple see that they are not the problem but that the problem is the problem. This brings about a different relationship between the client and their problem.
4. The therapist tries to help clients re-story events by immersing them in discussions about the alternative stories until those stories gain more power.

5. Therapy is a collaborative process, and therapists are not experts but coresearchers, trying to search out better ways of envisioning the issue (Kazdim, 2000).

6. Narrative therapists try to create stories that encourage clients to see choices rather unchanging certainties (Brunner, 1986). The therapist does this by challenging limiting beliefs, using empowering language, and looking at behavioral alternatives (Freedman & Combs, 1996).

7. Cultures have dominant theories about what is good and bad, sick and well, healthy and unhealthy. There are other stories that are equally valid to the ones that society tells you. Narrative couples therapy is openly "and decidedly political (or politicizing) experience designed to liberate relationship partners from the restrictive, limiting and oppressive assumptions of the larger culture, especially those involving notions of maleness and femaleness" (Gurman, 2003, p. 499). Because reality is socially constructed, clients are encouraged to share their new empowering stories with their social network or "preferred story audience" (White & Epston, 1990).

Emotionally Focused Couple Therapy

Emotion is the music of the couple's dance.
Johnson and Denton, 2002, p. 222

Emotionally focused therapy originated at the University of British Columbia in Vancouver when two couples therapists, Les Greenberg and Susan Johnson, began to recognize that when couples could express their emotions to each other in a safe environment change occurred. Although therapists such as Virginia Satir (1983) had emphasized the importance of affect in family interactions, this focus had been lost in the cognitive and behavioral revolution of the 1970s and 1980s. The cognitive–behavioral emphasis largely ignored emotions or felt that they were detrimental to progress (Mahoney, 1991). To include emotional change along with cognitive and behavioral change, Greenberg and Johnson actively engaged couples in becoming aware of their emotional states. What is unique about emotionally focused therapy is that it tries to go back and forth between validating the feelings and viewpoint of each client while addressing the relationship issues as a pattern.

Emotionally focused therapy is an integrative approach drawing its ideas from gestalt therapy, family systems therapy, attachment theory, and experiential psychotherapy (Johnson & Denton, 2002). These ideas are blended in the premises of the therapy described below. One of the major strengths of emotionally focused therapy with couples is that its effectiveness has been established by several studies (see Johnson, Hunsley, Greenberg, & Schlinder, 1999). It is attractive to therapists who recognize that the ways that couples express their emotions is part and parcel of their interaction pattern, predicts divorce (Gottman, 1998), and makes their mutual life a heaven or a hell. Emotionally focused therapy's emphasis on attachment has led to its use with depressed partners, posttraumatic stress disorder in one of the partners, and violence in relationships (Johnson & Denton, 2002).

Definition of Key Terms

There are few original terms in emotionally focused therapy because it is integrative, or eclectic. Still, some terms deserve mention because they are derived from attachment theory, which may be unfamiliar. Others are the unique names given to techniques.

attachment injury When one member of the couple asks for comfort and the other does not provide it.

bonding event An experience a couple has that transforms their relationship, reestablishing trust and security. This may occur in or out of the session.

disorganized attachment strategy Many couple problems are the result of ineffective strategies that a client uses to get comfort or connection. A therapist might help a couple understand their problems as disorganized attachment strategies rather than the result of pathology.

exploring and reformulating emotion The general tactic a therapist uses to help clients deal with strong emotions that are separating them from their partner. An emotionally focused therapist might reflect, validate, use gestalt techniques to enhance awareness of the emotion; heighten the emotion; or use interpretation to help clients see their reaction in a different way.

restructuring intervention The emotionally focused therapist uses reframing, or restructuring, as a key intervention strategy along with exploring and reformulating emotion. The therapist might ask the clients to reenact or replay their interactions or reframe their interactions in terms of attachment theory.

secure attachment or **secure bond** Attachment theory à la Bowlby (1988) says that people are motivated to be connected to others. Those who have insecure attachment experiences are tentative and fearful in relationships. Secure attachment allows for autonomy and flexibility in relationships. Couples with secure bonds can express their feelings without fear of abandonment and ask for support when they need it. In such circumstances, couples can begin to develop a worldview that sees others as trustworthy and the self as worthy of love and care.

soothing interaction When one member of the couple asks for comfort and the other provides it.

Some Premises of Emotionally Focused Theory

1. The aim of emotionally focused therapy is to create a more secure bond between the couple. If the bond is more secure, it is more flexible and resilient, allowing the couple to jointly face the tasks and developmental challenges of life. The best way to do this is to get the couple to express emotions, including those such as fear, which often lurk behind angry outbursts.

2. Having attachment needs, regardless of their origin, is normal, and meeting them is healthy. What causes problems is that one or both members

begin to feel insecure and their interaction becomes self-defeating. For example, if one member hides annoyance because, in a former relationship, this led to rejection, the other member might feel insecure because he or she senses that they are not getting the whole story.

3. The therapeutic relationship is one of collaboration because this allows the couple a safe haven to readjust their relationship. The therapist is more of a consultant/facilitator than an expert.

4. The focus of the therapy is on the relationship, and the therapist tries to move neutrally between focusing on the expression and regulation of emotion in one member and focusing of the pattern between the couple. Thus, the therapist might reflect the following: "Your anger right now is a way of protecting you from being hurt again even though it becomes a barrier between the two of you."

5. Relationship cycles or patterns exist, and emotion is key to understanding how they are maintained. The therapist helps the couple reduce the negative interaction patterns, deal differently with negative emotions, and increase the positive emotions in their interactions.

6. Change is the result of emotional experiences that couples have in the therapy session or in their interactions with each other. For example, a bonding experience can renew a sense of trust and improve communication. This change is not the result of "insight into the past, catharsis or negotiation" (Johnson & Denton, 2002, p. 229) but a transformative experience.

CONCLUSION

In this chapter, we looked at two major groups of therapies for couples: structural strategic and constructivist as well as two newer ones, narrative and emotionally focused. The structural and strategic therapies held center stage in the early development of family therapy. Minuchin's structural approach advocates "joining" or creating a relationship with a couple and then "kicking." *Kicking* refers to disrupting patterns, boundaries, and alignments. Haley's strategic approach is more devoted to "pure change." Using this approach, the couples therapist assigns ordeals and prescribes other pattern-disrupting measures to get couples out of their persistent cycles. These were radical approaches 30 years ago, but structural and strategic therapies are now considered traditional today (Gurman & Jacobson, 2002).

Structural and strategic approaches are not the focus of current research and writing in couples therapy. While the interest in the strategic school has given way to solution-focused and brief therapy, structural therapy's major contributions about changing boundaries and alignments seems to be left out of most discussions of couples therapy these days. Structural therapy is still worthy of study because it helps us understand the variety of family and couple structures in an increasing diverse culture with more and more different family configurations.

With the death of Steve de Shazer in 2005, the solution-focused approach has lost its prime innovator, but it is now well established. Solution-focused therapy is popular due to its brief, positive approach, which appeals to students and therapists (Lipchik, 2002; Pichot & Dolan, 2003). Its future influence depends on how it can meet the demands for more quantitative evidence of effectiveness and its ability to generalize to a variety of counseling situations. In couples therapy, the solution-focused approach takes criticism for failing to recognize the role of a couple's history in their issues and for being too focused on the behavioral changes and ignoring the affective ones (Young, 2005). Still, it has had a mighty influence on therapy and couples work in general at a time when clinicians were looking for a way out of pathological formulations.

Finally, the narrative and emotionally focused couples therapies are described here in outline. These two methods are having an important impact on the field. They are relatively new, but they seem to have fastened on to missing aspects of the picture. Narrative therapy has reminded us that the stories that we tell are influencing how we see the world and that these stories are not truth but versions of reality—learned from others and swallowed whole. On the other hand, emotionally focused therapy has made an important contribution by shifting our attention to the affective realm that is so important to the couple and is a barrier to reconciliation. In the next chapter, we take elements of these therapies and integrate them in our brief therapy model for couples.

4

An Integrative Model
for Couples Therapy

KEY CONCEPTS

- An integrative model draws on other theoretical positions, bringing together "what works" into a coherent system.
- The model rests on a circular notion of causality, which brings with it less emphasis on blaming one of the partners.
- Assessment of both past and present issues is considered to be a critical precursor to therapy.
- The model emphasizes the couple as a team and asks therapists to help couples find their hidden resources.
- For couples to be satisfied that change has occurred, both feelings and behaviors must be improved.
- The integrative model also addresses cognitive change in its emphasis on an evolving definition of the problem
- Even when change has occurred, the couple must be trained to maintain the change.
- A major task for the therapist is to help the partners keep hope alive as they move through the process of therapy.
- The five-part integrative model moves from assessment to goal setting to intervention to maintenance to validation.

In the previous two chapters, we examined theoretical positions that help us conceptualize how change occurs. One of the conclusions that could be made from the theoretical discussion is than an integrative approach might be a practical way of incorporating the best ideas. If a successful integration occurs, it could also allow the use of the newest and most progressive methods and techniques from a number of theoretical positions. The integrative therapist has more freedom because he or she is not confined to a single theoretical view (Young, 1992, 2005).

The challenge is to develop an approach that provides a coherent system synthesizing key concepts in an understandable and logical way. The metaphor of quilting helps explain this kind of integrative approach. There are two ways to make a quilt: Simply pick up pieces of the patchwork and put them together until you have some kind of blanket or develop a design and then select the pieces that you need to complete it. The integrative approach in this book starts with a design or treatment plan that is fashioned in the first few sessions and then, using the clients' goals as the pattern, finds techniques and interventions to address the clients' specific problems. The integrative model proposed in this chapter and developed in this book is a structured method that draws from several theoretical positions. Many of the premises of the model are drawn from the traditional therapy schools discussed in Chapters 2 and 3, including solution-focused therapy and narrative therapy.

COMMON THREADS OF THE THEORIES

Thus far we have reviewed the ideas and languages of the most influential theories in couples work. Some practitioners accept the tenets of a single theory and proceed to practice in accordance with that perspective. Other therapists merge two therapies or hold to a single theory and bring in other techniques, language, or perspectives from several theories.

In this chapter, we describe an integrative model for couples therapy and apply it through all the later chapters. In developing this model, we chose specific aspects of several theories that we believe are compatible. In short, we have not created a new theory but have tried to bring together theoretical ideas, techniques, and clinical experience into a teachable and learnable model that can be used to structure the sometimes-baffling experience of couples therapy. From the theories that we have reviewed, we have identified the following eight building blocks, or elements, of our integrative approach.

A Circular Model of Causation

A basic premise of our model is a circular, or recursive, process of assessment, treatment planning, and therapeutic intervention. This idea of circularity is consistent with "systems thinking" and characterizes nearly all the mainstream approaches to couples counseling and family therapy. *Circular* and *recursive* are two words used to mean that the interactive patterns of the relationship form a type of feedback-loop response system. Instead of a linear cause-and-effect view, in which A affects B and causes C, the recursive viewpoint emphasizes mutual causation of events (Landis & Young, 1994). Thus, each individual influences and in turn is influenced by another individual in a circular pattern: "A may cause B, but B also affects A and C and so on" (Goldenberg & Goldenberg, 2002, p. 96). Like gears in a clock, the behaviors of each person influence the functioning of the other and the relationships they have (Young, 1992). Crises, the environment, organizations, and other individuals outside the relationship also have a significant impact on the couple.

Circularity when applied to couples therapy implies that the therapist focuses on the interactions of the relationship and how the couple is affected by the continual action and reaction of each partner. For example, Roberto is not the sole cause of Marta's depression. Roberto plays basketball while Marta spends time with her mother. Roberto is angry that Marta spends so much time with her mother. Marta is hurt that Roberto does not accompany her to her mother's house. Roberto regrets that they do not have intimate time together, and Marta expresses feelings of rejection that he does not want to be with her. All of the beliefs, behaviors, and feelings of each member are interacting factors in the problem.

Circular questioning is a technique that focuses the couple on their relationship and is based on the premise of circular causation. Instead of asking the question, "How did the fight start?" (a linear question), the therapist asks questions that remind the couple of mutual causality, such as "What effect does fighting have on your relationship?" The question may influence the couple to examine arguing in the context of the way they relate to each other rather than "Who started the fight?" (Methods for using circular questioning are described in Chapter 6.) These questions may also serve an assessment function for the therapist, who can gain information about the couple's interactions (Tomm, 1984a). The concept of circularity and circular questioning has been widely embraced in relationship therapy (Hoffmann, 2002; Keeney, 1983, 1985; Papp, 1983; Tomm, 1984a, 1984b). Sometimes just an awareness of the reciprocal relationship of behaviors may promote spontaneous change (Palazzoli-Selvini, Boscolo, Cecchin, & Prata, 1980; Penn, 1982; Tomm, 1984b). This awareness can allow the couple to develop a new perspective on old problems, which can lead to rapid change. When couples begin to view the problem as a relationship problem instead of individual personality flaws, they may better understand the need for mutual change and feel a freedom from criticism and guilt.

Blame Is Not a Useful Concept

Blame implies linear causation. Whose fault is it? Unfortunately, couples spend a great deal of time in their private lives and in the early stages of therapy using a linear approach to solving their joint problems, trying to determine who caused the problem and who is to blame. From the very beginning in the integrative model, the couple is shown that, just as it "takes two to tango," it takes two to solve problems.

We blame others to avoid our own guilt and responsibility (Kottler, 1994). Although it might be self-protective to blame one's partner, it also produces a high degree of helplessness for the blamer. There is no sense of responsibility for creating a solution. We believe that a primary task of couples therapy is to define the problem *interactionally* so that there is emphasis on the reciprocal, or shared, nature of the relationship. The aim is to help both partners feel empowered to resolve the problems in the relationship. This notion is consistent with solution-focused therapy. A principle goal of therapy is to foster a sense of mutual responsibility for the problem and mutual contribution to the solution.

The Therapist Remains Neutral

Neutrality is a one of the key concepts of the Milan, or systemic, school of family therapy. *Neutrality* means that the therapist maintains a nonjudgmental view of the problem and does not ally with either partner. For example, if John and Alan are each blaming the other for the lack of time that they devote to the relationship, the therapist would refuse to take sides and would instead help the couple examine how each can contribute to the solution.

There are of course some cautions to expressing neutrality when dealing with issues of domestic violence. Neutrality does not mean that the therapist either fails to take a stand against damaging behavior perpetuated by one partner or asks the couple to share the blame for the problem (see Holtzworth-Munroe, Meehan, Rehman, & Marshall, 2002).

Assessment Is a Crucial First Activity

Assessment involves (1) a statement of the problem from each person's point of view and (2) assessment of the couple's background, patterns of interaction, mental health status, history of violence, and substance abuse. Both Bowenian and object-relations theories recommend looking at past relationships so that both partners can recognize that they have inherited ways of interacting that may not be appropriate to the current situation. In this text, we recommend using a genogram to obtain this background information and as a quick screening instrument, but there are other ways of conducting background assessments, which we also discuss.

It is also useful to find out what has worked for the couple in the past. If we have been successful in solving a similar problem, why not implement those strategies again? Strategic therapy and behavior therapy are most concerned with looking at problem-maintaining behaviors. In other words, what are we doing to keep the negative patterns going? How are they being rewarded? In this integrative model, we recommend assessing both past influences and present patterns to help attack the presenting problem. In addition, it is obvious that we must assess for domestic violence, substance abuse, and the presence of major mental disorders. These three issues can undermine all our efforts if they are not identified.

The Couple Must Form a Team

The narrative approach has given new life to the idea of externalizing problems, and this approach works especially well in couples and family therapy in which family or couple cohesiveness is required. *Externalizing* means that the partners learn to attack a problem together rather than looking for the flaw in the other person. The therapist reframes the problem as something external to the couple, not in each partner. In this sense, externalizing can be seen as an outgrowth of nonblaming circular thinking (White & Epston, 1990).

Central to the team concept in our integrative model is the notion that the couple should inventory their assets as individuals and as a couple and recognize how these assets can be used to solve problems. This is a strength-based approach.

This change in thinking is based on the Milan school's notion of *positive connotation,* or the concept of reframing promoted by the strategic therapists. Couples are asked to see differences in their abilities and personalities as strengths in the relationship. Couples must then see that the solution to their problems lies in pooling all of their varied resources.

Feelings, Behaviors, and Cognitions Must Change

Most therapists would agree that behavioral change is part of what we mean by lasting change. This is a central tenet of the behavioral school, but the brief therapy and strategic therapy schools also recommend dealing with presenting problems, which are often behavioral in nature. Changes in behavior are often signs to the partners that change is possible and progressing.

Affective change, or change in feeling, is also critically important to couples. Although couples want to manage negative feelings, they also come to therapy wanting to feel intimacy, happiness with each other, companionship, and romance—the crucial intangibles of couplehood. Therapists should consider positive-feeling states not as luxuries but as necessities. Couples may not feel that therapy is complete until these positive feelings have returned and the negative feelings are in check.

In addition, change is often accompanied by or caused by a change in perspective or cognition. Thoughts about one's partner and the relationship are salutary signs. In the integrative model, couples are asked to reframe their difficulties as joint goals. It is believed that by changing thinking, feeling, *and* behaving, the change is likely to be more lasting (Prochaska, Norcross, & DiClemente, 1994).

Couples Must Learn Maintenance Tasks

The behaviorists tell us that old learning is stronger than newly acquired skills. In a pinch, we are most likely to revert to old patterns unless our new behaviors are rewarded. A couple's exhilaration at dealing with a difficult problem can plummet when the first argument occurs and the partners believe that they are "back to square one." Cognitive therapy calls this "black-or-white" or "all-or-nothing" thinking, the tendency to think that either our situation is idyllic or doomed. Couples must be challenged to see the progress that they have made and not overemphasize minor setbacks.

Couples Must Develop Joint Solvable Problems

For the integrative model to work, the premises must mesh and form a rational whole. As we see it, the "whole," or organizing, idea is a constructivist one—each couple comes to therapy with a perspective about the relationship and its problems. The therapist's job is to guide the couple to reframe each individual's problems, not as dissatisfaction with the other person but as a joint work project. Then the therapist helps the partners envision the problem as external to them (externalizing) and as a problem that they can jointly attack. Finally, the couple is challenged to view the problem as significantly resolved yet needing continuing maintenance to prevent its return. The model suggests that, because each couple is unique, the methods and techniques used to achieve these redefining tasks will vary. The hall-mark of the integrative model is that it is not wedded to a few theoretically pre-scribed techniques but is flexible in its methodology to achieve the aims of therapy.

Therapists Must Foster Hope

Writers from Bowenian to solution-focused theories have underscored the signifi-cance of overcoming demoralization when working with couples. Hope is power-ful medicine, especially for couples (Ripley & Worthington, 2002). In our model, we see it as vital from the first phone contact. Initially, the therapist lends hope to clients by noting progress and predicting success. At Stage 2, couples are asked to set goals. Goal setting itself gives the couple a feeling that the overwhelming prob-lem has been identified and mapped into solvable pieces. Finally, at the end of ther-apy, couples are challenged to develop realistic views about change, celebrate their successes, generalize them to other problems, and congratulate each other.

AN INTEGRATIVE MODEL FOR COUPLES THERAPY

Figure 4.1 is a graphical representation of the five-part integrative model of cou-ples therapy. The stages are sequential, and normally therapy proceeds from assessment to validation. At the center of the model is the couple's changing view of the problem. As therapy proceeds, this view becomes modified through inter-actions with the therapist and with each other.

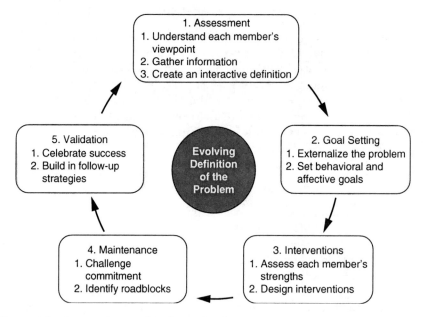

Figure 4.1   Integrative model of couples therapy

Stage 1: Assessment and Identifying a Shared Definition: "We Have a Problem"

The initial phase of the integrative approach is devoted to understanding a couple's background, patterns, mental health issues, potential for violence, and substance-abuse concerns. The reasons for assessment are simple: We want to determine if this couple is suitable for couples counseling. Couples that are not suitable for brief integrative approaches like ours include

- "Out-of-the-door" couples who have already decided to separate but come to counseling to prove that the relationship is hopeless.
- Couples who have other issues that need to be treated first and take precedence—namely, substance abuse, domestic violence, or a major mental disorder in one of the members.
- Couples who have trouble desisting from arguing (these couples can be very difficult but not necessarily unsuited for this work).

We also suggest examining solutions that have not worked for the couple in the past. Previous attempts may have been based on what worked in each partner's family of origin or what worked for them in prior stages of their relationship. When a therapist recommends something that the couple has already tried, the therapist is seen as less competent. (Chapter 5 is solely devoted to assessment issues with couples, and we describe the guidelines, mentioned here, in more detail.)

Understanding Each Member's Viewpoint

Following this screening, the therapist asks each partner to define the problem from his or her perspective. Some typical questions that the therapist asks during this part of Stage 1 are the following:

"I would like to hear from both of you separately about what prompted you to make this appointment."
"Let me hear from each of you—your own perspective—on the problem that has brought you in today."

Most of the questions by the therapist at this stage ask for information (orienting questions), but the therapist might also ask some circular questions such as

"When your partner yells, how do you respond?"
"What effect does your withdrawing have on the relationship?"

Each member of the couple is allowed time to give his or her version of the story. Although these accounts may be unfair, overstated, and extreme, it has been our experience that, unless the couple has an opportunity to fully express their concerns, the remaining time will be spent in returning to these complaints. During this period, the therapist keeps each member on track and does not allow the other partner to object. The therapist explains that it is important for each person to have his or her side heard. Although it is useful to hear these complaints, no more that 10 minutes or so per person should be spent in this activity. Otherwise, the session takes on a negative tone, and the couple begins to feel a sense of dread that this will be just like the arguments that they have at home—unproductive. Thus, the therapist tries not to end the first session with complaints. There should be a period in which the therapist summarizes what he or she has heard and is able to infuse some measure of hope. For example,

> "It sounds like the concerns that brought you in today are serious. But based on what I have heard, I also have a feeling that there is a good deal of hope that things can improve. You both believe that a lot is invested in this relationship and your coming today is a message to the other person that you are willing to try."

Developing a Shared Definition: The Big Reframe

The interactive, or shared, definition is the centerpiece of the integrative model. It is the basis upon which the couple first begins to see that they are talking about the same issues. During the recitation of complaints and when looking over the couple's background data, the therapist is mentally formulating a way to reframe each person's concerns into a joint definition that both people can agree to.

We all need this agreement, or buy-in from others, to get what we want. We need to have buy-in at work from our boss or from a committee if we want to start a new project. We want buy-in from our family about where we vacation. *Buy-in* is also a buzzword in business today; it is defined as another person's "understanding, commitment and action in support of our goals" (Walton, 2004, p. xv). It means that when workers at a company believe that they have a stake in a company's profits, they will work harder, be more loyal, and work for the greater good.

In the same way, each member of the couple must have buy-in for couples counseling to take place. This is a prime reason for therapist neutrality; we want both partners to buy-in. When we have this commitment and both people see their potential gains, a fundamental shift has already occurred. The couple now sees the problem as a joint problem or shared work project. The blaming diminishes and the focus is on the problem.

The therapist cannot stop here. To assure the other partner that buy-in has occurred, the therapist must hold both partners' "feet to the fire." The therapist repeatedly asks the couple to indicate their willingness to work on the problem through such questions as

> "Although you are still angry, you have said that you want to work on the credit card problem as a team. Can you each tell me how committed you are to making this happen?"
>
> "If this problem were solved, what would each of you personally get out of the new arrangement?"

Is This Really Couples Counseling?

Unless the therapist can deliver an interactive definition that satisfies both, one member of the couple may merely be acquiescing to the other or attempting to appease the therapist. Without this testing, the couple may spend several unproductive sessions continuing their arguments. No one has really required them to commit to binding arbitration. We argue that the acid test for determining whether two people need couples counseling is whether they can form and buy into an interactional, or shared, definition of the problem.

Example

Emeric: Although we live together, I don't want to get married right now. I have a lot of problems with my career. I am not sure whether I should go back to school or not. I am recovering from the effects of a car accident. The relationship has become one more responsibility I have to deal with. I believe it should be going smoothly and am not sure I have the energy to work on problems all the time. For me, the decision to live together was mostly a convenient solution, but now it seems she wants me to change and orient my whole world around her.

Nicola: I thought when we moved in together, this was the next step; later we would get engaged and then married. But he is dragging his feet. I don't know whether I am wasting my time here or not. When I threaten to leave, he changes his tune. But he never really changes his behavior. He acts like we are roommates.

Emeric's statement on the surface suggests individual counseling rather than conjoint couples counseling. But in reality, more assessment is needed before we can finally make this decision. Does the couple see themselves as a couple, and would they be willing to work on the relationship?

In the integrative model, we recommend that the therapist push each member to test his or her willingness to work on the relationship with the understanding that we might discover that these are two people with individual problems without an interactive definition. In this case, the interactive definition that the therapist might try to promote is "It sounds as if the two of you have never decided about whether you are staying together or just marking time." This puts pressure on them to decide whether they want relationship-oriented counseling.

How It Works in Therapy

Learning to reframe the couple's problem as interactional, or shared, takes practice. It is an intuitive process and frequently involves trial and error. The therapist presents the reframe to the couple, and one or both may reject some part. Then, the therapist returns to a listening, assessment role until the "light bulb comes on." Listed below are two examples, which are each person's statement of the problem. See if you can formulate an interactive definition that encapsulates the essence of each person's concerns. Remember, there is probably not one correct interactional, or shared, definition. It is formed from your hunches and is right only when you get confirmation from both members of the couple.

An example in dialogue

Isabel: You never want to go with me to see my mother. I am getting embarrassed because I feel I have to make excuses. I go with you to your family's get-togethers, and I don't feel it is fair to always reject them. When you do come along, you sit in the corner and read or make a long face, looking at the clock. Do I do that at your parents' house?

David: When I go with you to your parents' house, I feel so alone and isolated. You grew up with three brothers and two sisters. It's like a madhouse. You go off with your sisters and watch TV, and I am stuck trying to make conversation with your father. He hates me because I am not Brazilian. I am from a Southern white family and, I admit, I am used to a little more courtesy.

Possible interactive definition: You don't have a way of interacting with her family as a unit. Neither one of you is happy with the way you interact, but you haven't found a way that will make both parties comfortable.

Another example   Sam and Rachel have difficulty when they argue. They admit that she attacks and uses name-calling when she gets mad, and he sulks and won't talk to her for several days. In the first session, when they each were asked to describe the problem, they complained about the other person's behavior during arguments and described each other with terms like *immature* and *punitive.* Using the genogram, the couple was able to discuss the fact that Sam's family did not openly express anger, whereas Rachel's family arguments were ways for the family to ventilate. Both believe they do not have good models for resolving difficulties in their families of origin; one family kept everything hidden, and the other exploded but did not solve problems constructively. When Sam and Rachel were asked about ways that they had tried to solve the problem previously, they admitted that they had never seriously attempted to openly disagree with each other and try to compromise. Instead, they wait for things to cool off, apologize, and then forget about it until the next argument. Unfortunately, arguments are becoming more frequent.

Possible interactive definition: "You have never found a productive way to disagree and stay with an argument until it is solved. You both are nervous about arguing, and so you avoid bringing up divisive issues."

Summary of Stage 1
The therapist follows these steps:

Step 1: Obtain each person's definition of the problem.
Step 2: Gather important assessment information.
Step 3: Create a shared (interactive) definition of the problem based on the information that the partners have provided from their personal perspectives and assessment data.

Stage 2: Goal Setting: "We Have a Common Goal"

In this stage, each partner identifies the desired outcome of therapy. In other words, each is asked to decide what would be different if the problem no longer existed, to imagine life without the problem. The purpose of this stage, beyond focusing the troubled couple on a hopeful scenario, is to help transform a problem statement into a goal. One step in this direction is to externalize the problem so that blame is decreased and the couple can work together. Next, therapists help clients start thinking about the problem as a goal. Finally, the couple can identify behavioral and affective aspects of the goal and set clear and concrete targets.

Externalizing the Problem

Externalizing means helping the couple think about the problem as separate from themselves; this puts both partners on the same team. Michael White (1989) pioneered this approach that is fundamental to narrative therapy. The therapist begins to talk about the problem as if it is an outside force keeping the partners apart. Soon, couples begin to talk about the "arguing problem," "the money monster," or "the in-law dilemma." As partners externalize the problem, they can move closer together in order to conquer it. Through externalization, the blaming and concomitant emotions are lessened. When emotions are running high, it is difficult to set goals. Externalization has the effect of reducing emotional arousal around the issue.

The notion of externalization has appeared in Japanese tradition as *Kane Mushi* (Tomm, 1991) and is based on the folk idea that a worm gets inside and causes the misbehavior of a mischievous child. Because it is the unacceptable behavior (or the worm) that is criticized, rather than the person who exhibits it, the child can retain a positive self-image, and the parents do not worry about periods of misbehavior. In therapy this method provides them with an explanation for their behavior that they can rectify by "conquering" the problem together. In the examples that follow, the therapist attempts to lead the clients to externalize the problem and set a goal.

"We have discovered that your arguing over minor and unimportant issues is a concern. Can you tell me about some ways that arguing interferes with your goal of spending more time together?"

"What we have decided is that the two of you have a pattern where Nela gets jealous and Clayton's reaction is to distance himself further. The result is a cycle of increasing jealousy and resentment. What might the two of you do together to attack this jealousy-resentment cycle?"

Although externalizing is important at this stage, it is a technique that the therapist uses continually as a way of evoking the team concept and reminding the couple that they are working on a joint project rather than overcoming personal problems.

Setting Behavioral and Affective Goals

A problem is a set of symptoms, and a goal is a vision of the future. Both goals and problems are revisited throughout the therapy process. Just as the board of trustees must deal with problems in company production, the couple must try to solve difficulties that hinder everyday functioning. But the exciting thing about managing a business is moving the company to produce greater profit or create new products through research and development. The emphasis on goals in a couple's relationship reawakens interest about what the relationship could be and helps counterbalance the chore of dealing with problems. Too often, couples get stuck on "What is wrong with us?" and the relationship begins to take on a negative valence. At this juncture, the partners are asked to examine "how we would like our relationship to be."

The solution-focused approach to therapy has, as a central tenet, the belief that when couples talk about what a positive future looks like, they are ipso facto setting goals. These goals are generally stated positively as the presence of something rather than the absence of something. In the beginning, a couple may state the problem as "We fight too often and too emotionally about minor problems"; when they set a goal, they will say, "We want to solve minor problems and feel positive about each other when we are finished." You can see that goal setting in the integrative model is defined interactionally, as a shared vision. Our approach is to ask that partners identify both *behavioral* and *affective* changes that they would like to see and then state them in simple and concrete terms. When such goals are defined, both members have a clear notion of what they are trying to achieve. Successful goal setting can go a long way in counteracting the demoralization and frustration that brought them to therapy.

Here are some examples of how couples can transform problems to goals with behavioral and affective components:

"We will complete a new budget together by next week (behavioral) so that we can feel more competent (affective) as a couple and be more responsible with our finances"

"We will spend one night a week going out to dinner and taking a walk (behavioral) so that we will feel closer to each other (affective) and have more fun in the relationship."

Most therapists believe that substantial and long-lasting change is established when transformations occur in all three areas of human functioning: the affective (emotional), the behavioral, *and* the cognitive realms. So you may be asking yourself, what about cognitive or perceptual changes? Is it not important that the couple change in their thinking and perceptions about the relationship as well? We agree. That is why the interactional, or shared, definition of the problem is the starting point of the model. It is a big (cognitive) reframe of the problem from a personality- or pathology-oriented definition to a joint definition. Our model addresses cognitive or perceptual changes directly by a constant focus on asking the couple to view the problem and the goal differently at each stage of therapy, to abandon the problem-saturated story and adopt a goal-oriented vision of the future.

Summary of Stage 2

To change their view of the problem, couples follow these steps:

Step 1: Externalize the problem.
Step 2: Set behavioral and affective goals.

Stage 3: Interventions: "We Have a Solvable Problem"

In Stages 1 and 2, the couple has had a chance to air their grievances. The therapist has made an initial appraisal of the couple, helped them identify a shared definition of the problem, and worked with them to develop a joint positive goal. Stage 3 involves implementing interventions proposed by the therapist and guided by the couple's needs and background, which help them reach their goals. It becomes clear at this stage that unless the therapist really understands the couple, the interventions, however clever, will not be effective if they conflict with the cultural (religious, language, and ethnic) or idiosyncratic differences of the couple.

Identifying Strengths

One specific technique that is fundamental to this stage of treatment is the identification of strengths. In counseling and therapy, talking about strength-based approaches is popular these days, but there are relatively few specific techniques. Therapists employing the integrative model have used this method. They have found it to be effective because it furthers the overall aim of the model, which is to bring the couple together toward a jointly desired aim. The technique involves asking each member of the couple to list the positive characteristics of his or her partner. When this has been done, the couple jointly decides how they might be used to achieve the goal. By searching for and identifying the positive assets of each partner and how those assets have been helpful in similar situations in the past, the partners can view each other and the situation more positively. In addition, the therapist gets the couple to consider their joint assets. What strengths do they have as a couple? What issues have they previously mastered that could help them in the current situation?

Of course, this technique also has its pitfalls. If the couple is very angry and resentful, they may have a difficult time identifying anything positive about the other person. This is the reason for allowing each member of the couple to air his or her grievances in the initial stage of counseling. Still, it may be necessary, in such cases, to spend more time with a particularly alienated couple. One way of getting around this is to get the couple to talk first about a time when they were getting along and then move into individual strengths. For example,

Therapist: Tell me about the time when you first met?

Jen: We found a lot to talk about. We couldn't wait to see each other, and we would talk for hours on the phone when we couldn't be together that particular day. Every day was an adventure."

Therapist: In the story you told about how you met, what were the strengths in Jonah that you admired most?

Jen: Well, I found him very easy to talk to, had a sense of humor and was stable, someone to count on.

Therapist: If Jonah were able to bring some of his strengths to help achieve the goal we have been working on, what would that be?

Jen: Well, our goal is to spend more time together so that we can feel closer again. I guess he could remember how to be a good listener again. I just don't think he cares about my feelings any more.

Therapist [focusing on the strength]: So, when you do spend time together, he could let you know he is listening, and that would mean a lot because it would mean that he cares.

The couple can adapt the positive attributes from these stories for future possibilities and new outcomes. It reminds the couple that his or her partner is not without redeeming qualities. With a more respectful and positive view of each other and a clearer idea of desired outcomes, the couple can continue to reduce, if not eliminate, blame. The couple generates specific and concrete possibilities for the relationship as they shift from reminiscing and storytelling to a specific here-and-now plan for change.

In short, identifying the positive attributes of the relationship and its past is not only a tactic to encourage the couple but also a real "nuts-and-bolts" technique to identify who will be responsible for which changes. It evokes the best qualities of each. For example, Leila and Bob might move from a story about their ability to be romantic with each other before the children were born to a romantic picture of how it might be when the children are grown. Then they can bring the romantic notion to the here-and-now by exploring possibilities for honeymooning once a month while the children are cared for by the grandparents. They must describe exactly what they expect from each other based on the identified strengths that they have attributed to each other. In this case, they must decide how they will set aside the time together, who will arrange it, who will arrange child care, and what kinds of plans they can make for spending time together.

Designing Interventions

The integrative model allows for a variety of interventions designed by the therapist and approved by the clients if they all believe that the method will further the therapy goals. In Chapters 2 and 3, a number of techniques associated with the major therapies were described. A therapist implementing the integrative model might use any of these theories if they seem to be appropriate for the couple and are directly applicable to the goal. Let's consider the following three specific techniques (each is described more fully later in the book, along with many others). Each technique includes a goal that might mesh well with this intervention:

> Communication training: The couple wants to be able to discuss the parenting of his child from a previous marriage (behavioral) and at the end feel good about their relationship (affective).
>
> Divorce mediation: The couple wants to end the marriage (behavioral) in a way so that both partners feel that they have been treated fairly and that they can retain some positive feelings toward each other (affective).
>
> Referral for sex therapy: The couple wants to have sex more frequently (behavioral) so that they can feel more satisfied and intimate (affective).

Summary of Stage 3

The therapist follows these steps:

> Step 1: Help the couple identify strengths and introduce the notion that the couple can use each other's resources to achieve the goals of therapy.
>
> Step 2: Match goals with interventions that are appropriate for the couple and enlist their aid in implementing them until the goal has been reached.

Stage 4: Maintenance: "We Have a Solution"

Challenging Commitment

Stage 4 begins when the couple and the therapist agree that substantial progress has been made on the initial goal. In Stage 3, therapist interventions were designed to create movement and promote changes in the couple's relationship. Now, in Stage 4, a new set of tools is needed to keep couples from backsliding and to nurture the nascent changes. To get the couple to think about these issues, the therapist poses questions that ask the couple to imagine overcoming the hurdles:

"How big a part of you is willing to do this differently?"

"How will the two of you keep yourselves motivated to continue to work on this problem?"

"What will you each have to do in order to make the changes continue?"

"How serious are the two of you about keeping the ball rolling? What steps would you be willing to take to keep things moving?"

Maintenance may be the most delicate stage in the couple's progress because positive changes may easily be ignored when minor relapses occur. It is very easy for a couple to remember the complaints and see every step backwards as a sign of doom. They still need the therapist to help them remain faithful to goals and have faith in the relationship.

Identifying Roadblocks and Pitfalls

In the integrative model, Stage 4 involves challenging the participants to make a long-term commitment to growth while recognizing backsliding as a part of the process. A therapist at this point may ask the couple to write down their relationship maintenance plan detailing how they will handle the expected setbacks. Part of that plan might be to plan follow-up visits with a therapist, engage in marriage enrichment activities, or plan getaways.

To establish a viable maintenance strategy, the couple must focus on the roadblocks, or barriers, that could sabotage change in the relationship. Once the barriers are identified, plans to prevent them from influencing the change and ways to support maintaining the change are outlined. We could call this *relapse prevention* (Carlson & Ellis, 2004). If you tell the couple the ways in which they are likely to return to old behaviors, when the behaviors reappear, the couple is mentally prepared. When the therapist predicts relapses and "slipping," the couple will not be discouraged if there is a ready-made plan to implement. The questions that the therapist asks are sometimes directed at an individual member of the couple and sometimes to the couple as a unit:

"What other demands will pull you away from your commitment to the relationship?"

"What can you do when your boss puts pressure on you to work overtime?"

"How will the two of you handle it when Bill's mother comes to stay for the month?"

"At various points, you are going to feel like criticizing Marie even though it is not necessary or requested. How will you handle those feelings so that you don't slip back into that old behavior?"

Besides questioning, which gets the couple thinking about potential solutions to relapse, role playing can be used to get them to practice repairing the relationship when trouble appears. The therapist can devise a scenario in which the couple has returned to a previous pattern and now discusses how they can break out of it. This normalizes the process of backsliding and develops confidence in the couple's ability to handle their problems when the therapist is not around.

Summary of Stage 4

This is a critical stage in couples therapy where the therapist uses any and all methods to help couples recommit to the change process. Among the easiest methods to employ are the following:

Step 1: Reaffirm commitment and present questions that ask the couple how they will deal with relapses.

Step 2: Help couples identify common setbacks and develop, with them, a maintenance strategy to cope.

Stage 5: Validation: "There Is No Problem"

Celebrating Success

Stage 5 is a time for celebration. At this point, the couple may not have completely solved the problems that brought them in, but they have made a dent in them and they are feeling better about the relationship and more hopeful. Here, the therapist asks them to compare the goals set at Stage 2 with the current state of the relationship. Individuals are requested to congratulate themselves and their partners for their success in conquering the problem as a team and for enacting new, positive behaviors. The therapist underscores also the importance of using maintenance strategies outside of therapy to "keep the ball rolling."

Building In Follow-up Strategies

At this stage, couples may still lack confidence in their ability to handle things on their own. The therapist's faith and conviction make the transition toward termination less difficult. Some couples will complain that the problem is not entirely eliminated, partially because they fear that things will return to chaos. That is why we like to use the statement, "You have made a dent in the problem." In brief therapy, we hope to make a dent and have the couple continue their progress independently. A long-term maintenance plan with the couple can include reassuring periodic visits with the therapist at 3-month and then 6-month intervals. Listed below are some therapist statements that (1) help validate the couple's success and (2) ask the couple to validate the changes they have made:

"It is important to congratulate yourselves on the budget you created and followed for the past two months. It sounds like you have created more confidence in your competence as financial planners together."

"Lee and Jiang, what has been the most fun for you since you have been going out to dinner and taking walks together?"

Summary of Stage 5

Stage 5 is the final piece in the integrative model. It tries to help the couple make a cognitive shift by asking them to recognize success, however small. The two steps in this stage are

Step 1: Celebrate success. Ask the couple to celebrate joint success and recognize each other's efforts that led to that success.

Step 2: Build in follow-up strategies. Ask the couple to attend follow-up sessions and reinforce the need for maintenance.

OUR EXPERIENCES IN WORKING WITH THE INTEGRATIVE MODEL

Observation 1: Sometimes interventions are not effective because the couple is too angry or unwilling to work on the shared definition   The integrative model in Figure 4.1 graphically depicts the stages in the couple's perception of the focal problem. Although the movement of therapy is primarily clockwise, the couple may need to return to an earlier stage. For example, the couple may have reached Stage 3, intervention, where each is asked to look at the other partner's strengths, assets, and positive attributes. Suddenly they have great difficulty in identifying these assets in each other and become negative about their relationship. Actually, they are still harboring feelings of resentment and blame, which characterizes Stage 1, the assessment and obtaining a shared definition. The model suggests that the therapist should be flexible enough to shift gears and return to Stage 1 until the couple is capable of moving on. This "downshifting" is shown in Figure 4.2 by an arrow that travels from "Intervention" to the problem definition

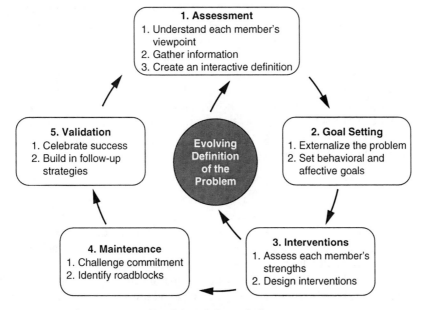

Figure 4.2   The integrative model and downshifting

at the center of the figure and then back to "Assessment." From there, the sequence of treatment resumes its course around the perimeter of the circle.

Downshifting to an earlier stage of therapy should not be thought of as a failure, nor should discouragement be transmitted to the couple. Experience will demonstrate that all couples travel at different rates, depending on the nature of their difficulties and on the unique qualities that they bring to therapy.

Observation 2: Some couples are not really couples   As we remarked earlier, when we begin to form an interactive definition of the problem, we may find that the couple has never made a basic relationship agreement. A few years ago, I (Mark) saw a couple for three sessions before it dawned on me that only one member of a cohabiting couple had any intention of remaining in the relationship. In short, they were not a couple. He considered it a temporary relationship, and she wanted therapy to try to convince him to make a commitment. Although the therapy was useful in bringing out each person's view of the relationship, none of their problems could be addressed because they had never reached the fundamental agreement: "We have a relationship." This issue was not identified in the initial assessment (and it rarely is) because the couple may not be entirely honest about it. It can short-circuit the process of therapy but may be a valuable revelation to the couple.

Observation 3: Some couples cannot buy into a shared definition   If a couple cannot identify a focal problem and cannot set clear interactive goals, this is possibly not a brief couples counseling situation. There are several reasons a couple cannot identify a joint, focal problem. Perhaps they are not really interested in working on the relationship. They may have outside romantic interests that make them unwilling to try and resurrect the primary relationship. Maybe they are comfortable with a distant relationship and fear that counseling will reignite a stage of fighting. The couple may also have so many areas of disagreement that identifying one small issue seems irrelevant. They need a giant step to convince themselves that things can be different.

One way to help a couple with an unfocused goal is to make goal clarification the issue to be worked on. This may keep the couple in therapy, but the intervention is probably not going to be brief. High-conflict couples and couples who cannot agree on a focal problem take much longer to move through the stages. In both cases, the couple must eventually stop what they are doing (fighting or avoiding) and find a way to agree on a common issue.

CONCLUSION

The integrative model is a synthesis of aspects of various theoretical perspectives with eight basic premises drawn from various schools of thought. The model provides a map for the therapist to identify the stages and steps for moving a couple from "He or she is the problem" to "There is no problem." The five-stage brief therapy model is based on constructivist thinking and drawing from solution-focused, narrative therapy, systemic therapy, and strength-based approaches. The model encourages therapists to use reframing to create a change in attitude about the problem to focus away from blame and recrimination. The couple then begins the hard work of achieving behavioral and affective goals. The therapist uses the language of success and change to help couples identify pitfalls in the maintenance stage of therapy and celebrate success when change has occurred.

You do not need to adopt the integrative model to use the techniques presented later in the book or benefit from the research about specific couple problems. The integrative model was designed to help those who want to learn couples counseling to approach it in a systematic and step-by-step way. Its benefits include flexibility in the types of techniques that it uses and its sensitivity to the needs of the couple. We hope that you will consider using the integrative model as an initial framework and see if it works for you.

5

The Assessment of Couples and Their Problems

MARK E. YOUNG AND JOANNE VOGEL

KEY CONCEPTS

- Assessment is not a one-time project but an ongoing process in couples therapy. It is interwoven with treatment and is vital to achieving successful outcomes.
- We bring our own biases, assumptions, theories, and prejudices to the assessment task.
- Assessment acts like a funnel with a wide variety of information pouring in and being squeezed by our constructions into useful packages that we call diagnoses or problems.
- We can choose to assess both members of the couple, the problems in their relationship, or the overall quality of the relationship.
- The integrative therapist casts a wide net, using as many sources of data as possible.
- A key assessment method for the couples therapist is the use of the interview.
- The genogram also functions as an important assessment tool that, along with the interview, provides important historical data and information about the present family structure.
- A number of available assessment tools exist including standardized tests and semistructured methods that can be added to the repertoire of the couples therapist.

Too often we map our clients' prison, but not their escape.
Waters and Lawrence, 1993, p. 53

Assessment courses such as Tests and Measurements are some of the most unpopular courses in a therapist's academic training. As Boen (1988) notes, many counselors and clinicians have a bias against testing. More specifically, therapists who see couples and families seem even more leery of psychological tests than other helping professionals. For one, many measurement devices label *individuals* and do little to help with the problems that bring couples or families to counseling. This skepticism about testing does not mean that couples therapy does not need an assessment component. If you begin treatment without an assessment, you are saying that all clients will benefit from the same treatment. In a way, you are supposing that all clients are the same. Those who emphasize assessment believe that differences are important.

Assessment allows us to ferret out the uniqueness of each individual, couple, or family so that we may apply the appropriate treatment. An integrative model incorporates this philosophy of difference and diversity. We believe that the couples therapist must adapt to the attributes of the clients rather than forcing clients to adapt to our treatment regime. Clients differ on the basis of history, culture, adherence to traditional gender roles, readiness for treatment, and any number of factors that affects the treatment selection. Similarly, each couple is different and deserves the time that a comprehensive assessment takes.

ASSESSMENT IS AN ONGOING PROCESS

As the integrative model diagram shows (see Figure 4.1), assessment is the first step in the therapy process (see also Ivey & Mathews, 1986). Unfortunately, a two-dimensional model like this one cannot adequately represent the fact that assessment is *not* a one-time activity of the therapist. Assessment is an ongoing process, beginning with the first telephone contact, the first sight of the client, and probably the initial seconds of the first encounter. This process continues with each additional piece of information that we learn about the couple and their experiences, whether through standardized instruments or informal assessment tools. Of note, we often gather important information in later sessions when clients feel more trusting and open up more.

Although assessment is continuous, there are two important points where it is critical. The first point is at initial *screening* where the therapist is attempting to rule out serious problems such as psychosis, substance abuse, and physical violence. Following this assessment, the therapist decides whether the couple is appropriate for couples therapy or if individual therapy, hospitalization, or some other specialized treatment might be more effective. At this point, the therapist is aware of the most important issues facing the couple. The second point for assessment occurs when couples therapy has been decided upon and the couple has negotiated a goal statement with the therapist.

Even though several issues may have emerged during the initial screening, some areas are put aside for the moment, and the therapist makes a more intense scrutiny of a single issue or two. To use a metaphor, screening is like using binoculars to scan the whole horizon broadly. But once a particular area has been selected, we engage in a more specific process of *problem assessment,* which could be compared to a microscope. Similarly, Snyder, Heyman, and Haynes (2005) advise sensitivity over specificity in the initial screening phase to avoid overlooking potential issues then selecting narrower measures to pinpoint specific sources of concern. Finally, they follow with strategies to analyze how individual and relationship concerns affect each other and relate to other situational factors (Snyder et al., 2005).

ARE ASSESSMENT AND TREATMENT REALLY SEPARATE?

To complicate things a bit further, assessment and treatment are not as separate as we like to believe. Although it is useful in the integrative model to identify these as separate steps, assessment methods have therapeutic effects. In fact, assessment can be considered the beginning of the therapeutic process (Sarnoff & Sarnoff, 2005). If you ask members of a couple to write down every time they make disparaging comments about their partner during the day (assessment task), researchers tell us that couples will make fewer such remarks to each other as they become aware of what they are doing (treatment). Conversely, treatment often becomes assessment. Let's say we give a couple the homework assignments to read to each other nightly from a certain self-help book about marriage. When the clients return to the next session, we find that they have not done the assignment but instead present us with a journal of the issues that they fought about during the past week. We have learned (assessed) something about the couple's response to therapist-initiated directives, what they see as major problems, and perhaps discovered that they enjoy certain kinds of homework assignments.

To further this point about the intertwining of assessment and treatment, we find that many assessment devices, such as the family genogram, are both assessment tools and intervention methods. The genogram is a tool discussed in detail later in this chapter. It is a pictorial representation of the client's family tree and maps out the relationships between family members. For example, during a workshop presented by the authors, one of the participants revealed that she had come from an alcoholic family. At age 30, she sought individual therapy for some personal problems. During her first session, the therapist used a genogram, and the client could identify long-standing problems and issues in the family as well as understanding something about the history of her own difficulties. She could relate this information to her current interpersonal problems and, after this single session, believed that she no longer needed the assistance of a therapist. We are not advocating one-session therapy for everyone, but the experience of this client suggests that assessment devices can bring about "Aha!" experiences for individuals and couples. Similarly, Gordon (1986) reports the effectiveness of a "dispassionate assessment" as a means of allowing couples who are contemplating divorce a way to consider couples therapy as an alternative.

In light of this discussion, should we conclude that couples therapists need to become less skeptical of paper-and-pencil tests and embrace the measures of psychopathology embedded in these tools? Our answer to this is no. Most standard psychological measures aimed at individuals are not worth the time when working with couples in the *problem-assessment phase*. However, it is prudent to employ certain standardized screening tools to identify major mental disorders, the presence of violence, substance abuse, and other issues that should be treated prior to couples therapy. In addition, well-selected assessment tools can be a beneficial supplement to a counselor's clinical judgment (Hawley, 1995). They offer an additional perspective to counselor observation (Olson, 1977) and save time through providing a wealth of diagnostic information (Olson, Fournier, & Druckman, 1986).

In conclusion, we are hoping that the reader will consider that assessment is a crucial and indispensable activity of the therapist. It plays a vital role in couples counseling (Hawley, 1995). We have suggested that assessment with couples has two major parts: an initial screening and a more careful look at the particular problem. Second, we have suggested that assessment is more than testing. The interview, observations, and questions of the therapist are part of the assessment process and sharpen the picture of the couple's issues throughout the therapy process. In fact, a case can be made for the use of multiple assessment methods such as self-report, interview based, observational, and other report (Cromwell & Peterson, 1983; Grotevant & Carlson, 1989; Hawley, 1995; Snyder et al., 2005). Finally, assessment can be valuable as a treatment tool as well. It can help couples become aware of positive and negative aspects of their functioning that they have ignored or have become habituated. While it is understandable that many couples counselors and family therapists have rejected traditional assessment techniques, we propose that assessments are necessary to guide and enhance the therapeutic process. We need to keep an open mind to assessment methods that lead our clients to greater awareness and help us as therapists make good treatment decisions.

BIASES AND ASSUMPTIONS IN ASSESSMENT

When therapists begin a therapy relationship, we bring our own history, assumptions, biases, and prejudices with us. Our value systems, biases, and assumptions affect the therapy process from the very beginning, including the assessment phase (Mayer, 1989; Rigazio-DiGilio, 1999). These biases may lead to misunderstandings, misdiagnosis, and selection of ineffective interventions (Bernal & Castro, 1994; Ho, 1995). Notably, bias can occur when responding in either a positive or negative direction to either partner (Guanipa & Woolley, 2000). It can also affect our ability to screen effectively in such areas as domestic violence (Hamberger & Phelan, 2004; Sugg & Inui, 1992). Although paper-and-pencil tests are not free from bias or cultural constraints, these offer an adjunct to the therapist's observations. Using multiple sources of information for assessment decreases the likelihood that any one source will overwhelmingly bias our judgments.

Besides personal biases, therapists adopt theories with built-in assumptions about human nature. If you believe that the couple's relationship is improved by treating the intrapsychic conflicts of each individual, the Minnesota Multiphasic Personality Inventory (MMPI) might be administered to both members of the couple, and the resulting data would become the basis for one or two individual therapies. If you believe that all of a couple's problems result from attitudes and learning in the family of origin, a genogram or family history will be the first order of business. Liddle (1983) compared various systems of family therapy based on their diagnostic/assessment approaches. He points out that the assessment function is the point where theoretical systems begin to differentiate themselves. Below is a summary based on Liddle's look at the issues that various theories identify in the assessment phase:

1. Bowenian theory assesses issues such as
   a. The family's level of anxiety and emotionality
   b. Differentiation of each person from the family
   c. The general coping ability of the past three generations
2. Structural theory (Minuchin) focuses on
   a. Organization of family rules, boundaries, alliances, and subsystems
   b. The family life cycle
   c. A search for strengths
3. Strategic theory (Haley) is mainly concerned with
   a. The presenting problem
   b. The family life cycle
   c. Specific sequences of interaction
4. Brief therapy (MRI) looks primarily at
   a. Presenting symptoms, not history
   b. Observable interactions
   c. Symptoms as the result of failed problem solving
   d. Life's transition points
   e. Communication levels, rules, and congruency

Thus, assessment is not free of one's biases, prejudices, theories, or assumptions about human nature. Besides thinking about the various theories and their perspectives on couple problems, it is important to examine our own intrinsic theories to see if they promote a productive viewpoint or are merely "baggage." In Figure 5.1, the funnel of assessment, the diagram depicts how information obtained during assessment is filtered through our personal "lenses" that affect our diagnoses or hypotheses about a couple's problems. Listed below are a series of questions to stimulate your thinking about some of the lenses, or attitudes, that you bring to couples therapy. Answer by writing True, False, or Not Sure next to the question and then explain your answer underneath. You may wish to discuss your answers with fellow learners. In that discussion, list the implications for *assessment* that arise from each statement.

Self-Assessment of Assumptions About Couples

1. If each individual is happy and self-sufficient, the relationship will be a good one.

   _____

2. An interracial marriage is "asking for trouble."

   _____

3. Most difficulties in couples are due to irrational ideas or dysfunctional belief systems that clients have learned.

   _____

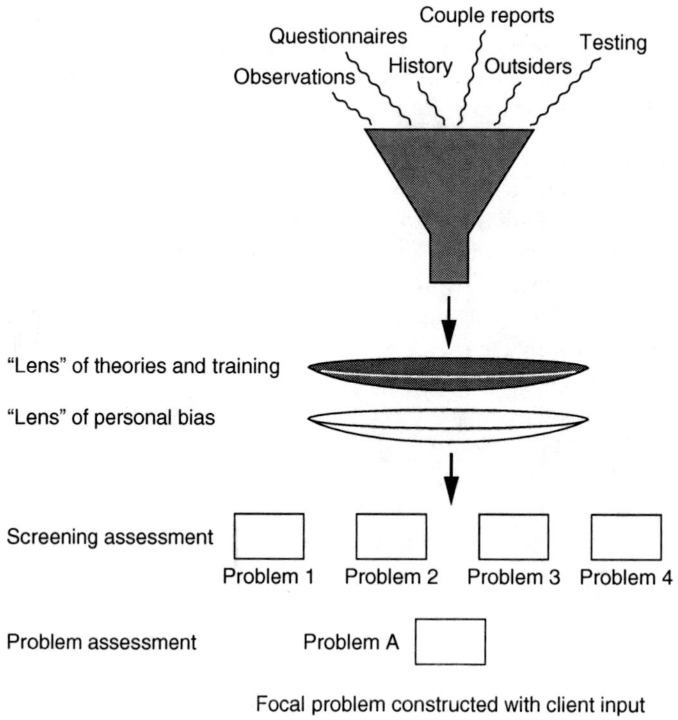

Figure 5.1   The funnel of assessment

4. Tracking down their roots in the family of origin can treat most couple problems.

_____

5. Good couple relationships are made up of two people who are very similar.

_____

6. Marriage is a sacrament and not just a legal contract; therefore, one must understand the spiritual dimension in order to help a troubled relationship.

_____

7. Most couple problems can be solved by better communication.

_____

8. An "open marriage" in which the couple agrees to have other intimate and even sexual relationships, while remaining married, is a workable arrangement for some people.

_____

9. In order to have a healthy relationship, men and women must have an equitable or "peer marriage."

_____

10. Some marriages are so troubled that a therapist should recommend divorce.

_____

There are no easy or correct answers to the questions posed above. The purpose of the exercise is to make you aware of biases, prejudices, or assumptions that you may carry with you. How can we ever escape from them? The answer is that we probably cannot actually step outside of our conceptual frameworks. We cannot truly be objective (Crosby, 1991). But, we may learn to become aware of when our prejudices are affecting our actions. Here, we hit upon the major problem with prejudices. We often do not know we have them. So, at the very minimum, we should become aware of our attitudes and biases by examining our own history and present belief systems. We can do this through personal therapy, good supervision, or entering a relationship enhancement seminar with a partner. This blindness to our own point of view is the reason why many therapists continue to seek supervision from a trained supervisor periodically throughout their professional lives.

ASSESSMENT USING THE INTEGRATIVE MODEL

The Funnel of Assessment

Figure 5.1 shows a funnel with information flowing into it from a variety of sources. Among these potential sources in couples therapy are the following:

1. Therapist observations based upon the couple's spontaneous interaction or during interactions introduced by the therapist
2. Questionnaires completed by the couple outside of the session
3. The couple's reports to the therapist regarding their behavior outside of the session
4. Historical data from the genogram or from client histories
5. Reports from other sources such as family members, the courts, or police reports
6. Results from paper-and-pencil testing

In Chapter 6, we look at how assessment and goal setting are linked. For now, let's consider assessment as a separate enterprise during which the therapist keeps an open mind to all information flowing in and searches to gain the most complete picture of the couple's total functioning.

DIRECTION FOR COUPLES ASSESSMENT: INDIVIDUALS, PROBLEMS IN THE RELATIONSHIP, OR QUALITY OF THE RELATIONSHIP?

Assessing Individuals

Why must we even think about the individuals if we are treating a couple? The answer is that sometimes one member's problems can be treated individually, leading to better couple functioning. Also, some unresolved personal problems could undermine your efforts with the couple. For example, a couple came into our office due to a crisis surrounding the husband's infidelity. We began immediately to help the couple deal with the crisis in the relationship, trying to repair the damaged trust and supporting each individual. During the initial session, the wife appeared very depressed, and the therapist's attention turned to her to determine the depth of her distress. The session immediately changed when it was determined that she needed to be hospitalized to prevent a suicide that she was planning. We did not return to couples therapy for several months until the depression was under control. So, before we can successfully treat a couple, we need to determine if each individual is healthy enough to engage in the process. Specifically, individuals need to be screened for three major impediments:

1. Is there a safety risk? Is either one of the partners suicidal or suffering from bulimia, anorexia, or other life-endangering disorder? Is there violence in the relationship?
2. Is the client psychotic, severely disturbed, and cannot distinguish between delusions and reality? Is one of the partners suffering from some other major mental disorder such as agoraphobia or bipolar disorder that will strongly influence the effectiveness of couples therapy?
3. Is the client under the influence of drugs and alcohol to the extent that progress in the couple's relationship will be limited?

When screening for these issues, divergence exists as to whether the initial assessment should be conducted conjointly or individually. It is suggested that interviews be conducted individually whenever violence or substance abuse is suspected (Snyder et al., 2005). This allows for more open disclosure about the presence of these issues and the degree of danger (Holtzworth-Munroe, Meehan, Rehman, & Marshall, 2002; Rosenbaum & O'Leary, 1986). Although individual interviews may offer victims an opportunity to disclose violence, some victims will not acknowledge these issues due to embarrassment, minimization, or fear (Ehrensaft & Vivian, 1996). Other reasons may lend to partner violence going undetected such as the therapist's discomfort, unwillingness, or failure to ask in addition to confusion over terminology or what constitutes violence (Straus, Hamby, & Warren, 2003). In any event, assessment of violence needs to be an ongoing process with the ability to ask specifically and confidently about these issues whenever violence is suspected or detected. It is not unusual for violence to be revealed later in treatment once trust has been established.

In our research and clinical work at the Community Counseling Center at the University of Central Florida, we use a combination of conjoint and individual interviews when gathering information about suspected violence. At the outset of therapy, couples take the Revised Conflict Tactics Scales (CTS2) (Straus, Hamby, Boney-McCoy, & Sugarman, 1996), along with other measures of couple functioning. Couples are instructed to complete all assessments individually, without collaborating, and are placed at opposite ends of the room or in separate rooms when space permits. If the assessment from either partner indicates physical assault, injury, or sexual coercion, the therapist completes a structured interview addressing additional risk factors associated with violence. Depending upon the level of violence disclosed on the CTS2, the therapist decides whether to complete the structured interview individually or conjointly. The presence of violence necessitates providing the victim with a safety plan along with community referrals. Moderate to severe levels of violence or injury cause us to refrain from offering couples treatment until the batterer receives and completes appropriate intervention. Most authorities (for example, see Willbach, 1989) advocate addressing violence as a prerequisite for further treatment.

Whereas the issue of physical danger and psychotic problems clearly must be brought under control before couples therapy begins, the issue of alcohol and drug abuse is less clear. Lukas (1993) suggests that the therapist ask about substance abuse in every intake session. The usual protocol is to address this issue during the first interview or by questionnaire and to then refer the individual for addictions treatment if needed before ever beginning couples therapy. It is difficult, though, to distinguish between those individuals who must go through treatment and those who maintain their lifestyle despite "recreational use" of drugs and alcohol.

We once treated a couple who had reconciled after a long separation. The husband admitted to a history of drug and alcohol abuse, but we were told that he was no longer abusing these substances. We suggested that he attend Alcoholics Anonymous (AA) and that she continue with Al-Anon. She did attend Al-Anon, but he refused to participate in AA. The couple was successful in reuniting and clearing up many of the bad feelings from the past, but it soon became clear that he was smoking marijuana on a daily basis after work. He did not feel that this was a problem, but it was definitely affecting the relationship. He began to lose interest in couples therapy and many of the maintenance behaviors that were suggested. Consequently, the relationship began to stagnate. He was fired from his job, which propelled him into treatment for his marijuana use, temporarily ending couples therapy.

Drugs and alcohol, by reducing anxiety and motivation, are in direct conflict with the focus of couples therapy, which attempts to teach people to deal with their conflicts together. Alcohol temporarily relieves the discomfort and creates a behavioral syndrome (sometimes called codependency) in the affected others. Sober partners of alcohol and drug abusers take on most of the responsibilities for the household and for maintaining the relationship. This imbalance produces resentment and a parent–child relationship. In sum, screening of alcohol and drug use is critical because it must be treated before couples therapy begins or when it is discovered. Otherwise, couples therapy may be derailed or ineffective until the issue of chemical dependency is resolved.

Assessing Relationship Problems

Assessment of relationship problems involves focusing on a different level of functioning than those explained by individual characteristics (Vincent & Carter, 1987). This type of assessment emphasizes relationship processes and interactions (Snyder et al., 2005) such as problems with in-laws, parenting an adolescent, or dealing with finances. Box 5.1 lists a number of tests in this area, along with a brief description of their focus.

Box 5.1
Some Clinically Useful Assessments for Couples Therapy

STANDARDIZED ASSESSMENT INSTRUMENTS:INDIVIDUALS

Family of Origin Scale (Hovestadt, Anderson, Piercy, Cochran, & Fine, 1985). Clients rate their family of origin on ten scales: trust, empathy, conflict resolution, positive tone, ability to express feelings, willingness to deal with separation and loss, openness of family boundaries, respect, personal responsibility, and clarity of expression.

Myers-Briggs Type Indicator (MBTI) (Briggs & Myers, 1977; Briggs-Myers & McCauley, 1985). This instrument measures clients on four dimensions: Introversion versus Extroversion, Intuition versus Sensing, Thinking versus Feeling, and Judging versus Perceiving.

16 Personality Factors Questionnaire (16PF) (Institute for Personality and Ability Testing, 1967). The Institute for Personality and Ability Testing offers a Couples Counseling Report based upon the 16 PF. This seven- to eight-page computer-generated assessment assesses the personality of each individual then looks at the interactions (similarities, dissimilarities, and potential conflicts) of these personalities.

SPECIFIC PROBLEMS OR STRESSORS

Scale of Marital Problems (Swenson & Fiore, 1982). This scale assesses problem solving, decision making, goal setting, childrearing and home labor, relatives and in-laws, personal care/appearance, money arrangements, affection, and relationships with people outside the marriage.

Marital Activities Inventory (Birchler, Weiss, & Vincent, 1975). This inventory identifies how spouses allocate their time.

Area of Change Questionnaire (ACQ) (Weiss & Birchler, 1975; Weiss, Hops, & Patterson, 1973). The ACQ identifies 34 specific behaviors and asks about the amount of change that each person wants.

Marital Agendas Protocol (Notarius & Vanzetti, 1983). This assessment probes the areas of conflict in the marriage, expectations, blame, and level of agreement about the seriousness of problems.

Sexual Interaction Inventory (SII) (LoPiccolo & Steger, 1974). This 102-item inventory assesses the frequency of sexual activity and satisfaction.

Derogatis Sexual Functioning Inventory (DSFI) (Derogatis, Lopez, & Zinzeletta, 1988; Derogatis & Melisaratos, 1979). The DSFI is a 254-item inventory gauging sexual knowledge, sexual attitudes, and sex drive.

(Continued)

Golombok–Rust Inventory of Sexual Satisfaction (Golombok, Rust, & Pickard, 1984). This inventory measures global sexual functioning, impotence, premature ejaculation, anorgasmia, and vaginismus.

Revised Conflict Tactics Scales (CTS2) (Straus et al., 1996). The CTS2 is the most widely used measure of couple aggression. This 78-item assessment tool includes scales for negotiation, psychological aggression, physical assault, injury, and sexual coercion. It can help differentiate between minor and severe levels of assault and abuse.

THE QUALITY OF THE RELATIONSHIP

Marital Adjustment Test (MAT) (Locke & Wallace, 1959). The MAT is one of the oldest and most widely used measures of marital satisfaction. This 15-item test gauges happiness and agreement.

Dyadic Adjustment Scale (DAS) (Spanier, 1976; Spanier & Filsinger, 1983). This 32-item scale is the most frequently used measure of relationship satisfaction. It looks at cohesion and affectional expression but also proves useful for discussing specific problems.

Marital Satisfaction Inventory-Revised (MSI-R) (Snyder, 1997). This 150-item true/false assessment of relationship functioning looks at the nature and intensity of distress. Some initial studies have shown evidence of reliability and validity for the Spanish version for use with Mexican, Mexican American (Negy, Snyder, & Diaz-Loving, 2004), and Spanish populations (Reig-Ferrer, Cepeda-Benito, & Snyder, 2004). Additionally, the MSI-R has German, Russian, and Korean translations.

PREPARE/ENRICH Inventories (Olson, 2002). This program offers five different types of enrichment assessments targeting premarital couples, cohabiting couples, premarital couples with children, marital couples, and older couples. The computer-generated report offered via paper and pencil or online identifies strengths and growth areas in the couple relationship.

Personal Assessment of Intimacy in Relationships (PAIR) (Schaefer & Olson, 1981). The PAIR inventory identifies seven kinds of intimacy.

Marital Problem-Solving Scale (Baugh, Avery, & Sheets-Haworth, 1982). This scale measures satisfaction with decision making and problem solving in a marital relationship.

Golombok–Rust Inventory of Marital State (Rust, Bennun, Crowe, & Golombok, 1988). This 28-item assessment focuses on the overall quality of the relationship.

Marital Status Inventory (Weiss & Cerreto, 1980). This assessment measures the tendency of the couple toward divorce.

Relationship Assessment Scale (Hendrick, 1988). A seven-item scale providing a global evaluation of the dyadic relationship.

Ordinarily in the interview situation, a linear approach to assessment of problems seems the logical approach. At the heart of a linear model is the idea that if we gather enough information, we will be able to determine "why" a problem occurred. This is, of course, the basis to psychodynamic thinking. We begin to try to discover the "who, what, where, when, and how" of the problem. For example, if the couple is having difficulty with finances, it would be useful to know who is in charge of finances, what the couple's financial situation is, where and when they fight about it, and how the couple thinks the problem originated. The search for a cause might lead you to understand one partner's impoverished family background, which makes him a miser now, and the other partner's need to acquire possessions as a symbolic way of getting love. Solving such deeply rooted problems is the individual, linear approach to therapy. A systemic approach suggests that the vain search for causes leads to blaming and rarely leads us to a solution of the problem because what is critical is the interaction of two people rather than simply the individual issues of each person.

Assessing the Quality of the Relationship

Literally hundreds of measures of marital quality and happiness exist in the literature on couples therapy (L'Abate & Bagarozzi, 1993). They ordinarily yield an overall score of general satisfaction with the marriage. These are self-reports from each member of the couple. Each person's score is compared with the partner's and sometimes to group norms. It often occurs that one member of the couple is satisfied and the other is not. In these cases, are we really assessing the relationship or the viewpoint of one member? Another problem with such scales is that they rarely help the therapist identify specific problems. Also, these scales may promote the irrational idea that happiness is an enduring trait of the relationship rather than a more realistic idea that satisfaction is a discovery one makes from time to time during life.

Attempts have been made to define more clearly what is meant by satisfaction, but the concept remains murky (Spanier & Lewis, 1980). For example, Crosby (1991) points out that the term *stability* has been shown to be separate from the idea of happiness or satisfaction in a marriage. Stability is the tendency of the couple to stay together or maintain the couple bond. There are stable relationships that are unhappy, and there are happy relationships that are not stable. If measures of satisfaction do not show us how the couple interacts, what their specific problems are, or whether or not they are likely to split up, how much usefulness can be claimed for these overall indicators? Nonetheless, a proliferation of articles focusing on the concept of marital satisfaction has emerged since the last edition of this text.

Perhaps the most notable drawback to measures of marital quality, for the clinician, is that they emphasize the viewpoints of the individuals in the relationship rather than the relationship itself. One alternative that has been tried is to develop observational checklists. A trained observer records data from watching live or videotaped interactions of the couple and then applies these observations to a measurement tool in order to draw conclusions about the functionality of these behaviors. Although it seems that observational methods are useful and valid, standardized observational measures are often too time-consuming and expensive for ordinary clinical use (L'Abate & Bagarozzi, 1993; Mash & Foster, 2001).

Another method that has been explored is called conjoint marital testing (L'Abate & Bagarozzi, 1993). This is a testing situation in which both members of the couple work together on the same task. Once again, these tests have not made their way into clinical practice because of time and money limitations. More recently, Sarnoff and Sarnoff (2005) have proposed an informal assessment of creativity in couples called the Couples Creativity Assessment Tasks (C-CAT). This assessment incorporates both individual tasks (for example, Early Memories, Future Visions) and a self-assessment (Creative Problem Solving) in addition to a conjoint Divergent Thinking Task.

Notwithstanding these flaws, measures of marital quality may still be useful to the couples therapist. They can be useful in determining the seriousness of the couple's problems and can signal improvement. Box 5.1 includes references for a number of the best and most concise standardized methods available. One of the best uses of the construct, marital quality, would be to repeat testing with a brief measure at two or three points during the course of therapy. Besides gauging progress, positive results might help to encourage the couple that some headway is being made.

Assessment During a Crisis

When a crisis occurs, extensive history taking and in-depth individual assessment are put on hold. Incidents of substance abuse, acts of violence, or discoveries of infidelity are the most usual crises that propel a couple into the therapist's office (Hendrick, 1995). The usual intake procedure is put aside, and the therapist begins to defuse the incident. Assessment in a crisis mainly consists of determining the extent of the damage and how to prevent imminent danger or psychological abuse while giving the couple support and hope. In this book, we deal with the protocols for these three usual crises (substance abuse, violence, and infidelity) in separate chapters. At this point, let's note that a crisis requires a brief assessment and immediate reduction of stress rather than the normal sequence of couples therapy depicted in the integrative model.

USING TESTS AND INFORMAL TOOLS TO ASSESS COUPLES

Testing Couples

With regard to choosing appropriate methods, Beavers and Hampson (1990), Corso (1993), and Grotevant and Carlson (1989) make several suggestions for the appropriate use of assessment techniques in family therapy. We have included six suggestions in the list below and modified the wording to focus on couples therapy:

1. Examine the needs of the couple being served and fit the assessment device to the kinds of problems that the couple is experiencing.
2. Use information gained during assessment to determine what areas warrant examination in therapy rather than labeling the couple.
3. Choose instruments that are easy to administer while understanding that shorter is not always better.

4. Remember that timing is important. Use assessment instruments (especially tests and questionnaires) as early in therapy as possible while the couple is becoming oriented to the process. This allows assessment information to be used when planning treatment.

5. Select a combination of measures in order to be thorough. Use screening tests that measure a wide array of potential problems.

6. Be particularly aware of ethnic variations among clients, differences in social class, gender, and disabilities. All these factors influence therapy, but they also affect the validity of instruments when substantially different from the norms of the test. For example, the Marital Adjustment Test (MAT) (Locke & Wallace, 1959) uses middle-class couples in its norm group. The scoring may not be valid with other kinds of couples.

Box 5.1 summarizes some clinically useful tests for the reader to explore. Because space does not permit a discussion of each test, a reference is given next to the brief description. We have chosen tests that represent the briefest and most psychometrically defensible ones available. Still, this does not exempt them from the six considerations mentioned above. Any of these tests may be inappropriate for a particular couple.

Sharing Assessment Data With Clients

At the conclusion of the initial interview, the usual procedure is for the couples therapist to share the major issues identified during the assessment phase. Boen (1988) recommends that couples receive a copy of the results of any testing along with an explanation of the results. However, this may not be appropriate for every instrument. At times, couples may misuse the assessment results (Boen, 1988). Additionally, they may misinterpret the results, become overwhelmed, or feel that their situation is hopeless. Olson (2002) prohibits giving clients a copy of the PREPARE/ENRICH report due to copyright restrictions, lack of client training in reading and analyzing the results, and possibility that clients could use the results as a "club" against their partner. Some of the assessments administered to clients are temporal and offer only a current "snapshot" of the relationship. Having such results may not provide a valid picture of the relationship following any amount of intervention. Nonetheless, therapists have an ethical obligation to provide an appropriate amount of feedback to their clients following the administration of assessments. Too often, instruments are used that clients never see again. In these days of brief and briefer therapy, we must use our time and our clients' time wisely. For this reason, assessments should be chosen based on the couple's needs and implemented as a time-saving device in helping identify the focus of or track progress during treatment.

Other Considerations

Some of the assessments listed in Box 5.1 and others used for couples counseling offer computer-generated reports. Computers make scoring easier and can provide useful information about normative data. Using computer printouts alone, without adequate training, is an unethical practice and is potentially harmful to clients. Computerized interpretation is not a substitute for experience and training in the use of any evaluation instrument. Personality tests, such as the Meyers-Briggs and the Cattell 16PF in particular, must be properly explained because there is greater potential for psychological damage when reports are misinterpreted. For instance, clients who find a high score on the Schizophrenia scale of the MMPI are not necessarily psychotic, but a trained therapist is needed to give the proper interpretation of the scale's meaning in the context of the other scales and based on the background of the client.

The Myers-Briggs Type Indicator

The Myers-Briggs Type Indicator (MBTI) is described in some detail here for several reasons. First, it provides one example of the interrelation of assessment and treatment in couples counseling. Second, it is perhaps the most popular indicator of psychological style (Fredman & Sherman, 1987). It is used in a variety of settings and for many different purposes in management seminars, team building, career counseling, and individual therapy. Third, the Myers-Briggs is simple. It is based on four dimensions of personality preferences: *Introverted (I) versus Extroverted (E), Sensing (S) versus Intuition (N), Thinking (T) versus Feeling (F), and Judging (J) versus Perceiving (P).* The combinations lead to 16 possible personality types. Finally, the MBTI has some history in couple's therapy, and the publisher provides a relationship report when both members of the couple take the test.

The MBTI Relationship Report includes more than 10 pages of interpretation with individual and couple summaries. The report outlines similarities and differences for the couple on each of the four dimensions. Let's say that in a couple Jane is an ENFJ and Luis is an ISFJ. The couple enjoys *similarity* on two dimensions (F and J) and *differs* on the first two dimensions. It is this notion of similarities and differences in type that is the main thrust of MBTI interpretation. In general, similarities mean a shared viewpoint, whereas differences suggest conflict or complimentarity. In the next few paragraphs, we outline some ways of interpreting the MBTI to a couple. As with other assessments, good interpretation is based on education and familiarity with the instrument as well as graduate training.

Interpreting the MBTI

An assessment session using the MBTI would begin by having each individual complete the answers separately and without input from the other partner. Usually, the instrument would be scored between sessions, and the couple would return for an interpretation session on another day. This gives the therapist time to consider the results. Provost (1993) provides one of the best sources of information about the use of the MBTI in couples therapy. Some of her suggestions regarding the interpretation of results with a couple are listed below:

1. Make sure that the couple understands the reason for taking the MBTI and is open to the concept that they can learn to appreciate differences.

2. Explain the concepts of the MBTI, the idea of preferences, and what the different key words mean.
3. Explain all dimensions (for example, Extroversion versus Introversion) and ask each member of the couple to guess their preference and that of their partner.
4. Present the partners with their actual scores and discuss any discrepancies between their own and their partner's perceptions of the scores.
5. Give couples outside reading about psychological type (for example, Provost's *Work, Play and Type: Achieving Balance in Your Life,* 1990).
6. Have couples complete homework such as observing how each approaches a joint task and ask that they report back at the next session. It is important to remind the couple to avoid blaming or using one's own psychological type as an excuse.

What Else Can the MBTI Tell Us?

As indicated above, the MBTI functions as both an assessment and treatment tool. It can help a couple become aware of differences and similarities in their psychological types. An individual may gain some understanding of the uniqueness of their partner and learn to appreciate the differences as strengths rather than merely points of conflict. They may see that there are different ways to achieve similar ends. Williams and Tappan (1995) suggest a clinical framework for using the MBTI in couples counseling incorporating the following steps: (1) Discuss the personality types, (2) depathologize differences, (3) take the other's perspective, (4) find a compromise, (5) strengthen the less developed side, and (6) warn couples about times of stress. The assessment allows couples to apply their personalities directly to common issues of conflict. It clarifies that no type is better or worse while looking at the strengths that various preferences offer.

Some Cautions

Although MBTI proponents do not like to call it a test, the MBTI is a personality test. All personality tests are attempting to measure stable characteristics. If improperly interpreted, the results can make clients believe that their situation is unchangeable. Some possible reactions to MBTI scores are "My partner and I are too different," or "See, he'll never change. He's an introvert," or "She'll never be able to meet my affectional needs because she's such a thinker." Worse, clients can come to the same conclusions about themselves: They cannot change. In addition, it would be unreasonable to presume that similarities in psychological type are going to predict perfect compatibility. Differences in values, background, and other kinds of preferences may cause conflict between people. Living successfully in a relationship is always a matter of acceptance, appreciation, and tolerance of differences.

Use of the MBTI seems best suited for couples experiencing low to moderate distress (Williams & Tappan, 1995). As a popular assessment and intervention with couples, it was described in greater detail. Nonetheless, it should be part of a comprehensive assessment and interpreted carefully to achieve maximum effectiveness and avoid potential harm. In the area of testing, a little knowledge *is* a dangerous thing. No test or assessment device should be used alone or exclusively, and as noted earlier, test results can be misinterpreted or can simply be wrong.

Informal Assessment Tools for Couples

In this section, we consider tools for assessment other than paper-and-pencil tests. Here, we have included a range of methods from more structured tools such as the genogram to projective techniques like family photographs and imagery. Box 5.2 lists a number of informal assessments that we have found to be clinically useful. The genogram and clinical interview are both informal methods of note. Because these are normally tasks of the first session, we included that material in Chapter 6. More information on these methods can be located in the references provided.

Box 5.2
Informal Methods for Assessing a Couple

INDIVIDUALS

The mental status examination (see Trzepacz & Baker, 1993)
Questioning (see Tomm, 1987a, 1987b)

SPECIFIC PROBLEMS AND TYPES OF COUPLES

The interview (see Chapter 6)
The genogram (see Chapter 6 for an example of substance-abuse
    issues in the couple's family of origin)
Marital history (see Gottman, 1999)
Number of repairs during a 10-minute discussion (see Gottman, 1999)
Couple's myths
Sexual problems

Medical examination
History of the sexual problem (see L'Abate & Bagarozzi, 1993)
Sexual history of the couple (see L'Abate & Bagarozzi, 1993)
Individual sexual histories (see L'Abate & Bagarozzi, 1993)
Structural diagrams (drawings of boundaries, alignments, and power
    arrangements; see Friesen, 1985)

Couple's images (see Sherman & Fredman, 1986)
Family photographs (see Sherman & Fredman, 1986)
Couple's joint tasks

Other Tools

This section contains some additional assessment devices suited to couples therapy that you may wish to learn about. In each section, a separate assessment tool is described. Key references are included. Some of the tools that serve a dual assessment/intervention function, like couple's imagery, are described in more detail in other chapters.

Couple's Myths Assessment

Couples bring myths and irrational beliefs to their relationship. Cognitive therapists will assess the dysfunctional belief systems that dictate an individual's understanding of couple relationships. Many of these myths surround the notion of romantic love. For example, a couple might come to believe that once romantic love has ebbed, it can never be revived. There are a number of ways to assess myths including testing, interviewing, examining favorite fairy tales, short stories, movies, and so on (Bagarozzi & Anderson, 1989).

Couple's Joint Tasks

Some couples therapists like to assign couple's joint tasks to work on outside of the therapy session. The couple returns and reports the outcome. The way in which the task is completed, organized, and scheduled tells us a great deal about the negotiating style of the couple. Sometimes the therapist may ask the couple to plan a weekend getaway in order to assess the couple's communication, negotiation styles, and skills. In marriage enrichment classes, sometimes couples are asked to paint a picture together or model something out of clay. Introducing the element of play does not seem to interfere with the serious intent of exposing the way that the couple interacts. Not much has been written on this area. It remains more of an informal method used by clinicians.

Family Photographs

The use of photographs in family therapy is based on several hypotheses (Anderson & Malloy, 1976; Kaslow & Friedman, 1977). Three of these are listed as they might apply to couples:

1. Couples tend to take photographs and films at important times during the life cycle of the relationship.
2. During stressful times, fewer pictures are taken.
3. There is a reason that couples select certain photographs. They depict something that the clients would like to portray.
4. Photographs are symbolic communication and express hidden meanings about the relationship just as dreams and slips of the tongue give access to the unconscious.

One way of using photographs in couples assessment is the "show-and-tell" method. The couple is asked to bring in photographs to show the history of the couple, high points in the relationship or pictures that best describe their relationship. Each member discusses the photographs that he or she selected and explains their meaning to the therapist. From the photographs, the therapist can learn about the couple's extended family, children, and home environment while getting a feeling for the nature of the relationship.

Couple's Imagery

Family therapist Peggy Papp uses imagery to work with couples. This method is described in Sherman and Fredman (1986). Briefly, the couple is asked to close their eyes and to think about their relationship and interactions that characterize their togetherness. They are then instructed to imagine themselves and their partner as something other than humans, either animate or inanimate. After each member of the couple verbally describes his or her images, they act them out in the therapy room. After each member of the couple has enacted the fantasy, the implications are discussed with the therapist.

Imagery techniques yield information not obtainable in other ways because such techniques are nonrational and bypass defenses. The results provide potentially useful information in the assessment process and can be used in therapy. For example, one of our clients, Hans, imagined himself as a turtle and his wife, Marie, as a poodle. In his fantasy, she was always running ahead and coming back to tell him about what lay ahead, asking him to make a decision about which path they were going to take. He was always hurrying to keep up and did not want to make a decision until he got there himself. His fantasy revealed his perception about their two different decision-making styles.

CONCLUSION

In the opening paragraph of this chapter, we indicated that marriage and family therapists have underutilized assessment in working with couples. We hope that this chapter illustrates the importance of assessment in helping determine and focus in on the most crucial problems for treatment. In addition, we believe that after reading this chapter you will see assessment not only as the administration of paper-and-pencil tests but also as a wider process that involves interviewing and gaining information from outside resources. Furthermore, you have learned that personal assumptions, biases, and choice of theoretical orientation affect the assessment process. Finally, we have introduced both standardized and informal assessment tools. These are points to keep in mind as we move to Chapter 6 and examine the link between assessment activities and goal setting.

6

Diagnosis, Goal Setting, and Treatment Planning With Couples

KEY CONCEPTS

- As the assessment phase closes, the couple's task is to trade in each individual version of the problem and develop an interactive definition.
- Diagnosis, as we define it, is a collaborative process between clients and therapist in which the therapist's theoretical knowledge and experience blends with clients' needs to identify key problems or goals.
- *DSM-IV-TR* diagnostic categories for couples' problems focus on symptoms or impaired functioning by a person in a relationship.
- *DSM-IV-TR* "V" codes and adjustment disorder diagnoses are categories that encompass some of the problems that couples face, but they cannot be used as diagnoses for relationships.
- Marriage and family therapists tend to use their own diagnostic categories to describe dysfunctional relationships.
- The funnel of assessment and treatment planning is a way of visually depicting the process of gathering information and refining it through interaction with clients until a set of solvable goals is reached.
- The interactive definition of the problem is a key feature of the integrative model because it is this negotiated goal that drives the treatment plan.
- There are a number of practical questions that therapists must ask when devising treatment plans, such as "Which problems should be addressed first?"
- One helpful notion for developing goals is that clients are at various states of readiness, and sometimes their partners' readiness must be heightened before they can receive the maximum benefit from therapy.
- When interactive definitions are formed, the therapist's job is to help transform these problems into goals or positive statements of how the couple would like the relationship to develop.

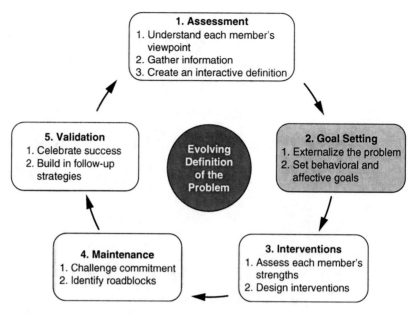

Figure 6.1   The integrative model of couples therapy

- The integrative model focuses initially on "cognitive" change, getting clients to see that they are each contributing to the problem and that they can team up to make changes.
- Most couples want to achieve concrete behavioral changes, and they want to experience positive feelings or emotions about their partner and their relationship. These behavioral and emotional changes are described as goals.

In Chapter 5, we looked at both formal and informal methods of assessment for couples. In this chapter, we link the assessment process with what is usually called *diagnosis* and *treatment planning*. Some therapists do not like these two terms because they imply a medical model, and so they prefer to use the expression "identifying problems and goal setting." We begin in the traditional direction by describing various methods of diagnoses used in couples and family therapy, and then we present our own ideas from the integrative model that are much more consistent with a nonmedical paradigm. Figure 6.1 shows the integrative model with the goal-setting stage highlighted.

FORMS OF DIAGNOSIS

The *Diagnostic and Statistical Manual Training Revision (DSM-IV-TR)*

In Chapter 5, we identified *assessment* as a general term to describe the gathering of information about clients from six sources of data:

1. Observations made by the therapist based on the couple's spontaneous interaction or during interactions introduced by the therapist
2. Questionnaires completed by the couple outside of the session
3. The couple's reports to the therapist regarding their behavior outside of the session
4. Historical data from the genogram or from client histories
5. Reports from other sources such as family members, the courts, or police reports
6. The results of paper-and-pencil testing

Diagnosis, on the other hand, is a transformation of data; it is the art and science of grouping findings into categories. The term has unfortunate medical implications because it suggests that two different people with a mental disorder have the same or similar features and nearly identical treatments.

DSM-IV-TR, the most recent *Diagnostic and Statistical Manual of Mental Disorders* of the American Psychiatric Association (APA, 2000) is a listing of more than 300 mental disorders and the criteria for assigning a person to a category. A *mental disorder* is defined as a set of symptoms or a syndrome (a disease) that interferes with social or occupational functioning or creates significant distress. It is important to note that in *DSM-IV-TR* only an individual person can be described as having a mental disorder. Families and couple relationships cannot be diagnosed as pathological because they involve more than one person. Karl Tomm, a seminal thinker in family therapy, proposed that the *DSM-IV-TR* list a number of "PIPs," or *pathologizing interpersonal patterns,* such as abusive relationships. Unfortunately, his and similar suggestions were not included in the recent *DSM* revision, although Kaslow (1996) published an influential book of family diagnoses.

Conditions, or V Codes, in *DSM-IV-TR*

V codes are *DSM-IV-TR* diagnoses for issues that are a focus of clinical attention but that do not reach the level of a mental disorder. The capital letter V appears before the numbers in the diagnoses, which indicate that a *person* (not a couple) can have a "relational problem" or a "problem related to abuse or neglect." The political issue connected with this category is that V code diagnoses are not normally eligible for insurance reimbursement, regardless of the seriousness of the abuse or relationship problem. Therapists who treat couples are being encouraged by the third-party payment system to identify mental disorders in individuals and treat them individually rather than solve them as couple problems (White, 2002). Box 6.1 shows the *DSM-IV-TR* V code diagnoses most often used to diagnose couple problems in an individual.

DSM-IV-TR Adjustment Disorder Diagnoses

An *adjustment disorder* is a mental disorder that arises in response to psychosocial stressors. To be classified as a disorder, it must appear within 3 months of the stressor's appearance, and the client must also show a level of distress that exceeds

---

Box 6.1
DSM-IV-TR *V Codes for Relational Problems and Problems Related to Abuse or Neglect*

V61.9 Relational Problem Related to a Mental Disorder or General Medical Condition The client's problem is caused by interacting with a significant other who possesses a medical problem or a diagnosable mental disorder.

V61.1 Partner Relational Problem A person shows clinically important symptoms or functioning is negatively affected by the relationship with a spouse or partner. Communication problems may or may not exist.

V61.20 Parent–Child Relational Problem The client shows clinically important symptoms or is negatively affected in functioning by problems with a parent or a child.

V61.18 Sibling Relational Problem The client's functioning is negatively affected or shows clinically important symptoms as a result of the way that siblings interact.

V62.81 Relational Problem Not Otherwise Specified Problems in a relationship not covered in the other categories of relational problems.

PROBLEMS RELATED TO ABUSE AND NEGLECT

V61.12 Physical Abuse of Adult This includes spouse abuse and elder abuse. If the person is the victim rather than the perpetrator, the diagnosis numbers 995.81 are specified.

V61.12 Sexual Abuse of Adult This is the category for rape or sexual coercion. If attention is on the victim, the therapist must specify 995.83.

ADDITIONAL PROBLEMS THAT MAY BE THE FOCUS OF CLINICAL ATTENTION.

V62.89 Phase of Life Problem This catchall can be used when the client shows important symptoms or is negatively affected in functioning by a change in life circumstances. These circumstances can include marriage, separation, or divorce.

---

what would normally be expected from this stressor. There must be impairment in job, social, or academic functioning, and the symptoms must not last longer than 6 months nor be caused by bereavement. Box 6.2 lists the adjustment disorder diagnoses. Any of these are possible diagnoses for an individual with couples' problems. To make this diagnosis on Axis I of the *DSM-IV-TR,* the therapist must

---

Box 6.2
Adjustment Disorders in DSM-IV-TR Related to Couples' Problems

309.0 With Depressed Mood (tearful and sad)
309.24 With Anxiety (nervous, worried)
309.28 With Mixed Anxiety and Depressed Mood (a mixture)
309.23 With Disturbance of Conduct (the client violates rights of others or societal rules)
309.4 With Mixed Disturbance of Emotions and Conduct (may be depressed, anxious, or both with conduct disturbance)
309.9 Unspecified (for example, withdrawal from social contact)

---

also code the stressors on Axis IV. Couples' problems are generally categorized as "problems with the primary support group." Here is an example of a four-axis diagnosis of a fictional client who is experiencing depression as a result of marital separation:

Axis I: 309.0 Adjustment Disorder With Depressed Mood
Axis II: V71.09 No Diagnosis
Axis III: None Known
Axis IV: Problem With Primary Support Group (marital separation)

Family Therapy Diagnoses

Although most couples therapists believe that diagnostic formulations are stigmatizing and do not capture the whole person, marriage and family therapy as a profession has its own diagnoses. Just because the diagnosis is made for a family or couple does not mean that it is not a label. Marriage and family therapists often use special terms like *schism, skew, triangulation,* and *enmeshment* (see Chapters 2 and 3) as labels for unhealthy relationships. The notions of "dysfunctional family" or "codependent relationships" are diagnoses applied to a family in the same way that "neurosis" came into common parlance in earlier times. On the other hand, the marriage and family therapy field has sought to identify interactional patterns between people rather than blaming specific individuals, and more emphasis has been placed on the patterns of family interactions. As Willi (1982) suggests, couples and families "collude" in creating their problems. In addition, tremendous effort has been made to avoid the medical terminology that identifies couples, individuals, and families as "sick."

Diagnosing Problem Patterns

Diagnosis is a transformation of data from specific bits to labels that suggest larger patterns. Patterns emerge from all forms of assessment including the interview, the Sexual Interaction Inventory, and the genogram. The notion of a pattern suggests that it is a recurring behavioral sequence involving two persons who both play parts in the problem. Listed below are a number of commonly observed couple patterns.

1. *The parent–child relationship.* This relationship is characterized by one partner taking care of the other and assuming the bulk of the responsibility for most maintenance tasks. The "child" may have physical or mental disorders. Such a pattern is often present when one partner is a substance abuser. A lesser form might be called the responsible–irresponsible relationship.

2. *Siamese twins.* In this pattern, the partners are so involved with each other that they have no life outside of the relationship, have few friends, and exercise little autonomy.

3. *Victim-victimizer.* The victim–victimizer pattern is typical of some long-term abusive relationships. The treatment for this pattern is normally individual therapy for the victimizer and supportive therapy and assertiveness training for the victim before addressing the relationship issues.

4. *Pursuer-distancer.* This is a classic pattern in which one member of the couple is always seeking more intimacy than the other seems to want. When the pursuer moves toward the partner seeking closeness, the distancer moves farther away. It is a frustrating experience for both members of the relationship. We discussed this pattern earlier when discussing Gottman's study of the complaint–withdrawal cycle (see Gottman, Driver, & Tabares, 2002).

5. *The A-frame relationship.* In this pattern, both members of the couple lean on each other, supporting each other like two sides of the letter *A*. Each has strictly defined roles typical of traditional couples, but each is "lost" without the other. In contrast to the "Siamese twins" couple, it is an asymmetrical relationship. Both partners may have separate lives but depend on each other in some significant way.

6. *The parallel relationship.* Sometimes called the "marriage of resignation," couples sometimes develop a pattern of distancing themselves and leading nearly completely separate lives. The relationship may be stable, but the partners do not experience much caring, intimacy, or friendship. Gigy and Kelly (1992) studied the reasons that people gave for divorce. More than 80% identified a pattern of slowly growing apart, loss of closeness, and not feeling loved. Only 40% of these couples identified intense fighting as contributing to the divorce.

Besides these commonly observed patterns, we identified a number of patterns associated with particular theoretical orientations in Chapters 2 and 3. They are listed again here.

Couple Patterns Observed by Theorists

I. Behavior therapy
  A. Maladaptive communication patterns
    1. Coercive exchanges
    2. Withdrawal
    3. Retaliatory exchanges
    4. Cross-complaining (summarizing self-syndrome)
    5. Low rates of mutual reinforcement/high rates of mutual punishment

II. Psychodynamic theories
   A. Complementary neurotic patterns
      1. Spouse as superego
      2. Spouse as devaluated self-image
      3. Spouse as ego ideal
      4. Dominant–submissive dyad
      5. Detached–demanding dyad
      6. Romantic–rational partnership
      7. Spouse as parent
      8. "Love-sick" wife/"cold-sick" husband
III. The Bowen theory
   A. Chronic conflict pattern
      1. Distancer–pursuer pattern
      2. Triangulating
      3. Overfunctioning–underfunctioning pattern
IV. Structural/strategic theory
   A. Asymmetrical pairings
      1. Introvert-extrovert
      2. Flirtatious-jealous
      3. Assertive-nonassertive
      4. More involved–less involved
      5. Dependent–independent others
V. Transactional analysis
   A. Game playing
      1. "If it weren't for you"
      2. Many others

ASSESSMENT AND DIAGNOSIS: A PRECURSOR TO TREATMENT PLANNING IN THE INTEGRATIVE MODEL

Table 6.1 lists five key therapist activities that are involved in completing the assessment and goal-setting phases of the integrative model. Notice that the first step refers to the six sources of client information. Figure 6.2, the funnel of assessment, shows the kinds of information that the therapist tries to gather in the assessment phase. In this phase, each member of the couple has had the opportunity to express his or her own viewpoint. As assessment activities are completed, however, the therapist challenges the couple to combine the viewpoints into a single problem or two. We could compare this to looking through binoculars. Each lens provides a different viewpoint, but when both lenses are viewed together, a wider, three-dimensional picture emerges. Similarly, in the assessment phase, each member's perspective is recognized, but the assessment process is not complete until a joint vision of the problem is identified (Figure 6.3). The therapist's role at this phase is to take the clients' concerns and use his or her knowledge and skills and the results of the assessment to help the couple achieve the most useful and solvable statement of the problem available. The therapist guides the clients to find a

Table 6.1   Key Therapist Activities in the Treatment Planning Process

Stage	Activity
Assessment	1. Therapist obtains information from six sources.
	2. Therapist obtains each individual's view of the problem.
	3. Therapist constructs an interactive definition of the problem with the clients' goal setting.
Goal setting	4. Therapist helps clients refine definition. (This is a precursor to Step 5. Externalizing is another step in this stage, but it is not strictly treatment planning. Its main purpose is to join the couple and to help them view the problem as external and as something to conquer.)
	5. Therapist helps clients change problems to create behavioral and affective goals stated in a solvable form.

constructive way of looking at their difficulties, a way that leads to resolution of problems rather than further confusing, pathologizing, or discouraging the clients. This positive outlook is a key feature of the integrative model elaborated in this book.

In constructing an interactional definition of the problem, the therapist feeds back to clients the essence of their individual perspectives on the problem using foundational counseling skills like paraphrasing and reflecting feelings

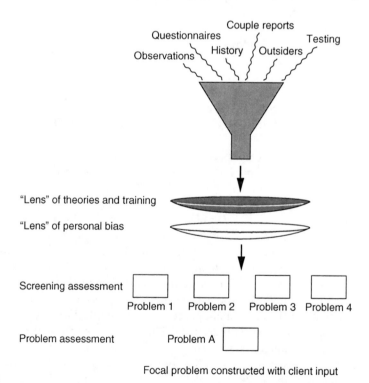

Figure 6.2   Funnel of assessment and treatment planning

Figure 6.3   The goal-setting process

(Corey, 2004; Young, 1992, 2005). Meanwhile, in the therapist's mind, the raw assessment information is being transformed into larger concepts such as patterns, games, or common problems, depending on one's theoretical orientation. The therapist develops hunches about what is and is not working in the relationship and what needs to change to create a significant change for the better.

STAGE 1: FORMULATING AN INTERACTIVE DEFINITION IN GOAL SETTING

We believe that an interactive definition of the problem is the centerpiece of the treatment plan in the integrative model and the therapist's input into the construction and definition of the problem is crucial. The therapist is an expert in human relationships (Guanipa & Wooley, 2000) and can negotiate a well-stated interactive definition that will move couples toward agreement and help them believe that they can each receive gains from a positive solution to the problem.

The integrative model is founded on the premise that therapy should begin with the client's definition of the problem, but that creating an *interactive* definition is the result of a confluence of three perspectives: those of each partner and that of the therapist or therapists involved (see Figure 6.3).

Case Example: Bill and Wanda

Perhaps the process of arriving at an interactive definition is best grasped by looking at a case example. We have chosen the example of Bill and Wanda, whose treatment plan is described throughout this chapter.

Bill and Wanda, both in their early 30s, have been married for 7 years and have come for therapy to deal with Wanda's affair with a coworker 6 months ago. The couple has been arguing unproductively for several months. Wanda feels pressured and Bill is anxious and mistrusts her. The couple seems to have the most difficulty when they have been apart for some time. Bill usually initiates troublesome discussions when he becomes agitated after ruminating over the past. Wanda "closes down" when confronted and becomes uncommunicative. After the first session, the therapist formulated the following hypotheses, or preliminary diagnoses:

1. Bill and Wanda are experiencing a pursuer–distancer type of pattern; he attacks and she withdraws.
2. Bill feels weak and ineffective, while Wanda feels guilty.
3. The couple is socially isolated (having moved recently).
4. Wanda's mother is very involved in the couple's life and supports Wanda, blaming Bill for her affair.
5. The couple has difficulty dealing with finances.
6. The couple reports several years of a positive and mutually supportive relationship that deteriorated about 1 year ago.
7. They share several joint interests including backpacking and photography. Some of their best times have been during their wilderness adventures.
8. They are very concerned that their teenage son is smoking marijuana.

Deciding Which Problems Should Be Addressed First

Couples who come for therapy typically have multiple problems. Which are the most important? As we indicated earlier, crises involving physical risk, mental disorders, or substance abuse are normally dealt with first. However, many couples like Bill and Wanda have no such issues, and the therapist is confronted with several options. The integrative model suggests first dealing with the issues that the couple feels "ready, willing, and able" to attack. "Ready and willing" refers to motivation; "able" asks the question "Do the clients have the necessary skills to complete the goal?" Box 6.3 lists a number of guidelines that therapists can use to think about priorities in goal setting.

Ready and Willing

Although we think we know what is best for our clients, they may not be willing or ready to accept our goals for their lives. We have learned that the greatest chance for success and change is to adopt those goals that are important to the

---

Box 6.3
Goal-Setting Guidelines

1. Choose goals that the couple is ready, willing, and able to achieve.
2. Tackle crises first. As Maslow points out, you cannot deal with higher-order needs, such as intimacy, when you are being evicted from your apartment.
3. Advocate for goals that lead to general improvement rather than goals that are Band-Aids.
4. Set goals to represent the presence of something rather than the absence of something. Make goals simple things that the couple can really do and feel.
5. Translate vague words into action and connect with feelings. For example, "How do you expect to feel when you find you are spending more time together?"
6. Reframe therapy as a joint project that requires hard work rather than as a painful medical procedure. The couple will see this as a familiar learning process, not as "magic" performed by the therapist.
7. Make sure that the goals are important by asking the couple, "How will we know when therapy is completed?" The answer should include completion of the majority of therapy goals.
8. It is all right to tell couples that you are searching for an interactive definition and a goal for therapy. Enlist their help.
9. Assume that therapy is going to be a success. In your discussions with clients, use terminology such as *when* and *yet*.

---

clients. For Bill and Wanda, we may believe that resolving issues related to the affair are the most crucial to their general well-being. But it is important that the problem initially identified is one that the couple is ready to attack. If Bill and Wanda are determined that their key issue is a teenage son's smoking marijuana, this would probably be the very place to begin.

Earlier, we quoted Gottman's statistic (Gottman et al., 2002) that the vast majority of couples' disagreements are about perpetual issues that call for acceptance rather than change (Dimidjian, Martell, & Christensen, 2002; Jacobson & Christensen, 1996). Most people are familiar with the serenity prayer of Alcoholics Anonymous that says we should change those things we can, accept those that we can't, and prays for the wisdom to know the difference. The couples counselor must try to identify whether the members of the couple should attempt to change or adjust to the other. Thus, sometimes the chosen goal is to understand, to develop empathy and accept each other's differences.

More on readiness: Six levels of change   The emphasis in the therapy literature that is now being placed on readiness signals a shift in the way that we have conceptualized the change process. Previously, we ignored the client's motivation when selecting treatments. For example, we tried to get all alcoholics into inpatient or intensive outpatient treatment. Prochaska, Norcross, and DiClemente (1994) developed a six-part model based on research about how clients reported they made lasting changes. The model is circular and proposes that change takes place in six successive levels. The key implication is that clients at different levels of readiness respond to different kinds of interventions:

1. In the first level, precontemplation, clients feel resentful and angry when it is suggested that they have a problem. Their reaction is "I can handle it!" They lack awareness of the issue, which we could call denial.
2. At the contemplation level, there is some dawning awareness that a problem exists but also a feeling of confusion about what to do. The client is anxious and slightly uncomfortable but not quite ready to change: "I'm stuck!"
3. At the preparation level, the client knows that change is necessary but is unsure how to begin. "I'll stop drinking tomorrow" is a familiar phrase associated with this stage.
4. In the action level, the client makes a commitment to change and takes some action to change the problem but is very scared about the new territory.
5. At the maintenance level, the client is dealing with the fear of relapse while experiencing some of the rewards of having made a significant change.
6. Finally, termination takes place when maintaining change is nearly effortless. Even though there are temptations to return to earlier behaviors, the change lasts.

Carlson and Ellis (2004) caution that clients who make lasting change must focus on relapse prevention and maintenance of the gains they have made. These gains provide possibilities for continued focus on skills training, relational strengths, and progressive movement to resolve the issues that brought the couple to therapy (Hackney & Cormier, 2001). The six-part model proposes specific therapist activities at each stage that helps couples progress to termination.

For example, two clients who had been married for only 6 months consulted us because they were concerned that they did not know how to make something productive come out of their disagreements. Normally, they would get into a spat, and it ended as they both became angry and gave each other the "silent treatment." They were not interested in couples therapy because they said that they were happy in their marriage and did not feel that they needed that kind of assistance, but they wanted to work on "better communication." The couple was seen twice and was given a set of videotapes about communication and negotiation. During the sessions, they discussed their communication patterns and identified some changes they would like to make. This level of treatment (education) was in keeping with their minimal level of readiness for therapy (contemplation). They did not wish to make a third appointment, but we recommended that they come back if problems reemerged.

Are you buying or just looking?   Steve de Shazer (1988) made an important conceptual breakthrough when he announced the "death of resistance." De Shazer and his colleagues at the Brief Family Therapy Center felt that lack of progress in therapy is often blamed on clients through use of the term *resistance.* Instead, de Shazer (1988) believed that clients are at different stages of motivation, which he described as having three levels. He called some clients "Visitors," some "Complainants," and some "Customers." Visitors lack motivation and often arrive at the therapy appointment at the behest of some third party. Complainants are experiencing discomfort and understand the need to change but are unwilling to take the necessary steps. Customers are those who come to therapy ready to take action. De Shazer's view, like that of Prochaska and colleagues (1994), was that therapists must select interventions based on clients' state of readiness. In general, visitors need education, and complainants need to become more aware of how the problem is affecting them so they can better see the need for change. Customers are ready to respond to the suggestions to change.

Ripeness   Dym (1995) has elevated the concept of readiness to the central feature of his work with couples. The term *ripeness* is used to illustrate a client's degree of readiness. In the book *Readiness and Change in Couple Therapy,* Dym (1995) cites a long tradition in family therapy, religious customs, and groups such as Alcoholics Anonymous that support the simple truth that people are most likely to change when they are ready. As Shakespeare said, "Ripeness is all!"

According to Dym (1995), a relationship is comfortable when it is stable. As long as things are stable and discomfort is minimal, the couple is unlikely to change. Dym compares trying to change a stable couple to trying to budge a 400-pound sumo wrestler who is standing firm. Dym proposes that readiness to change comes about only when the couple is off balance or in a state of disequilibrium. The disequilibrium may already be underway when the couple enters therapy, often because of a crisis or a new life situation or life-cycle stage. Dym's insight is that during the assessment and goal-setting phase of therapy we should be aware of what issues clients are ready for and begin with the "hot issues." In the goal-setting phase, the therapist encourages the couple to set goals that both people seem to be ready for. Because chances for success are greatest when readiness is high, we can bring about early success that helps overcome initial skepticism and helps build hope.

Helping Couples Decenter

Getting couples to identify a common issue is probably the most difficult part of couples therapy. For one thing, couples may be angry, hurt, or vengeful. They often see the therapist as the judge who is going to find their partner as guilty and themselves as innocent. The skills called for at this point in couples therapy are not so much negotiation skills as skills in listening and reflecting thoughts and feelings. Negotiation implies that we give and take in a compromising, businesslike fashion, but what is really needed is for each member of the couple to understand and validate the other person's concerns. *Decentering* is a word taken from the moral development literature that means the ability to transcend one's own point of view. Similar to empathy, it means learning to "walk in the other person's shoes." For example, a couple came in with the following difficulty: The husband was very jealous and believed that his wife was being unfaithful to him. He had no evidence beyond his suspicions, but he was adamant that the infidelity issue must be solved. She was angry and hurt but relentlessly stuck to her story that he was unduly suspicious. Therapists can easily get trapped into seeking to determine who is telling the truth, but the real task is to construct a "joint truth" that can be approached productively. In this case, the partners were able to rename their problem as the distrust–distancing pattern and began to work on it in therapy. For this to work, both partners must have the opportunity to express themselves (get past overwhelming feelings) and to feel fully understood. Often, it is necessary to cover the same ground over and over and to stop and check each person's understanding because often each one believes that he or she has the proper perspective. Here is a different example:

> *Ximena:* I am tired of being the only one who tends to family obligations. When your mother is sick, I am the one who sends flowers and goes to see her.
> *Carlos:* If you don't want to visit my mother anymore, just say so!
> *Therapist* [to Ximena]: Could you repeat your statement to Carlos again? [To Carlos]: This time I'd like you to listen carefully and repeat back to her what you think her major concern is.

This example points out that angry feelings prevent us from decentering and hearing the other's point of view. Often it useful for the therapist to reflect in Rogerian fashion: "Carlos, I understand that you are feeling angry and maybe a bit guilty when you hear Ximena's complaint, but what is she really saying?" The therapist's job is to acknowledge these feelings and eventually bring each person back to the task of seeing the other's viewpoint.

While this kind of empathy training is basic to the relationship education programs we discussed in Chapter 5, we include it here to show that frequently (especially in perpetual problems) the goal of therapy is to join the couple so that they can keep their dialogue alive.

COLLABORATION ON THE INTERACTIVE DEFINITION OF THE PROBLEM

In the first stage of the integrative model, each member first expresses his or her view of the problem and listens to the other partner. Then the therapist helps move the couple toward combining the two perspectives. An interactive definition means that the partners have identified an issue that they are ready to work on and that can be expressed in interpersonal terms. Listed below are some common statements that are made during the initial phase of assessment when each person is giving his or her own account of the difficulties. Each person's account is followed by an interactive definition that the couple has arrived at as the assessment phase moves into the next stage of goal setting.

Examples of Individual and Interactive Definitions of Problems

Couple 1: Individual Definitions

"She is impossible to live with, always depressed, and never wants to go out or do anything."

"He doesn't want to be with me anymore. He wants us to spend all our time with friends. He is always going and doing, like he's trying to avoid me."

Couple 1: Interactive Definition

"We have forgotten how to do the things that we used to enjoy, and our relationship has become focused on the things we disagree about."

Couple 2: Individual Definitions

"He has such a bad temper. Every time we disagree, he gets mad and walks out."

"Whenever we have an argument, she starts calling me names and brings up things I did years ago. It's just not worth it."

Couple 2: Interactive Definition

"We can't seem to solve minor problems because our arguing gets in the way and is not a productive way of solving our problems."

Couple 3: Individual Definitions

"The problem is that he is a spendthrift. We can't keep our heads above water because he can't control himself."

"I work hard and I don't like to feel pressured that every dime is accounted for. She wants to save for furniture; I'd rather be able to enjoy life a little. Sometimes when I get a little depressed, I like to buy something."

Couple 3: Interactive Definition

"We need to identify and negotiate financial priorities. We have never really compromised in our decision making. It has been more of a win–lose struggle over every issue."

Refining the Problem

As therapy progresses, clients tell us more as they develop more trust. Carl Rogers once said that in the beginning clients talk about "the thing next to the thing." In other words, the initial "calling card" issues are not necessarily the ones that will provide the avenues for meaningful change. As time goes on, our assessment becomes more accurate, trust develops, hidden issues surface, and we begin to detect larger patterns in seemingly unrelated incidents. Clients also begin to have greater awareness of the key issues when they get everything out on the table and they begin to listen to their partner's side of the story.

The fact that initial formulations of client problems are only temporary hypotheses or beginning formulations is the reason that problem *refining* is at the heart of the integrative model. The model suggests that we must sometimes

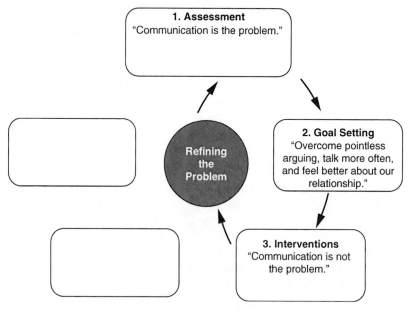

Figure 6.4   Refining the problem: returning to an earlier stage

return to an earlier step (such as assessment) as we gain a clearer view of the problem, following side routes on the model rather than traveling in a straight clockwise path (Figure 6.4). You might think we are suggesting that to go two steps forward in therapy we must go one step backward, but that is linear thinking. The circularity of the model does not mean that the process is always a forward-moving, step-by-step progression. Refining often means a return to the first step of the integrative model, assessment. From there, the therapy process proceeds in a clockwise fashion around the perimeter of the model. Experience tells us that the problem may be refined two or three times during the first six therapy sessions.

The need to return to an earlier task does not reflect a failure on the part of the therapist; it is a normal part of couples therapy. The therapist conducting an assessment is very much like a sketch artist; every so often, it is necessary to hold the picture up to the client and ask, "Now, is this it?" Similarly, as time progresses, the clients are constantly erasing and changing their idea about the focal problem at the center of the model. As this problem evolves, it moves from an amorphous cloud to a distinct and solvable issue.

Let's say that it is the third session in couples therapy with Bill and Wanda, and the therapist has spent a good deal of time understanding the couple's "money problem." As the therapist begins introducing budgeting and negotiation exercises, the couple balks. Bill and Wanda believe that the major issue is that they have different basic values (a perpetual problem). This information from a couple may make a beginning therapist panic over the thought of abandoning the way the problem is being viewed and embracing a whole new concept. Eventually, we become comfortable with the fact that this is part of the process of refinement of the problem that lies at the center of the integrative model. In this case, a solution to come up with a budget probably will not work because of the values clash. The therapist, instead, helps the couple find a way to deal with the difference and connect with the other person's viewpoint.

Recall that one of the assumptions of the integrative model is a constructivist philosophy; the therapist is trying to help the clients construct a workable goal based on a shared perspective. It is not a compromise but a "new promise," meaning that the new goal is a novel way of thinking about the problem. The therapist is under no illusion that he or she can determine "the truth." If it seems that the clients want to call the problem "agreeing on financial priorities" rather than "managing money better," the therapist respects this change because it is just as useful in achieving the goals of therapy. Clients reword problems to make them fit better into their framework and worldview. As long as the refined problem is constructive and solvable, the therapist must remain flexible and adapt as the couple's picture of the problem evolves.

STAGE 2: SETTING GOALS

Our experience in couples therapy suggests that most couples seek counseling when they are demoralized and "at the end of their rope." Thus, instituting hope is an important and immediate healing activity of the therapist (McCabe & Priebe, 2004; Parry, 2004). Therapists must collaborate with and support the couple as the goal-setting process begins (Weeks & Treat, 2001) because their expectations and energy may be low.

We believe that the therapist's overarching goal of couples therapy is to help couples use their strengths to identify and resolve present issues and learn problem-solving strategies that will help them with future concerns (Mecca, Rivera, & Esposito, 2000). This solution-focused approach to goal setting (Fischer, 2004) is compatible with the goal for couples that their goals must reflect their core beliefs and values and be important to their life perspective and worldview (Kilpatrick & Holland, 2003). Lew and Bettner (1999) describe a goal as similar to a mission statement. Each partner and couple should reflect on what they want from their relationship including their core values and beliefs about themselves, their relationship, and others.

Goals are most effective when they are possible, realistic, specific, concrete, and achievable (De Jong & Berg, 2002; Eckstein, 2001; Thomas, 1999; Zetik & Stuhlmacher, 2002). Having set clear and achievable goals with the support of their therapist, clients immediately feel a sense of relief and can become more involved in the change process (Carlson & Ellis, 2004; Thomas, 1999). Reaching even small goals helps them feel encouraged that they are finally out of the rut of endless arguing or distance that has characterized their relationship.

Well-established goals also promote self-regulation and systematic efforts toward thoughts, feelings, and actions (Zimmerman, 2000). As self-regulation is enhanced, it affects motivation and self-efficacy (Myers, Sweeney, & Witmer,

2002; Schunk, 2002). This confidence inspires people to continue to set challenging new goals (Schunk, 2002).

Effective goals are also based on individual and the couple's strengths and resources and must represent the beginning of something new in the couple's life rather than an end to be achieved and then forgotten (De Jong & Berg, 2002). White (2002) believes that the way to focus on strengths is to externalize the problem and identify the necessary strengths required to conquer it.

Transforming a Problem Into a Goal

During the 1960s, a very effective television advertisement for the Peace Corps asked viewers to decide whether a glass of water was half full or half empty. This is an intriguing idea because we know that both statements are true; but which viewpoint is the most constructive and hopeful way of looking at the situation? Similarly, in the integrative model, we begin by allowing couples to have their "say" and to identify the troubling issues confronting them; we allow them to talk about the half-empty view of their relationship (see Figure 6.1). We do this because we need to understand the severity of the problem and they need to feel understood. But it is easy to become bogged down in blame and recriminations. Eventually, we ask couples to transform their problems into goals: to identify not what is missing in the relationship but what they want to have. Here is an example:

Interactive Definition 1
"When we argue, it escalates into name-calling, and we end up saying things that hurt each other without solving the problem."
(Viewpoint: Arguing is the problem in our relationship.)

Goal 1
"We want to be able to keep our arguing on the topic and stay with it long enough to solve the problem."
(Viewpoint: We could have a relationship in which we could disagree effectively.)

Choosing the Kinds of Goals

Because many clients present with multiple problems, it is often difficult to decide which to deal with first. Although we have suggested that "hot goals" are best, there are some other guidelines for deciding the ordering of goals that might be helpful when reflecting on a treatment plan for a couple (see Box 6.3).

When goals are established, the integrative model recommends breaking them down even further into behavioral and affective components. This fits with the commonsense notion in therapy that real change involves change in all three areas of human functioning: cognitive, behavioral, and emotional (Lew & Bettner, 1999; Page & Eckstein, 2003; Zetig & Stuhlmacher, 2002). Figure 6.5 shows the interaction of cognitive, affective, and behavioral changes. Regardless of where we decide to change—behavior, emotions, or cognitions—a change in one produces changes in the other. For example, people who quit smoking (a behavior) feel

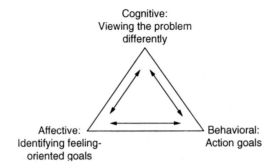

Figure 6.5   Interaction of cognitive, affective, and behavioral change

pleased, happy, and confident (emotion) and see themselves as having more self-control (change in perception). We believe that lasting change is best achieved when the therapist seeks change in all three arenas.

Cognitive Components

Cognitive change in our model comes about through the process of reconstructing the problem situation in interactive *goal language*. As clients change their view from blaming to a joint work project, they have made an important shift in their thinking (Fennell & Weinhold, 2003). The collaborative reconstruction of the problem between therapist and clients is a shift in perception that continues as the view of the problem evolves. The next step is to make sure that clients actually change their behavior and feelings about each other and the relationship.

Behavioral Components

Couples come to therapy hoping for the best, but they are often skeptical that things will really change. They want and need to see tangible results. Most therapists (not just behaviorists) see behavioral change as an important sign of real change. Even Freud admitted that sometimes clients must get up off the couch. But one of the most important reasons to focus on observable change in couples therapy is to keep the couple's hopes alive. Seeing new behaviors in oneself or one's partner engenders hope and optimism. Success breeds success. When setting goals, behaviorists suggest making goals quite specific and observable so that there is no question that they have been reached (Eckstein, 2001; Thomas, 1999; Weeks & Treat, 2001). In couples therapy, a couple may identify a goal of spending more time together. In setting a behavioral goal, the therapist tries to get the couple to be simple and specific. An example of a specific behavioral formulation of the couple's goal to spend more time together might be stated as "We will spend two evenings per week going for a long walk in our neighborhood."

Emotional Components

Before describing affective goals, a discussion of the role of emotion in couples therapy is warranted. Some people have viewed emotions as the enemies of the relationship. The equivalent of the Four Horsemen of the Apocalypse for marriage have been described as critical anger, contempt, fearful defensiveness, and sullen withdrawal (Gottman, 1991). Couples become involved in creating cycles of emotional interaction, as when one person ends up feeling angry and the other defensive. These patterns are difficult to resolve, and couples find it very difficult to change these patterns on their own (Johnson & Greenberg, 1994). Gottman (1999) has used technology to assess the physiological signals of emotional arousal during arguments. Using heart rate–monitoring equipment, a person's arousal around a certain topic can be identified and discussed.

Aside from trying to escape from the throes of negative emotions, couples want to regain the initial good feelings that they had about their relationship and about their partners. They do not simply want their partner to stop annoying habits; they also want to feel some of the old attraction, closeness, contact, and intimacy. In fact, the quality of a couple's emotional contact is a better predictor of whether they will stay together than is how much they argue. It appears that even if couples do not resolve their issues during disagreements, they tend to stay together if they can remain in emotional contact and not become defensive and distant (Gottman & Krokoff, 1989). In sum, emotions appear to be significant factors in couples' decision to stay together, and emotions can form an important source of dissatisfaction that brings couples to therapy.

Next we turn to the therapist's role in evoking clients' emotions for the purpose of bringing about change. Through reflecting feelings and helping clients focus on their emotional reactions, therapists help couples give vent to strong affect by expressing sadness, grief, anger, and joy. The experience of emotional arousal and the consequences of expressing feelings form an important curative factor in all forms of counseling and psychotherapy (Fennell & Weinhold, 2003; Frank & Frank, 1991; Young & Bemak, 1996). This phenomenon has been referred to by various names, including *catharsis* and *abreaction*. In the therapy session, therapists often encourage clients to express deeply held feelings, hoping that this unburdening will bring about new awareness and a sense of relief. Techniques from psychodrama and gestalt therapy have been widely used for this purpose. More important, when one member of a couple expresses these feelings, the other member sees the pain of the other, and there is the possibility of empathy and reconciliation.

In the family therapy field, Virginia Satir (Satir, Banmen, Gerber, & Gomori, 1991) made experiencing and transforming feelings a major part of her theory. Satir was aware that when one member of a couple expressed strong emotions, it had an effect on the partner. Emotion-focused marital therapy (EFT) (Greenberg & Johnson, 1994) recommends that couples be asked to disclose their previously unacknowledged thoughts and feelings about their partner. As a result, partners experience a change in their view of the other person when shown this hidden side (Denton, 1991). The partner who expresses feelings receives the benefits of emotional release and startling self-awareness, while the other partner has the opportunity to become aware of the other's viewpoint and to develop empathic closeness. Of course, strong emotions with negative messages expressed toward the other partner can be hurtful rather than beneficial. It is the therapist's job to encourage the expression of emotions when it is clear that they will lead to greater closeness, address an important issue, or lead to greater understanding for the couple. It may be critical for a person to hear how another's actions hurt them, but it may be quite destructive to hear the juicy details of an affair with its attendant emotions.

The presence of the therapist—aside from providing a safe environment—somehow makes the expression of strong feelings more of a landmark experience, just as affirming wedding vows "before witnesses" becomes a watershed event in a relationship. When the therapist evokes one partner's feelings, the other partner can take a less defensive stance. Because the emotions are not aimed at the partner, he or she finds it easier to accept and understand them.

To summarize, emotions play an important role in couples therapy. Negative emotional cycles propel couples into therapy and are a primary source of dissatisfaction; good feelings, intimacy, and closeness help couples weather difficult storms. Evoking emotions and allowing a partner to see underlying feelings seems to be a powerful method or technique to help couples regain closeness. Finally, we have seen that couples come to therapy to feel better about their relationship, not just to accomplish behavioral goals. Lew and Bettner (1999) refer to these feelings as qualities that are equally important as behavioral goals. Feeling close, respected, loved, cared for, and connected are examples of the qualities of affective goals. A prescription for a better relationship thus includes planning for and expecting better feelings about the relationship.

Affective goals   The integrative model recommends including affective, or emotional, goals when behavioral goals are formulated. For example, a couple wants to manage finances better, but both members also want to feel more in control and more positive about their ability to solve problems as a couple. Another couple wants to improve both partners' sexual satisfaction, but they also want to experience feelings of closeness, not just more orgasms. In the integrative model, we recommend setting clear goals for therapy so that as each goal is reached the couple feels the renewed sense of being on a winning team. Couples do not wish to change the other person's behavior; they also want to be happy with each other.

The emotional goals, facilitated by the therapist, can be clearly stated as part and parcel of the desired outcome of therapy. We now present a dialogue with our fictional couple Bill and Wanda. This session depicts how a therapist moves a couple from (1) viewing each person's version of the problem, (2) to constructing an interactive definition of the problem, (3) to changing problems to goals, and (4) to establishing behavioral and affective goals.

Case Example: Bill and Wanda (continued)

Bill and Wanda have been working on the lack of trust in the relationship since Wanda's affair with a coworker. The couple has changed the problem into the goal of leaving the past behind in order to feel more bonded in their relationship. But because the past still haunts them, it was deemed useful to discuss the specifics of where, why, when, and how the issue arises—that is, to do more assessment and gain a more refined version of the problem.

> *Therapist:* So, we were talking about how you two get into fights, usually after work, is that right? You get into fights when Bill has been home alone for a while. Tell me about that.

Bill: Well, yeah, I've been at home, thinking about the past, you know, and getting myself worked up. And then when she comes home and I am almost looking for something—some way that she is lying. And she just acts mysterious, like it doesn't bother her.

Wanda: I get the third degree.

Therapist: What do you mean, Wanda?

Wanda: Well he starts in with the questions. "Who were you with after work?" "What did you do today?" et cetera, et cetera, and then I just clam up.

Therapist: Right now I would like to sort of trace the way in which this problem surfaces. But remember, just because we identify a beginning and an end to your pattern, that is really artificial. Couples interact all the time, so I don't want you to think that just because we start with Bill, for example, that he is to blame for the problem. It takes two people to create it. So let me understand the way you two set up the distancing problem. Let's call it that because that's how it ends up. You are both confused and distant. Right?

Bill: Right.

Wanda: All right, but if he wouldn't start, things would be a lot better.

Therapist: Well, right now, that's what I want to avoid—blaming. [pauses] Okay, it happens like this: Wanda comes home, probably a little wary, and Bill, who has been brooding and alone, starts asking leading questions because he is feeling jealous and suspicious. Wanda feels guilty and angry because Bill's first contact with her is to start asking questions. The result is that you two are distant and mistrustful. And what you want is to be closer [interactive definition of the problem]. Is this right?

Wanda: Right.

Bill: Yes.

Therapist: So, how would you like it to be?

Wanda: I would like us to have fun again.

Bill: I am not sure we could.

Therapist: But is that what you want too, Bill?

Bill: Sure.

Therapist: Give me an example of what that would be like—what would you be doing.

Wanda: Well, we would be going out together, or we would just spend a night together without bringing up that tired old subject.

Therapist: How's that, Bill?

Bill: Yeah, I would like that. We would be able to have a normal discussion about her job and my job without ending up in a fight.

Therapist: Okay, I think I see that. You'd like to be able to have a discussion about work and end up feeling good about it. And you'd like to do something different so that you could feel closer. Am I on the right track?

Bill: Yeah.

Wanda: I don't think we are ready to have a normal discussion about work yet. I don't trust Bill not to blow his top. It will just end up like before.

Therapist: Okay, if it's agreeable to you, Bill, we'll put that part off for now and concentrate on finding a way for you to get out or do something different so that you can feel that you're on the same team again.

Wanda: Just comfortable again.

Therapist: All right, so my understanding is that this week, on two occasions, you two will try to find something to do together during which you'll try to relax and just be comfortable with each other. I might suggest that each of you choose one of the activities but both of you strive to have fun and relax with each other. When we get back together next week, we'll see how it's going.

At the end of the session and with the therapist's help, Bill and Wanda have

1. Negotiated an interactive definition of the problem: "We have a 'distancing' problem."
2. Changed the problem to a goal: "We want to feel closer and have more fun together."
3. Added behavioral and affective components: "On two occasions this week we will agree on something that will allow us to feel relaxed and comfortable with each other."

CONCLUSION

Treatment planning with an individual client involves assessment and then diagnosis. The treatment plan is then dictated by this diagnostic formulation of the problem. In the integrative model, our focus is on getting the couple together as a team to meld their individual complaints and jointly attack a mutual issue called "the interactional definition of the problem." Because this is a more solution-oriented, positive approach, the therapist guides the couple to translate this problem into a solvable goal, a vision of what the future would hold if the problem were solved. To reach that vision, the couple must articulate behavioral steps and feeling outcomes that will tell them when the goal has been reached. Only after these cognitive, behavioral, and affective goals have been identified can specific treatment strategies be matched with the goals and implemented during therapy.

TWO

COMMON ISSUES IN THE LIFE OF THE COUPLE

7

Treatment Strategies

BRIGID M. NOONAN AND LYNN L. LONG

KEY CONCEPTS

- Creative treatment strategies offer counselors multiple options for treating couples.
- Treatment strategies must be grounded in theory in order to provide a basis for a coherent change plan.
- Learning how to select and implement appropriate strategies is critical to the counseling process.
- The uniqueness of the couple should be considered when selecting treatment options.
- Reframing and using metaphors are useful tools for counseling couples.
- Role reversals and role rehearsals help couples examine and practice new behaviors.
- Storytelling and narrative strategies help couples actively change and reshape their lives.
- Talk therapy is not always the best strategy for effecting change in a couple's interactions.
- Dance, movement, and psychodrama can provide ways for couples to express their struggles without words.
- Art therapy and music therapy are also positive ways to explore feelings, attitudes, beliefs, and interactive patterns.

THE NEED FOR CREATIVE TREATMENT STRATEGIES

Selecting appropriate treatment strategies for counseling couples is an integral component of our integrative model. The selection process includes examining patterns, making meaning of the couple's experience(s), understanding the culture in which the couple lives, understanding the couple's similarities and differences, creating new meaning and context, instilling hope, promoting growth, and eliciting change (Bobes & Bobes, 2005; Murray & Rotter, 2002). Most important, treatment strategies foster new possibilities for productive ways of loving, working, and living.

Treatment strategies are grounded in theory, and it is important for counselors to be cognizant of their theoretical orientation when selecting different techniques (Murray & Rotter, 2002). However, having knowledge about the different strategies and the implementation of them is not enough to assist clients in making change. Thompson (1996, p. 27) notes that "techniques alone merely produce a technician skilled in gimmicks, not a therapist whose intention is to effect change."

Using several theoretical orientations, the integrative model provides counselors with a framework for clarifying which technique(s) to use when working with couples. As the stages of the model progress from assessment to goal setting to interventions, maintenance, and validation, counselors choose which strategies will best suit the couple at each stage. Hackney (1992) points out that success in which strategy to use depends on how that strategy matches the client's experience of the problem.

Decisions about "client fit" occur in Stage 1 of the integrative model as a shared, interactive definition of the problem is formulated. The shared definition is based on each person's view of the problem, family influences, and individual beliefs. Offering hope, reframing, exploring exceptions, and using metaphors are some strategies that may be useful in this stage. In Stage 2 (goal setting), select strategies that help couples define and clarify what they would like to change in their relationship. Reframing problems into achievable goals is central to this stage. Stage 3, intervention, helps couples realize that the shared problem is solvable. It is in this particular stage that the counselor's expertise in selecting appropriate strategies to meet the goals set forth by the couple comes into play. Using play and humor, contracting, creating intensity, de-escalating conflict, role reversal, role rehearsal, storytelling and narrative techniques, and many of the nonverbal therapies such as dance, art therapy, and music therapy are useful at this time. Stages 4 and 5 (maintenance and validation) move from recognizing that there is a solution (maintenance) to celebrating that the identified problem is a solution and helping couples validate their success (validation). Techniques that assist with these stages include contracting, therapeutic compliments, narrative techniques, storytelling, and the use of rituals.

Learning how to select and implement different strategies requires consultation from experienced and competent practitioners. We believe that obtaining high-quality supervision is an important part of a couples counselor's learning experience (Stevens, 2000). Whether implementing role reversals, rituals, or art therapy, counselors must know how and when to incorporate a strategy.

Culture also plays a role in the selection of treatment strategies. Counselors are required to understand couples' cultural experiences. Arredondo & Arciniega (2001) remind us that having a thorough knowledge of the multicultural counseling competencies is an important aspect of a counselor's training. Specifically, awareness in three major areas assists counselors in establishing which treatment strategies to use. These three areas are (1) counselor awareness of own cultural values and biases, (2) counselor awareness of client's worldview, and (3) culturally appropriate intervention strategies (Arredondo & Arciniega, 2001).

Becoming culturally competent is a circular process that involves support of a culturally competent supervisor. Because no one strategy will work for couples of the same culture, counselors must be cautious in making generalizations about cultures (McCarthy & Holliday, 2004). In addition, it is important to discern cultural influences and individual differences prior to intervening with couples. If the counselor is unfamiliar with the particular cultural background, it is particularly important that he or she engages the couple in finding out about that culture so that they can collaborate on creative strategies. Asking pointed questions such as "How would that work for you?" or "Would that be something that you both would be comfortable with?" are important because many cultures have values and traditions that are not Westernized. Checking out these strategies with the couple begins the rapport building within the counseling relationship.

Many of the creative strategies described in this chapter balance traditional talk therapy (Murray & Rotter, 2002) with nonverbal methods. Although extremely valuable, talk therapy focuses on the verbal, whereas nonverbal counseling techniques (for example, music, psychodrama, dance arts) emphasize the couple's active participation in the counseling process.

Murray & Rotter (2002) also note that employing creative techniques can in fact speed the counseling process by providing an interactive environment that elicits change from undesirable behaviors to more healthy living patterns.

In this chapter, we provide examples of treatment strategies based on cognitive, affective, and behavioral change. We have selected many possibilities for helping couples achieve more satisfying relationships. However, other useful strategies have not been included in this chapter.

REFRAMING

Reframing, also referred to as *relabeling,* is a technique that helps change perceptions by altering the context of a situation (Becvar & Becvar, 2000; Gladding, 2002; Hanna & Brown, 2004; Sherman & Fredman, 1986). The actual facts of a situation do not change by viewing them from a different lens, however, they can be perceived more favorably. For example, when a partner describes the other as "stubborn," the counselor can alter the word and instead describe the person as "strong willed," This alteration may help foster a more positive attitude toward the characterization and toward the partner and, as a result, create an environment for change (Gladding, 2002).

Reframing is one of the most widely used strategies in couples counseling (Weeks & Treat, 2001). It helps counselors at various stages of counseling provide a greater likelihood of success. During the initial sessions, Brown and Hanna (2004) suggest that relabeling problem behaviors quickly offers new meaning to the definition of the problem. For example, "jealousy" can be described as "caring," or "working too much" can be framed as "being a good provider." In addition to offering new meaning to problem behaviors, deficits can be relabeled as strengths. A person who is "slow to act" or may "procrastinate" can be described as a "careful thinker." This reframing helps couples get unstuck from rigid, non-productive patterns and beliefs that have become a part of the problem (Brown & Hanna, 2004). Once the couple accepts the description of a "careful thinker," they can begin to explore new ways to problem-solve and come to a resolution more quickly without one partner feeling blamed.

To offer successful reframes, counselors must carefully assess the problem so that they have a clear understanding of the symptom (Weeks & Treat, 2001; Young, 1992). Of particular interest are problems that are presented by the couple as unsolvable or unmanageable. The negative presentation suggests that a person does not possess the personal resources to conquer the problem. If the couple enters counseling with much of their energy invested in arguing and disagreeing, a counselor might state, "It seems as if the two of you have a lot of passion in your relationship. It appears that you are using your energy in a way that is not making you feel better or is not helping you find a solution to your problem. Let's find a way to channel that energy to explore some positive alternatives." Building a bridge from the old view, "constant fighting," to a new view, "we have energy and passion that needs to be redirected," offers a solvable problem with positive rather than negative connotations. In future sessions, the couple discusses ways that they can use their energy and passion productively and stop themselves when they waste that precious energy on nonproductive arguing.

In many situations, a counselor presents the reframe as a directive or invitation:

> Directive: "I want you to write down three ways that you can focus your energy on doing something positive together this week."
> Invitation: "Would you be willing to explore at least three ways that you might put some love and passion in your relationship this week?"

These suggestions about positive energy and passion should be reinforced throughout the counseling sessions. When the couple backslides and talks about "fighting all the time," the counselor can correct the language by gently reminding them "that kind of use of your energy doesn't really help you get where you want to go, does it?" Or "You must have had a lot of energy this week that needs to be redirected. What kind of excitement can you create that would be loving rather than argumentative?"

This method of reframing does not resolve the underlying anger and resentment that are part of the arguing cycle. These feelings must be explored so that the situation can be externalized and resolved. Remaining stuck in the pain and anger is not useful if the couple wants to seek resolution and enjoy a more satisfying relationship. If a couple continues to argue despite the counselor's attempts to use positive reframes, they are possibly getting some type of payoff by remaining embroiled in the battle. This pattern should be explored because it may lead to further dissatisfaction in the relationship. At times, the counselor may recommend that the couple discontinue counseling until they are ready to move forward.

METAPHOR AND IMAGERY

The use of metaphor and imagery are important means for creating experiences that lead to greater self-awareness and change (Inkson & Amundson, 2002; Lyddon, Clay, & Sparks, 2001). Brown and Hanna (2004, p. 207) define a *metaphor* as a "word or phrase that represents another condition by analogy . . . . [When] using metaphorical tasks, the [counselor] chooses an activity that resembles the stated problem." A metaphor can also "explicate what is implicit" (Bayer & Thompson, 2000, p. 39).

Cormier and Cormier (1991) describe six steps for designing metaphors:

1. Examine the nature of the presenting problem so that the counselor can use the theme to create a parallel metaphor.
2. Choose a representation for the metaphor (for example, animal, object, situation).
3. Use words in the metaphor that match the couple's frame of reference.
4. Develop an interactional process that matches the interactions observed in the problem situation.
5. Embellish a situation in order to emphasize the metaphor.
6. Create some type of mystery or transformation in the metaphor.

In one situation, a couple came to counseling with an identified problem of not being able to find the spark and love that they once shared. The couple complained that they were bored and overworked and that they had developed very predictable patterns. They stated that they did not know what to do to find their love again. The counselor decided to use a metaphor of embarking on a treasure hunt to find their stolen or hidden passion. Life had robbed them of their passion, and they needed to join together to reclaim it. In a counseling session, the couple stated that "we can't seem to discover what makes us excited anymore" and "we have lost our way together." The counselor responded by using a parallel theme that involved a treasure hunt: "It seems that you have lost the map that you developed when you first got together. Let's imagine that you create a new map together. What would be some of the clues that you could give each other about where to find your passion?" Other therapeutic queries or invitational responses that might be useful include

"How can the two of you uncover some of the hidden treasures that you each contribute to your relationship?"
"What plans can you jointly create in order to journey to the hidden treasure?"
"What will you do with the treasure when you find it?"
"How do you make certain that you always have a treasure in your relationship?"

By posing these types of queries, the counselor assists the couple with collaborating on an adventure to uncover personal and relational strengths, excitement, and passion together. In future sessions, the couple can identify ways to revitalize their relationship and to develop specific steps to implement change. The use of a treasure-hunt metaphor parallels the search for passion and helps create a non-threatening language for expressing and solving the dilemma.

Imagery, similar to metaphor, is a representation of something fanciful. It is a tool to help couples create their own notions of reality. From a guided description of images and ideas, couples can formulate new ideas, options, or actions (Sherman & Fredman, 1986). Imagery also transforms abstract feelings and thoughts into concrete experiences so that couples can more readily identify and resolve issues by objectifying and externalizing the problem. In addition, this technique offers a more flexible and creative way of viewing the problem.

For example, Chance and Soirel came to counseling to address poor communication issues in their relationship. In the first session, they described themselves as animal lovers. They also admitted that they look at the animals as their children. The counselor determined to use an animal imagery technique in order to provide a context for talking about their communication issues (Henderson, 1999). First, the couple was asked to bring in photographs of dogs from magazines. They were asked to choose those that represented likenesses of themselves and of their partner. In the session, the counselor explored with them the characteristics that most represented their physical, symbolic, or behavioral characteristic. These canine images provided a framework for discussing personal traits, feelings, habits, and coping styles of each partner. The images helped facilitate discussions and uncovered incongruent aspects of self and views of their partner. They could also identify with the theme of animal traits characteristics that they would like to possess in order to resolve their issues.

Both metaphor and imagery serve as therapeutic strategies that enable couples to develop an alternative language and context for implementing change. These strategies promote creativity and flexibility that open future possibilities for growth.

ROLE REVERSAL

Role reversal helps couples view a situation through the eyes of their partner and emotionally "experience the role of the other" (Sherman & Fredman, 1986, p. 140). The style that individuals portray when enacting the role suggests the way they view themselves and their partner. Role reversal allows thinking, feeling, and acting in a situation rather than talking about the feelings of the other party. The goal of role reversal is to increase empathy and understanding of the other and experience a greater awareness of how each person's behavior affects the other. It is particularly useful to help focus on themes of sadness, anger, and conflict (Fow, 1998).

For example, the following scenario might occur with a couple in conflict about the way they spend time together:

> *Therapist:* In this activity, I am asking that each of you assume the role of
> your partner. You are to respond to my questions by expressing feelings
> and reacting as you think your partner might feel or react. Later, we
> will explore how you have portrayed each other, and we will take the
> opportunity to offer feedback to each other about the portrayal. Reuben

and Elfriede, please have a discussion as your partner about how you
would like to spend this weekend.

Elfriede [as Reuben]: Well honey, let's just wait to see what happens. I don't
really want to make any plans because I might have to work or my boss
might come into town.

Reuben [as Elfriede]: You spend more time at work than you do with me.
I'm just not your top priority. You never want to be with me anymore.

Elfriede [as Reuben]: That's ridiculous. My work is important. You know
that. You are the most important person in my life.

Reuben [as Elfriede]: I don't see it that way. Let's go to dinner and a movie on
Saturday night. You could see your boss on Sunday if he comes to town.

Elfriede [as Reuben]: I don't know. I just hate to make a plan and have to
break it. It's not that I don't want to be with you.

Therapist: Okay, so we can see where it breaks down.

Reuben [self]: I guess I don't make a lot of plans, but my work is so
demanding. I do want to spend time with Elfriede.

Elfriede [self]: Yes, but that means that we stay home every weekend just in
case you need to work.

Reuben: Maybe we could try Saturday evening if I can reserve Sunday for work.

Elfriede: Where do you want to go?

Reuben: Well, I don't know. What movies are playing?

Elfriede: I'll check the newspaper tomorrow.

Therapist: Would the two of you be willing to sit down tomorrow evening
and make a plan for Saturday? Try not to stop the conversation until you
have determined what movie you will see, what time it begins, and where
you will go to dinner. Be as specific as possible.

Elfriede: That seems to be the piece we leave out of our conversation. We
end up arguing over not wanting to spend time together, rather than
making a plan. When I know we have a plan to spend time together, I
feel more important to Reuben.

Reuben: I always think you are important. I want to do well in my job and
be in line for a promotion next year. I will try to make more plans with
you. One weekend I would like to go to the beach like we used to do.

This example demonstrates how the use of a role-reversal technique highlights
the way that the couple detours from making specific plans to spend time together. It
allows them to view the situation from the other's perspective and then react by
attempting to correct and change the behavior that is getting in the way of a solution.

ROLE REHEARSAL

Kipper (1996, p. 1) describes *role rehearsal* as a "manifestation of the effort to master
the world around [us]." We display our feelings and behaviors by acting them out.
Role playing is a way of helping couples express their present life circumstances and
their hopes for the future. Couples can reenact stories or situations, and they can

often convey the message more clearly. It has the potential to relieve helplessness and uncertainty, reduce fears, instill hope, promote healing, and contribute to a better understanding between two people (Kipper, 1996). In addition, practicing new behaviors and acting them out can contribute to a greater likelihood of success of the targeted skill.

Enactment techniques that focus on practicing new behaviors can result in achieving longer-lasting results. This process includes the "acting as if" principle that helps couples try out new behaviors that may be uncomfortable or unfamiliar to them (Kipper, 1996).

Kipper (1996) describes the role-rehearsal process in four stages:

1. Prepare couples. Help them realize that the technique can help them achieve new ways of behaving
2. Select a target situation. Ask couples to describe the goal behaviors in detail so that they can identify what specific skills they need to practice.
3. Help couples understand that rehearsal is a gradual shaping process that may require a continuum of skills practice. Counselors offer modeling and coaching techniques and, at times, a role reversal as described previously.
4. Have couples practice new roles in real-life situations. The results will be discussed in subsequent counseling sessions.

One benefit of role rehearsal is that the counselor can give immediate feedback that may shape corrective action in the future (Gladding, 2002). Role rehearsal can also reveal relationship conflicts and can help produce new options and insights into conflict situations (Fennell & Weinhold, 2003).

Counselors set up a role rehearsal by asking the couple to identify a change that they would like to make in their interactions with each other. Let's consider a couple who comes to counseling in order to change their communication pattern to a more productive one. In the past, one partner has attempted to control the thoughts and feelings of the other, and as a result, an emotional shutdown has occurred.

Therapist: Would the two of you be willing to try something new in the way that you communicate with each other so that we can identify where you need more practice or new options for behaving?
Couple: Sure, what do you want us to do?
Therapist: Let's use a recent example to explore your communication style.
Couple: Okay.
Therapist: Coretta, how are you feeling about the situation with John yesterday?
Coretta: I feel disappointed because I think he is trying to cut me out of a promotion.
Therapist: It sounds like you are annoyed with him.
Coretta: Absolutely! He made me look really foolish in front of my boss. I was embarrassed.
Robert: I don't blame you for being angry.
Therapist: Robert, maybe you should ask her more about being embarrassed and how she handled that.
Robert: How did you handle it?

By practicing and trying new ways of communicating with the counselor as a coach, Robert can acknowledge Coretta's feelings without telling her how to feel. Coretta can explore her feelings without Robert interrupting or dominating the conversation. She can focus on her own reactions and possible solutions rather than responding negatively to Robert. This technique offers multiple practice opportunities until changes are made.

RITUALS

Although we have described the use of rituals in previous chapters, it is worthy of inclusion in a chapter focusing specifically on treatment strategies. *Rituals* are prescribed directives that dramatize memorable events and positive aspects of couples' relationships. The behaviors associated with rituals will impact cognitive and emotional reactions. As a result, these symbolic actions help couples embrace change and reaffirm relationship cohesiveness (Gladding, 2002; Goldenberg & Goldenberg, 2004; Viere, 2001).

Winek and Craven (2003) describe the use of rituals for healing when extramarital relationships have occurred. Consider the situation of Jamal and Darnelle who have come to counseling after Darnelle had an extramarital affair. The couple has been married for 16 years. They determined early in their marriage not to have children because they both have very demanding careers. Jamal is a real estate developer who works 60 hours each week. Darnelle is a tax attorney. Over the years, they began to define themselves and their relationship based on their careers and the demands of their careers. They found little personal time or time for each other.

Two years ago, Darnelle had a brief extramarital affair with Tony. The relationship began as the two of them worked on an auditing project for a local financial firm. As the affair ended, Darnelle told Jamal about the relationship with Tony and complained to him that they just didn't have "a spark" anymore in their marriage. Jamal was hurt and angry, and he suggested that they seek counseling. In counseling they identified the shared view of the problem as "putting their life energy in their work" with little time for each other. The affair was convenient because it was associated with the workplace and highlighted the lack of intimacy in their relationship. Jamal and Darnelle both would like to rekindle their relationship. Through counseling they identified their hurts and struggles and the strengths that they can use to create a more fulfilling marriage. After many counseling sessions, the couple was ready to celebrate their changes together.

The counselor described the need for a ritual, or symbolic, experience to convey their success (Barnett & Youngberg, 2004). They were asked to separately go through all of the photographs they have collected over the past 16 years, emphasizing the positive experiences they have shared. Next, they were required to bring the photographs to their counseling session. They were then asked to share some of their positive memories associated with the experiences. They were instructed to return home and to create a photograph album of some of the highlights of their relationship. They returned to counseling 2 weeks later and processed the experience of making the album. The counselor directed them to spend 20 minutes each week for the next month reviewing the photos together. In addition, the photo album symbolized the need to continue to provide experiences together and capture the events on camera. Once a week, they planned a date time together, alternating with each partner participating in the planning of their time together. Twice a year, they must plan a vacation as an additional way of adding to their positive memories.

Wiener (1999) describes the therapeutic use of pictures and art in rituals. These rituals help couples visualize change in a creative manner in order to redefine and reconfirm our present, past, and future (Imber-Black, 2002). Jamal and Darnelle have infused fun and creativity into their relationship, and they have learned to connect intimately. Finally, they have learned to find solutions to their problems without bringing in a third party to complicate their lives.

CONTRACTING

Contracting with couples is a behavioral approach that identifies particular behaviors desired in a relationship (Carns & Carns, 1994; Fennell & Weinhold, 2003; Weeks & Treat, 2001). Specifically, *contracting* assists couples in making behavioral changes that contribute to affective and cognitive changes (Weeks & Treat, 2001). There are many ways that counselors can use contracts with couples. One is a *therapy contract*. This particular contract is written and discusses the administrative details pertaining to the therapeutic relationship. Issues such as day(s) and time(s) of therapy, costs, vacations, and goals of therapy are discussed within the contract. This approach capitalizes on couples' strengths by outlining what will take place over the course of their time together in therapy (Fennell & Weinhold, 2003).

Another type of contract is the *contingency contract*. As discussed by Fennell & Weinhold (2003, p. 157), "Contingency contracts help couples establish a mutually reinforcing *quid pro quo*. When one partner does something positive, the other partner reciprocates." The assumption with contingency contracts is that couples are able to work reciprocally in an effort to improve their relationship. If unable to maneuver these possibilities, this approach may not be viable option to use.

Glasser (2002) notes the importance of keeping written contracts simple between counselors and clients. Using contracts often assists in defining clear goals as determined by the couple. For example, one particular couple cannot listen when having heating discussions. Angie and Calvin talk over one another and do not listen to what the other says. The counselor outlined a contract for them that each would write out three things that they wanted their partner to do while having a discussion. The following is their contract:

> I will listen to what you have to say for up to 5 minutes. I will ask questions, as it relates to the discussion if needed. I will continue to listen if my questions are being answered. At the end of our 5 minutes each, we will discuss possibilities for a next step or come up with a workable solution. If we are able to listen to each other for those 5 minutes each, we will celebrate by taking a walk together.

Each signed and dated the contract. For Angie and Calvin, it was important that they begin to learn to listen to what the other had to say and not "jump in" to the discussion before the other was finished. Many times, couples need to relearn how to communicate, and the contract is a specific behavioral technique that gives them a step-by-step approach to change certain negative behaviors.

CREATING INTENSITY

Creating intensity is an opportunity for counselors to offer couples a different view of their relationship. Couples mired in a repetitive process of conflict can create intensity that helps them learn a new, more positive way to manage their conflict. This particular technique should not be used with couples in which a pattern of abuse is evident. Creating a safe environment for both parties is an essential element. As noted by Weeks & Treat (2001, p. 70), "Generating intensity within a therapy session requires sensitivity to process issues and the ability to use cognitions and emotions creatively in the couple-therapist interaction."

For example, a couple came into therapy because one felt ignored by the other. Tonya and James have been married for 8 years and feel "stuck" in their relationship. James feels that Tonya does not pay as much attention to him as he thinks he needs. They both work full time, and Tonya is also pursuing a master's degree. What little free time they had, James thinks that Tonya cares more about school than him. In creating intensity, the counselor offers the following directives to the couple:

Therapist: I'm going to ask you all to re-create a recent time when you felt ignored. I want you to continue the scene as long as possible. You may begin to feel a little foolish, but I want you to continue until I ask you to stop. I want you to discuss how you feel ignored.

James: I just don't feel like she cares about me at all; I mean, I come home, there isn't any dinner, or if there is, it's leftovers.

Tonya: We talked about this; we agreed that during my school semester, we would share kitchen duties. I haven't once seen you cook. I feel like I'm doing everything.

James: Yeah, but I didn't think it was going to be like this. I thought it would just be a couple of days, not *every* day.

Tonya: I'm home every day; I don't go anywhere, except work and school. I don't know why you're so angry. I thought that we agreed that I would support you during your school, and you would support me. I don't feel supported.

James: My school only took one year; yours is taking a lot longer. I just want my wife back.

In this example, Tonya and James were able to focus on the fact that they both felt ignored and resented not each other but that their work and outside activities (Tonya's schooling) took time away from their relationship. They were able to create a schedule that helped map out time to rediscover their relationship each week.

Attempting to create appropriate emotional intensity between couples and their counselor is a significant aspect of the counseling relationship. Too much emotional intensity does not give the counselor an opportunity to intervene constructively, nor does it assist the couple in learning how to communicate in a positive manner. Conversely, too little intensity can shift the therapy from having focus, which affects how the couple engages on an intimate level (Weeks & Treat, 2001).

DE-ESCALATING CONFLICT

De-escalating conflict is useful to help couples see how destructive their communication patterns have become. One technique is to have a couple who argues incessantly argue within the session to an empty chair. One at a time, for approximately 5 minutes, each will argue their position. After each has argued their position, the therapist asks them to describe what they saw and heard.

Having the couple talk about their observations further helps them explore what has been working, as well as what has not been working. This helps separate the process from the problem and helps the couple see that their communication style may not be healthy. Asking the couple questions concerning how these communication patterns have worked for them, versus how they have not worked, also enables them to explore different styles of talking with each another. Similar to narrative techniques, the language that is used is important for the counselor to point out to the couple.

USING STORYTELLING AND NARRATIVE TECHNIQUES

Narrative techniques are designed to emphasize the re-storying of the couple's past and present relationships in order to help promote the opportunity to invent, reinvent, or create a present and future history with a focus on the couple's relationship reality. Storytelling and narrative techniques are goal directed by helping the couple explore how their language both constructs as well as maintains the problem/issue. To help make their experience understandable, the couple's experiences are collapsed into stories that provide a frame of reference (Etchison & Kleist, 2000). Instead of viewing the problem as a problem, narrative techniques facilitate the separation of the couple from the problem. Allowing the couple to create an alternative story shifts the focus from the problem and helps them explore different ways of behaving, in addition to resisting or disputing the problem, or how to negotiate the relationship with the problem differently (Etchison & Kleist, 2000).

Many times, couples present with negative narratives about their lives. These narratives can include myths, self-defeating behaviors, feelings of inadequacy, feeling overwhelmed, justifying why they cannot change, and negative self-labeling, to name a few (Goldenberg & Goldenberg, 2004). To make change, couples are asked to create alternative positive narratives that further help them consider how to make change as it relates to their values, beliefs, and assumptions of their life experiences. This process frequently fosters new views about more positive possibilities, which "actively change or reshape lives" (Goldenberg & Goldenberg, 2004, p. 343). Through questioning, the therapist asks a couple to reflect on their feelings associated with their story at various times with various individuals, as well as under various circumstances. Emphasizing the positive points of the story is important; however, many times the couple's story may not be positive. Issues of trauma, loss, grief, and depression may play major roles in the story. It is important to accommodate those aspects of the story that are painful, which can further affect values, beliefs, and assumptions (Goldberg, 1999).

DANCE/MOVEMENT THERAPY

Dance/movement therapy is the psychotherapeutic use of movement to further emotional, cognitive, social, and physical development. Awakening our senses and rediscovering parts of ourselves that have been lost or unavailable for some time address these aspects of personal development. Dance therapy nurtures the wisdom and power that lies within us and empowers us to utilize our personal resources to change behaviors, thoughts, and feelings about the past, present, or future. It punctuates the couple's strengths by complimenting their teamwork (Bobes & Rothman, 2002). In addition, it offers a playful and freeing vehicle for change (Olshansky, 2000).

A renewed optimistic view of life often emerges and is instrumental in helping us see new facets of ourselves. As personal insight grows, underlying problems become clearer, and new ways to release or convey feelings occur. Dance also promotes flexibility and change, keeps couples healthy and fit, and provides new possibilities for the future (Gladding, 2002).

Based in theories such as gestalt, Adlerian, social learning theory, and family systems theory, dance is the "rhythmic interaction that enhances or impedes one's overall functioning" (Gladding, 1998, p. 37). Communication and interactional skills are described as the dance of the couple (Lerner, 1985a, 1985b). Lerner describes two very powerful interactions in the books *The Dance of Anger* (1985a) and *The Dance of Intimacy* (1985b). The premise is to change the dance step in order to change the relational pattern. Such metaphors are pervasive in family therapy.

The "it takes two to tango" approach to dance therapy is particularly useful for couples who have become out of step with each other or are unaware of the steps they are taking. Often these steps can be interrupted and modified to create a more healthy couples dance.

Consider the case of Amalie and Robard who come to counseling because Amalie feels restricted and isolated in her relationship. Robard works outside the home, and Amalie owns a craft company that she operates exclusively through the Internet. The couple does not have children. They spend most of their time on their careers. Robard is unhappy when Amalie leaves the house without him, and he quizzes her if she goes to the grocery store or runs errands during the day. She feels confined and mistrusted, yet Robard states that he is protective of her because "you can never be too careful with all the psychopaths loose out there." Through the use of dance movement, the counselor helps Amalie express her feelings and then helps them learn a new dance together.

> *Therapist:* I am going to try something a little different with the two of you today. I would like to have both of you stand up; then, Amalie, please take Robard's hands and act as if you are dancing. Show us what that dance looks like right now when you feel confined in your relationship.
>
> [Amalie places them in a tight pattern, squeezing them tightly with their feet locked together.]
>
> *Therapist:* Okay, now try to glide across the floor.
>
> [Amalie and Robard attempt to move but get tangled with each other and remain stationary.]
>
> *Therapist:* Amalie, is this how it feels at times in your relationship?
>
> *Amalie:* Yes, I never thought of it this way, but I can't move, I can't breathe.
>
> *Therapist:* You can't move forward together. Robard, how do you experience this?
>
> *Robard:* I guess I can see what she is doing. I just want to protect her.
>
> *Amalie:* You are strangling me.
>
> *Robard:* But I love you, Amalie.
>
> *Therapist:* Let's try something else. Hold on to each other, not too tightly, but hold on, nevertheless. Also, each of you take a step backwards giving your feet room to move, but hold on. Now, how does that feel?
>
> *Amalie:* A little more free.
>
> *Robard:* I don't know . . .
>
> *Therapist:* Now, try to move across the floor.
>
> [The couple moves across the floor, and Amalie smiles.]
>
> *Therapist:* What is the smile about, Amalie?
>
> *Amalie:* We can move now. We aren't on top of each other. But look, we are still connected and we are right here together.
>
> *Robard:* Well, I want to know that we are together, that you won't leave.
>
> *Amalie:* I'm not going anywhere. *We* just need room to breathe. Otherwise, we will just smother each other.
>
> *Therapist:* Robard, could you hold on, but not quite so tightly?
>
> *Robard:* What do I need to do?
>
> [They begin a discussion on what specific changes they will make in their relationship, referring to the restricted feelings of the first dance and the free but connected feeling of the second dance.]

This is but one example of how dance and movement therapy can be helpful to couples. Counselors can use their creative talents to incorporate dance and movement into their personal counseling styles.

PSYCHODRAMA TECHNIQUES

Many techniques of psychodrama can be used in working with couples. One such technique is called *mirroring*. This particular technique helps individuals realize the difficulty they may be having with their interpersonal relationships. If working with a couples group, this technique is extremely helpful because the individual having the difficulty (in psychodrama, this individual is known as the protagonist) is asked to watch while someone else from the group plays their part (mirror) (Gladding, 2005; Hamamci, 2002). The counselor asks group members to come forth to enact a scene. Once a person or couple is identified, the individual or couple is asked to engage in a number of enactments. From performing a soliloquy, to acting out a monodrama (where they play all the parts of the particular enactment), to role reversal (discussed earlier), to performing a double or multiple-double (where the protagonist's alter ego is expressed), psychodrama is beneficial because the focus is on the present and requires couples to be spontaneous and creative when acting out their feelings. Gaining insight is the key component to psychodrama and is achieved when these enactments empower couples to fully express their feelings, thereby helping them grow within their relationships.

ART THERAPY TECHNIQUES

Art therapy can help couples express and explore feeling, thoughts, and behaviors through the use of art media and imagery (University of Louisville, 2005). It is a nonverbal, expressive therapy that focuses on the process, rather than a product. The aim of art therapy is to help effect personal growth and awareness, heal emotional pain, and create change in a nonthreatening, facilitative environment (Edwards, 2004; Sobol & Williams, 2001). Through the use of art, couples can increase their self-awareness, understand their relationship better, cope with stress and conflict, and address traumatic life incidents (Edwards, 2004).

Couples create objects and images that clarify meaning in their relationship in a different way than talk therapy. As in any expressive treatment, couples are required to process together any materials, which they create, that stimulate thinking and new ideas (Gladding, 2005). They also examine the process that they used and how that process is different than the way they normally relate in their daily lives.

Counselors use artistic methods to diagnose relational struggles and explore motivation for change. The depictions that emerge from the use of art are often richly symbolic and offer multiple levels of meaning for listening, speaking, and interacting with each other (Wiener, 1999). One basic use of art is to ask couples to draw their relationship. One rule is that they cannot use stick figures. The sizes and shapes of the figures, the size of the paper, and the chosen colors can provide information for future conversations (Jordan, 2001; Wiener, 1999). All forms of paint media, fingerpaints, crayons, chalk, clay, play dough, and other forms of artistic media may be used. Olshansky (2000) describes the use of quilting as an example of art therapy.

The Joint Family Holiday Drawing Technique provides counselors with a way of observing couples' interactions and problem-solving skills. Materials needed are large sheets of paper (such as poster board), colored pencils, felt-tipped pens, crayons, and pencils. Couples are asked to work together on a drawing with a theme of how they spend their holidays together. Counselors instruct couples that they may not speak during the activity after they have identified the holiday they will depict. A time limit is normally set for the activity. The completed drawing offers information about how they work together and how they each experience their time together. During the processing time after the drawing, such questions (adapted from Jordan, 2001) are posed as

"What was this experience like for the two of you?"
"How did you make decisions about the drawing?"
"How did your partner influence you as you created your picture?"
"What roles did you each play in the development of the picture?"
"How did you solve different opinions in the picture?"
"What did you learn about yourself and your partner from this experience?"
"How would you change the picture if you could?"

Another example of art therapy is to use the Joint Scribble. In this task, couples are asked to make scribbles on a piece of paper and then unify them into one picture (Gladding, 2005). The unification is a way of looking at interactional styles, decision making, conflict resolution, and how they incorporate each other's needs in their relationship. In addition, they can explore how they make space for each other and how they arrive at solutions, or an end result (the unified picture) (Gladding, 2005).

An additional activity is to ask couples to make a collage about their relationship together. It is necessary to have magazines and poster board available. Any topic can be used for the activity. An interesting topic is to ask them to depict happy times in their relationship. Together they must choose pictures or shapes that represent those times and create a visual representation of them without verbal communication. Later, they verbally process the experience, and they explore their ideas about positive times together. This activity can also be used to represent emotions (create a picture of depression, anger, jealousy, and so on). Externalizing internal emotional struggles is often a first step toward healing because it provides a media for exploring and discussing the underlying individual and relational tensions and conflicts.

MUSIC THERAPY

Music is a form of therapy that fosters "inspiration, relaxation, motivation, and integration" (Darnley-Smith & Patey, 2003, p. 8). It helps couples integrate different experiences, beliefs, attitudes, and feelings about the quality of their lives together. **Music therapy** is goal directed and involves the use of music activities such as singing, humming, tapping, playing musical instruments, listening to music, composing music, moving to music, or discussing lyrics and characteristics (J. S. Peters, 1987). It allows feelings to be revealed that may not come forth in traditional talk therapy.

Counselors can use music in many ways. Asking couples to select songs that express how they feel is a projective technique that can reveal underlying emotional distress or conflicts. Couples can bring CDs to the counseling session that reflect their emotional states. Counselors can ask how the music speaks to them or for them and can help them examine the lyrics, rhythm, melody, or a combination of all of these musical components (Gladding, 2005). Counselors can also provide music and ask couples to close their eyes and express what it means to them. Couples who are musical may bring in composed songs, or they may bring in musical instruments to play that reflect their relationship.

Music is also used to help create a certain mood such as using uplifting music to crowd out negative thoughts (Miles, 1997). Couples can move to the rhythm, sing along, and imagine joy. Relaxing music is often used to set a mood for intimate time together at home or to diffuse anger and frustration. Lively music may help address depression or sadness or help couples express freedom and happiness. Music can help couples speak more freely; escape negative thought patterns; vent feelings or frustrations; manage aggression; reveal repressed anger, depression, and grief; or help develop new habits for self and relational care (Miles, 1997).

Counselors can prescribe examination of a particular song that may reflect relational issues or ask couples to recite song lyrics and express how they are representative of what is happening in their relationship. Some possibilities for lyrics that provide food for thought include the following:

> I've had bad dreams too many times,
> to think that they don't mean much anymore,
> Fine times have gone and left myself home,
> friends who once came, just walk out the door.
>
> Bonnie Raitt, "Love Has No Pride"
> —*The Bonnie Raitt Collection*

> I keep on fallin' in and out of love with you
> Sometimes I love you, sometimes you make me blue
> Sometimes I feel good, at times I feel used
> What you're doin' makes me so confused
> I keep on fallin' in and out of love with you.
>
> Alicia Keys, "Fallin'"
> —*Songs in A Minor*

> Have I told you lately that I love you
> Have I told you there's no one above you
> Fill my heart with gladness
> Take away my sadness
> Ease my troubles, that's what you do.
>
> Van Morrison, "Have I Told You Lately"
> —*The Best of Van Morrison*

> Okay, I forgot about the trash
> I didn't trim the long hairs on my moustache
> I did buy you a ring, I believe it was back in '93
> Alright, I admit I forgot our anniversary
> But I did pick up the baby this morning at the nursery
> That ain't no big thing but it's a gold star for me

You get tired and disgusted with me
When I can't be just what you want me to be
I still love you and I try real hard
I swear one day you'll have a brand new car
I even asked the Lord to try to help me
He looked down from heaven and said to tell you please
Just be patient I'm a work in progress.

Alan Jackson, "Work in Progress"
—*Drive*

EXPLORING EXCEPTIONS

Exploring exceptions is based on the work of the poststructural/postmodern or social constructivist theorists. In particular, exploring exceptions is part of a solution-focused approach to counseling (DeJong & Berg, 1998). *Solution-focused counseling* centers on "the counselor's confidence in the client's ability to make positive changes in his or her life by accessing and using inner resources and strengths" (Lewis & Osborn, 2004, p. 82). When asked to explore exceptions, couples deconstruct the issue/problem by looking for exceptions to the rule. That is, when was the couple able to keep the issue/problem from occurring, or when were they able to control the problem or issue? In other words, having the couple explore when the problem was not present creates an exception that helps them to reconstruct how they view the problem/issue (Dzelme & Jones, 2001). This is also known as the *miracle question*. The therapist poses a question in this way:

> "If you were to wake up tomorrow and a miracle happened and the problems in your relationship were solved, how would your relationship look? What would be different about the relationship, and how would you know that your relationship was different?"

The couple directs the goals for therapy by answering the questions that help them create strategies to solve or reduce the issue. Constructing solutions by focusing on these exceptions helps them realize or discover their strengths and competencies and directs them to achieve more realistic and healthy goals. By having the couple discuss how to solve the problem (explore exceptions) rather than talk about the problem, they are better able to see the problem in a different light. The therapist and couple are cooperative in their work, and this cooperation is a key aspect of the therapeutic process.

In one particular situation, a couple came into therapy because their careers were beginning to build resentment. Amanda and Terry have been married 5 years, and both work full time. They have a 3-year-old son (Ben) who spends 3 days at day care and the other 2 days with Terry's mother. Both are tired at the end of the week. Terry does not want to "do chores" on their 2 days off, but Amanda feels obligated to take care of their home because "that's what you do." When the counselor asked the miracle question, each came up with responses:

"For Amanda and me to be able to enjoy each other and our son during the
week, as well as on the weekend."

"For Terry and me to be able to communicate better about what we both
would like our home to look like."

"For us to be able to engage in activities that we enjoy doing together and
separately."

"For us to not feel guilty about leaving Ben during the week."

By exploring exceptions, the counselor was to help the couple point out possible exceptions taking place regarding their behavior. For example, Amanda and Terry were asked if they could think of a time when they both were home and didn't communicate. Both quickly answered that although they may be tired, they always spend at least part of the evening talking about their day.

In this type of intervention, the counselor is the student, whereas the couple (client) is the teacher. It disputes the notion that the counselor has all the knowledge and the client is the sponge in obtaining the information. By having the couple examine resources that are readily available to them, they are empowered to further discover their strengths.

THERAPEUTIC COMPLIMENTS

Similar to exploring exceptions, using therapeutic compliments is also a method used in solution-focused counseling (Campbell, Elder, Gallagher, Simon & Taylor, 1999; Quick, 1998). Compliments in counseling are used to normalize a couple's experience as well as reframe issues and emphasize their strengths and competencies in solution building.

Campbell and colleagues (1999) indicate a template that can be used for developing compliments when working with clients:

1. Normalizing statements
2. Restructuring statements
3. Affirming client competencies
4. Bridging statement
5. Providing between-session suggestions (if appropriate)

The authors note that, depending on the situation, the flexibility of the format can be changed. The first, normalizing statements, helps couples realize that their problem/issue is not as unique as they may believe and that their reactions are normal.

In one situation, a couple was at an impasse regarding their relationship because each felt neglected by the other. Diana and Beth are actively involved in parenting three children. Diana works full time, and Beth works part time in order to care for the children. The counselor responded that "no wonder you are feeling neglected, you both are putting all of your energies into raising and caring for three beautiful children. It's a great deal to handle, plus you both work outside the home." This helps them see that their situation was not something unusual.

By normalizing their stress, the counselor can assist Diana and Beth in changing their perspective from what is deficient in their relationship to their capacity for change.

Restructuring statements is another technique used to help couples rethink the problem/issue. Many times, couples limit their solutions when trying to solve the problem. Restructuring offers possible options for thinking differently, and allows a couple to actively restructure their thinking (Campbell et al., 1999).

Affirmations are also used to assist couples to accept how their personal and social resources can be used in building solutions to the problem/issue. For example, the counselor might say, "Staying sober is incredibly difficult, but you both are using the tools (AA and Al-Anon meetings) you learned to really make a positive change in your relationship because you want the relationship to work." The counselor focuses on what each had begun to learn in recovery to articulate their new competencies in building a stronger relationship.

Bridging statements are used to look at previously discussed information, the next steps necessary for growth, and the connection between the two (Campbell et al., 1999). The key component to bridging statements is for the counselor to offer new meaning for couples.

Finally, between-session suggestions help couples remain open to change. Between-session suggestions should focus on a couple's strengths and competencies. For couples who are not open to change, focusing on simple tasks (whether homework or observations) helps them recognize their competencies.

INSTILLING HOPE

Instilling hope with couples who have experienced emotional stress for a long period of time is an essential component of the counseling process. If counseling is to be successful, couples need to believe that they can make the necessary changes in their lives. Brown and Hanna (2004) indicate that 15% of successful therapeutic outcomes are related to a client's sense of hope. In fact, the counselor's position should be "hopeful and curious." Cunningham and Henggeler (1999) use the term *gift giving*, which they borrowed from Sue and Zane (1987), as a way to achieve a hopeful therapeutic environment. Gift giving is when the counselor provides some immediate relief through normalizing feelings, reducing guilt, or breaking down presenting issues into more manageable components. The relief offers motivation for commitment to change (Hanna & Brown, 2004).

Solution-focused counseling emphasizes focusing on possibilities as a means of instilling hope. Being future focused is a way to help couples look toward better times rather than remaining stuck in the past or the present. In addition, focusing on couples' strengths can help foster a hopeful view of the future. Bobes and Rothman (2002) use the strategy of inquiry of what attracted them to each other as a way of recalling strengths.

Snyder (2002) conceptualizes hope as a goal-directed cognitive process. They are "hoped for ends" that reflect what couples desire to get, do, be, experience, or create. A first step toward building hope, according to Snyder (2002) and Irving et al. (2004), is to identify goals for counseling. In Stage 2 of the integrative couples model, we identify cognitive and behavioral goals. However, instilling hope begins with the initial phone conversation and continues in Stage 1 as the shared view of the problem is defined. Identifying the problem in relational terms neutralizes blame and promotes the notion that the situation is solvable. White (1989) describes externalization of the problem as a way to move away from blame and place the problem in a context that allows couples to gang up on the problem together or to conquer it.

The therapist may use the following comments to instill hope at all five stages of the integrative model:

Stage 1
"It sounds as if the two of you have taken a big step in attempting to resolve your differences. You are to be commended for that."

"It seems as if the two of you would like to identify a solution together and, in my experience, if we are all on the same page about what it is you would to see happen, it will be easier for you to have a successful outcome. As you think about your relationship, what would you like for it to be like in the future?" (What do you envision your relationship to be in one year?)

Stage 2
"Describe what you would like to accomplish in counseling."

"How will you feel, and what will you do differently?"

"How can you join together to resolve your differences?"

Stage 3
"Tell me about your initial introduction to each other. What attracted you to each other?"

"What traits did you admire the most in each other?"

"What traits in your partner drew you to him/her?"

"What are your partner's strengths?"

"What are your strengths together?"

Stage 4
"When you get caught up in life and backslide a bit, what will you do to get back on track?"

"What skills will you draw on in order to move forward when you get stuck?"

Stage 5
"How can you continue to use your new skills in the future?"

"How can you create a ritual together to symbolize your success?"

"What can you each do to keep your relationship fresh and focused toward the future?"

"How can you enjoy your time together as you continue your life journey?"

These queries in all stages of the model help couples remain positive, goal directed, and hopeful about their relationship together.

PLAY AND HUMOR

Games are an important aspect of play. What many couples do not realize is that often they engage in zero-sum game playing. This particular type of game is based on competition sports, meaning that if one person wins, another loses. In relationships, if placed in this situation, life is made acrimonious because the issues of fairness, tolerance, and trust are not established. Couples need to be taught non-zero-sum games in which no one person wins or loses simultaneously. In other words, "losses and gains do not cancel each other out. This means that their sum may lie above or below zero" (Gladding, 2005, p. 178). Teaching couples how to cooperate within the counseling relationship so that they can cooperate outside of the counseling relationship is an important part of relationship growth. For example, sharing household chores allows couples to further enjoy their relationship with one another as well as with their children.

Humor, if used in a healthy manner, can also strengthen a couple's relationship (Eckstein, Junkins, & McBrien, 2003). There is a physical benefit to healthy humor in addition to the emotional benefits. Humor and laughter can have immense effects on the immune system as well as lower blood pressure, trigger beta endorphins (which can induce euphoria), and increase muscle extension. On the other side of the coin is unhealthy or "toxic humor" (Eckstein et al., 2003, p. 302). This type of humor has many negative consequences within relationships. Toxic humor is "demeaning, degrading, or is designed to be aggressive or show superiority over the other person" (Eckstein et al., 2003, p. 302). It is important for couples to understand the differences between healthy and unhealthy humor. By coming to an understanding of how and when to use play, humor, and laughter, couples can increase their understanding of the issues presented and use these techniques as a way to encourage and support each another as they build a stronger relationship.

One specific exercise discussed by Eckstein and colleagues (2003, p. 303) is entitled "Belly Laughter for Couples":

> Stand facing your partner. Place one hand on your partner's arm or shoulder. Place the other hand on your belly (or theirs if you prefer). Look your partner in the eyes and, on the count of three, begin to laugh. Fake it until it becomes the real thing. Cut loose with your "pretend" laughter so it is deep and belly shaking. After you stop laughing, pause and feel the feelings you have inside. Pay attention to the feelings you have for your partner. Enjoy them a moment and then share some of those feelings with one another. Wind up with a nice, warm hug. If you begin and end your days this way, your relationship will benefit and so will you.

The power of levity many times brings insight, as well as tension relief, into the situation and creates an intense experience (Gladding, 2002). Furthermore, using these techniques provides counselors with an opportunity to help promote positive change for the couple.

All techniques described in this chapter offer opportunities for counselors to treat couples based on their unique presenting issues while drawing on the creativity and skill of each counselor. All techniques can be adapted to meet couples' needs. Remember that some of the techniques may require additional training.

CONCLUSION

This chapter is devoted to treatment strategies for couples that can be used within the framework of the integrative couples model. We have focused attention on a variety of strategies based on cognitive, emotional, and behavioral aspects of functioning. Of particular importance are the nonverbal strategies such as dance and movement, psychodrama, art therapy, and music therapy because these methods can be very effective with couples who are frustrated with traditional forms of talk therapy. These methods offer new possibilities for expression that help couples move forward when stuck in their conflicts. All strategies, however, must be based in your theoretical framework and must enhance relational functioning. Otherwise, they are merely a collection of activities that are not goal related and do not help achieve overall relational success.

8

Communication and Relationship Education

KEY CONCEPTS

- Good communication is essential for problem solving, sharing information, and support in the couple relationship.
- The history of communication in couples therapy includes a strong influence from social learning theory and other skills-training approaches.
- The work of John Gottman and associates has had a major impact on couples work. He has traced specific communication problems and strengths to divorce proneness.
- Besides communication training, couples need skills in learning to negotiate and to increase the amount of positive interactions.
- Nonverbal communication plays a special role in a couple's communication and can accentuate a couple's messages or create a roadblock.
- There appear to be gender differences in communication that may play a role in the ways couples misunderstand each other.
- Self-disclosure is an interpersonal skill that some couples need to address if they wish to be more intimate.
- The linear model of communication allows us to look at the key features of sender/receiver, feedback, and lets us examine the importance of intent and impact of messages.
- Communication is misunderstood because people are indirect in their sending of messages. They also play games, create distance, and erect smokescreens with communication.
- Often communication is disturbed because there are hidden agendas that the couple needs to address directly but have not been brought out into the open. This includes unspoken dreams.
- Communication can be assessed in several ways including the use of inventories, through identifying barriers, and with video recording.

- Communication barriers are standard patterns identified by experts, which couples can use to examine their own interaction.
- Positive communication skills are just as important. The general approach has been to present these in psychoeducational groups, but they can be taught in an ordinary couple's therapy session.
- Several packaged communication training programs for couples and many marriage enrichment seminars are available.

"I MISS YOU MOST WHEN WE ARE TOGETHER"

Communication is the currency of the intimate relationship. It connects, reassures, alerts, and comforts. Yet, on a very practical level, communication also allows couples to discuss and solve problems and exchange important information. For example, a couple who cannot disclose their feelings toward each other will have difficulty discussing sex. If they constantly use blaming as a method for problem solving, they will have difficulty navigating the course of parenthood. Couples who cannot communicate will often end up in cycles of unfinished business if they cannot bring disagreements to agreements. When couples have open lines of communication, they can support each other and be sounding boards for personal and work problems.

While recognizing that good communication is essential to a good relationship, most of the time, when we talk about communication in couples work, we are referring to breakdowns and impasses. For decades, therapists and couples say that communication is the most common and destructive problem in troubled marriages (Jacobson, Waldron, & Moore, 1980). Looking at this the other way around, one thing we discover is that when couples have other kinds of problems, they develop communication problems too.

Couples tend to communicate less when they are having a serious problem. They detach and lose touch because the price of becoming emotionally aroused is too high. Because less information is exchanged, possibilities for misunderstanding increase. It is truly a "Catch-22." Communication can heal problems between people, but when couples are troubled, their communication becomes impoverished in quality and quantity and they become less able to use the tools that can help them. Because communication is so vital to the couple relationship, you might want to consider the questions in Box 8.1 before you read the rest of this chapter. These questions provide an opportunity for reflection about how you might communicate as part of a couple.

COMMUNICATION AS SKILLS

A major emphasis in communication enhancement has been to look at communication as a set of skills to be learned and to provide them in workshop and group formats (Crowe & Ridley, 1990; Hunt, Hof, & DeMaria, 1998). By the end of the 20th century, nearly a third of U.S. adults had attended some form of relationship

---

Box 8.1
Questions to Consider

1. Suppose you are married, living together, engaged, or involved in an intimate relationship. On a scale of 1 to 5, with 5 being the most difficult to discuss, rate each of the following topics on how uncomfortable it would be to talk about the issue with your partner:
   a. Your feeling that your partner spends too much money
   b. Your need to spend more time together
   c. Your sexual preferences
   d. Your partner's sexual likes and dislikes
   e. Your need to have privacy
   f. Your negative feelings about your partner's family
   g. Your partner's personal cleanliness
   h. Your partner's bad habits
   i. Your worst fears
   j. Your past relationships

2. If you needed to talk to your intimate partner about one of the more difficult issues in the list above, what might stop you from bringing up the problem? Discuss your answers with fellow learners.

3. Draw three concentric circles on a sheet of paper. Place a dot in the center of the innermost circle. Think of the outer ring as acquaintances, the middle ring as friends, and the inner ring as your closest confidantes. What sorts of things do you discuss with the acquaintances, versus friends and confidantes? How many people are there on this inner circle? Can you confide everything in this group, or are there many things you keep to yourself? What keeps you from including more people in your inner circle? Compare your answers with members of the opposite gender. Do you see any patterns or differences?

4. Do you think there might be other ways of increasing communication in couples rather than teaching them new skills? Write down some things you might have done to improve the quality of a relationship that did not involve either person learning a new behavior.

---

education (Halford & Moore, 2002). In most of these enrichment/education programs, couples are taught to communicate less defensively, negotiate, and solve problems. In this chapter, we refer to them as communication-training programs but elsewhere they might be called marital education or marriage enrichment.

In the last 10 years, John Gottman and his colleagues have challenged the assumption that communication training really helps couples. Drawing on his considerable research, Gottman in his book *The Marriage Clinic: A Scientifically Based Marital Therapy* (1999) asserts that successful couples, who he calls "masters of marriage," do not communicate the way that communication-training programs instruct couples to communicate. His assumption is that communication training should be based on what successful couples do, not what experts think they should do. He has carefully analyzed couples and has been very successful in identifying those who stay together and those who will divorce. He has also criticized the relapse rates of many of these programs and the lack of empirical support for their claims.

In addition to this rebuke of the many couples communication programs, Gottman also rejects the idea that problem solving should be the major focus (Miller, Wackman, & Nunnally, 1983). He says that 69% of the problems that couples discuss are perpetual, having to do with personality and other basic differences (Gottman et al., 2002). Because the majority of what couples disagree upon is unsolvable, couples need to learn to live with most problems, like one learns to live with chronic back problems (Gottman, 1999). Gottman believes that couples need to establish a positive dialogue about problems rather than solve them.

Gottman's research cannot be adequately summarized here, and every couples counselor should be thoroughly familiar with his work. Gottman is an innovator who uses quantitative methods to back up his claims, and he has prompted other relationship education programs to follow suit. Whether one adopts his total program or not, there is a library of nearly 50 interventions that can be incorporated into an integrative approach (see Gottman, et al., 2002). Later in the chapter, we describe Gottman's methods in a little more detail, along with some other popular relationship education programs.

A SHORT HISTORY OF COMMUNICATION IN COUPLES THERAPY

As early as the 1950s, Gregory Bateson had noticed that dysfunctional families had dysfunctional communication patterns. Among the first to be identified was the "double-bind." The double-bind is exemplified in the old joke where a parent buys the son two shirts. When he tries on the blue one, the parent asks, "You didn't like the red one?" No matter what you do, you can't win. Such communications lead people to frustration and withdrawal in intimate relationships (Bateson, Jackson, Haley, & Weakland, 1956).

Virginia Satir, the family therapist, extended the work of the "communication school" of family therapy pioneered by Bateson and popularized it among therapists (Satir et al., 1991). One of her main contributions was that she helped families focus on changing their communication patterns and not on healing their personalities. This was a true paradigm shift from the psychodynamic viewpoint that was built on identifying the interlocking pathologies of the members. This led other theorists to examine the pathology of communication between people rather than "in" people.

Eric Berne (1961), founder of transactional analysis (TA) in the 1960s, focused therapy on the "transactions," or exchanges, of recognition and affection between people and the elaborate games involved in getting attention and intimacy. He diagrammed communication patterns between client ego states and saw bad communication mainly as "crossed transactions" and good communication as coming from "complementary transactions." For example, complementary adult-to-adult transactions are good for exchanging information ("Do we have enough money to pay the bills?" "Yes, we do"). Child-to-child transactions are necessary for a couple to have fun together. A crossed transaction exists when she says, "What do you want for breakfast?" (adult to adult) and he replies, "Why should you care?" (child to parent). Berne got us to look at the *intentions* and the payoffs involved in elaborate communication games.

The behaviorists had a major impact on the development of communication training for couples by taking communication out of the realm of therapy and reclassifying it as skills. Behaviorists such as Weiss (1975), O'Leary and Turkewitz (1978), and Gottman and colleagues (1976) made contributions to research and training by identifying the specific skills involved in better communication for couples and in conducting research on the effectiveness of such programs.

In 1994 Gottman turned his attention to what communication patterns were associated with marriages that succeed and fail. His research suggests that successful couples maintain a 5:1 ratio of positive to negative interactions. Gottman compares this conceptualization to taking the pH of soil. It does not matter how much acid is added to the soil, the ph remains the same if a neutralizing amount of alkaline is thrown in. When the negative interactions increase beyond this magic 5:1 ratio, a marriage destabilizes. This formula accounts for an enigma we often encounter: those volatile couples who argue a lot but stay together. According to Gottman, stable marriages of this type have a counterbalancing helping of passion and positive interactions.

Gottman then asked the question "What were stable couples doing that maintained this balance?" He found that stable couples were much less extreme when expressing negative feelings. Overall, they showed less contempt, were less critical, and were better listeners. But more important, these couples showed their "positivity" by openly expressing positive feelings.

COMMUNICATION FUNDAMENTALS

Nonverbal Communication

Therapists have long known that nonverbal communication can be as powerful as the words people use. In addition, one of the most important aspects of our messages is the emotional tone. Mehrabian (1972) found that about 7% of the total feelings conveyed are done so by verbal means, 38% is vocal, and 55% is facial. Nonverbal communication adds the punctuation to our verbal statements. Saying you are concerned about someone and putting your arm around them can accentuate your message. Emotional intimacy is communicated largely through nonverbal communication. Therapists face clients squarely, mostly show open, uncrossed postures, and maintain eye contact for the purpose of increasing intimacy and facilitating self-disclosure by their clients.

Earlier it was pointed out that distressed couples communicate less when they are having problems. This is also true for nonverbal communication. Distressed couples use far less eye contact than those who are not having problems.

Satir often asked couples to pay attention to their physical messages. She felt that when sending a message to the partner, the nonverbal aspect could communicate sincerity and "anchor" the verbal message. Satir would sometimes demonstrate this to couples by asking them to sit back to back and discuss a problem. She then gave them a contrast by asking them to sit eye-to-eye, hold hands, and repeat the verbal message. Nonverbal messages can also be manipulations or can be used to dominate or increase the emotional distance in a relationship. A too-common family pattern is when one member is a "rage-aholic" who uses his or her aggressive nonverbals such as loud voice tone and angry postures to get what is wanted.

It has often been said that we cannot not communicate. We are constantly communicating, but listeners may not easily recognize all our nonverbal behaviors as communication. In couples, very often one member is not aware that his or her communication style is aggressive or has some other effect on their partner. By watching videotapes or receiving other kinds of feedback, couples can become more aware of the messages they are sending. Couples can easily misinterpret the nonverbals of their partners. Research suggests that couples who are having problems, "distressed couples" as they are called in research studies, often interpret all kinds of messages as more negatively than the partner intended. This must also be true of nonverbals. Sometimes the raising of eyebrows, the tone of voice, silence, or an inflection can be enough to set off an argument when one member of a couple reads the nonverbal as extremely negative. In couples, a good example is the ways couples communicate about sex. Couples may use words to initiate or refuse sexual interaction. But nonverbals are used more frequently than verbal methods (Sprecher & McKinney, 1993). Given that nonverbal communication can be ambiguous and the sexual relationship may be imbued with tension, misunderstandings can quickly develop. When communication about sex is more satisfactory, the sexual relationship and the relationship as a whole are judged as more satisfactory by the couple (Cupach & Comstock 1990).

Gender Differences in Communication

Much has been made of male–female differences in communication. Whatever one's evaluation of this pop psychology book, *Men Are From Mars, Women Are From Venus* (Gray, 1993), it has struck a chord with an American public who believes that men and women do not communicate well because of their different gender styles. Deborah Tannen in her books, *Gender and Discourse* (1994) and *You Just Don't Understand: Women and Men in Conversation* (2001), addresses these differences in a very scholarly way. One of Tannen's contentions is that men communicate facts (report talk) and women communicate to maintain relationships (rapport talk). These two different agendas cause confusion. When she says, "Sit down, I want to talk to you," she may mean, "Let's be close for a minute." His response is likely to be, "What do you want to talk about?" Another of Tannen's discoveries is that women cover one topic in depth while men tend to cover many.

In addition, women see men as not listening when they are, but men are not necessarily giving off the cues that they are listening. This is typical of the conversational culture when men talk to men. What women find belittling in a conversation with their peers, men accept as much less negative when it comes from their friends. When women talk with each other, they expect support and agreement. When men talk to women, they often give a competing view, which women find disturbing. Tannen (2001) concludes that male–female conversation is cross-cultural communication.

Gottman's (1999) research has revealed that divorce could be predicted in relationships in which men do not accept influence from (share power with) women. Whether the wife accepted influence from the husband predicted nothing. This is probably because the wives in the study were already sharing power with their husbands. According to Gottman (see Coan, Gottman, Babcock, & Jacobson, 1997), this does not mean that the husbands were merely going along with whatever the wife wanted but were striving for "give and take."

Gottman has also found that men think about the recent negative interactions and hurts more than women do. Men also escalate their negative emotions when women complain. During conflicts, women are more likely to criticize and men to withdraw emotionally when the emotional climate gets too hot. This has been called the female criticism–male stonewalling concept (Gottman et al., 2002). Gottman and Levenson (1988) hypothesize that men react more strongly to stress than women. They found that in relationships in which men were able to calm themselves down or were soothed by their wives, there was a more positive outcome in the relationship.

With this knowledge in mind and knowing that women are more likely to bring up problems than men (Ball, Cowan, & Cowan, 1995), Gottman and colleagues recommend a "softened startup, which is mainly aimed at women. *Softened* means that the problem bringer does not begin with criticism but with language about a personal problem. This is very similar to recommendations that other relationship programs have about criticism and blaming versus sending an "I" message or personal concern.

Self-Disclosure and Male–Female Relationships

We often define our relationships as close or distant. By *close,* often we mean the degree of self-disclosure that exists in the relationship. Self-disclosure normally deepens over time in a relationship, but sometimes it develops rapidly. Self-disclosure in a relationship means sharing one's emotions as they are felt but also includes such things as admitting to bad habits and sharing aspects of one's past and one's hopes, dreams, and ambitions (Waring, 1988). Where couples are concerned, there appears to be a positive relationship between disclosure and marital satisfaction (Hendrick & Hendrick, 2000). Because of the relationship between intimacy and self-disclosure, many marriage enrichment programs try to improve relationships by helping couples disclose more to each other.

Self-disclosure has been considered important to the well-being of relationships and as a general barometer of mental health (Jourard, 1964; Pennebaker, 1990). On the other hand, we find that disclosure is not always helpful and can be destructive (Gottman, 1994). When unrestrained, self-disclosure can cause severe damage. Telling the brutal "truth" perpetuates many wrongs. Sharing too many negatives about the relationships can lead to dissatisfaction (Levinger & Senn, 1967). More often, self-disclosure causes a problem in a relationship when it is too little, leading to a lack of intimacy and misunderstanding by the other person.

Fitzpatrick (1988) has identified three patterns of disclosure in relationships. "Traditionals" are couples who are very interdependent. They share many things, but where conflict is concerned, they communicate nonassertively. "Independents," on the other hand, also share a lot but have separate lives and tend to be assertive and confrontive in their communication. Finally, "separates" are much less interdependent, are limited in their assertiveness with each other, and avoid open conflict. These patterns may keep the couple in a state of homeostasis and allow for the degree of closeness that the couple desires.

Women are more disclosing in same-sex friendships than men and in general have closer relationships. Research suggests that women disclose more throughout their lives (Hendrick & Hendrick, 2000). For example, it is acceptable for girls to shed tears, but such expression for a teenage boy would be considered weak. Hendrick and Hendrick (2000) claim that penalties for self-disclosure of emotions are also higher for adult men than for adult women. Crying on the job or losing one's temper carries a greater stigma for a male, so men learn not to express. Male images of success and strength show men not as performing despite fear and self-doubt, but like James Bond, these heroes laugh in the face of death. The problem comes in a marital situation in which the woman highly values self-disclosure and wants it from a man. In the typical case, the man values it less and produces less than what is wanted by his mate.

The Linear Model

The well-known conceptualization of the communication process is called the linear model. The model is useful because it simplifies a single set of communications and allows us to look at them as if they are in a linear/temporal sequence. He says, she says, he responds, she responds. In reality, verbal and nonverbal messages are flowing back and forth between sender and receiver simultaneously. While she is speaking, he is turning away. She responds to that and changes her message. Although recognizing this back-and-forth flow is useful, there is no good way to depict this, so we use the linear model because of its simplicity and teachability.

The linear model illustrates that there are listeners and receivers, messages, channels, and feedback loops (Figure 8.1). A sender originates a message and sends it through a particular channel to the receiver. A channel is the way a sender encodes a message. Encoding is done because of the past experiences of the sender. For example, one might learn to send an "I message" rather than a "you message." An "I message" such as "I get annoyed when I see those dirty dishes piling up" is likely to be better received than "You are a filthy slob." But the channel someone chooses is often based on his or her beliefs and family history. In one couple who we worked with, she came from an Italian family where great emphasis was placed on being honest and straightforward. He came from a rather quiet Maine Protestant family. When expressing her anger, he was surprised to find that

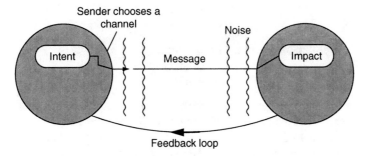

Figure 8.1   The linear model of communication

she did not quietly confide her concerns but instead engaged in name-calling and explosive outbursts of emotions. The channel she chose to send her messages of anger were based on her cultural/family history, and she couldn't really understand why this was so unpalatable to her husband because what she said was "true" and because that's how everyone in her family acted. People encode their messages and send them through familiar channels. They assume that decoding will be easy. For example, a husband once said to his wife, "You are a good person to be away from." He chose a confusing channel for his communication. He was trying to express that he felt comfortable when he was away from his wife and looked forward to seeing her on his return. She decoded it as "I like being away from you."

Communication would be easy if we were only sending what we meant to say. But *noise* interferes with our reception or decoding of the message. Just as in a radio broadcast, we cannot hear the message when static is interfering. We cannot hear intimate messages when we are listening to thoughts and past experiences that distort what others are saying. Noise is shown as wavy lines on Figure 8.1, and they appear to be outside of the sender and the receiver. But in reality, noise is anything that interferes—including loud sounds in the environment; a hearing disability in one of the partners; one person worrying about another appointment, perceptions; and cognitions; and past experiences that make it hard to read the intention of the message. As we said before, cultural and family background provides noise and filters the messages coming in from others.

The fact that there is noise in human communication makes a feedback loop necessary. A feedback loop is actually "metacommunication," communication about communication. The feedback loop is a statement by the receiver to the sender asking for confirmation about the sender's message:

"Am I hearing that you do not intend to go to the party with me?"
"Are you saying you want to be alone right now?"
"What I am picking up is that you would rather invite your family here for Thanksgiving rather than go to my parents' house. Is that right?"

Feedback is a nonblameful restatement of the message heard and asks a question for confirmation. It is best constructed so that it does not raise the defensiveness of the other person. Sometimes anger masquerades as feedback as in the following examples:

"You couldn't care less about me, could you?"
"You don't want to spend any time with me, do you?"
"You hate my family, isn't that true?"

The questions in these examples are rhetorical. They pretend to ask for confirmation, but they are really expressing anger. This is what makes intimate communication so confusing. We respond to the verbal message "You hate my family, isn't that true?" by saying "I like your family" rather than responding "You feel hurt and angry about my plans to spend Thanksgiving with my side of the family." Very often, the feeling is the real message one person is trying to send.

Feedback: The Way Out

The emergency exit from confusing cycles of bad communication is to focus on the feedback loop (see Figure 8.1). According to Gottman and his colleagues (1976, p. 2), feedback is "when the listener tells the speaker about the impact a message had." By comparing *impact* and *intent*, then we can see where miscommunication occurred.

Case Example: Levon and Maria

The case of Levon and Maria illustrates a simple but common miscommunication sequence, which allows us to examine impact and intent. Figure 8.2 shows the linear model applied to this couple.

Levon: I heard that the party isn't going to be that good.

Levon's statement is chosen as a way of easing into a difficult conversation. He may be afraid to say "I'm tired; I want to stay home" or "I feel more like going to a movie." He chose a channel that he thought would open up conversation without committing himself to a course of action. Another way of saying this is that Levon's *intent* was different than the message he sent. Figure 8.2 shows Maria and Levon's exchange in terms of *impact* and *intent*.

Maria [option 1]: You don't want to spend any time with me.

Maria feels angry and, instead of asking for feedback in a nonblameful way, accuses Levon, hoping that he will feel guilty. Perhaps she is just retaliating because she feels

Figure 8.2   One-way communication showing intent and impact

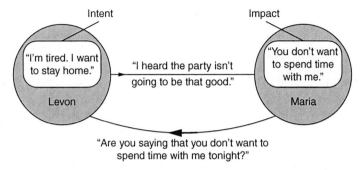

Figure 8.3   Two-way communication: Maria using the feedback loop to check intent of message

hurt. The *impact* on Maria's side was based on the confusing message that she heard, but it was perceived by her in a much more negative way than was intended.

> *Maria* [option 2]: Are you saying you don't want to go to spend time with me tonight?

(See Figure 8.3.)

Using the feedback loop in 8.4, she clarified the message that Levon was really sending:

> *Levon:* No, I am just tired. I want to stay home.

(See Figure 8.4.)

Now that the couple better understands Levon's basic message they are on the road to clear communication. Although they may not have solved the problem about whether they are staying home or going to the party, some of their needs are more out in the open. Much of the content of couples communication training is aimed at teaching couples this process: to stop the action, obtain a clear idea of the intent and impact of messages, and to work out reasonable compromises.

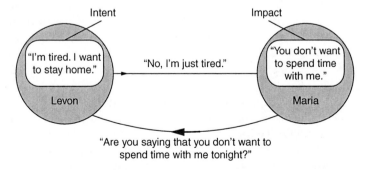

Figure 8.4   Two-way communication: Levon responding honestly to Maria's feedback

Games, Smokescreens, Dreams, and Manipulations

Referring again to the impact, or perception, of Maria's that Levon does not want to spend any time with her, her underlying feeling of disappointment and perhaps anger in option 2 is translated into an accusation: "You don't want to spend any time with me, do you?" The purpose of the accusation might be to make Levon feel guilty. If he feels guilty, then he will accede to her wishes. Maria may not be aware of the fact that she is manipulating (asking Levon to act because of guilt). The problem with this communication is that Levon is not straightforward, Maria's response raises Levon's defenses, and it gets off the topic of going to the party and on to who cares about whom. The therapist must watch for these "games" as Eric Berne called them. They can be elaborate ways to get attention or other needs met or bring excitement into the relationship or merely a confusing loop where both members feel frustrated and alone.

The impact of Maria's response to Levon's message may seem unreasonable to an outsider. Why must she be so unreasonable? But Levon's message may have particular meaning for Maria. There may be a hidden agenda, an unfulfilled dream, or underlying issue. For example, Maria may be feeling ignored in general. Rather than dealing with "feeling ignored" separately, it emerges whenever the couple tries to communicate. It is not only *this* party but also all the times that Levon has not wanted to go out with her that she is responding to. Similarly, why has Levon shaped his message in such an obscure way? Why doesn't he just honestly state his preference? Once communication has clarified the original intent of Levon's message, the couple must then evaluate why this message had such an impact on Maria and why Levon was so cagey.

Indirectness and Culture

Why do people send such indirect messages? Why can't Levon tell Maria that he is tired in the first place? Sometimes the answer lies in one's upbringing. Tannen (1986) claims that people choose indirect channels because they are afraid of the effect that their words will have on the other person. So we drop hints to see how the other person feels. In Levon's case, he may feel that if he says he is tired, Maria will go to the party without him or that she will be angry and he will have to contend with that for the rest of the evening. So rather than expressing his feelings, he tests the water with his initial statement. Levon may also have been willing to go to the party and did not wish Maria to feel that he would be miserable.

Politeness is a cultural matter. Tannen (1994) has suggested that the stereotype of Jewish people as "pushy" may be due to their directness and confrontive communication style, which conflicts with the indirect Anglo-Saxon style. An Indian acquaintance related another example. Within his north Indian culture, one did not make direct requests of one's parents. Such a thing would be met with silence and would be considered very unkind. It implies that the parents are not taking adequate care of their children. Consequently, when he wanted a radio, he planned a hint-dropping strategy to his father, which extended over several days. On one day, he would say, "You know on the radio there are many interesting broadcasts about current events." On another day, he might have related the fact that a friend with a radio had cited one of the programs in a school term paper. One day his father told him that he had chosen a radio and that it could be picked up at a certain shop. This may seem an elaborate way to send a message, but it maintained the respectful relationship between parent and child and the message was communicated.

Cultural problems in communication often occur because of different use of nonverbals. We are all familiar with the fact that certain nonverbal gestures in one country have opposite meanings in another. But communication, verbal and non-verbal, is full of many nuances that are not so easy to detect. Voice tone, volume, voice speed, and choice of words all convey special culturally specific meanings (Tannen, 1986). Recently, I (Mark) found myself becoming annoyed at an acquaintance from Germany. I was asking him about various aspects of his country, and he very often responded, "Of course!" These words and intonation in America suggest that the speaker is correcting the other person for asking such a stupid question. This was not the intention of his message as it turned out. He had learned "Of course!" as a synonym for the word *yes*. This is what makes therapy with someone from a different culture such a challenge. In a couple where each member comes from a different cultural background, there are linguistic and value differences that can be sources of enrichment or conflict.

ASSESSMENT OF COMMUNICATION PROBLEMS AND STRENGTHS

There are three avenues to the identification of couple communication strengths and difficulties. One method is to look at questionnaires such as the Primary Communication Inventory (PCI), a 25-item self-report inventory (Navran, 1967), or the PREPARE/ENRICH scales, which are commercially available. (Some of the screening instruments listed in Chapter 5 contain communication scales.) A second direction is observational coding systems in which videotaped records of a couple's reactions are examined and coded to analyze communication. A third, more commonly used assessment is to look for standard maladaptive patterns and strengths, identified by couples experts, which we summarize in the next section. Inventories and identifying patterns both have their shortcomings. Research suggests that both self-report and classifying communication patterns into types fail to get at the real nuances when compared with the videotapes of couples trying to communicate (Baucom & Adams, 1987). Not all couple communication problems fit very neatly into the categories that we identify. But observational coding is far too time-consuming for a clinician, and a short sample can be very unreliable about how the couple really communicates. Both of these methods tend to ignore the cognitive aspects of the communication. That is, what did each person mean by their message? What did they perceive the intentions of their partner to be? One way out of this issue is to use screening inventories and report back to the couple the results as a starting point in the discussion. Even in a 1-hour therapy session, a clinician can include 10–15 minutes of video assessment of the couple's communication.

Videotaped Assessment

The presence of a video camera in the therapy office sets everyone's nerves on edge, even the therapist's. If the therapist can introduce the presence of a video camera into the session as a natural part of therapy, then clients will be more receptive. One way to do this is to have the camera in the room with the lens cap on for several sessions before the taping takes place. Begin taping early on in the session, and when some particularly good interaction between the couple has been filmed, the therapist can stop, perhaps halfway through the session, and play back the tape for the couple. One way that the therapist can get clients to look at intentions and perceptions is to stop the tape and ask the following kinds of questions:

"What were your intentions when you said, . . . ?"
"Tell your spouse what you mean by . . . ."
"Were you suggesting a change, or were you trying to hurt your spouse?"
"Was this statement constructive or destructive?"
"How effective were you in getting your point across? What ways would work better?"
"If you were going to use a listening response, what would you have said instead?"

Here are some actual examples from a recent session:

"Fred, when Sara said, 'Just like always, I have to take care of everything,' how did you feel?"
"Sara, you perceive yourself as having to take care of all the difficult tasks. When you say to Fred, 'I have to take care of everything,' what are you requesting from Fred?"
"Sara, can you think of another way of expressing how angry you are and asking for a change?"

Gottman, who helped pioneer videotaping in looking at couple's communication, likes to see them on tape for an entire weekend if possible. But he also recommends a 10-minute observation session during a normal couples counseling session (Gottman, 1999). In its most simple form, the clinician could merely watch and record positive behaviors as the couple talks with each other about a significant issue confronting them. The therapist then gives the couple feedback on their behavior with suggestions for improvement. This part of the session could take about 20–25 minutes.

Who Should Receive Communication Training?

Another important aspect of assessment in communication training is to determine which kinds of couples ought to be included and excluded from such training. For couples in which there is a significant substance-abuse problem, they will not benefit. This issue must be treated first. Where there is violence in the couple relationship, communication training is only a Band-Aid approach. Violence must be treated separately. Improving a couple's communication is no substitute for treating violent individuals. Communication training is also usually a waste of time for couples who have recently experienced an affair. That wound will need some healing before couples can address other issues.

COMMUNICATION PROBLEMS IN COUPLES

Common Problems

This section describes some of the common roadblocks to communication that have been identified by researchers and couples therapists. Most communication programs help couples identify these "negative skills" as well as building "positive skills." Gottman (1994) says that the most negative communication patterns fall under four broad categories, which he calls the "Four Horsemen of the Apocalypse." The presence of these helped predict divorce with 85% accuracy. They are the following:

1. *Criticism versus complaint.* This is the problem of attacking the person rather than the behavior. Usually this takes the form of an accusation: "I can't have any fun because you don't like to dance." A complaint might be "I really enjoy dancing. I wish you and I could dance more or take dancing lessons."

2. *Contempt.* The difference between criticism and contempt is the *intention* to psychologically wound or hurt your partner. Insults and name-calling, hostile humor, mockery, and contemptuous body language are the signs of contempt.

3. *Defensiveness.* When defensiveness sets in, the couple is not acting as a team. They deny responsibility, make excuses, and use methods such as cross-complaining. Couples at this stage have a difficult time solving problems because they leave many things hanging as they walk away in frustration.

4. *Stonewalling.* When couples reach the point of giving up, one member may turn into a "stone wall" and remove him- or herself from the conversation. Turning into a stone wall conveys contempt and is both retaliation and a gesture of helplessness. Many people "stonewall" occasionally during the course of a relationship but habitual stonewalling can become a serious problem.

Other Maladaptive Problems

Mind reading   Mind reading occurs when one member of the couple consistently acts on the perceived intent of the other person without using the feedback loop. For example,

"I didn't even tell you about the free tickets to the ballet because I knew you wouldn't want to go."
"I could tell by the look on your face that you didn't want to eat at that restaurant."

Mind reading occurs in couples that have known each other for a long time and those that have been together a short time. It is a short circuit in the communication process because one person reacts to a message without checking out its intent.

The panel discussion   The panel discussion is a tendency for a couple to be excessively rational in their discussions so that the underlying feelings are not expressed. Such couples may be dual career, highly educated, or merely place a great deal of value on being civil and avoiding conflict. An example might be the following:

> *Vincent:* The thing that is the most troublesome is that Denise never calls me and tells me that she is going to be late. I don't know how to plan the evening. [*Intent:* I am annoyed and lonely.]
>
> *Denise:* I would suggest that you assume that if I am not home by seven o'clock that you can make plans that don't include me. [*Impact:* I feel angry and pressured.]

Treatment involves helping them express and reflect feelings.

Being right   The more unhappy a couple is, the more they believe that they are right and justified in their viewpoint (Noller & Vernardos, 1986). Although inflexibility can be the problem of individual members, it can be addressed as a couple's problem in which each person is trying to be right.

The summarizing self syndrome, or cocktail listening.   Like people at cocktail parties, some couples are rehearsing what they want to say and are waiting until the other person stops talking so that they can say their piece (McKay et al., 1994). The summarizing self syndrome (SSS), identified by Gottman (1994), is another way of describing this interaction. It pertains to couples who continue to reiterate their same complaint without reacting to their partner's statement. For example,

> *Renee:* I said "ABC."
> *Manny:* I said "XYZ."
> *Renee:* But I said "ABC."
> *Manny:* But I said "XYZ."

Cross-complaining   Cross-complaining sounds like a response to the other person's complaint, but it is a defensive reaction rather than responding to the concern. Cross-complaining is answering the other person's complaint with one of your own:

> "I wish you would not spend so much money on golf."
> "Well, I wish you wouldn't invite your mother over every week."

Incongruent messages   Incongruent messages contain positive and negative aspects or contain verbal and nonverbal messages that do not carry the same meaning. For example, one member of a couple verbally encourages the other person to talk and meanwhile continues to watch television.

The "stinger" pattern   The stinger is an incongruent message containing a positive statement with a criticism at the end:

"Sure, you want to spend a lot of time with me now, but why couldn't we
  have done this five years ago?"

Name-calling and nonsupportive statements   It would seem to go without
saying that character assassination and questioning the other person's motives and
abilities would build greater walls between people. In many families, this is unfortunately the norm. People who originate in such families bring this kind of communication pattern to a marriage and have to become aware of the damaging
nature of such insults.

Not hearing the positives   For many distressed couples, there is a common
cycle in which compliments, praise, and recognition are given, but the other
member hears the negative aspects of the communication. Therapists like to "stop
action" when they find that couples are responding only to the negative aspects of
the message. Couples can then become more aware of the intent and impact of
their communication.

Kitchen sinking   When a couple begins an argument on a certain topic,
sometimes other issues that they have been saving up are thrown in. Without
some restraint, everything but the kitchen sink is complained about at once.

Harsh start-up   In Gottman's research (1999), only about 4% of negative
interactions changed course and became positive. Thus, how one starts the conversation is critical to how it ends. As we noted earlier, there are gender differences in how negativity is perceived and reacted to.

POSITIVE COMMUNICATION SKILLS

Repairs   According to Gottman (1999), repairs are efforts to keep the interaction going and soothe the partner. This can be done by smiling, using humor,
conceding a point, or recognizing the other's point of view. Couples who can
repair their conversations are more likely to stay in the relationship than those
who fail to repair. During videotaped segments, observers can count the number
of repair attempts that each person makes and discuss with the couple about how
to make more attempts and to respond favorably.

Perspective taking   Perspective taking is the ability to understand the point
of view of another. Perspective taking is similar to empathy except empathy seems
to include the ability to access the emotional experiences of others. Perspective
taking asks that we understand another's thinking and intellectually put ourselves
in another's place. Perspective taking seems to be important to good relationships.
Research suggests that in distressed marriages men are often low in perspective
taking (Long, 1993). This skill is a repair attempt that combats several negative
communication practices including "being right" and the SSS.

The speaker–listener technique   In the speaker–listener technique, couples take turns with the role of sender and receiver of communication. Couples are given the following instruction: A listener cannot become a speaker until the speaker indicates that he or she has been properly heard. Then the couple switches roles.

When you are a speaker, you

- Describe the problem in a nonblameful way.
- Stay on one topic.
- Express your feeling.
- Don't insult or criticize the other person.

When you are a listener, you

- Pay careful attention.
- Don't interrupt.
- Try and understand their perspective.
- Use good listening nonverbals.
- Reflect and paraphrase for accuracy (use the feedback loop).

The floor technique   The floor technique is designed to give couples feedback on the impact of their communication on the other person (Gottman et al., 1976). Couples first decide on an issue they wish to discuss. They then label three index cards. One says, "The Floor," another says "Positive," and the third is labeled "Negative." Whoever holds "The Floor" card is the speaker and talks without interruption until he or she is finished. The speaker may hand over "The Floor" at any time if asked. The listener holds up the "Negative" or "Positive" cards to let the speaker know the impact of the current message. When the listener holds up the "Negative" card, this often leads to a change of floor because the speaker now wants to get feedback on what was negative about their message. It is useful to stop the action at these points and see why intent and impact are not matching. At first, couples should practice with the therapist present, who serves as both a referee and coach.

Giving affection, praise, and admiration to your spouse   In Chapter 2, we reviewed the importance of increasing the positives in the relationship. When couples are troubled, they stop noticing the positives altogether. As recommended by the postmodern theories of psychotherapy, couples can view their relationship more positively if they are asked to notice the positives, the way the other person is trying, instead of noting only what is lacking in the relationship.

Editing: The art of being polite   We cited research earlier (Birchler et al., 1975) claiming that we are more polite to strangers than to those closest to us. Politeness in this context does not mean "walking on eggshells." It means editing out the negative aspects of one's messages and learning to pare it down to include only things that are constructive. Gottman and his colleagues (1976) recommend nine rules of politeness, which are summarized here:

1. Be direct: Say what you can do and want to do.
2. Show appreciation in a sincere and positive way.

3. Be considerate and courteous.
4. Show interest in the other person's activities. Listen and ask questions.
5. Say things you honestly feel and that might be important to your spouse.
6. When you feel you were wrong, admit it but don't criticize yourself because this requires your spouse to offer support.
7. Keep your focus on the present, not the past.
8. Let your spouse finish speaking before you respond.
9. Try to understand your spouse's point of view, his or her needs and desires.

Editing is the skill of looking at one's own statements and determining if they fit these nine rules of politeness. Couples can review transcripts, see videotapes, or give written responses to stock situations in order to learn to edit their responses according to the rules.

COMMUNICATION-TRAINING AND RELATIONSHIP EDUCATION PROGRAMS

A number of couple's communication and education programs (most often called marriage or marital education) are commercially available (L'Abate & Weinstein, 1997). Most are group psychoeducational formats that require some sort of certification for trainers. A complete listing of these is updated on the Smart Marriages website (www.smartmarriages.com). Through Smart Marriages, you can obtain certification for many of these programs at their annual convention and purchase recordings of the originators. In this section of the chapter, we briefly examine five of the major programs: Gottman's Sound Marital House theory, Olson's PREPARE/ENRICH, the PAIRS program, Markman and Stanley's PREP program, and Guerney's Relationship Enhancement system.

Sound Marital House

Gottman's research-based approach has been discussed throughout this chapter because of its contribution to communication in couples. Gottman and colleagues (see Gottman.com) offer couples workshops four times per year and training sessions for therapists who want to become certified in the Gottman method of working with couples. Gottman offers these workshops in Seattle, Washington, and training for therapists takes place around the country. There are more than 100 Gottman-certified therapists in the United States.

The workshop for couples is based on the Sound Marital House theory. The theory is relatively new and is graphically described as a seven-story house:

Story 1 (the house's foundation) is the "love map," which is a technique and admonition to get spouses to know each other better and periodically update their knowledge of each other.

Story 2 is the "fondness and admiration system," which is used to counter contempt.

Story 3 is "turning toward" versus "turning away." In daily contact, spouses set up a tendency to make contact and develop an emotional bank account with their spouse.

Story 4 is the "positive perspective," helping couples enter conflict situations with a positive orientation to the other so that previous negative interactions do not bias the person against their spouse's present responses.

Story 5 involves dealing with conflict. Part of this involves helping couples realize that some problems are perpetual and that they must adjust to each other.

Story 6 is "making dreams and aspirations come true." This phase involves helping couples recognize that if they want to keep an emotional connection, they must understand the other person's values and the symbolic nature of certain conflicts. The couple may not be able to compromise because they are gridlocked on some fundamental issues that must be confronted.

Story 7 is "creating shared meaning: dreams, narratives, rituals of connection, myths and metaphors." This involves two couple interviews where they discuss the meaning of emotions, roles, and goals. Culture clash and the family's own culture are explored. These narratives, myths, and metaphors have importance to the other six stories of the Sound Marital House.

PREPARE/ENRICH

PREPARE/ENRICH is an inventory-based program. Participating couples take a series of tests to learn more about each other and themselves. There is substantial research on the inventories and the program (see Olson & Olson, 1997). Counselors or clergy can be certified to deliver PREPARE/ENRICH training (see prepare-enrich.com) and can score their clients' inventories online. Based on the type of couple, a separate set of tests is available (see below), but they all assess the same 13 areas: communication, conflict resolution, personality issues, financial management, sexual expectations, marital satisfaction, leisure activities, children and parenting, family and friends, expectations/cohabitation issues, idealistic distortion, role relationship, and spiritual beliefs. The following tests are designed for different types of couples:

- PREPARE: premarital couples
- PREPARE-MC: premarital couples with children
- PREPARE-CC: cohabiting couples
- ENRICH: married couples
- MATE: couples over the age of 50

Because PREPARE/ENRICH is based on inventories, it is relatively easy to use with a single couple in a therapist's office. A group format is now available (Olson, Dyer, & Dyer, 1997). Couples can also purchase materials online and self-administer an aspect of the training independently.

Prevention and Relationship Enhancement Program

The Prevention and Relationship Enhancement Program (PREP) began in 1980 at the University of Denver and has its origins in the work of Gottman and his colleagues (1976). It has gone through several revisions and is now one of the best-researched couples enrichment programs (Halford & Moore, 2002). The long-term studies (3- and 4-year follow-ups) seem to show that couples who have gone through the program are more likely to stay together than controls and show less negative communication (Markman, Renick, Floyd, Stanley, & Clements, 1993). The program is skills based but also considers getting the proper attitude set for couples. It asks them to think about improving their relationship as skills that can be acquired. It asks them to consider small modifications and builds on successes. PREP uses research data to convince participants that real improvements are possible. PREP also comes in a Christian format called CPREP and a Low Income PREP for economically challenged individuals (frequently, women who come alone). PREP trainers can be trained in a 2- or 3-day training process. There is also a master certification to train trainers.

Some of the major topics addressed in the program include

The intent–impact model
Effective speaking and listening (speaker–listener format)
Destructive and constructive styles of communication
Giving specific feedback
Examining expectations that may affect the relationship
Hidden issues behind the surface topics
The role of fun in maintaining the relationship
Problem solving
Team building: positive ways to increase intimacy and commitment
Spiritual values of honor, respect, intimacy, and forgiveness
Communication in the sexual relationship
Practicing skills and maintaining skills

There are three formats for couples. The training can be given in a 1-day, a 2-day, or an extended format. In the extended format, 4 to 10 couples attend six weekly sessions lasting 2–2½ hours. In all formats, there are brief lectures on the topics listed above. Later, every couple is given a "communication consultant" who coaches them when they practice skills together in a separate room. In a large-group format, up to 60 couples come together for the lecture portion over one weekend. Couples normally stay at the hotel and practice the skills on their own in their rooms (Floyd, Markman, Kelly, Blumberg, & Stanley, 1995). There are also two trade books used in the course. The first is *Fighting for Your Marriage* (Markman, Stanley, & Blumberg, 1994), and the most recent is *12 Hours to a Great Marriage* (Markman, Stanley, Jenkins, Blumberg, & Whitely, 2004). A number of video and audio materials are available on the Prepinc.com website.

Relationship Enhancement

Bernard Guerney, Jr., and colleagues (Guerney, Brock, & Coufal, 1986) have developed a relationship enhancement (RE) program based on a psychoeducational model of therapy. They believe that most human problems can be reframed as skills deficits. The technique taught to couples is mostly communication skills but requires a trained facilitator to recognize and reflect feelings. The company, called

The National Institute for Relationship Enhancement, has a website (nire.org) that advertises weekend workshops for couples and certification for trainers.

Basic Principles Taught in the Program

Expressive skills (teaching appropriate self-disclosure)

Empathic skills (teaching listening and reflecting feelings)

Mode-switching skills (learning to change from listener to speaker depending on who has the problem)

Problem–conflict resolution skills (creative problem solving, negotiation, and compromise)

Self-change skills (self-monitoring and setting personal goals)

Helping others change skills (supporting the other person's goals)

Generalization-transfer skills (using skills learned in other interactions to help the couple relationship)

Teaching supervisory skills (training others in social environment to use good communication skills so that clients can practice and use these methods)

Maintenance skills (relapse prevention skills, helping clients practice problem solving and use preventive measures including relationship enrichment activities)

Practical Application of Intimate Relationship Skills

Not all couples' communication and relationship enhancement programs are based on behavioral or social learning theory. The Practical Application of Intimate Relationship Skills (PAIRS) program is an eclectic blend of experiential, psychotherapeutic, and educational elements (Gordon, 1990). Therapists conduct a 16-session mastery program, meeting weekly. Shorter options are available taking as little as half a day. The program accepts singles as well as couples and is aimed at helping people develop intimacy skills such as self-awareness, couples awareness, communication skills, sexuality/sensuality awareness, fair-fighting skills, and negotiation. It is a strength-based program that incorporates group process with behavioral change and communication training (DeMaria, Hannah, & Gordon, 2003). PAIRS leaders must be licensed clinicians. Clergy and others can be certified for shorter presentations as instructors. (For more information, see their website at Pairs.org.)

Marriage Encounter and Marriage Enrichment

Marriage encounter programs similar to relationship education programs are now conducted under the auspices of several religious denominations. They vary from a single weekend to several months. They also vary in the degree to which professional therapists are involved. You will find more information and home pages for marriage encounter on the Internet in the following denominations: Roman Catholic Church, Lutherans, Seventh Day Adventists, United Methodist Church, United Church of Christ, and Jewish Marriage Encounter, as well as many others.

ACME (Association for Couples in Marriage Enrichment) is a unique marriage enrichment organization. Married couples who have been through the program and have received additional training facilitate weekend enrichment courses for couples. During these weekends, the couples address problem solving, communication, intimacy, spirituality, and sexuality. The couples work as a group and then split into couples to discuss the topic. It is marriage encounter but not necessarily in a religious setting (see www.acme.gekos.com).

CONCLUSION

Communication problems are what most couples complain about when they come for help. Every couples therapist must be thoroughly familiar with specific couple communication problems and how to treat them. In this chapter, we said that couples counselors have always recognized that how the couple relates is critically important to whether they solve problems and whether they stay together. We discussed good communication and bad communication practices. We also touched on how gender and cultural differences can affect the communication process.

But how should the couples therapist deal with communication knots when they see them in the therapy session? One approach is to tackle communication as part of therapy involving only the therapist and the couple. Alternately, a group psychoeducational approach might be used. The selection of treatment venues is a judgment that a counselor must make with the clients' input. Some couples are too fragile or distressed to attend a group session. Some may benefit from the encouragement of a group.

Since the last edition of this book, much has occurred in the field of relationship education. Federal funding of marriage education programs has expanded their scope. A new organization, Smart Marriages, has become a clearinghouse for marriage education and promarriage activities. Gottman has added startling new findings to the prediction of divorce based on marital communication. As a result, many of the most popular relationship education programs are gathering research to support their approach. The couples therapist today has many more choices if he or she wishes to receive training in relationship education and enhancement. Better-researched and -formatted programs are available. Because of the rapid changes in this area, therapists must keep tabs on the growing body of research and the group psychoeducational programs that are proliferating.

9

Intimacy and Sexuality

KEY CONCEPTS

- Intimacy and sex are interlocking concepts, but it is possible to have one without the other. Generally, couples want both in their relationships.
- There may be gender differences in the way that intimacy is expressed, which may lead to misunderstandings.
- Three key elements of love are passion, commitment, and intimacy.
- Therapists assess the degree of intimacy in the couple's relationship and help them enhance closeness.
- Most sexual problems and dysfunctions are based in the couple's emotional struggles.
- Because some dysfunctions are medical problems, it is always important to have sexual problems medically checked before treating the problem in couples therapy.
- Sex therapy is a specialty that requires specific training. Couples therapists should understand the causes and treatments for major sexual dysfunctions.
- Two ways to assess a couple's current sexual functioning are to take a sexual history and create a sexual genogram.

INTIMACY

Most couples entering counseling and therapy identify a more intimate, loving relationship as a primary concern. Their definitions of intimate relationships, however, are typically very different from each other and often lead to confusion and doubt about their love for each other and how to become closer to each other. Intimacy is at the heart of nurturing and emotionally nourishing relationships and is linked with a more positive and satisfying relationship (Heller & Wood, 1998). Waring (1980) defines couples intimacy as composed of the following eight elements:

1. Affection—the degree to which feelings of emotional closeness are expressed by the couple

2. Expressiveness—the degree to which thoughts, beliefs, attitudes, and feelings are communicated within the relationship
3. Compatibility—the degree to which the couple can work and play together comfortably
4. Cohesion—a commitment to the relationship
5. Sexuality—the degree to which sexual needs are communicated and fulfilled
6. Conflict resolution—the ease with which differences of opinion are resolved
7. Autonomy—the couple's degree of positive relationships with family and friends
8. Identity—the couple's level of confidence and self esteem

Counselors help couples explore and understand these elements and identify some level of agreement about ways they would like to express their intimate relationship.

Gender Issues

Gender plays an important part in influencing intimate relationships. Gender refers to cultural, social, and emotional aspects associated with being male and female (Gilbert & Sher, 1999; Long, Burnett, & Thomas, 2006). Andersen (2003, p. 33) describes gender roles as "the expectations for behavior and attitudes that the culture defines as appropriate for women and men." Young girls and boys learn their gender roles from their parents through verbal mimicking and modeled behavior (Andersen, 2003; Long et al., 2006). However, intimacy is still somewhat influenced by a patriarchal relationship structure that is usually biased in a power differential favoring men. Traditionally, men have controlled the money that created power over their spouses. Because perceived equality is a key ingredient for the development of intimacy, many women have not felt equal in their relationships and have not viewed their relations as fair or supportive.

According to Tannen (1994), men traditionally value independence over emotional intimacy, and most women are better than men at creating and maintaining intimate connections. It has been said that men typically use communication to preserve independence and maintain their status, whereas women use conversation more often to express and create intimacy (Gilligan, 1982).

In addition, different values are placed on emotional disclosure for men and women. For example, women have been socialized that it is permissible to cry and talk about hurt and disappointment, whereas men have been told to be quiet and stoic when they hurt or are disappointed. In general, women are more comfortable talking about personal issues, and men typically do not easily disclose personal information. This does not mean that men are opposed to or cannot learn greater openness; they are simply unfamiliar with the methods of disclosing and have been taught to fear the consequences of lack of closeness as autonomy.

Because of the stereotype that women are more active in seeking closeness and intimacy with their partners, a woman is often identified as the pursuer where emotional issues are concerned. A man has been characterized most frequently as the distancer in such relationships. For example, a woman may be more inclined to initiate talks about feelings, love, hurts, and other personal information or inquiries in an attempt to feel more connected with her partner. A man may be more inclined to turn his feelings inward and protect his self-esteem by refusing to talk on a personal level or by refocusing a conversation toward concrete issues. As a woman presses to talk to her partner, she may follow him from room to room in an attempt to initiate conversation. Consequently, he is more apt to leave the room or become angry so that conversation is discontinued. In other words, the more she pursues, the more he distances.

Although the "dance" they engage in may be divided along these traditional gender lines, it is sometimes the case that the man is the pursuer and the woman is the distancer. Interestingly, when the female stops pursuing, the male may begin to move toward her. This change in the usual behavior of the couple creates a space or opportunity for achieving greater closeness as one partner changes the step of the dance. Both partners participate in the "dance of intimacy" out of fear. For pursuers, the fear is that they will be rejected or abandoned if they do not push for closeness. Men are primarily distancers either because they fear that they will be engulfed or overwhelmed by an emotional female or because they fear that they may reveal too much information that could potentially harm them or trap them in the future (Bowlby, 1973).

Sternberg's Triangular Model of Love

Sternberg (as cited in Weeks & Treat, 2001) describes a triangular theory of love based on the components of intimacy, passion, and decision/commitment. The theory suggests that the amount of love each individual experiences is based on the strength of the three components. Furthermore, the type of love each person experiences is relative to the interaction of the three dimensions, shown in Figure 9.1. It is suggested that stable, loving relationships contain all three components of passion, friendship, and commitment.

Intimacy, Passion, and Decision/Commitment

Intimacy includes self-disclosure and feelings of connection and emotional bonding with each other, but passion involves erotic interest in another (Harvey, 1995). The

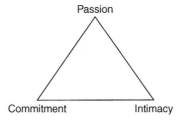

Figure 9.1   Sternberg's triangle of love

Source: From *Couples in Treatment,* by G. Weeks and S. Treat, p. 103. Copyright 1992 by Brunner/Mazel. Reprinted by permission of Routledge/Taylor & Francis Group, LLC.

Box 9.1
Suggestions for Helping Couples Develop Intimacy in Therapy

1. Help partners assign good intentions to each other while they strengthen their intimate relationship.
2. Teach them active listening skills and how to paraphrase, summarize, and reflect feelings as they attempt to understand each other.
3. Explore gender myths and resentments.
4. Teach them to use "I" statements and to avoid blaming each other.
5. Help the couple understand that difference is a positive factor that keeps the relationship alive and interesting.
6. Help the couple create time to talk and problem-solve as well as time for play and relaxation.
7. Encourage expression of feeling as a key ingredient in solution-focused discussions.
8. Eliminate unfair tactics from their conflicts such as blaming, diversions, silent treatments or negation, grocery-listing complaints, interruptions, humiliation tactics, and mixed messages.

Source: From *Solving Problems in Couples and Family Therapy,* by R. Sherman, P. Oresky, and Y. Rountree. Copyright 1991 by Brunner/Mazel. Reprinted by permission of Routledge/Taylor & Francis Group, LLC.

---

energy leading to romantic love, physical attraction, and sexual feelings can be described as *passion* (Weeks & Treat, 2001). Passion may be initially present for some couples, but it can wane in a long-term relationship. Intimacy develops over the course of the relationship and often includes a decision of loyalty to the relationship. The decision/commitment component refers to the decision to be with one partner, to deny any other partners, and to maintain the relationship above all else.

Therapeutic Interventions

Counselors and therapists must assess the couple's degree of intimacy, motivations behind fears, avoidance strategies, and distancing techniques before a plan can be developed to increase the levels of closeness and connection in the relationship (Watzlawick, Weakland, & Fisch, 1974). Box 9.1 lists some suggestions for helping couples become more intimate. A genogram can also be used to uncover expectations about gender roles, communication patterns, and male–female modeling in each partner's family of origin. After the messages and patterns have been identified, couples learn how they can communicate effectively and reduce anxieties and distancing behaviors through the use of behavioral, modeling, rehearsal, and contracting techniques. As trust develops, couples regain a sense of understanding and empathy for each other rather than distrust and disharmony (Zimmer, 1987).

The achievement of a healthy balance between too much togetherness and separateness also increases intimacy and promotes clearer boundaries for couples.

In counseling, couples practice role reversals in order to develop a greater appreciation for their partners, and they learn to view each other in a way previously hidden behind the routine behaviors of daily living (Long et al., 2006). Couples must also acquire healthy conflict skills so that they can trust each other, thus increasing self-disclosure and feelings of connection (Atwood & Dershowitz, 1992; Atwood & Weinstein, 1989).

Case Example: Amy and Greg

Amy and Greg have been married for 6 years. During the first year of their marriage, they lived with Amy's parents because Greg had been laid off from work and was having a difficult time finding another job. There was a high level of stress in the relationship during this time. Amy's parents argued frequently and expressed all their emotions freely. Greg had difficulty with open expression of feelings because his parents had not been affectionate in front of him, nor had they argued openly.

Two years before the couple came to therapy, Amy's mother died. Amy had been very close to her mother and had visited her and confided in her often. Shortly after her death, Amy and Greg began to fight more frequently. They came to counseling with issues of increased conflict, feelings of "drifting apart" emotionally and physically, and confusion about how to be intimate with each other.

Application of the Integrative Model: A Problem of Intimacy

Stage 1: Assessing the Problem

From Amy's perspective, the problem is the unresolved conflict between the partners and her feelings of being unheard and unimportant. Greg described the problem as his difficulty feeling close to Amy, increased feelings of distance, and fear of closeness. After exploring patterns in their families of origin, they realized that they each brought different ideas about intimacy to the relationship.

Greg recognized that his desire to distance himself during conflicts stems from his discomfort with his own emotions. Living with Amy's parents had allowed Amy and Greg to deflect their feelings from each other and create distance from each other. Amy became aware that her overinvolved relationship with her mother contributed to the distance that she and Greg created. Greg reported that he never felt "good enough" in Amy's mother's eyes, and so he distanced from Amy when she spent time with her mother. They did not openly discuss the issue with each other.

Amy and Greg now see that they "let a lot of things get in the way of being connected and close to each other" (interactive definition of the problem). Amy notes that when they tried to solve the situation by talking, it turned into an argument and remained unresolved. Greg reports that he has tried to "fix" the relationship by walking away from disagreements, but he acknowledges that this action has only created more distance.

Stage 2: Goal Setting

Amy and Greg agree that they learned how to be intimate from their families and that they now desire to create their own definition of intimacy so that they can learn to communicate clearly, problem-solve more successfully, and feel more connected (behavioral and affective goals). They are hopeful as they realize they have the power and knowledge to make these changes.

Amy and Greg can accept joint responsibility for a solution to their struggles once they reframe the problem and view it as a roadblock on a highway that they must go around, rather than as an obstacle that impedes their journey. They can view their problem as not understanding how to overcome the roadblock, and in attempting to move forward, they had gone in different directions. Now they are excited about traveling the highway together and about finding a better way to navigate around the roadblocks.

Stage 3: Adopting New Perceptions and Behaviors

Greg, a draftsperson, is organized and creative. Amy works as a technician in a veterinary clinic and is required to make quick, sound decisions and display a caring attitude at all times. Together they are adaptable and have worked well together in other areas, such as teaming up for road rallies when sharing responsibilities for mapping a route is critical (positive assets). Amy and Greg report that they feel most connected and intimate when they work side by side cooking dinner and then share the meal talking quietly. The therapist suggests that most couples who have different ideas about how to create and maintain intimacy will encounter roadblocks; however, as they see the obstacles more clearly and anticipate them, it is easier to navigate around them *together.*

Stage 4: Maintaining New Perceptions and Behaviors

Greg and Amy report that they really enjoy the feelings of being closer and connected and are hopeful for continued improvement. Amy feels more important in Greg's life, and Greg feels safer sharing his thoughts and feelings with Amy. They are both aware that obstacles may interfere with these new feelings and behaviors. Greg knows that if he begins to guess about Amy's motives or keeps feelings to himself and does not share them with Amy he will build resentments. Amy knows that she must monitor her communications and that if she becomes accusatory or blaming she risks stilted couple communication. The two are also aware that both of them are responsible for the solution. They both will need to identify clues that indicate they are not feeling as close as they would like (relapse prevention).

Stage 5: Validating New Perceptions and Behaviors

The couple realizes that their hard work has paid off. Greg likes spending time with Amy and is feeling more relaxed. Amy feels more secure and accepted after recognizing that Greg will not abandon her. Because of these connected and united feelings and the open, clear, and solution-focused communication, the partners feel comfortable enough to use their new skills to discuss their financial concerns and their sexuality. They feel confident about success with these other relationship issues because they have new tools with which to problem solve and to express their true feelings. Greg and Amy like the growth and change and have accepted that the relationship will be in a constant state of change and will always require their attention and nurturing (K. Schoening & J. Schoening, personal communication, May 1995).

Considerations for Working With Intimacy Problems

This checklist can be used during the assessment stage to address important issues related to intimacy.

1. Is the couple aware of the messages that both partners received from their families of origin regarding the expression of intimacy?
2. Are the partners willing to explore the myths of gender expectations and negotiate an equitable relationship rather than allow one partner to have all the power?
3. Can the partners communicate about the ways in which they would like to demonstrate closeness and attempt to meet each other's needs?
4. Are the partners willing to self-disclose and trust their partner with their feelings?
5. Can the couple learn problem-solving skills and conflict resolution to promote solutions?
6. Is the couple willing to share responsibility for problems and solutions in the relationship?
7. Can the couple create a healthy balance between a strong self-identity and a couple identity?
8. Can both partners value the other's contribution to the relationship?
9. Is the couple willing to create time together to nurture their relationship?
10. Does the couple provide romantic situations to promote a continued "honeymoon" period throughout the relationship?

SEXUAL ASPECTS OF RELATIONSHIPS

Love, intimacy, and sexuality are interrelated aspects of close relationships that influence each other in both positive and negative ways. For example, if love and intimacy are high, physical sex is most likely satisfactory. If the level of intimacy is low, sex may seem mechanical or purely physical, without emotional responsiveness. Although it is possible to have good sex without intimacy and love, the most gratifying sexual relationship occurs within the context of love (Hendrick & Hendrick, 2000). Sexuality is an integral part of self-expression that is informed by our views of self, sexual choices, identification as male of female, and our physical selves (L'Abate & Talmadge, 1987; Long et al., 2006). The act of sex is an activity that is influenced by biological and physiological functioning and is only one aspect of sexuality.

Often, sexuality is a presenting problem that couples express when they come to therapy, and it is usually related to a problem of intimacy in their relationship rather than to a physical sexual problem.

SEXUALITY AND THE COUPLE

Sexuality refers to both personality and sexual characteristics, including biological, psychological, and social attributes (Weinstein & Rosen, 1988). In sexuality therapy, the therapist helps the couple explore conjointly their sexual feelings, values, responsibilities, needs, and behaviors (Weinstein & Rosen, 1988, p. 1;

Long et al., 2006). Social influences such as multiple family constellations, changing gender roles, dual careers, media exposure to sexuality, and a high frequency of substance abuse all play a role in a couple's sexual satisfaction, responsiveness, and sexual performance and affect the degree of sexual intimacy in their relationship (Wincze & Carey, 2001).

Social Issues and Sexuality

One of the most important factors for couples to consider is that sexual problems are not necessarily internal conflicts manifested in their sexual relationship, nor are they necessarily physical dysfunctions. Most often problems are a result of social influences that affect a couple's emotional states and interfere with healthy sexual functioning (Leiblum & Pervin, 1980; L'Abate & Talmadge, 1987; Long et al., 2006). Sexual scripts from early childhood development based on familial messages, social influences, and peer relationships strongly shape sexuality. These scripts are challenged and edited throughout the life span (L'Abate & Talmadge, 1987). Life circumstances such as the death of a loved one, family illness, job stress, the birth of children, or economic worries may precipitate the onset of sexual problems. Similarly, hurt feelings, anger, hostility, and jealousy directed toward a mate can adversely affect sexual relationships.

Communication and Sexuality

A couple's quality of communication is closely linked to the overall quality of their relationship (Barbach, 2001). Their skill in communicating about sexuality is important in order to maintain sexual satisfaction and general satisfaction in the relationship (Harvey, 1995). Clearly, if partners can be direct and honest in their relationship, there is less likelihood that ambiguous messages and other unclear communication patterns will develop in their sexual relationship.

Different communication agendas can often create confusion and disappointment in relationships. For example, a woman may state "We need to spend more time together" when she means "I don't want you to go to the ball game with your friends." His response might be, "So what do you want to do? We spent all day yesterday with each other." Often, couples use nonverbal messages by avoiding eye contact with each other or by maintaining a stiff posture if approached by the other. One partner might also begin doing chores or turn attention to the children as a way to avoid or reject sexual advances (Long et al., 2006).

Practical considerations must be considered and communicated about when couples address sexual issues. These include the "where, when, and how often" aspects of sexual relations that must be determined, particularly if there are rigorous demands on the couple's time. For example, couples with small children or who both have demanding careers may find it necessary to plan time to be intimate. Specific issues include deciding which partner will initiate lovemaking, what each will give up in order to make time for the other, and what both will do to keep the relationship exciting and passionate.

Finally, performance issues may arise if there are fears of pregnancy, fatigue from chronic illness, aging concerns, disabilities, worry over infections or sexually transmitted diseases, or impairments from medications (Long et al., 2006).

The Development of Sexual Problems

Sexual problems, like other relationship problems, often develop as a consequence of vicious cycles of imbalance in partner's styles of loving—in particular, their sexual styles (Roughan & Jenkins, 1990). Early in the relationship (the honeymoon stage), couples rarely experience desire problems. As the relationship develops and external factors such as work and children intrude, one or both partners may find themselves less physically available for each other. If only one is less available, the other may feel hurt and attempt to entice the other to respond more sexually.

If the imbalance persists, over time couples may become more polarized and distant and begin to experience hurt, disappointment, and frustration. One may tend to blame the other for the lack of sexual intimacy so that neither is interested in initiating the sexual relationship. For example, one partner may believe that frequent sexual activity is an indication of how close they are as a couple, while the other believes that spending time together and talking often is the most important indicator of an intimate relationship. As the frustration develops over time, they might argue, "You never want to have sex with me anymore." "Why would you say that when we have not even been out together or had a conversation that was not about the children in weeks." These vicious cycles can continue to escalate until either they reach a crisis and create resolution to the problem or there is a breakdown in the relationship. Sometimes the relationship becomes stalled because neither partner wants to risk the breakdown. The couple may decide to retain the unsatisfactory relationship pattern indefinitely or until another crisis brings the problem to the forefront (Roughan & Jenkins, 1990).

Dysfunction or Problem?

It is difficult for couples to establish a satisfying sexual relationship if there is a diagnosed sexual dysfunction. Sexual dysfunctions are impairments, either physical or psychological, of one of the three phases of the sexual response cycle. These dysfunctions consist of disorders such as erectile disorder, premature ejaculation, male orgasmic disorder, and sexual aversion disorder in males; orgasmic disorders and vaginismus in females; and dyspareunia and hypoactive sexual desire in both males and females (American Psychiatric Association, 2000).

If a dysfunction exists, couples can explore options to improve their love relationship either through couples therapy, self-help manuals, physiological changes such as a new medication, or specific behavioral-learning techniques designed to improve sexual interactions. It is important to seek a medical opinion from a qualified physician before any diagnosis or treatment is initiated.

Often the problem is not physiological but is emotionally based. These sexual difficulties can include differences in partners' sexual preferences including frequency, setting, timing, preference of sexual positions, length or presence of foreplay or afterplay, degree of passion expressed, and type of communication style employed by each partner (Karpel, 1993). Anxiety about any of the above mentioned sexual problems—as well as distress about other societal and family based issues such as early messages, sexual misinformation, childhood incest or rape, coping with the aftermath of an extramarital affair, or faulty communication—can result in the development of a sexual dysfunction (Dove & Wiederman, 2000).

THE PROCESS OF SEXUALITY THERAPY

Assessment and Diagnosis

Determining whether a couple has a sexual dysfunction or a sexual problem is an important step for therapists in the assessment stage and prior to developing any course of treatment. However, often it may not be evident in the early stages of therapy and is diagnosed at a later stage of therapy. Remember that assessment continues throughout the counseling process (Drummond, 2000; Young, 2001).

Sexual dysfunctions require medical attention and the services of a trained professional experienced specifically in treating dysfunctions. Treatment strategies for sexual dysfunctions are usually behaviorally based. In many instances, a combination of psychotherapy and behavioral strategies is utilized. If partners experience no difficulty in the desire, excitement, or orgasmic phases of their sexuality, then a dysfunction is probably not present. A sexual problem or an unresolved relationship problem should then be considered (Heiman, LoPiccolo, & LoPiccolo, 1976; Kaplan, 1983). Specific questions about sexuality must be asked to determine the diagnosis. Some common general content areas for questions include the following (Leiblum & Rosen, 1984):

1. Current sexual function and satisfaction for both partners
2. Family-of-origin message and sexual practices for both partners (see "Sexual Genogram")
3. Relationship history that includes major events in the relationship such as divorce, separation, pregnancies, deaths, and so on
4. Effects of contraception, pregnancy, illness, medication, and the aging process
5. Current sexual concerns and relationship concerns.

If the presence of a dysfunction is discerned, the couple should be referred for a medical evaluation and to a licensed sex therapist. If a relationship problem is determined, then couples therapy can be directed toward the development of goals to include increased sexual pleasure and responsiveness.

All therapists, whether or not they are experienced and qualified sex therapists, must be familiar with the most prevalent sexual dysfunctions in order to determine a course of treatment. In addition, after couples have undergone treatment for a particular sexual dysfunction, they may require therapy for relationship issues that have surfaced. Thus, therapists must also be familiar with treatment procedures.

Sexual Genogram

A sexual genogram is a useful assessment tool for collecting information about both partners' family-of-origin messages and critical events in their sexual development (Duhl & Duhl, 1981; Hof & Berman, 1986; Sherman, 2000). It combines information from a family history and a sex history that helps provide data about family taboos, secrets, childhood abuse or sexual assault, and expectations about sexual interactions (Long et al., 2006). Also, a sexual satisfaction time line can be created, with the years of the couple's relationship noted at regular intervals on the line. The therapist can then ask the couple to describe sexual satisfaction and problems at each point in time.

Goal Setting for Sexual Problems in Therapy

Blame and guilt are two factors that negatively influence a couple's' sexual satisfaction. To reduce feelings of blame and guilt, therapists create a shared, interactive definition of the sexual problem so that the couple can look at their problem as a joint one and begin to conceptualize changes that they will make as a collaborative effort. Only then is it productive to develop goals for therapy.

Goals are stated as shared experiences that couples will achieve during therapy. Goals are stated in behavioral and affective terms so that the couple is clear about what they will do and how they will feel when they accomplish them. Goals can include changing the intimate time the partners spend together, challenging negative messages from their families of origin or the relationship, or making specific changes in their sexual behavior. Common feelings associated with these behaviors include feeling closer, more connected, more intimate, more understood, more supported, and so on.

MALE AND FEMALE SEXUAL DYSFUNCTIONS

In this section, we identify the most common sexual concerns that couples bring to therapy, as well as some of the most common methods of treatment. (We would like to acknowledge J. Palelog's contribution to this section.)

Male Dysfunctions

Erectile Dysfunctions

Inhibited male orgasm, more recently referred to as *erectile dysfunction,* occurs in the excitement phase of the sexual response cycle and is present in "20 to 30 million men in the United States" (Epperly & Moore, 2000, p. 3). It is described as the continued or repeated delay in achieving or maintaining an erection sufficient for the purpose of intercourse (Lefrancois, 1993; Weinstein & Rosen, 1988). Primary erectile dysfunction means that a man is never able to achieve an erection sufficient for intercourse. With secondary erectile dysfunction, a man has at one time in his life been able to achieve an erection but, for some reason, is now unable to do so. With situational erectile dysfunction, the man is able to have sexual intercourse in some circumstances but not in others (Weinstein & Rosen, 1988).

Causes   Male erectile dysfunction is caused by physical factors such as fatigue, diabetes, medication, low androgen level, narcotics or alcohol, neurological diseases (multiple sclerosis, spinal cord injuries, diabetes, renal failure), and endocrine deficiencies (Coleman, 1988; Wincze & Carey, 2001). Physical causes can occur alone or in conjunction with other psychological factors like anxiety or guilt, excessive maternal or paternal dominance in childhood, or inhibitory religious doctrines (Kosch, 1982; LoPiccolo, 1985; Spector & Carey, 1990; Wincze & Carey, 2001).

Treatment   The goals of treatment for erectile dysfunction involve (1) removing the man's fears about sexual performance, (2) helping him be an active participant in the sexual experience, and (3) relieving the woman's fears about the man's performance. Usually asking the couple to refrain from sexual intercourse removes the fear of performance so that the couple can focus on giving and receiving pleasure in other situations. This step is called *sensate focus,* and it provides a relaxed atmosphere for the couple to engage in pleasurable acts without a goal of intercourse. Later, the couple is instructed to assume a female-superior position, manipulate the penis to a semierect state, and then manually insert the penis into the woman's vagina. Initially, the woman thrusts and slowly stops so that the man may begin to thrust. Sometimes the partners are instructed to stop if an erection occurs, but eventually they learn to maintain intercourse with the goal of pleasure rather than an erection (LoPiccolo & LoPiccolo, 1978; Masters & Johnson, 1970). Desensitization training is also used for prolonged erectile problems (Althof, 2000).

Oral medications can be used to increase the flow of blood to the penis. These include apomorphine, phentolamine, trazodone, Viagra, Levitra, and Cialis (Strong, DeVault, Sayad, & Yarber, 2005). It is important to encourage men who use these medications to communicate with their partners and to explore the effects of these medications on the overall functioning of their relationship.

Premature Ejaculation

Premature ejaculation is the inability to control ejaculation. Ejaculation occurs before the individual wishes it because of recurrent and persistent absence of reasonable control during sexual activity. When a man believes he has ejaculated too quickly, he becomes frustrated and develops a fear that the pattern will continue (Weinstein & Rosen, 1988). It is the most common male disorder and is often of most concern to female partners (Polonsky, 2000).

Causes   If primary premature ejaculation exists and the man has never experienced control during sexual experiences, it is unlikely that the problem is organically based. On the other hand, with secondary premature ejaculation, where there has been a prior history of control, the problem may be caused by medication or other physiological factors. Psychological causes such as power struggles, unconscious anger, or low self-esteem may also affect the ejaculatory control (Leiblum & Rosen, 1989).

Treatment   If the couple's problem is premature ejaculation, the squeeze technique is prescribed after the couple completes sensate focus exercises. The woman is instructed to stimulate the man to full erection and to immediately apply pressure to the penile glans, with her thumb on the frenulum and the first and second fingers adjacent to each other on either side of the coronal ridge. This effectively eliminates the man's urge to ejaculate.

During the next step, the woman brings the man to an erection two to three times while in a female-superior position. Thereafter, the woman inserts the penis into her vagina and remains motionless. If the man feels the urge to ejaculate, the woman uses the squeeze technique again. Then, the woman initiates low-level thrusting in a non-threatening way. As the man maintains prolonged ejaculatory control, the woman can thrust more vigorously (Masters & Johnson, 1970; Weinstein & Rosen, 1988).

Retarded Ejaculation

Retarded ejaculation is the man's inability to ejaculate and achieve orgasm during intercourse. With primary retarded ejaculation, the man has never experienced ejaculation during intercourse; with secondary retarded ejaculation, the man was previously able to ejaculate during intercourse but is now unable to do so.

Causes   Physical responses are rarely the cause of retarded ejaculation. Psychological factors include a subconscious fear of being injured, anxiety, problematic relationships, trauma during early sexual experiences, or inhibitory religious practices (Leiblum & Rosen, 2000; Kelley, 2004).

Treatment   Sensate focus is the first step in treating this problem. The woman manually stimulates her partner so that she can be viewed as a pleasure-giver. The woman manually stimulates the man just short of ejaculation and then assumes a superior position and inserts the penis into her vagina. She initiates thrusting until the man ejaculates. If he does not, she returns to manual stimulation and repeats the procedure (Masters & Johnson, 1970).

Common Female Sexual Dysfunctions

Inhibited Sexual Desire

Inhibited sexual desire is a deficiency or absence of desire for sexual activity or fantasy. Although men can experience this problem, it is more common among women and is considered by many therapists to be the most difficult to treat (Pridal & LoPiccolo, 2000). There are two subtypes of this dysfunction: (1) primary—those who have never experienced sexual desire—and (2) secondary—those who have had an interest in sexual activity but for some situational reason no longer feel desire or those who feel desire in certain circumstances but not in others (Weinstein & Rosen, 1988).

Causes   Physical causes for inhibited sexual desire include alcohol, narcotics, and antiandrogens and diseases that affect testosterone and pituitary functioning (Kaplan, 1979). Psychological causes can be prior negative conditioning related to sexual experiences (Masters & Johnson, 1970), such as rape or incest in early childhood. Negative messages from parents regarding sexual practices like masturbation or oral sex can also affect adult sexual functioning. Other causes are sexual anxiety stemming from lack of knowledge, unrealistic expectations, guilt, or performance concerns (LoPiccolo, 1985; Weinstein & Rosen, 1988).

The presence of desire also depends on biological drive, adequate self-esteem, previous positive experiences with sexual activity, a suitable partner, and a positive relationship in other areas with a sexual partner (Leiblum & Rosen, 2000). Unresolved issues in a relationship such as affairs can also lead to unsatisfactory sexual functioning.

Treatment   Often, problems of inhibited sexual desire require relationship therapy to address the issues preventing the woman from desiring sexual activity with her partner. Intrapsychic issues from her past or current issues regarding intimate time together, finances, children, work, or other factors may be dealt with in therapy (Pridal & LoPiccolo, 2000). Once those issues are resolved, the partners must make time for sexual activity together. Sensate focus exercises and general physical, nonsexual touching is a good way to begin creating desire. Later, more erotic sexual touching should be initiated including the use of sexual fantasy (Byrne & Osland, 2000), leading to intercourse or other forms of sexual pleasure. Communication between the partners about what they like and dislike is a part of this process (Leiblum & Rosen, 2000).

Orgasmic Dysfunction

A woman suffering from *orgasmic dysfunction* shows signs of sexual arousal yet does not experience orgasm (Leiblum & Rosen, 2000). There are three subtypes: (1) primary—the woman has never reached orgasm; (2) secondary—the woman has previously achieved orgasm but currently cannot do so; and (3) situational— the woman can achieve orgasm under specific conditions, such as through masturbation.

Causes   Physical causes include hormonal patterns, drugs (such as alcohol), antidepressants, alpha adrenergic agents, nerve damage, and advanced diabetes. Psychological factors include lack of sexual knowledge, poor communication about sexual needs, guilt, fear of losing control, overt anger, and unconscious motivations (Comer, 1998; Leiblum & Rosen, 2000).

Treatment   Sensate focus exercises followed by stimulation of the woman's genitals by her partner in a nondemanding position is initiated early in treatment. Continued touching combined with communication about pleasurable feelings follows as the woman is able to feel a warmth and security with her partner. If all proceeds well, intercourse follows, with the woman in a superior position with her partner. Sexual play should ensue, interspersed with periods of rest. Finally, lateral positions and prolonged periods of sexual activity that may result in orgasm are initiated. Other conjoint treatments including anxiety reduction, sexual training, and continued relationship therapy may also be indicated (Leiblum & Rosen, 2000; Masters & Johnson, 1970).

Vaginismus

Vaginismus is defined as a disorder in which an involuntary contraction of the muscles of the vagina prevents intercourse. Women experiencing vaginismus have little or no difficulty becoming aroused, and they can experience varying degrees of discomfort or pain. It can occur at any age and can range from a tightly shut vagina to pelvic pain (Long et al., 2006). Penile entry may be difficult and can be very painful for both partners; sometimes entry is not possible at all. In some instances, even the use of tampons and pelvic examinations are impossible without pain. Other women have reported that although penile penetration is impossible, they are able to use tampons or engage in sexual practices that include digital penetration (Kaplan, 1983).

Causes   Endometriosis, vaginitis, herpes, pelvic tumors, childbirth, and surgical injuries of the genitals are some of the physical causes of this dysfunction (Kaplan, 1983; Weinstein & Rosen, 1988). Psychological causes include social factors related to religious practices, fear of pain, or a partner's repeated erectile dysfunction.

Treatment   After a thorough medical examination has indicated a diagnosis of vaginismus, a woman can use dilators to increase her ability to open her vaginal muscles and reduce her anxiety about intercourse. Dilators come in graduated sizes and are used in the privacy of the couple's home under nonstressful conditions. Sexual intercourse is not attempted until the woman has success with the dilators, usually at least 6 weeks into the program (Weinstein & Rosen, 1988). Desensitization training helps couples unlearn the connection between anxiety that produces vaginismus and the situation that produces the physical reaction to intercourse (Bourne, 2000).

OTHER PROBLEMS IN SEXUAL RELATIONSHIPS

Sexually Transmitted Diseases and Infections

Sexually transmitted diseases (STDs) and infections (STIs) are serious and painful and can cause significant damage to the sexual and reproductive organs if left untreated. Sometimes there are no outward signs or symptoms of the disease. STDs are spread during sexual activity, usually through intercourse, oral sex, and anal sex. Most STD germs live in warm, moist areas, so they are often found in the mouth, rectum, vagina, vulva, penis, and testes (Crooks & Baur, 2002; Hillier & Holmes, 1999; Hook & Handsfield, 1999).

Couples who report any symptoms should be referred immediately to a medical doctor or clinic for treatment. Although there are more than two dozen diseases referred to as STDs, the most common are chlamydia, gonorrhea, and herpes.

Acquired Immunodeficiency Syndrome

Acquired immunodeficiency syndrome (AIDS) is caused by the human immunodeficiency virus (HIV). HIV is an organism that appears to mutate rapidly, so it is difficult to treat. At present, the disease is incurable and fatal. It is transmitted through the exchange of body fluids, principally blood and semen, but it can also be found in vaginal fluid, breast milk, and menstrual blood. The HIV virus breaks down the immune system, creating a susceptibility to common infections and unusual cancers. An infected person may be symptom free for years but is still contagious. In the final stages of AIDS, a person may exhibit symptoms of prolonged fever, weight loss, diarrhea, and swollen glands. The transmission of HIV can be prevented through abstinence, monogamy, use of condoms, and, for intravenous drug users, avoiding the sharing of needles (Ambroziak & Levy, 1999; Crooks & Baur, 2002; Marr, 1998).

Alcohol and Sexuality

Although alcohol has been regarded by some as a powerful facilitator and disinhibitor for sexual behavior, it has some destructive and detrimental consequences (Crooks & Baur, 2002; Leiblum & Rosen, 2000). Alcohol use can be associated with impairment of erectile response as well as the impairment of communication necessary to understand each partner's needs. In addition, alcohol diminishes the intensity of a woman's orgasm and can depress her arousal. Certainly, chronic use of alcohol has a negative effect on the relationship because it promotes denial, poor communication, and poor coping styles for resolving relationship problems.

Infertility Issues

Infertility is the inability to conceive after 1 year of intercourse without the use of contraception or the inability to carry a pregnancy to live birth (Speroff, Glass, & Kase, 1994). It is a difficult life crisis for couples, and it can result in intense grief and emotional pain. It can also influence sexual relationships in profound ways (Diamond, Kezur, Meyers, Scharf, & Weinshel, 1999). Psychological reactions include denial, grief, helplessness, anger, denial, and guilt (Cooper-Hilbert, 1998; Long et al., 2006). Therapy focuses on helping couples explore their beliefs about family and their reactions to the possibility that they may not be able to create a biological child. They are encouraged to develop a support system and explore medical options. It is also useful to help them explore other options such as adoption, in-vitro fertilization, or surrogate parenting.

Aging Issues

Age-related issues impact couples' sexual functioning. These issues include physical changes and life-event changes. Many physical changes result from a decline in the production of estrogen for women and decreased testosterone levels for men. Women may experience reduced vaginal lubrication resulting in painful intercourse or decreases in breast swelling and intensity of orgasm, while men may notice a decrease in the size and firmness of their testicles along with reduced sperm reduction. Aging men may also address prostate difficulties such as prostate cancer or excessive development of the prostate (Stone, 1987). Life events include the loss of a partner, changes in living arrangements due to aging, retirement, or chronic illnesses that impair sexual interactions. These issues can lead to depression and despair for some couples. Therapists should help aging couples address their challenges and identify some of the positive aspects of aging. Couples may experiment with a variety of sexual interactions or techniques previously unknown to them. They may attempt to infuse playfulness in their sexual relationship while acknowledging the physical limitations they possess. Clear communication is a key to the success of creating new options for aging couples.

Childhood Sexual Abuse and Therapy

When treating a couple in which one partner has a history of childhood sexual abuse, key questions concern identification of the problem, the effect of the therapist's gender, the modality of treatment (individual, conjoint, or group), and the process of interventions (Ainscough & Toon, 2000; Maltz, 2001; Wilson & James, 1992). Organic sexual dysfunctions may be present and must be diagnosed by a medical doctor. Specific sex therapy may be indicated, in addition to relationship therapy.

If individual therapy is recommended, the couple may return after sex therapy to resolve the relationship conflicts. If possible, it can be useful to provide treatment for both partners so that the nonabused partner can learn about the effects of the abuse on the partner and can learn specific triggers that may reenact or recall the prior abuse. Sometimes a certain touch or phrase can trigger the recall (Maltz, 2001; Rencken, 2000; Roland, 2002;). In addition, it is important to be aware of the literature on false memory syndrome so that therapists do not contribute to emotional trauma as a result of childhood sexual assault (Loftus, 2003; Roland, 2002).

A goal of treatment is to help the couple identify ways in which the problem currently affects their relationship. Interventions to ameliorate the situation may include communication techniques, sensitivity training, behavioral strategies, and intimacy development enhancement (Ainscough & Toon, 2000; Maltz, 2001).

Checklist for Treatment of Sexual Dysfunction

1. Does the couple report a sexual dysfunction or a sexual problem?
2. Have appropriate questions been asked to ascertain the problem?
3. How willing or open is the couple as the two discuss their sexual relationship?
4. Have they explored their sexual messages from their families of origin?
5. Is there significant blaming by one partner, or do they both accept responsibility and desire change together?
6. Do they have correct sexual knowledge in order to understand what they desire?
7. Is there excessive use of drugs or alcohol or other medications that may have an impact on sexual functioning?
8. Has either partner experienced any childhood sexual abuse?
9. Do the partners appear willing to address their sexual problems conjointly?

ETHICAL CONCERNS FOR COUNSELORS
TREATING SEXUAL ISSUES

Only experienced and qualified therapists should treat sexual dysfunctions. An appropriate referral should be made once a diagnosis or tentative hypothesis is ascertained. To be certified to treat couples for sexual problems, many states require that therapists complete a certain number of academic hours of training in sexual issues.

It is important to remember the caveat "first, do no harm" and take all presenting concerns seriously (Corey, Corey, & Callanan, 2003). Couples must never be told that the problem is "all in their heads" or that they are making up problems. All concerns are to be taken seriously and treated respectfully by the therapist. At no time should the therapist promote a sexual practice or side with one partner on the appropriateness of a sexual action. Clearly, couples must determine how they wish to express themselves sexually. If a conflict exists, the therapist's goal is to help clients problem-solve and negotiate successful resolutions to their sexual problems (Corey et al., 2003).

To provide competent services, therapists are ethically obligated to explore their own values, beliefs, and behaviors about human sexuality so that we do not impose our values on our clients. These values should be recognized so that we are able to work with diverse types of couples' issues without judgment or without influencing the sexual behavior of others (Baruth & Manning, 2003).

Case Example: Charlotte and Frank

Charlotte is 24 years old, and Frank is 26. They were married while Charlotte attended college, and she is currently in graduate school. Since Charlotte began graduate school, Frank has been working two jobs in order to make ends meet financially. Charlotte also works full time and maintains a full class load. They have no children, and they have not had sex for 3 months.

Application of the Integrative Model: Working With a Sexual Problem

Stage 1: Assessing and Obtaining an Interactional View of the Problem
Frank complains that Charlotte is too busy and never wants to have sex. Charlotte asserts that Frank does not understand how stressed she is. An interactional view is that the two have allowed themselves to overload and they have not found a way to create intimate time together.

Stage 2: Goal Setting
The therapist developed the following goals with Frank and Charlotte:

1. Charlotte and Frank want to create more time together for cuddling and being close, as well as for sexual activity so that they feel more intimate with each other.
2. They will set aside 2 hours a week to share their thoughts and feelings about daily events of their lives so that they will feel more connected to each other.

3. They will do some long-range planning and create future goals to be implemented when school has ended. This will provide a sense of anticipation and
feelings of hopefulness for the relationship.
4. They agree to wage battle against the time clock and create more balance in
their lives. School, career, and couple time will be reapportioned so that they
can feel a sense of control of their lives.

Stage 3: Adopting New Perceptions and Behaviors

The couple noted Charlotte's skill at creating time-management plans for her coworkers. Frank is more flexible and can create blocks of time if he is aware in advance of the
need to do so. The two practice a written time-management plan that they have created;
then they plan one "sabotage" of a work or school time when they will sneak away
together for couple time. This way, they do not feel so controlled by their schedules.

Stage 4: Maintaining New Perceptions and Behaviors

Frank and Charlotte agree that the priority must be on maintaining the couple relationship. School and career are necessities and responsibilities that must be achieved
but cannot dominate their lives. They agree to each take a turn planning and implementing fun time in the relationship.

Stage 5: Validating New Perceptions and Behaviors

They compliment each other on taking control of their lives and vow not to let the time
clock regain control. They are eager to use the same system to plan their future once
school is over. Charlotte's planning and Frank's flexibility and fun-loving nature will
keep them on the right track. Finally, they decide to reevaluate their success every 3
months (J. Najafian, personal communication, May 1995).

CONCLUSION

Emotional and sexual intimacy is at the core of most couple relationships.
Decision making and intellectual processes also play a part but are less significant,
particularly in the honeymoon stages of the relationship. Social factors such as
family messages, religion, career, childrearing, and financial stressors also have an
impact on the couple's intimate life.

Many people have been hurt and have a fear of closeness. As couples, these
partners often create a dance of closeness and distance so that they do not become
intimate with each other. Distancing occurs from fear—fear of being hurt, of
anger, of dependency, of loss of control, and of rejection by one's partner.

Sexual problems may be evidenced when partners fear intimacy and do not
feel connected to each other. It is important to distinguish a sexual problem from
a sexual dysfunction because problems are often created from the relationship and
dysfunctions may be organically based. A thorough medical examination is necessary to rule out organic causes. Other factors such as childhood abuse, inhibitory
religious practices, family messages, or a series of unsuccessful extramarital affairs
can create sexual dysfunctions.

Therapists must determine an appropriate referral, when necessary, but must also be knowledgeable about sexual dysfunctions and their treatments if they are to be helpful to couples who have experienced or who are currently experiencing these problems. Specificity and empathy are two of the most valuable tools that a therapist can possess when working with sexual problems. These tools can help therapists provide an arena for couples to set goals and attempt new methods for achieving emotional and sexual intimacy in their relationships.

10

Conflict: Negotiation and Resolution

KEY CONCEPTS

- Conflict within the couple is a natural function of differences. Conflict cannot be avoided, but it can be managed to produce positive negotiated outcomes.
- Conflict can result from tension caused by forces external to the couple, as when economic conditions lead to conflicts over finances.
- Conflict also occurs when one member of the couple perceives inequity or experiences an imbalance in rewards.
- Anger can be a signal of underlying problems. It can also be a manipulation. Constructively dealing with anger prevents abuse and violence.
- Verbal abuse can occur with or without physical violence. It involves criticizing, name-calling, and belittling the partner.
- Physical violence in the relationship is a cue to separate the partners and treat each individually. Power and control issues for the male batterer must be dealt with.
- Strategies such as reframing, use of metaphors, relationship contracting, and role reversals may be employed to deal with a couple's conflicts.

Healthy couples experience conflict (Christensen & Jacobson, 2000; Sween, 2003; Weeks & Treat, 2001). Because no two people think, feel, and behave exactly alike, it is inevitable that differences will occur. Differences occur around the definition of a problem, each partner's style for addressing problems, how each partner thinks the problem should be solved, and even the expected outcome of the solution to the problem. Values, desires, perceptions, and dreams also play a part in a couple's conflict. Disagreement ranges from less serious issues such as the proverbial who squeezed the toothpaste from the top, to serious differences such as childrearing, money, career issues, or lifestyle concerns.

"Paradoxically, those we love are often the ones we are most likely to hurt. It is a rare person who does not, at some point, feel 'hurt,' 'let down,' 'betrayed,' 'disappointed,' or 'wronged' by [a] relationship partner" (Fincham, Beach, & Davila, 2004, p. 83). These feelings often pose challenges as couples learn how to be connected and how to be different. In fact, it is usually in the process of maintaining connection and expressing differences that conflict occurs. Expressions of differences can be described on a continuum of responses ranging from mild disagreement to violent conflict. Over time, an inability to resolve these differences effectively leads to erosion of intimacy and an ultimate breakdown of the relationship.

Research suggests that some kinds of conflict are more harmful to relationships than are others. For example, the more intensely heated the conflict (in terms of physiological arousal), the more likely a couple is to break up within a 3-year period (Cahn, 1992; Gottman, 1991). Counselors help identify the sources and styles of conflict so that couples can determine effective ways of resolving their conflicts and feel less fearful that each disagreement will destroy their relationship. It is not the disagreement that is destructive to a couple's relationship, it is the way in which the disagreement occurs that leads to distress.

SOURCES OF CONFLICT

Social Context

Change is an inevitable process that either presents opportunities for adaptation and growth or leads to defensiveness and withdrawal. Either way, change is initially stressful for individuals and relationships. Changing roles within relationships present challenges for most couples. Social changes such as dual careers, shared parental responsibilities, economic stressors, and societal mobility are also potential sources for conflict (Christensen & Jacobson, 2000).

Situational Stress

Sometimes foreseen and unforeseen life events require adaptive or coping behaviors. Although the resulting anxiety from these life events does not stem from the relationship, it can trigger conflict (Gilbert, 1992) Chronic illness, death, aging parents, financial crisis, or child-related problems are often conflict triggers. The degree and intensity to which stress is evidenced depends on the couple's conflict-coping skills.

Perceptual Differences Theories

One reason conflict develops is that two parties initially view a situation differently (L'Abate, 1999). Conflict begins with perceptual differences and it is expressed in emotions and behaviors. There are basically two types of perceptual theories: motive-centered and action-centered models. *Motive-centered* definitions view psychological states as the cause of conflict, whereas *action-centered* orientations view behavior as a central focus.

Equity Theory

Equity theory provides the conceptual framework to link perception to conflict behaviors (Adams, 1965; Levi-Straus, 1969; Murstein, Wadlin, & Bond, 1987). An individual's perception of fairness in the relationship is determined by an appraisal of the outcomes. In other words, a person looks at what he or she is getting out of a relationship and what their partner is receiving. If one perceives the relationship to be inequitable or unbalanced, psychological tension results and tension leads to conflict. In a dual-career couple, one member may, for example, perceive inequity in the distribution of household tasks, providing more free time to the other partner.

Exchange Theory

Exchange theories explain that conflict arises when one partner in a relationship is dissatisfied with the exchange achieved and uses hostility as the ultimate bargaining move (Scanzoni, 1978). Exchange theory as applied to interpersonal relationships suggests that conflict is the result of looking at a psychological balance sheet: How much I am putting out compared to what I am getting in return (Murstein et al., 1987)? Each partner wants to maximize the rewards and minimize the costs (Brown & Christensen, 1986). The relationship is maintained by the provision of rewards to both partners ("I'll scratch your back if you scratch mine"). Some of the rewards that couples exchange include money, goods, services, love, status, and information (Argyle & Furnam, 1983).

Attribution Theory

Attribution theory suggests that people's responses to a problem are very often based on their ideas about what caused the problem. Attributing the cause of a problem to one's partner and not taking personal responsibility for conflict is a common way of feeling better about oneself without resolving the conflict (Baucom & Epstein, 1990). Field studies and laboratory experiments on conflict have found that when people perceive that they have some control over the resolution of the problem, they can cope more effectively with negative events (Langer & Rodin, 1976; Schulz, 1976).

Behavior/Event Theories of Conflict

In contrast to perceptual theories, behavior/event theories of conflict contend that it is important to understand the action of each partner during conflict and then seek new behaviors to manage the conflict (Patterson, Hops, & Weiss, 1975; Satir, 1964; Turner, 1970). Successful management of the conflict includes clarifying rights and obligations, setting interpersonal boundaries, promoting shared decision making, and using open communication (Coser, 1956; Deutsch, 1973; Simmel, 1950; Sprey, 1971; Vuchinich, 1984). A situation that illustrates this theory is a partner who belittles and criticizes, while the other just leaves the room rather than verbally confront the behavior. Instead of resolving the conflict, the partner leaving the room only increases the conflict. The focus of behavior theories is to change the behavior of both partners.

Negotiation Theory

Negotiation theory has some relevance to understanding the causes of couples conflict. Negotiation theory indicates that conflict is the result of failed bargaining strategies (Scanzoni & Polonko, 1981). Bargaining strategies and tactics such as verbal persuasion may be ineffective in a relationship (Scanzoni, 1978; Straus, 1979). The negotiation behaviors themselves then, rather than the underlying needs, become the reason for the conflict. An example of these behaviors is seen in the relationship of Gustav and Anella. Anella would like Gustav to remain home during the evenings, and she rewards him for staying home with sexual activity. She is attempting to meet her needs of having him home with her by offering more sexual play as a solution that benefits both of them. If she is unsuccessful, Anella might begin to complain when Gustav goes out with his friends, thereby pushing him more toward his friends. She might then retaliate by decreasing sexual activity as a way of punishing him for being unwilling to accept her solution to the problem.

Developmental Theory

According to developmental theory, conflict results as a couple experiences stress at predictable and unpredictable stages of development. It is during transitional phases in the family life cycle that conflict in relationships will most likely emerge. The more problematic the transitional issue is for the couple, the more intense the conflict is. For instance, a couple who have just borne their first child may come to counseling complaining of increased distance and disagreement in their relationship. Both partners feel hurt, and they are confused about why their relationship is deteriorating at such a happy time for them. As their confusion grows, their anxiety increases and they begin to misunderstand each other.

VERBAL CONFLICT AND ANGER

Conflict and anger are intimately related. Many of us fear anger because it associated with losing control and being destructive, but anger is a signal that is worth heeding. It can be a message that we are hurt, that our rights are being violated, that our needs or wants are not being adequately met, or simply that something is just not quite right (Lerner, 1985). It is not anger that is the problem but how we express it.

Couples can be taught to deal constructively with anger in their relationships. For most of us, our style of anger comes from two sources: from our families of origin (Harris & Dersch, 2001; Mones, 2001) and from our relationships with others. An anger genogram can be used to understand the family-of-origin perspective or the following questions may be asked to explore the couple's typical ways of dealing with angry feelings:

1. What is anger?
2. What does it mean when you are angry?
3. What does it mean when you are angry with your partner?
4. What does it mean when your partner is angry?
5. What does it mean when your partner is angry with you?
6. How do you respond to your partner's anger?
7. How do you respond to your own anger?
8. How do you let your partner know you are angry?
9. How long does your anger usually last?
10. What other feelings are associated with anger?

An Anger Genogram: Questions to Ask

1. How did your parents deal with anger or conflict?
2. Did you see your parents work through anger or conflict?
3. When members of your family got angry, how did others respond?
4. What did you learn about anger from each of your parents?
5. When a parent was angry with you, what did you feel and do?
6. When you got angry, who listened or failed to listen to you?
7. How did members of your family respond when you got angry?
8. Who was allowed and who was not allowed to be angry in your family?
9. What is your best memory about anger in your family? Your worst memory?
10. Was anyone in your family ever seriously hurt when someone got angry?

This type of genogram reveals patterns in the family, including the expression or inhibition of anger, and can assist partners as they attempt to learn how these patterns affect the way they currently deal with conflict.

Anger as Manipulation or Defense

Many times anger is used as a defense against hurt and pain; it also may be used to give a person a sense of power and control, as in abusive relationships. Sometimes a partner uses anger to create distance in a relationship, to punish, or to be left alone.

Anger can function in a healthy way when it is a signal that boundaries are violated. For example, one partner might become annoyed when the mother-in-law repeatedly calls in the evenings during dinner. Anger can be a signal that one partner has violated the other's freedom (Weeks & Treat, 2001).

Sometimes anger serves as a motivator for resolving differences. It is viewed as a barometer that indicates underlying unresolved feelings that must emerge. Anger is a helpful reminder to deal with such deeper issues as hurt, fear, disappointment, or self-reproach (Wile, 1993).

Withdrawn Partners

One common conflict style is withdrawal. Sometimes this affects the relationship, and both partners become demoralized and back away from each other. Withdrawn partners typically suppress their thoughts and feelings. They fear humiliation or do not feel entitled to their feelings. They may also be fearful that by expressing conflict they will hurt their partners or that it will lead to an unmanageable argument. These fears are often based on experiences from their families of origin or repeated unsuccessful attempts to resolve conflict with their partners.

Alternately, some individuals are seen as withdrawn by their partners because they have fewer social needs or perhaps they have little faith that they can solve problems through negotiation. Others have learned that withdrawal is a powerful tool to exercise control over their partner, and they use it to establish a classic pursuer–distancer relationship with their mate (Wile, 1993).

Consider the situation with Dave and Sandy. During her childhood, Sandy's mother told her that "men cannot be reasoned with" and that "it is better to pretend you agree with them and then just do what you want to do." Sandy was also told that if she persists long enough, "men will break down and give you what you want." Dave, on the other hand, watched his father leave the house each time there was any tension. It is easy to understand how Sandy has become the pursuer and attempts to get what she wants through manipulative tactics rather than by negotiating with Dave. It is also apparent that Dave is following in his father's footsteps; he goes to the other room and watches television each time there is conflict. Because neither of them has seen positive problem solving modeled in their families of origin, they are playing out the patterns from their early childhood training.

In addition to identifying anger and withdrawal as indicators of verbal conflict styles, we must look at other behaviors that can vary in their intensity and duration.

Characteristics of Verbal Abuse

Verbal abuse is hurtful and attacks the abilities of the partner. It is often manifested by overt, angry outbursts, or it may be very covert and couched in sincere terms that only the abused partner can discern. It is insidious and manipulative. Verbal abuse is also unpredictable, and it can be expressed in double messages. Finally, verbal abuse becomes the problem in the relationship rather than the process of disagreement. For example, when a couple is having a disagreement about money and one or more of the abusive tactics is employed, the issue no longer is about the money but is centered on the way one partner treats the other (Evans, 1992). Verbal abuse is characterized by the following behaviors:

1. Discounting the partner's ideas
2. "Put-downs" disguised as jokes
3. Blocking and diverting
4. Accusing and blaming
5. Judging and criticizing

6. Trivializing the partner's viewpoint
7. Threatening
8. Name-calling

Verbal abuse can be associated with physical abuse and couples violence if the couple cannot manage conflict in more appropriate ways. Verbal abuse inhibits a couple's intimacy, communication, and problem solving. For example, Ryan and Allyson have been having a disagreement about Allyson's forgetting to pick up the weekly dry cleaning. Gradually, as Ryan continues to berate her, he accuses her of being stupid and a worthless human being. He also insinuates that he is not getting ahead at work because she is not a "good enough wife." Allyson cries and promises to do better. This verbally abusive interaction could be considered as a coercive cycle that results in rewarding abusive behavior by one partner "giving in."

CONFLICT ISSUES AND PATTERNS

Control, Power, and Equity

The major conflicts in a marriage "center in the problem of who is to tell whom what to do, and under what circumstances" (Haley, 1963, p. 27) and who is to have the power. Couples make informal and formal rules and assign roles regarding who is to control each situation in their relationship. Control issues center around resources such as space, money, and children (Christensen & Jacobson, 2000), and couples often get involved in win–lose struggles over these topics rather than negotiating their differences. If one partner "wins" more often, the other may feel worthless, frustrated, and angry. Consider the situation of Ken and Babs when they entered therapy. Ken has a job that requires that he travel most of the week, and he has continued this pattern for 3 years. Babs has made a life with her female friends when Ken is away and she is not always at home when he calls her. Ken has become angry and has insisted that Babs remain at home and wait for his call each evening. Ken confides that he feels unimportant in Babs's life and wants to regain control of his relationship by this symbolic act, indicating her subservience. The counselor's job in such situations is to help couples understand the sources of these feelings and then learn to negotiate new rules rather than act on outmoded ones.

Blame

Blame is an attribution that the other partner is the cause of the problem. Thus, blame is a form of denial about one's personal responsibility for the conflict. Rather than lead to productive negotiation, blame sidetracks the couple on the issue of what or who caused the problem.

The following four methods of blame have been identified as contributors to relationship distress (Strong & Claiborn, 1982; Weeks & Treat, 1992):

1. *Justification* is the practice of assigning negative behaviors to external situations; for example, "I cannot help the way I act," or "It is your fault I got angry and broke the vase. You shouldn't get me so upset."

2. *Rationalization* is the practice of denying one's behavior as harmful; for example, "I did it for your own good," or "I have to leave home without telling you where I am when you act like that."
3. *Debilitation* refers to statements indicating that one is helpless because of the other's behavior; for example, "I go crazy when you do that and I can't help it," or "You kill me when you act like that in front of my friends."
4. *Vilification* is when the other person is made the villain by attributing negative intent; for example, "I know you try to feel superior to me, so you make jokes in front of your friends," or "I know you don't want your family to like me, so you tell them stories about me to make me look bad."

Often, one partner blames the other to protect his or her self-esteem. Blame makes us feel temporarily better about ourselves. Pointing out another's faults seems to affirm our own "goodness" (Johnston & Campbell, 1988). All these tactics interfere with solution-focused discussions between partners and instead foster avoidance, retribution, anger, and withdrawal.

Triangulation

When couples experience repetitive, polarized conflict, the struggles can become so great that they may attempt to ease the distress by drawing in a third element to the disagreement. This method, discussed briefly in an earlier chapter, is referred to as *triangulation*. The third element of the triangle can include excessive work, in-laws, friends, drugs or alcohol, children, or an affair (Dym & Glenn, 1993).

Triangulation is an avoidance strategy with destructive consequences (Prosky, 1991). One typical avoidance pattern of triangulation is "scapegoating," or shifting the focus to an innocent person as a way of lessening the intensity of the couple's conflict (Minuchin, 1974). The scapegoat may be a boss, a parent, or a social agency. Scapegoating can have devastating effects on children and fails to solve the real problem.

Another pattern involves one partner forming an alliance against the other partner. For example, a client may try to get the counselor to intervene in a conflict with a partner rather than dealing with the issue alone. If the counselor becomes a go-between, the tension is lessened, but the couple has not learned to deal with conflict. This pattern provides more power but creates less opportunity for conflict resolution because the other person feels "ganged-up on."

A very common pattern is to get one's emotional or sexual needs met through an affair rather than by addressing the problems of emotional distance or relationship issues. (Chapter 12 includes a more detailed discussion of some ways to manage this kind of triangle.)

Interactive Conflict Patterns

Another way of looking at conflict in a couple's relationship is to examine common conflict patterns. When the couple identifies the pattern, both partners can then begin to stop themselves when they see it emerge and implement better negotiating strategies. Listed below are a few of the most common patterns:

Pursuer–Distancer Pattern

This pattern evolves in couples when one partner becomes the aggressor in the relationship and constantly moves toward the other by attempting to involve him or her more intensely in the relationship. There are several ways to pursue. Initiating discussions or conflicts, overplanning the partner's time, following the partner throughout the house, initiating sexual interaction, or overcommunicating.

On the other hand, the distancer remains aloof from the relationship and commits little time to the activities planned, retreats for privacy in the home, deflects conversation if it becomes too intense, and finds excuses to divert sexual attention or intimate verbal communication with his or her partner. Together, these styles create a "dance" in which both partners contribute to a lack of closeness and intimacy in the relationship. Often, each will blame the other and fail to see the pattern they have created.

Reminder–Procrastinator Pattern

Also known as the overfunctioner–underfunctioner or overinvolved–underinvolved pair, this duo presents as one responsible partner who must remind the other to be responsible. Usually, the procrastinator eventually retreats from duties until reminded many times. This procrastination allows the person to underfunction in the relationship, yet he or she becomes resentful when the other partner nags. The more reminders given, the more dependent the procrastinator becomes. The "dance" promotes resentment and anxiety for the "reminder" and "resentment" and rationalization in the "procrastinator."

Parent–Child Pattern

Similar to the reminder–procrastinator pattern, this interaction is based on a critical "parent" attempting to place the other in a more submissive position in the relationship by criticizing, punishing, withholding praise and positive comments, or demanding certain tasks or responses of the other partner. The "parent" is angry and feels justified to treat his or her partner as an infant. The "child" may exhibit withdrawn or rebellious behavior or helpless responses to the "parent" rather than maintain a position of responsibility and equality. This cycle is destructive because each behaves in a way that requires the other to remain in the undesired role rather than change.

DEVELOPMENTAL STAGES OF COUPLES CONFLICT

One way of looking at conflict is in terms of how it escalates over time. Couples can be thought of as progressing to higher stages of conflict when they consistently fail to negotiate solutions to problems. The higher the stage, the more severe the conflict and the more some type of intervention is required.

Stage 1: Early Disagreement

Stage 1 involves a minimal degree of conflict and is usually present in couples who have been together for a short time. Conflict has generally not persisted longer than 6 months and has not created resentment or significant tension in the relationship.

Most of these couples are pre-clinical and will respond to psychoeducational approaches in therapy. Without the presence of significant anger, they are able to assimilate information required to produce change.

Stage 2: Repeated Conflict

Couples in Stage 2 are typically experiencing chronic conflict lasting more than 6 months. Communication between them is open, and both parties can express their dissatisfaction; however, blame and triangulation are present to some extent. Couples continue to spend time together and have fun, but resentment is evident. As a response to relationship stress, the couple may exhibit patterns of the pursuer–distancer, the reminder–procrastinator, or the parent–child. Counseling during this stage focuses on lowering anxiety and stress and reestablishing self-focus in place of partner blame.

Stage 3: Severe Conflict

Couples in Stage 3 present with severe conflict that has persisted well over 6 months with identified periods of intense anxiety and stress. Blame is evident, as well as polarization and power struggles. Anger and control are primary issues and may be diverted temporarily by increased triangulation of other parties or events. These attempts are an effort to reduce the conflict when it is most stressful. Communication is closed and trust is low. Therapy in this stage is centered on reducing the polarization and emotional reactivity and on reestablishing trust. This requires that any toxic issues be shelved temporarily until the couple has reduced blame and can use some degree of problem solving in the relationship.

Stage 4: Severed Couple's Relationship

Couples in stage 4 are characterized by the extremes of all the dimensions of relationship stress. That is, communication is poor, power struggles and blame are high, criticism is intense, self-disclosure is absent, and triangulation—which may be in the form of an attorney—is evident. Relationship counseling is usually not indicated because anger is extremely high. Instead, counseling may focus on negotiating concrete parent–children issues or the partners' reactions to the divorce process. Mediation, rather than an adversarial process, is the treatment of choice in this situation (Sperry & Carlson, 1991) because it can provide a more successful disengagement from the relationship.

VIOLENCE IN A COUPLE'S RELATIONSHIP

During periods of intense or violent conflict in relationships, it is necessary to provide individual counseling for each partner rather than couples counseling. It is the counselor's responsibility to assess the propensity for violence and make an appropriate referral for individual treatment if necessary. If one partner is abusing the other, the first issue is to make sure that the abused partner is in a safe place, such as a shelter, and she has notified appropriate authorities.

Scope of the Problem

A woman is physically abused in the United States every 9 seconds. In fact, 2000 to 4000 women are beaten to death each year. Domestic violence is the leading cause of injury to women and causes more injuries than car accidents, muggings, and rapes combined. The term *domestic violence* refers to a cycle of destructive thoughts, feelings, and actions that often involves physical battering accompanied by psychological, sexual, or property violence (Christensen & Jacobson, 2000). Men perpetrate most acts of violence toward their female partners; however, wives abuse a very small percentage of their husbands.

Definition of *Battering*

Battering is a pattern of behavior in which one person establishes power and control over another person through fear and intimidation, often including the threat or use of violence. Battering occurs when batterers believe they are entitled to control their partners (Figure 10.1). Battering includes emotional abuse, economic abuse, sexual abuse, manipulation of children, exercise of male privilege, intimidation, isolation, and a variety of other behaviors designed to maintain fear, intimidation, and power.

Recognizing a Potential Batterer

The following warning signs of a potentially violent relationship can help clinicians identify the profile of an individual who has the propensity for violence. The terminology used reflects the fact that most batterers are male and most victims are female.

1. Experienced physical or psychological abuse as a child
2. Had father who battered his mother
3. Displays violence toward other people
4. Uses guns for protection from other people
5. Loses temper frequently and more easily than necessary
6. Commits acts of violence against objects and other things rather than people
7. Uses alcohol excessively
8. Displays unusual amount of jealousy
9. Expects partner to be present or available at all times
10. Becomes enraged when he gives advice and it is not taken
11. Appears to have a dual personality
12. Exhibits a sense of overkill in his cruelty or kindness
13. The partner is afraid of his anger; preventing him from being angry becomes an important part of the partner's behavior
14. Has rigid ideas of what people should do, usually determined by male or female sex-role stereotypes

Figure 10.1   The wheel of violence

Source: Used by permission of the Domestic Abuse Intervention Project, 202 East Superior St., Duluth, MN 55802, 218-722-2781 www.duluth-model.org

Batterers tend to exhibit other identifiable characteristics including depression, anxiety, low self-esteem, dependence, paranoia, dissociation from their feelings, poor impulse control, antisocial tendencies, and hostility toward women. They desire close relationships, but they fear the intensity of relationships and the possible loss of control.

There are also passive batterers in relationships. Passive abusers tend to gravitate toward assertive women. These abusers are often resentful of their victims' life achievements, or they may feel jealous of the amount of education that their partners have received or jealous of the amount of money made. Overall, the abuser perceives a victim to be more efficient in life, often as a result of the abuser's low self-esteem (Marino, 1994; Walker, 1994).

The Cycle of Violence

The three cycles of battering are tension building, explosion, and love, and these cycles increase in duration and intensity and may also increase in frequency. It is not possible to predict the length of each cycle or the degree of damage that will occur the next time. In other words, just because an abuser has never used a knife, it is not safe to assume that the abuse will not reach that level the next time. Situational events, stages of life, and the partner's response all affect the timing and the acts committed.

Tension-Building Stage

In this stage, the victim (we will assume "she") begins to sense the man's edginess and begins to smooth over minor issues. She denies her anger and believes she can control the situation. He knows his behavior is wrong and is fearful she will leave him. She reinforces his fear by withdrawing so that she will not set him off. Tension rises. Some women report they begin to provoke attacks after a while just so they can "get it over." Provocation, in their mind, is a sense of control of the situation.

Explosion Stage

The abuser does not understand his anger and does not want to hurt his partner, but just wants to "teach her a lesson." He knows his rage is out of control but justifies it by her actions. Women may feel safer during this stage and may release their own anger and fight back. This is the shortest stage, which can last from a few hours to about 2 days. Women commonly deny their injuries, sometimes to soothe the batterer or because they are embarrassed and cannot accept the seriousness of the situation.

Love Stage

Both partners welcome this stage. The abuser is remorseful and fears his partner will leave him. He acts charming and manipulative. He believes that he can control himself and that he will not behave that way again. He convinces her and others that he is sincere. The victim wants to believe him because he is being nice to her and she wants to recapture the picture of love they once had. He acts dependent on her and says he cannot live without her. She begins to feel responsible for him as well as for her own victimization. She receives what she wants with overkill. He brings home flowers and candy, does errands, and may plan a vacation they have been discussing. They look toward the future and believe the abuse will not happen again. Unfortunately, as this stage progresses, tension begins to build again (Walker, 1994).

Reasons Why Women Stay or Return to Abusive Situations

Following are some of the reasons women may tolerate abuse from their partner:

1. She has low self-esteem; she thinks she deserves the abuse she has received.
2. She models her mother's behavior and considers it normal for women to be battered.

3. She believes she does not have enough money or other resources to leave.
4. She fears the abuser will find her and hurt or kill her.
5. She is dependent on her abuser's decision making and does not think she can manage by herself.
6. She loves him and believes she can change him.
7. She feels embarrassed to admit she has been abused.
8. Her abuser has agreed to seek therapy.
9. He "only gets abusive when he drinks."
10. She believes she has control of the situation ("he only hits me when . . .").

Counseling for Batterers and Victims of Domestic Violence

Once the counselor has assessed the presence of violence, couples counseling should cease. The overall goals are (1) to stop the violence, (2) create safety for the battered, and (3) help the abuser interrupt the violent cycle. Only then can couples therapy be reestablished.

The Batterer

The focus of treatment is on the cessation of the violence by teaching the batterer new skills for dealing with anger control, problem solving, and assertiveness. Old cognitive patterns are replaced with more effective ones. In addition, issues of self-esteem, jealousy, substance abuse, impulse control, and feelings toward women are addressed. Group and individual treatment are the methods of choice, and couples therapy cannot be reestablished until a safe environment has been created.

The Abused Woman

Discovering a plan for the victim's physical safety is the first priority. She should live apart from the batterer until he has acquired new skills and she has a safety plan in effect. She must accept the seriousness of the situation and understand that he will not stop the abusive behavior on his own. She must accept that the abuser does not understand what is happening and has displaced anger and rationalization, so he will not accept responsibility for his actions.

Group or individual therapy provides an arena for her to tell her story and have her feelings regarding the seriousness of the situation validated. Therapists can help her accept responsibility to protect herself when she is in danger and to recognize that danger. She should not be "rescued" but should be supported by the therapist. Treatment focuses on identifying her strengths, understanding how violence has affected her life and her behavior, and teaching her problem solving and assertiveness. She can look toward the future knowing that she may need to take care of herself economically and emotionally if he does not change. She should not be involved in couples therapy until she has accomplished these tasks and until the abuser has made significant changes. If he does not, she may desire assistance with divorce issues.

EQUITY IN A COUPLE'S RELATIONSHIP

Once all battering has ceased and the couple and their counselors have determined to resume relational counseling, it is important to help couples understand the principles of the wheel of equity. These principles are based on a relationship of negotiation, affection, division of labor, economic parity, respect, companionship, communication, and support (Figure 10.2). As counseling progresses, couples can assess the degree to which they are able to discuss and implement each component described in the wheel. Counseling interventions are often created as a result of candid discussions about these components and what changes are needed in the relationship so that both partners feel equal.

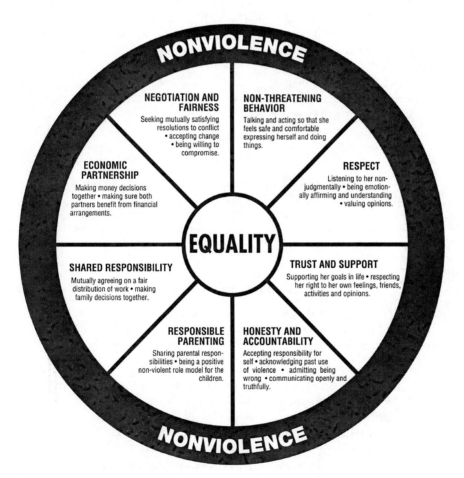

Figure 10.2 Equity wheel

Source: Used by permission of the Domestic Abuse Intervention Project, 202 East Superior St., Duluth, MN 55802, 218-722-2781 www.duluth-model.org

NEGOTIATION AND PROBLEM SOLVING FOR COUPLES

The ability to negotiate without reprisal is one of the important aspects of equality in relationships. Many interventions for couples related to decision making and conflict resolution have been based to some extent on concepts and assumptions basic to negotiation theory (Scanzoni & Polonko, 1981).

The aim of negotiation is to attain a convergence wherever a conflict of aims, goals, or behaviors is evident (Rubin & Brown, 1975). Each partner uses strategies or tactics to optimize the reward opportunities. The reward can be intrinsic (a feeling of rightness) or extrinsic (better couple relations). Couples who experience successful joint decision making can focus on an issue without bringing in extraneous arguments and feelings—for example, hurt feelings from other unresolved problems, anger, or current situations—that impede the process. Decision making requires that each partner feel a sense of equality so that input for the decision is valued by both parties. Use of "I" statements, uninterrupted time to speak, and the acceptance that the outcome (solution) may be an accommodation of both person's perspectives are essential components of the process. Rules for fair fighting must be established in relationships if that is to be part of the decision-making process. In addition, conflict training and couples contracting can be helpful interventions to produce positive negotiation and solutions for partners.

Conflict Training

Conflict training involves a shift from an emphasis on the individual to a view of the couple in which the individual is only a part (Cahn, 1992; Weeks & Treat, 2001). Engaging in couples communication skills training (see Chapter 8), learning a problem-solving model, and adopting principles of solution-focused discussions are all part of effective conflict training.

Problem-Solving Model

Successful problem solving is based on the partners' shared view of the problem and shared responsibility for its solution. These following steps for solving relationship issues increase the likelihood that a positive outcome will be forthcoming:

1. Clearly define a joint definition of the problem.
2. Brainstorm multiple possibilities for solutions to the problem (no idea is too unrealistic or too absurd).
3. Narrow the possibilities to three (one that one partner chooses, one that the other chooses, and one that is mutually agreed on).
4. Prioritize the possibilities (rank-order).
5. Choose one possibility with the understanding that, if it does not work, the second will be attempted.
6. Decide the particulars (who, what, when, where, how). Each person's responsibility for the outcome must be clearly stated rather than assumed.

7. Do it!
8. Evaluate the effectiveness of the solution attempted.
9. If the situation isn't resolved, try the second option.

This model allows both partners to participate in the formulation and resolution of the problem in a nonblaming process. Ideas are not "bad" or "stupid"; they either work or do not work.

Fair Fighting

One of the most important skills for couples to use is the ability to fight fairly. Most, however, do not have good role models and have little experience in how to accomplish this skill (Young & Long, 1998). When couples air their differences, certain rules must be established to protect the productivity of the disagreement and the feelings of each individual. A fair fight begins with the person who perceives a problem making an introspective assessment of feelings and beliefs associated with the issue.

During the first part of the fight, feelings must be expressed. Second, rules must be established so that blaming and name-calling are eliminated. Third, time and place must be established so that there are no distractions and full attention is available from both parties. Fights should not be hurried; they can be broken into segments, if necessary. Finally, after resolution is completed, the same issue should not resurface when there is a new problem to solve (Weeks & Treat, 1992). These steps ensure the safety of the interaction so that each person continues to feel valued and the relationship can be free to grow and flourish.

CLINICAL INTERVENTIONS

Reframing

Reframing, or relabeling, is a technique used to change a negative meaning into a positive one. It consists of changing the frame of reference against which a given event is considered or judged, thus changing the meaning and value judgment of the event without changing the facts (Paolino & McGrady, 1978; Sherman & Fredman, 1986; Young, 2001).

After observing the couple's language, worldview, and solutions to the problem, the therapist can offer information about the pattern of behavior in a different, positive context so that couples can hear it differently. Viewing it in another way can offer new possibilities and help couples think and feel differently about an issue. In turn, this may trigger optimism in approaching the situation (Mones, 2001).

Interestingly, the behavior that is reframed is the same behavior that the couple has defined as symptomatic (Weeks & Treat, 2001). For example, partners who come to therapy because they fight too much can see their problem differently if the clinician says, "You two must have a lot of passion for each other because your fights are so intense. There seems to be a lot of caring, or you wouldn't bother to fight."

With reframing of the event, it is possible to wonder what it would be like if the partners showed their passion in different ways. Determining those ways can be a goal of therapy and a positive attempt at problem solving.

Yet another example of a positive reframe is demonstrated in the case of Christophe and Celeste. Christophe complains that Celeste begins to cook when they start arguing. When she cooks, he becomes even more annoyed. Celeste explains that she does not understand why she cooks; perhaps it is a way to keep herself from saying something that she will regret. The therapist might reframe Celeste's behavior to suggest that cooking is her way of showing Christophe that she loves him, even when they are fighting. Celeste likes this idea and further states that she believes that she is doing something positive for the relationship. Christophe can now look at her cooking as a way that Celeste shows she cares rather than as a way to avoid a disagreement. By creating a positive explanation, the two can then determine whether or not they want to continue to handle disagreements this way. Blame and frustration are diminished, and they can look toward positive resolutions in problem solving.

Using Metaphors

A metaphor is a way of speaking in which one thing is expressed in terms of another, thereby casting new light on the character being described. The metaphor used in counseling couples must be congruent with the problem situation and must provide a possible solution in that context. Friedman (1990, p. 178) explains that metaphors or fables give the "reader or listener distance from his or her own real life encounters. Yet, through the distance they provide fresh perspectives on familiar human foibles."

Types of metaphors include metaphorical stories, fables, anecdotes, and short stories; analogies, similes, and relationship metaphors; tasks with metaphorical meanings; metaphorical objects; and artistic metaphors. Metaphors are also used because they are usually more interesting than direct messages and so can appeal to the receiver's imagination. Metaphors can be constructed to help clients try things or think about things in ways they have not viewed them before. Because metaphors are indirect, they can offer couples new perspectives in a less threatening way.

To use metaphors effectively to solve a couple's problems, the counselor must join successfully with the couples and have an understanding of the issues involved. The counselor then constructs characters equivalent to those of their actual clients. Table 10.1 shows the elements of a story about a client family with an anorexic daughter and other family problems. From this outline, a story might be constructed about the metaphorical family as a way of getting the couple to face the family problems objectively (Rosenbaum, 1992).

Counselors must also plan how to use the metaphor to help achieve the desired outcome. Because the solution cannot be apparent, the metaphor must demonstrate how the characters representing the real-life subjects made the changes that enabled them to overcome their problems. This is the *connecting*

Table 10.1   Sample Use of Metaphors in Therapy

The significant events of the case must be represented by equivalent events or incidents in the story. This is possible only when a full assessment of the case has been completed.

Real Family	*Metaphorical Family*
Carol will eat only vegetarian foods and is showing signs of anorexia.	Prince Christopher will eat only grains and vegetables and is getting very thin.
Linda is over involved with Carol's life.	The Queen and Christopher engage in many activities together, and the Queen has high expectations for the Prince.
Linda and Stu fight over Carol's work with the homeless.	
Linda and Stu fight in front of Carol about her work with the homeless, and Carol withdraws.	The King and the Queen fight over the Prince's work with the peasants.
	The Prince hears the King and Queen fight over the Prince's work with the peasants.
Linda and Stu do not have a life together without Carol.	
	He leaves and goes to a nearby village.
Carol and Stu do not have a good father–daughter relationship.	The King and Queen do not know how to relate to each other without the Prince's presence.
	The King and the Prince do not understand each other or have a good relationship.

Source: Adapted by permission of the author from *The Use of Metaphor,* by J. Rosenbaum (1992). Unpublished manuscript, Counseling Department, Stetson University, DeLand, FL.

strategy (Gordon, 1978); the story indirectly introduces ways that partners can deal effectively with their dilemma.

To conclude the metaphor, the counselor can either help the couple see how their own behaviors are similar to the ones in the story or can allow them to think about the meaning and implications of the story and discuss it at a later time.

Contracting

In an attempt to understand relationship conflict, Sager (1976) described *marital conflict* as a clash of different marital contracts. These contracts are a way of portraying the partners' beliefs in the relationship.

Relationship contracts help couples negotiate problems in an explicit, rational manner. They are based on bargaining, or exchange, theory. In other words, "To get what I want, I must be interested in what you want and accommodate with you" (Sherman & Fredman, 1986). Contracts are behavioral in form and require that both parties participate in the discussions and subsequent creation of the contract. The case example of Maria and Kimberlee describes a situation involving a good-faith contract; their contract is illustrated in Box 10.1.

Box 10.1
A Good-Faith Contract Resulting in Extrinsic Rewards
(Case Example Family)

Maria and Kimberlee both agree that the following specific tasks will be carried out in good faith by each member of this contract as it is specifically stated in writing below.

It is understood that Maria

- Will come home by 5:30 p. m. three times per week.
- Does not speak with Kimberlee for the first 20 minutes that she is home.
- Will not make any derogatory remarks about Kimberlee's friends.

It is understood that Kimberlee

- Will keep the bathroom and her own room as clean as agreed upon by Maria and Kimberlee in session.
- Must attend school 4 out of 5 days a week.
- Must call home by 10:30 on weekend evenings to let Maria know where she is, what time she will be home, or an appropriate friend's house at which she will be staying.

Signatures: _____

_____

Case Example: Maria and Kimberlee

Maria is a 37-year-old single mother with a full-time job. Her daughter, Kimberlee, is 17 years old. Kimberlee's father is described as a "deadbeat dad" whose whereabouts have been unknown since her birth. Maria initiated a request for family therapy, stating that "Kimberlee is out of control." Maria wants the two of them "to be close—like we used to be."

Maria describes the family as one in which tension has recently increased. Kimberlee does not come home or let her mom know where she is most weekends. Kimberlee, according to Maria, also skips school three to four times a week and is not completing her chores at home. Maria believes this change in behavior is associated with Kimberlee's new friends.

Kimberlee describes her family situation as extremely strict and punctuated with frequent screaming matches between mother and daughter. She believes that her Mom is too strict and is trying to live her life through her daughter. Both agree that tense feelings at home are associated with Kimberlee's absence from home and her avoidance of household responsibilities. Maria states that she also has been remaining at work long after the required hours in order to avoid a confrontation with her daughter. They agree to define their expectations and negotiate a new set of rules so that they can "get along better" and establish more positive feelings between the two of them. The therapist helps Maria and Kimberlee develop a contract (Box 10.1) so the expectations will be clear and specific.

Role Reversal

The use of role reversal in couples therapy helps each partner see the other's reality from a different perspective. When each is placed in an alternative role, it is easier to exercise self-control and view the situation in a more objective manner. This deflates the need to be right or wrong, an issue that frequently produces conflict for couples. When one partner "walks in the other's shoes," he or she may feel more empathy and may understand the problem in a different way. Concomitantly, the other partner may view himself or herself as if in a mirror because the self is seen through the other's perceptions. Thus, new insights are created.

A role-reversal strategy to encourage couples to consider viewpoints other than their own can be accomplished by having partners switch places, symbolically and physically. The partners might switch their seating arrangement and each take on the behaviors of the other. The therapist instructs both partners to communicate as if they are the other person, stating the other's views, even if logically they do not agree with them. Looking through a different lens can provide insight about the other person's belief system or behaviors and feelings. Finally, the partners should switch back to their real selves and process with each other what it felt like to be in the other's shoes and what they learned by the experience.

Bratter (1974) describes role reversal as driving a car 50 miles per hour and then shifting it into reverse to go the other way. It disturbs the equilibrium and provides a context for change. In couples therapy, the technique can be most effective in examining reciprocal roles such as pursuer–distancer, rescuer–scapegoat, parent–child, or other repetitive patterns that cause conflict.

Case Example: Morena and Saul

Morena and Saul have been married for 3 years and have been experiencing increasing conflict about Saul's hobby of collecting antique cars. Not only is it a very expensive hobby, according to Morena, but the time he spends working on them and purchasing them cuts away much of their couple time. Recently, Saul has rented a garage in which to store the cars, making him even less accessible to his partner.

Morena has begun to argue with Saul and is spending more time in the library researching careers in the travel industry. Saul will not discuss her career because he believes she will be away from home too frequently. Morena has recently met Tobias, a travel consultant who has offered to train her and allow her to travel with him on familiarization trips.

Application of the Integrative Model

Stage 1: Assessing and Obtaining an Interactional View of the Problem

Initially, Saul reports that Morena is being very hostile about his time away from her and she has begun to nag and complain when he is at home. He admits that he likes to get away from the house when she is acting so negatively. Morena complains that Saul is spending more time with his cars than with her. She claims that she is bored and would like to have a close relationship but does not know how to get back on track. Saul indicates that their sexual activity has been almost nonexistent.

After they each explain their frustrations, both agree that they would like to get closer and negotiate the time they will spend together. Morena wants to plan special dates; Saul extends the idea by including intimate time with more sexual touching as part of their new couple commitment.

Stage 2: Goal Setting

Together, Morena and Saul formulate the following goals:

1. They will plan time for talking and dating so that they can feel closer again.
2. They will have regular planning meetings so that they can negotiate the time they will spend on hobbies as well as the time together, to feel more included in each other's lives.
3. Morena will research the travel opportunities and discuss them with Saul before any future plans are made. They will feel more capable of problem solving when they complete this task.
4. The couple will plan a vacation independent from any auto rallies so that they can be more adventurous and romantic with each other. The vacation will provide an opportunity for feeling more connected and more playful.

The couple begins to refer to their problem as the "3-year marriage blahs," and they are determined to overcome their boredom and renew their interest in each other.

Stage 3: Adopting New Perceptions and Behaviors

In this stage, one of Morena and Saul's tasks is to negotiate and implement a written contract on their couple time. In addition, they have organized a trip for a romantic week in the Caribbean islands. Finally, the couple has determined to spend 30 minutes per day communicating with each other about their feelings and concerns for their relationship.

Stage 4: Maintaining New Perceptions and Behaviors

Both partners discuss each person's responsibility to continue working on the problems and vow to hold each other accountable if the day ends without "talk time." They decide to confront each other if the weekly date is not made a priority and discuss at a couple meeting what they have planned for the upcoming weekend.

Stage 5: Validating New Perceptions and Behaviors

Morena and Saul congratulate each other on their renewed commitment and identify Morena's free spirit and sense of adventure as their barometer if they should get off track with their plan for fun time together. Saul, the more serious minded of the two,

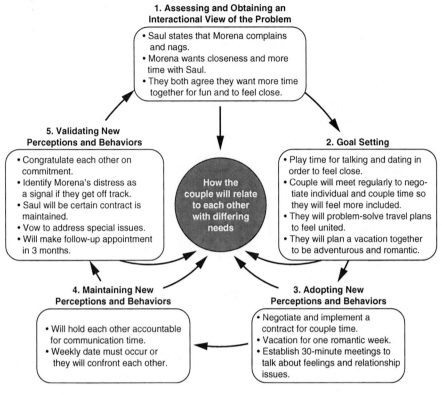

1. Assessing and Obtaining an Interactional View of the Problem

- Saul states that Morena complains and nags.
- Morena wants closeness and more time with Saul.
- They both agree they want more time together for fun and to feel close.

5. Validating New Perceptions and Behaviors

- Congratulate each other on commitment.
- Identify Morena's distress as a signal if they get off track.
- Saul will be certain contract is maintained.
- Vow to address special issues.
- Will make follow-up appointment in 3 months.

How the couple will relate to each other with differing needs

2. Goal Setting

- Play time for talking and dating in order to feel close.
- Couple will meet regularly to negotiate individual and couple time so they will feel more included.
- They will problem-solve travel plans to feel united.
- They will plan a vacation together to be adventurous and romantic.

4. Maintaining New Perceptions and Behaviors

- Will hold each other accountable for communication time.
- Weekly date must occur or they will confront each other.

3. Adopting New Perceptions and Behaviors

- Negotiate and implement a contract for couple time.
- Vacation for one romantic week.
- Establish 30-minute meetings to talk about feelings and relationship issues.

Figure 10.3   The therapy process with Morena and Saul

will gently remind them if they do not uphold their contract in every aspect. They also realize that they need more time to address the sexual issues of their relationship, and they have confidence that they can begin to work on the issue because they have been so diligent in this endeavor. (See Figure 10.3 for an overview of the counseling process.) Both determine to return to counseling in 3 months to assess their progress.

Considerations for Working With Couples in Conflict

1. Determine the causes of relationship stress and view it from an interactional perspective.
2. Assess the style of conflict each partner uses and attempt to design interventions that interrupt the pattern.
3. Assess the capability for violence in the relationship and cease couples therapy if violence is present.
4. Be aware of the destructive nature of verbal abuse and educate the couple of the destruction, if appropriate.
5. Assess the degree of power and control each person possesses and help both move toward an equitable relationship to promote problem solving.

6. Help the couple reduce blame by learning more useful communication skills.
7. Understand the stages of relationship conflict and provide appropriate interventions for each stage.
8. Know the cycle of violence and refer the batterer to individual or group therapy.
9. Assist the battered victim with a protective plan and a plan for individual or group therapy.
10. Use a psychoeducational approach to help clients learn fair fighting and problem-solving skills.
11. Be aware of the need for specificity with any relationship contracting.
12. Be familiar with reframing, use of metaphor, and role reversals as potential interventions to reduce conflict or channel it in more constructive ways.
13. Remember, conflict is necessary; it produces change. It is the negative way in which some couples conflict that is deadly.

CONCLUSION

Once couples can understand that conflict is a normal part of a relationship, they can begin to examine the way in which they disagree. If violence is not present, couples can learn effective problem-solving skills to foster long-term solutions. In addition, they can identify destructive interactional patterns and interrupt them for better results.

Counselors assist couples to explore the aspects of blame, power, and control and determine how these concepts influence their relationship. During the assessment stage, the counselor can identify the stage of marital conflict in which the couple is currently functioning and design interventions based on the nature of the conflict.

Strategies such as reframing, use of metaphor, relationship contracting, and role reversals may be employed to facilitate change with conflicted couples. As couples learn fair-fighting techniques through communication exercises and practice problem solving through the use of a stage model, they will be able to express their feelings, identify the stress or source of the conflict, and collaboratively create solutions without blame or inequities of power in the relationship.

11

Divorcing Couples

KEY CONCEPTS

- Couples use divorce stage theories to help them assess and design effective treatment strategies.
- Each partner may progress through the stages of divorce at a different rate.
- An integrative model of couples counseling helps provide a couple with a shared description of the presenting problem so that blame is not necessarily a central issue of the divorce experience.
- An integrative counseling model provides a systemic view of a couple's divorce process.
- Mediation and rituals are two specific intervention strategies to help a couple complete the divorce process.

SOCIOLOGICAL CONTEXT: THE PREVALENCE OF DIVORCE

The notion of couples living "happily ever after" has been challenged in the last 50 years with almost half of all marriages ending in divorce (Cottrill, 2004; Epstein, 2002; Paul, 2002; Roberts, 2004; Shulman, 2004). Of these divorces, more than half will remarry, and well over half of those who remarry will divorce again (Clapp, 2000). On the basis of these statistics, we can assume that a majority of couples coming to counseling will personally experience divorce or be affected by the divorce of a family member.

For most divorcing couples, the experience is painful and difficult, and it affects many aspects of each partner's life, as well as the lives of family members and friends. Disagreements during divorce range from issues related to money, children, sex, leisure time, career, and extended family. Cottrill (2004) refers to a 2001 DivorceMagazine.com poll in which 29% of the respondents cited infidelity as the reason for divorce, 22% blamed communication problems, and 14% said that emotional or physical abuse was the reason for the split. Shulman (2004) refers to couples' vastly different family backgrounds as a reason for relationship discord. This includes whether or not their parents have been divorced. Jacquet and Surra (2001) found that parental divorce is a factor for influencing relationship commitment and satisfaction. Because of the variances in family-of-origin lifestyles and values, Pittman (2004) refers to a need for "binocular vision," the ability to develop a perspective through your partner's eyes as well as through your own, which may not have been modeled in families who experienced parental divorce. When couples are unable to achieve such a vision, they often become disillusioned and feel unhappy in their relationships.

DIVORCE STAGE THEORIES

One way of understanding the divorce process is through knowledge of divorce stage theories. It is important that a couple understands the dynamics of divorce and the stages through which couples progress in order to effectively assess and design interventions for themselves. For example, the issues for a couple exploring the possibility of divorce will be very different from those of partners who have been emotionally detached from each other for a long period of time and who may primarily be seeking assistance with the issue of child custody.

Making the Divorce Decision

Internal Stressors

The decision to divorce is a result of the extreme internal stress of at least one partner, which may be influenced by unmet needs or goals, poor coping styles in handling life events, or the inability to communicate feelings to the other partner. These factors can affect one or both partners' ability to manage conflict and negotiation in the relationship.

External Stressors

In addition to internal difficulties within the couple or individual, couples may experience a variety of external stressors on the relationship. Some of these stressors involve career, community, and extended family. For example, a wife may be angry with her husband because he will not support her career by attending the charity events that she organizes in the community. Her husband claims it is not his style, while she believes it is critical for her career advancement. Over many months, she becomes resentful and more withdrawn in the relationship. Communication becomes strained and she spends more time at the office. Her husband complains, but eventually it becomes easier for him to be involved in his own activities. Finally, after a year and a half, she decides that she wants a divorce.

As trivial as the issues may seem, this is not an uncommon scenario. What counselors need to remember is that it is not usually the issue itself but the way in which couples attempt to resolve the issue that leads to a deterioration of the relationship. In this case, the partners did not seem to negotiate the relationship very successfully, nor did they manage conflict well. Gradually, the relationship eroded without either of them attempting to reconcile the differences. The wife may have become dissatisfied first, but clearly the husband played a role in the erosion of the marriage, even though he may not have wanted a divorce.

The decision to remain in a relationship or seek a divorce is the sole responsibility of the couple. Ethical standards prohibit a therapist from making such a choice for the couple. The therapist's role is to help couples make decisions about divorce. To be effective in this role, they must understand divorce stage theories and the experiences of each partner as they progress through the stages.

Hetherington (2002) describes five broad types of marriages and has identified the pursuer–distancer style as the most likely to end in divorce:

1. Pursuer–distancer marriages are those in which one partner wants to confront and address issues, while the other avoids and denies issues and becomes withdrawn.
2. Disengaged marriages are those in which couples do not share similar interests and activities. There is little conflict, but there is little interaction and little expressed emotion.
3. Operatic marriages involve partners who express intense emotion and are prone to volatility, arguments, and passionate lovemaking.
4. Cohesive–individuated marriages are characterized by warmth, equity, respect, and mutual support.
5. Traditional marriages have the least risk of instability. Typically, the husband is the provider, and the wife cares for the children and the home.

The Stages of Divorce

Most divorce stage theories focus on the emotions and experiences that each partner must resolve in order to progress to the next stage in the process. Although there is a sequence of stages through which individuals generally progress, one may repeat the stages, skip them, or experience them simultaneously. The intensity and duration of the stages may vary from person to person, and emotions experienced during a particular stage may resurface in other stages or during intense crisis periods in the lives of the divorced couple.

DEVELOPMENTAL MODELS OF DIVORCE

Differences between the developmental models of divorce are generally described in terms of points of emphasis (Landis, 1991). Some models focus more on the emotions that each individual experiences, whereas others emphasize thoughts and behaviors. Most models that emphasize feelings or behaviors hypothesize a sequence that typically progresses from denial to anger to depression and finally to acceptance (Crosby, Gage, & Raymond, 1983; Kaslow, 1984) within a 2- to 3-year time period. Generally the sequence of feelings and behaviors is described as three stages: (1) preseparation or predivorce decision-making stage, (2) transition–restructuring stage, and (3) recovery–rebuilding stage (Clapp, 2000; Kaslow, 1984; Sprenkle & Storm, 1983).

The Three Stages of Divorce

Preseparation or Predivorce Decision-Making Stage

In this stage, one or both partners experience a growing dissatisfaction about the relationship. Usually one partner begins to daydream or make plans for the future that do not include the other spouse. The dissatisfied partner may investigate the legal process of divorce and discuss the possibility of divorce with friends and family members. Women often experience this stage as more stressful than do men.

Transition–Restructuring Stage

This stage includes addressing the economic realities of divorce, the logistics of where each partner will live, and coparental and custodial issues if the couple has children. The result may be confused feelings as well as fear, loneliness, anger, and, at times, elation.

Recovery–Rebuilding Stage

It is during this stage that individuals begin to explore new life experiences, new identities, and new love objects. They clarify priorities, set new goals, and make lifestyle changes. Clapp (2000) refers to it as the "phoenix" stage when people rise from the ashes of divorce. Although it can be an exciting period for many, it can also be characterized by ongoing regret or long-term resentment.

A Diaclectic Model of Divorce

Kaslow and Schwartz (1987) have proposed a comprehensive, eclectic model of divorce that organizes behavioral dynamics, stage theory, and the emotional responses to divorce. Their model, highlighted in Table 11.1, includes five elements:

1. Temporal sequence
2. Stations of divorce
3. Intrapsychic dimensions
4. Behaviors/events
5. Therapeutic implications

Temporal Sequence

This element refers to the developmental stage through which partner's progress and the time frame typically required to progress through the stage. Most often, both partners do not experience the same rate of dissatisfaction or feelings associated with the disillusionment of the breakdown of their relationship.

Stations of Divorce

Stations include various aspects of divorce, such as emotional reactions, legalities, economics, coparenting, community reactions, and internal reactions of each partner (Bohannon, 1973). Often these stations are intertwined so that partners are reacting to intense emotional stress at the same time that they are receiving pressure from extended family, friends, or attorneys.

Intrapsychic Dimensions

These aspects encompass the feelings and emotional reactions each partner experiences during the stage of divorce. These feelings and reactions range from disillusionment, despair, shock, emptiness, anger, hopelessness, confusion, loneliness, excitement, regret, acceptance, independence, and autonomy.

Although certain stages of the divorce might be most often characterized by particular feelings, dramatic shifts in feelings and experiences can create a "rollercoaster" effect. For example, when one spouse first tells the other he or she wants to separate, there may be initial reactions of panic, anger, fear, or shock that can later turn to excitement and back to hopelessness in a matter of minutes or hours.

Behavior/Events

These elements refer to the actions taken or tasks in which the individual engages during stages of divorce. Some of these actions might be sulking, crying, confronting the partner, bargaining, threatening, grieving, making new friends, telling relatives, exploring new interests, and stabilizing new relationships. Behaviors are also quite confusing because one may vary from pretending that all is fine, to consulting with an attorney, and then to attempting suicide, all in a 24-hour period. It is a time to expect the unexpected.

Therapeutic Implications

Different interventions may be more or less appropriate at different stages of divorce. Interventions include marital therapy, couples group therapy, divorce therapy, individual adult therapy, child therapy, family therapy, parent–child therapy, and group support therapy for adults or children. For example, relationship (couples) therapy is useful during the preseparation or predivorce decision-making stage while the couple formulates a plan for separation. Later, family therapy may be indicated to help the children understand what is happening. Once the divorce has occurred, group therapy for either partner or for the children may help individuals address their feelings of hopelessness and fear and to begin to formulate plans for the future.

APPLICATION OF DIVORCE STAGE MODELS

As we discussed earlier, it is particularly useful for us to understand divorce stage models because both partners may not have agreed with the decision to divorce and may be progressing through stages very differently. One partner may have agonized over the decision to divorce for quite some time and may have experienced the disillusionment, anguish, and emptiness characteristic of the preseparation or predivorce decision-making period. These feelings, however, may be unknown to the other partner, who may be shocked when the other announces that he or she wants a divorce. Furthermore, the unknowing partner may perceive the other as cold, uncaring, impulsive, or unfeeling if he or she has already detached from the relationship and appears ready to take action, such as a physical separation or filing for divorce. The therapist's primary role is to help the

Table 11.1   Diaclectic Model of Stages in the Divorce Process

Divorce Stage	Station	Stage	Feelings	Actions and Tasks	Therapy Interventions
	1. Emotional divorce	1	Disillusionment Dissatisfaction Alienation Anxiety Disbelief	Avoiding the issue Sulking and/or crying Confronting partner Quarreling	Marital therapy (one couple) Couples group therapy
Predivorce A time of deliberation and despair		2	Despair Dread Anguish Ambivalence Shock Emptiness Anger Chaos Inadequacy Low self-esteem	Denial Withdrawal (physical and emotional) Pretending all is okay Attempting to win back affection Asking friends, family, clergy for advice	Marital therapy (one couple) Divorce therapy Couples group therapy
	2. Legal divorce	3	Depression Detachment Anger Hopelessness Self-pity Helplessness	Bargaining Screaming Threatening Attempting suicide Consulting an attorney or mediator	Family therapy Individual adult therapy Child therapy
During Divorce A time of legal involvement	3. Economic divorce	4	Confusion Fury Sadness	Separating physically Filing for legal divorce Considering economic arrangements	Children-of-divorce group therapy Child therapy Adult therapy

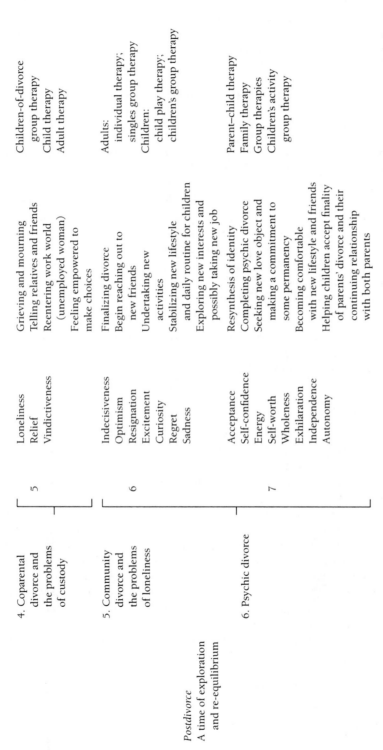

5	4. Coparental divorce and the problems of custody	Loneliness Relief Vindictiveness	Grieving and mourning Telling relatives and friends Reentering work world (unemployed woman) Feeling empowered to make choices	Children-of-divorce group therapy Child therapy Adult therapy
6	5. Community divorce and the problems of loneliness	Indecisiveness Optimism Resignation Excitement Curiosity Regret Sadness	Finalizing divorce Begin reaching out to new friends Undertaking new activities Stabilizing new lifestyle and daily routine for children Exploring new interests and possibly taking new job	Adults: individual therapy; singles group therapy Children: child play therapy; children's group therapy
7	6. Psychic divorce	Acceptance Self-confidence Energy Self-worth Wholeness Exhilaration Independence Autonomy	Resynthesis of identity Completing psychic divorce Seeking new love object and making a commitment to some permanency Becoming comfortable with new lifestyle and friends Helping children accept finality of parents' divorce and their continuing relationship with both parents	Parent–child therapy Family therapy Group therapies Children's activity group therapy

Postdivorce
A time of exploration and re-equilibrium

Source: From *The Dynamics of Divorce: A Life-Cycle Perspective,* by F. Kaslow and L. Schwartz, pp. 30–31. Copyright 1987 by Brunner/Mazel, Inc. Reprinted by permission.

couple communicate about the decision to divorce, even when both partners do not appear to have the same goals for the relationship. Remember, it takes two willing people to make a relationship work.

Counseling and the Stages of Divorce

When couples first come to counseling it is important to obtain a thorough history of the relationship including the development of conflicts, the style of conflicts, and the progression of the relationship from satisfactory or happy to irreconcilable. Friedman (2004) cautions that therapists must consider the potential for physical violence and choose counseling theories and interventions based on this data. It is not appropriate to conceptualize a conflict systemically and assign responsibility to both partners if there is a history of physical or emotional violence or intense conflict present in the relationship (Friedman, 2004).

During the preseparation or predivorce decision-making stage, the couple begins to consider divorce as an alternative to ongoing marital conflict. Usually, this decision has been made after the couple has struggled for some time, either alone or with each other. Guerin, Fay, Burden, and Kautto (1987) identified four developmental stages of marital conflict to describe the couple's decision to divorce.

1. Stage 1 typically occurs in the early years of marriage. In this stage, the relationship is characterized by open communication and a minimum amount of conflict. Negative reactivity toward each other and criticism are at low levels, and so therapy is not usually sought during this stage of conflict. Instead, couples attempt to negotiate their differences in a healthy way as they form their new relationship.

Issues such as how to spend time with each other, budgeting, in-law contact, career, and other household roles and rules are addressed. Most encounters between couples at this stage are through psychoeducational programs or marital enrichment courses sponsored by local churches, civic groups, and schools (Guerin et al., 1987).

2. In stage 2, the couple defines marital conflict as a problem. Couples in this stage experience anxiety and emotional arousal and argue openly with each other. Communication remains open, but there is more criticism and struggle for control. Although there may be some thoughts of separation or divorce, therapy more often is sought to address marital issues in an attempt to reconcile the differences.

If the therapist will be seeing the partners separately, it is important for him or her to discuss confidentiality issues with the couple before the sessions begin so that secrets do not emerge in individual sessions that cannot be expressed in joint sessions. A good rule of thumb is for therapists to tell both partners that all information brought forth in any session is to be considered joint information and can be shared with each other in a conjoint session. We do not advocate seeing couples separately because it can become difficult to maintain confidentiality and remember that the couple is the client.

A useful approach at this stage is a short-term couples group. This modality seems to help reduce the couple's tendency to cling to past hurts and battles and make excessive demands on each other and instead begins to create excitement and joy once again in the relationship (Kaslow & Schwartz, 1987). If the couple can resolve their differences and address historical problems, they will not progress to the point of divorce therapy.

3. Stage 3 is characterized by a dramatic emotional climate in the relationship. Anxiety is high. At times, one partner may appear to take an opposing view in order to fuel disagreement. The level of criticism is high at a time when both spouses have an impaired ability to communicate over day-to-day events. One or both partners may be bitter, and their lives run parallel courses as they pursue their own interests with minimum interaction (Guerin et al., 1987).

Couples at this stage experience confusion, ambivalence, and denial, and one partner may pretend that everything is fine while attempting to win back the spouse's affection. Chaos, confusion, inadequacy, and failure are prominent feelings (Kaslow & Schwartz, 1987). Often, individuals turn to their families and friends for emotional support or to enlist their help to induce the other partner to stay in the relationship.

Conjoint couples therapy is the treatment of choice at this stage until it is relatively clear that the relationship will end in separation or divorce. The role of the counselor is to help both partners clarify their confused feelings, help them determine any possibilities for the resolution of their difficulties, and help them make a decision that will be in the best interest of all parties involved. Custody may be a major issue during this stage, particularly if each desires primary custody of the children. Children can become pawns in the battle of divorce if custody disputes become the central focus.

Therapy can be difficult at times during stage 3 because of the intensity of emotions that the couple expresses. The initial goal is to reduce the anger, blame, and criticism that partners direct toward each other in the session so that the couple can make some decisions for the relationship. The therapist must also help both partners validate their pain and must instill hope for the emotional survival of both parties. If both partners can cooperate and work toward a solution that will focus on the "best interests" of all parties involved, they may begin to feel empowered to make their own choices. This process will enable them to experience more self-respect as they take responsibility and exercise choices for their futures (Kaslow & Schwartz, 1987).

It is also appropriate in this stage for the counselor to refer the couple to mediation for the resolution of their issues (Clapp, 2000). *Mediation* is the resolution of issues with the assistance of a neutral third party and is designed to reduce the couple's anger that is sometimes fueled by an adversarial court battle. (This intervention is outlined later in this chapter.) If mediation is not used and conflict remains high, adversarial legal proceedings are usually pursued. The couple may feel depressed, helpless, and pessimistic as the negotiating and problem resolution is now in the hands of attorneys, who may fuel the amount of anger, despair, and conflict by virtue of their adversarial positions (Landis, 1991; Palmer & Landis, 1989). The division of possessions, decisions over parental arrangements, and the loss of one's life dreams are very painful experiences for all involved.

Counselors must be aware that individuals can move from feelings of intense anger and retribution to extreme sadness and anxiety very quickly and without any apparent provocation (Landis, 1991). It is important to make couples aware of these dramatic mood swings and help them identify ways of managing these feelings when they arise. For example, one partner knows that when the other parent comes to pick up the children there is often a prolonged discussion that leads to anger and frustration. The partner might plan in advance to have the children ready and then immediately leave as soon as the children are in the other's care. A further plan might be to go to a movie with a friend in order to challenge impending loneliness and frustration.

4. Finally, stage 4 is marked by extreme conflict. One or both parties have usually engaged an attorney at this stage, and it may be most useful at this time to refer both parties to individual therapy. Continuing to see the couple conjointly is beneficial only if both are willing to work on unresolved joint issues affecting their children or the dissolution of their marriage. It is not recommended for the same therapist to retain either one of the parties for individual therapy. Confidentiality issues are confusing in circumstances where both parties have been prior clients, and any information about the therapy sessions requested by one partner requires a release of information form signed by both parties.

Another complication arises if one party believes that the therapist sides with his or her partner. The result may be a malpractice suit. At the very least, the counselor is faced with being subpoenaed by one party and becoming involved in a legal battle over what information can be used in court.

Because the divorce process can be a very chaotic time for most couples, it is important that therapists have a clear model for addressing a couple's needs. These needs can be addressed by the use of the integrative couples model outlined earlier.

THE INTEGRATIVE MODEL AND DIVORCE THERAPY

The following case example concerns a couple that comes to therapy during the preseparation or predivorce decision-making stage (Clapp, 2000). The partners are engaging in behaviors indicative of late stage 2 or early stage 3 of relationship conflict (Guerin et al., 1987). At this stage, emotionality is high, communication is low, and there is an excessive amount of blame directed at each partner.

Case Example: David and Marcy

David and Marcy have been married for 6 years. David initially made the appointment on the advice of his best friend, after confiding that Marcy has been working 50 to 60 hours per week for over 2 years and at times has been sleeping at the office after a long night of work. David reports that there is no excitement in the relationship and that the two have little in common. Sex has been almost nonexistent, and David has been the primary caretaker of the children for too long. He admits that he is lonely and would like female companionship, even if it were not with Marcy.

Marcy emphasizes that she loves her work and gets a lot of satisfaction from it, something that she does not experience as a wife and mother. She blames David for not being available to her because he is either playing with the children or playing tennis at the local club. Marcy is not interested in maintaining the relationship and would like to work out a separation so that the children, ages 3 and 5, will be minimally traumatized. David, on the other hand, would like to resolve their differences if at all possible.

Application of the Integrative Model: Divorce Therapy

Stage 1: Assessing and Obtaining an Interactional View of the Problem

During this stage of assessment, the therapist obtains information about each partner's perception of the problem. This is accomplished by the use of circular questioning. As both parties describe their version of the problem, the counselor gathers data about their families of origin and some of the early messages and interactional styles they brought to the relationship. This information may be useful later as the couple examines the early messages they have received from their families and identifies the personal strengths they have each developed to cope with life events.

David sees Marcy's work and her apathy about the relationship as the problem; Marcy views David's lack of excitement and diverted interests with the children and tennis as the focus of the problem. The counselor helps the couple begin to see an interactional problem so that they can share in the solution by jointly owning the problem. One interactional definition tentatively offered is, "It seems that both of you are lonely in your relationship and that you are seeking other ways to fill that loneliness. You both seem to have lost touch with each other to the point that one of you is ready to separate."

The therapist proceeds to obtain more information about the duration of the problem, the partners' commitment to trying to resolve the problem, others who are affected by the problem, and alternatives to a decision to separate. David claims that the children are afraid they will not see their parents anymore if their parents divorce. As the therapist finds out more about the couple, the couple explores attempts that have been made in the past to resolve the problem.

David states that he has tried to get Marcy more involved with the children and has tried to plan a family vacation together. He says that he also tried to teach Marcy to play tennis so that they could play together, but she claims that it hurt her arm and the weather was too hot. Marcy believes she tried to involve David more with her work-related activities that she says he found boring. They said that the only time they agreed on activities was when they participated together in a school carnival for the children.

Stage 2: Goal Setting

During this stage, the counselor asks David and Marcy to identify specifically what their lives would be like if the problem were solved. It is important to help the couple see the new picture of the relationship interactionally rather than as individually focused. It is not clear yet whether the focus will be on helping the couple remain together or helping them separate successfully. That decision is to be made solely by the couple. If the focus is on the couple remaining together, Marcy's statement that "David needs to spend more time with me away from the children" could be restated as "David and I need to find specific ways to spend time together as a couple and as a family with our children."

At the conclusion of this stage, the decision is made whether to continue with marriage therapy. David and Marcy decide to continue. The counselor then asks each partner to be more specific as they identify possible goals. David and Marcy identify the following goals:

1. They will set aside one night per week to pursue an activity together to infuse some excitement and joy in their lives. They will provide a babysitter and take turns planning the activity.
2. David and Marcy will sit down with the children and plan five activities they would like to do as a family and then plan a time schedule to complete the activities so that they feel more connected to each other.
3. The couple will spend time together talking about their intimate relationship, and they will set aside time at least once a week for a one-on-one activity, such as massaging each other, to feel more satisfied and more pleasure in their relationship.

These goals could be more extensive, but now let's assume that Marcy and David do not wish to work on the marital relationship. Instead, they would like to discuss a separation with the counselor. First, the counselor helps the couple understand what has led to their decision to separate and what barriers they have encountered in attempting to resolve the conflicts. The counselor can also help the couple be direct in their communications to each other so that there is a minimum of mixed messages and game playing about leaving the relationship. The couple must also entertain the challenge "Is there anything that can be done to save this relationship?" Usually this question spawns conversation about deep-rooted notions of love and intimacy.

If the couple is not interested in pursuing the relationship or if one is somewhat interested but the other is not, therapy will begin to move in a different direction. Both parties must be invested in making the relationship work, or there will be conflicting interests between the parties; it takes two to make the relationship work.

Therapy is now oriented toward helping David and Marcy explore and express their feelings about the divorce and the arrangements for the children. Goal setting with the couple now might be more like the following:

1. David and Marcy will discuss how they envision their lives as coparents and will develop a plan on paper before they talk to their children. This plan will help them feel more confident when they talk to their children and will help give them more direction about their future.
2. David and Marcy will talk with their children conjointly and answer any questions they can without blaming the other. The children will feel more secure as their parents describe what they can expect with regard to parental contact, where they might live, what school they'll attend, contact with grandparents, and so on.
3. David and Marcy will attend mediation sessions and will contact attorneys to finalize plans they make. This process will help them feel more collaborative rather than litigious as they separate their lives as marital partners.
4. Each individual will pursue friends and family to help them feel supported during this time. Neither person will blame the other in front of family or friends.

5. Divorce therapy will continue for at least five sessions to help them express their feelings and say goodbye to the marriage.

Specific goals for the couple during this stage help provide a focus and instill hope for a more positive coparenting relationship. A general goal or outcome statement might be "David and Marcy will seek all methods and support available for the two of them to divorce in the most collaborative, nonblaming manner possible so that they will feel more hopeful about the future and their children will feel more secure with the changes in their lives."

Stage 3: Adopting New Perceptions and Behaviors/Interventions

At this stage, the counselor facilitates a conversation as the couple draws on the strengths that both partners possess individually and as a couple to divorce successfully. Strengths in this case might include the ability to work on the school carnival together even when they were fighting, David's ability to be creative to find solutions, or Marcy's negotiating skills to find a middle ground. It can be useful to help the couple create their own story about how they want to parent their children and live their lives separate from each other. A conversation initiated by the counselor may progress like this:

Counselor: David, you said earlier that you two were able to work on the carnival together. Tell us what you saw as the most cooperative thing you did to make that happen.

David: Well, I took some time off and wrote a schedule of each event and who needed to perform each task.

Counselor: So, you were very clear about what you saw as each person's responsibility for the carnival events. How did you check that out with Marcy and come to an agreement?

David: She looked at the schedule and made some changes based on her time frame and how she thought it might run more smoothly.

Counselor: Is that how you see it, Marcy, that you were able to have a written plan and then make changes together to create a final plan?

Marcy: Well, basically. David is very good at planning a project, but sometimes he forgets about child care needed to implement his ideas.

Counselor: So you were able to help him make a plan that worked because you had more familiarity with that aspect of the plan.

Marcy: Yes, it went really well.

Counselor: I wonder if it would be possible now for the two of you to make a plan to include a parenting schedule flexible enough for all of you with your careers and with the children's activities.

David: I could make a chart of all the activities and a weekly time plan, and then Marcy could look at it to see what might be useful and where it might break down.

Counselor: Marcy, would you be willing to do that so that you could each have a part in the parenting schedule?

David and Marcy seem able to work things out. However, if the partners seek mediation at this stage, they focus on collaboration, not litigation.

Stage 4: Maintaining New Perceptions and Behaviors

In this stage, the focus of counseling is on how the couple will continue to work together during times of extreme stress. Questions about how much each wants to be successful with the divorce, how much each is willing to be different, or how much each is willing to give up the old picture and create a new one are helpful for underscoring the idea that often there is ambivalence about being different and remaining the same. One part of them would like to blame and be resentful, but another part would like to be cooperative. Therapy helps the couple acknowledge the inflexible reactions while emphasizing the flexible, creative side that exists in all people.

During this stage, questions are designed to help the couple identify the barriers, or "pulls to the old pattern." For example, "What do you each need to do to ensure that the plan you have created will work?" or "What will prevent success for you now?" or "What do you need from others to make this happen?" are effective questions to provoke thought about the barriers.

David and Marcy identify their work schedules, Marcy's mother, and David's bitterness as obstacles that get in the way of their interactions. The couple begins to discuss what they will do when work interferes, what Marcy might say to her mother if she is negative, or what possibilities exist for David, such as a support group or special friend to confide in when he feels bitter. The more specific the couple is as they identify barriers and solutions to the barriers, the more potential for resolution they create.

Stage 5: Validating New Perceptions and Behaviors

In this stage, the task is for partners to restate their goals for therapy and define their successes. David and Marcy have attempted to resolve their differences in therapy. They have attended mediation, identified their support systems, and have talked to the children together about the divorce without blaming each other.

The outcome statement directly addresses the statements they made in stage 2 as they defined their goals for divorce therapy. Both partners validate their collaborative success as well as their personal contributions to the successful resolution. Marcy says, "I am happy that we have been able to work together and that David has been so helpful about the scheduling," and David replies, "It seems like we really have a plan to work together for the children. I think Marcy has been very accommodating in making sure my parents see the children when they come down to visit." (See Figure 11.1.)

Ending therapy in a positive manner continues to provide the partners hope for the future that they will be able to work together on a variety of issues that arise. They are given a sense of accomplishment in the midst of grief, loss, and change. Although the feelings of grief and loss are dealt with only minimally in this model, this is not meant to suggest that these feelings are not central to the divorce process. Rather, it suggests that much of the individual feeling or grief work needs to be done individually. The focus of therapy in our case study, as stated in the goals, is to work together in order to parent the children effectively.

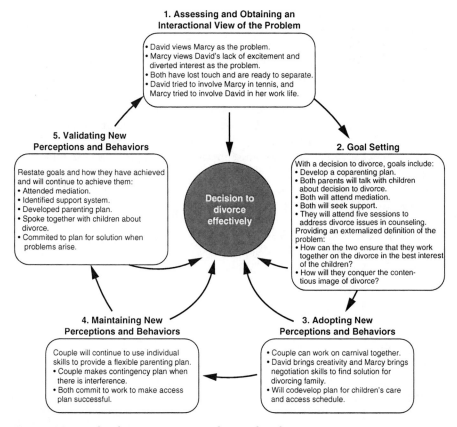

1. Assessing and Obtaining an Interactional View of the Problem
- David views Marcy as the problem.
- Marcy views David's lack of excitement and diverted interest as the problem.
- Both have lost touch and are ready to separate.
- David tried to involve Marcy in tennis, and Marcy tried to involve David in her work life.

5. Validating New Perceptions and Behaviors
Restate goals and how they have achieved and will continue to achieve them:
- Attended mediation.
- Identified support system.
- Developed parenting plan.
- Spoke together with children about divorce.
- Commited to plan for solution when problems arise.

Decision to divorce effectively

2. Goal Setting
With a decision to divorce, goals include:
- Develop a coparenting plan.
- Both parents will talk with children about decision to divorce.
- Both will attend mediation.
- Both will seek support.
- They will attend five sessions to address divorce issues in counseling.
Providing an externalized definition of the problem:
- How can the two ensure that they work together on the divorce in the best interest of the children?
- How will they conquer the contentious image of divorce?

4. Maintaining New Perceptions and Behaviors
- Couple will continue to use individual skills to provide a flexible parenting plan.
- Couple makes contingency plan when there is interference.
- Both commit to work to make access plan successful.

3. Adopting New Perceptions and Behaviors
- Couple can work on carnival together.
- David brings creativity and Marcy brings negotiation skills to find solution for divorcing family.
- Will codevelop plan for children's care and access schedule.

Figure 11.1   The therapy process with David and Marcy

Considerations for Counselors

Following are some guidelines for counselors engaged in counseling couples on divorce:

1. Determine the stage of divorce that each partner is experiencing and help the couple accept the differences.
2. Assess the stage of marital or relationship conflict, including frequency, duration, and intensity.
3. With the couple, determine joint as well as individual goals for therapy.
4. Design treatment plans based on the needs of both partners.
5. Assist the couple in the identification of support systems for each partner during the divorce process.
6. Help both partners identify appropriate therapeutic resources for each partner. These resources may include individual, family, or group therapy or community support groups.
7. Restate goals of therapy and define the success.

Counselors in training can identify the appropriate therapeutic goals and treatment strategies for a couple by using a role-play situation in the classroom to practice the "fit" of the goals, treatment plans, and therapeutic style of the integrative model that we have outlined. At the conclusion of the exercise, each class member can offer feedback based on the following guidelines.

Feedback Questionnaire

1. How well did the counselor assess the current stage of divorce and clarify the stage for the couple?
2. To what extent did the counselor assist the couple in defining the problem interactionally?
3. To what extent did the counselor address each partner's individual needs?
4. To what degree did the counselor assist the couple in identifying goals for therapy and a clear definition of success?
5. How well did the intervention strategies employed by the counselor help the couple move toward stated desired outcomes?
6. To what extent did the counselor make appropriate referrals?

INTERVENTION STRATEGIES

During the course of divorce therapy, counselors employ a variety of interventions to facilitate change. These interventions must be selected according to the unique characteristics of the couple. This section discusses mediation and rituals of separation because they may have specific application to divorce and separation issues. It is important to remember, however, that these interventions can also be used in other situations, depending on the couple's needs.

Mediation

Mediation is a process designed to assist separating couples in conflict to reach an agreement privately, confidentially, and informally. It employs the skills of a neutral and impartial third party, the mediator, who helps the individuals make their own decisions by providing necessary information, clarifying issues, helping them explore alternate solutions, and suggesting possible accommodations. Issues often mediated include child custody, primary and secondary residential parenting, child support, alimony or spousal support, division of assets, and taxes (Clapp, 2000; Palmer, 1993).

Goals of Mediation

The goals of mediation are to (1) reduce anxiety and other negative effects of the conflict by empowering the parties involved to devise a cooperative solution that best fits their needs and the needs of their children, (2) prepare the parties to anticipate and ultimately accept the consequences of their own decisions, and (3) promote an agreement for the future that all parties involved can accept (Palmer, 1993).

Advantages of Mediation

Mediation minimizes the potentially traumatic emotional and psychological effects of the adversarial process. Discussions between the parties can often proceed quickly, and an agreement can be reached in just a matter of one or a few sessions. For issues concerning children, the sessions are structured with the best interests of the child in the forefront of the discussion and in such a way that each partner can emerge a winner. Finally, mediation is much less expensive than traditional litigation proceedings.

What Mediation Is Not

- It is not therapy.
- It does not circumvent the legal system because both parties are encouraged to seek individual legal counsel at appropriate times.
- It is not primarily educational; rather, it is an interactive process with the primary focus on decision making, the establishment of a memorandum of understanding, and the development of a plan of action for the future.
- It is not arbitration. In arbitration, the couple authorizes a neutral third party to decide on a binding resolution of the issues. In mediation, the couple—not the third party—decides on the agreement that will govern the partners' relationship with each other in the future.
- It is not conciliation. People often use the two terms interchangeably; however, conciliation is a process whereby the couple meets with a neutral third party in an effort to work out the marital problems in order to continue the marriage. Mediation takes place after the couple has agreed that the marriage is over.

If Mediation Fails

If mediation does not bring about an agreement between the parties, any statements made during the sessions by any of the parties remain confidential. This means that a mediator cannot be forced to testify in court about the mediation process. If the parties cannot agree, the mediator will notify the court that agreement is not possible but will not comment or recommend further.

How Mediation Works

The process of mediation begins by an order of the court or by agreement of the parties. The mediator, though neutral and objective, plays an active role by assisting the parties in working toward their own settlement agreement. The parties are educated regarding what information is needed to achieve a fair agreement. The mediator clarifies and organizes details, prompts discussion and cooperative communication, and manages conflict. The purpose of the mediator is to help the couple identify issues, develop bargaining proposals, and conduct negotiations with the goal in mind of arriving at a settlement that best suits both partners' needs.

During mediation, the mediator uses such skills as managing conflict, referring the parties out for an expert opinion or advice, and sometimes just "directing traffic." Throughout the mediation, the mediator's function is to keep the parties task focused and mindful of the purposes, procedures, and scope of mediation.

The mediator does not make any decisions for the parties but facilitates the couple's own decision-making processes. When the issues have been resolved, the mediator drafts a memorandum of agreement. After review and approval by the parties, it is given to their attorneys for legal implementation.

The Counselor's Role

The counselor who is providing services for one or both parties seeking a divorce or modification can refer the couple to a certified mediator who will work with the couple on settlement of the issues relating to children and division of assets. The counselor may continue to see the couple for other therapeutic services, but the counselor should not attempt to mediate for either client while the couple is seeking therapeutic services. Therapy and mediation are two distinct services. It is important for counselors to be aware of mediators in their communities so that appropriate referrals can be made. We should note that a counselor can be a trained mediator. Training requires the completion of a prescribed course with some practicum experience, and in some states, specific laws govern training. It is not appropriate, however, for cocounselors—even if they are trained mediators— to provide mediation services once a therapy relationship has been established because mediation and therapy must remain distinct services.

The Attorney's Role

The mediator's role is neutral and is not a substitute for independent legal advice. The mediator does not represent either party but focuses on helping the parties reach their own agreement, so each party is urged to seek independent legal counsel throughout the mediation process. Although the decisions reached in mediation are made by the parties, it is important that they be informed decisions.

Attorneys may attend the mediation sessions, and at all times the parties are permitted to communicate privately with counsel. Upon completion of the mediation, the mediator will submit the memorandum of agreement to the parties' attorneys. If necessary, the attorneys will draft a settlement agreement from the terms of the memorandum for filing with the court.

The Cost of Mediation

The mediator's fee is usually determined on an hourly basis, and both parties are encouraged to share in the expense. The court may set the fee and determine the party responsible for payment when mediation is ordered. Occasionally, when the parties are indigent or qualify for financial assistance, low-cost services may be available. The important thing to remember is that mediation can be and frequently is less expensive in the long run, both financially and emotionally.

Who Uses Mediation?

Mediation is for parties who have made the decision to dissolve the marriage but who cannot agree on any or all of the many issues involved in the dissolution. Occasionally, mediation is used if the parties decide to separate for a period of time, when separation might result in dissolution. Frequently, parties have found mediation valuable in resolving differences that arise even after dissolution has been rendered. These postdissolution problems usually involve issues related to children (Palmer, 1993).

Rituals for Separation and Divorce

Traditionally, rituals have been associated with repetitive or symbolic behaviors designed to address a life event in a meaningful way for the individual or couple. Rituals can also be one of the most powerful socialization mechanisms throughout the life span (Laird & Hartman, 1988). Through rituals, we define and reaffirm our traditions and ourselves. Although rituals may employ language, they also take us beyond the conscious and cognitive domain to a more subconscious domain of myth, metaphor, and symbol. Rituals imply action and, being executed in the present, reflect the past and shape the future at one and the same time (Laird & Hartman, 1988). They can help individuals and couples express and create new realities without conscious awareness and can enable and impose change (Myerhoff, 1983). As rituals are enacted beyond our conscious awareness, they can be most effective for working with couples on issues of divorce.

Often in divorce, people become fearful and rigid and are reluctant to change. Both parties are confronting many new events, emotions, and situations in their lives, and there is a tendency to hold on to the life and behaviors from the former marriage, even when it is not feasible to do so. For example, Maya has always celebrated her birthday with Raoul at her favorite restaurant. This year, as a newly divorced person, Maya wanted to continue the tradition with one of her friends. But after the dinner, Maya was very disappointed with the emptiness that she experienced. Maya may be stuck in determining how she would like to commemorate occasions now that Raoul is not a part of her life. With the help of her counselor, she identifies a new tradition for her birthday that will elicit new meaning in her life without Raoul.

This is an example of how rituals can be powerful interventions in therapy when used to help clients effect change and provide alternatives to life situations. Rituals provide counselors a mode for helping people master life transitions, alter relationships, and construct more meaningful self-definitions (Laird & Hartman, 1988). They include a plan created by the counselor with the client to change a pattern in the present or the future.

Consider the following when creating a ritual:

1. Understand the context for the event that requires a ritual; did it come from the family of origin or from past behaviors of the individual or the couple?
2. Explore in detail with the individual or couple the old behaviors associated with the event and meanings ascribed to it.
3. Identify with the individual or couple the new context or manner in which they want to commemorate the passage of an event.
4. Identify the meaning the individual or couple would like to attach to the event.
5. Create a new behavior or way to commemorate the event that would ascribe new meaning to the event.

6. Explore with the client the barriers, or "blockers," for the completion of the task or ritual.
7. Evaluate the effectiveness of the new behavior and meaning of the behavior for the individual or couple in the past, present, or future, modifying the ritual accordingly.

Case Example: Kim and Lia

Kim and Lia are newly divorced. Kim initiated the divorce, and Lia was devastated. Finally, after 7 months, Lia is going to visit the mountain cabin that she and Kim had built during their marriage. Lia is taking her sons, Tyler and Stan, but she does not know what she will do without Kim to help her with them. Lia has considered asking her mother or a girlfriend to go with her, but she is concerned that she will get upset and does not want to be burdensome to anyone. She knows that she should be "getting on with her life" but feels uncertain and stuck. Lia has just begun to see a counselor and has decided to discuss her impending trip in her next session.

Intervention

After a thorough assessment, goal setting, and treatment planning with Lia, the counselor decides to help construct a ritual for Lia while she is on her vacation in the mountains. Because Lia was accustomed to Kim's company on the long drive to the cabin, she ordered a novel on audiotape that she could look forward to hearing while the children were sleeping. Lia also made plans to have an old friend stop and spend one night with her on the way home. Lia was most concerned, however, about the mementos that she and Kim had accumulated over the years in the cabin. Of particular importance was the arrangement of dried flowers they had collected on one of their hikes in the mountains.

As the counselor discussed with Lia the possibilities for change through a ritual, the following suggestions were made:

1. Lia will ask her friend to accompany her on a hike that she loves so dearly, but this time they will hike to a different destination on an unknown trail.
2. Lia will decide on a transformation for the dried-flower arrangement and will carry out the plan while in the mountains.
3. Lia will mark the transformation by some repetitive behavior or symbol while on the vacation.
4. Lia will select one friend with whom to share her feelings about her experience.

After much collaboration, Lia, with the counselor's assistance, decided to take her friend Carlita on the trip with her. She advised Carlita of her plan to choose a new hike, different from the one she previously took with Kim. Lia also decided to talk with Carlita about her fears and sadness about returning to the place she and Kim had shared so fondly.

After much deliberation, Lia devised a ritualized experience to mark the passage from her marriage to life as a single person. Lia decided to take the dried-flower arrangement and make a colorful potpourri. She will place the potpourri in three plastic bags. Next, the children and Carlita will accompany Lia on a hike and picnic in the mountains. While in the mountains and as the children are resting in their sleeping bags after lunch, Lia will disperse the potpourri throughout the hills, rocks, and streams. Finally, Lia will bury the vase in which she had arranged the flowers deep within the mountainous area. Through the ritualized transformation of the flowers that Lia had cherished with Kim, Lia chose to free them by returning them to their very origin, much as she hoped to feel after her divorce.

Symbolically, the burial of the vase meant the death and unavailability of the receptacle that had held the precious mementos, much like the end of her marriage. Having Carlita with Lia during the hike signifies the need for old friends, past experiences, and current events to ascribe new meanings to her present life.

This intervention has the potential for far-reaching effects if constructed in a meaningful way. Each ritual must be unique for the individual or couple so that clients experience new meaning and symbolism. Input from the client is crucial because it is the client alone who understands the meanings associated with particular events from the past.

CONCLUSION

With almost half of all marriages ending in divorce, counselors must become familiar with divorce stage models and important issues that couples face during this process; this is a critical area of learning for all counselors. The five-stage integrative model and its application for working with divorcing couples are reviewed in this chapter. The model includes (1) assessing and obtaining an interactional view of the problem, (2) goal setting, (3) adopting new perceptions and behaviors/interventions, (4) maintaining new perceptions and behaviors, and (5) validating new perceptions and behaviors.

In addition, two specific intervention strategies that have been adapted for divorcing couples are described in this chapter. Mediation as an alternative to adversity divorce proceedings is described in depth because clients often go through mediation and participate in therapy simultaneously. The use of rituals as a means of facilitating a couple's progress from one stage of divorce to another is also described. Finally, a case example illustrates how counselors can use this strategy to help divorcing individuals or couples.

12

Extramarital Affairs

MARK E. YOUNG AND ELIZABETH O'BRIEN

KEY CONCEPTS

- Extramarital affairs (EMAs) are common and when discovered are among the chief reasons for the break up of a relationship.
- Affairs begin with a great deal of excitement and promise but due to the conflicting responsibilities, the middle stages of an affair are fraught with tension. Affairs often end without resolution between the unfaithful partner and the lover.
- People enter into affairs for a variety of reasons. Sexual novelty and a wish for intimacy are two important motivations.
- Online infidelity is becoming a more prevalent mode for engaging in an affair.
- Society's code of silence about sexuality and media images support romantic ideas about affairs.
- Affairs do not necessarily mean the end of the couple relationship.
- Assessing culturally different attitudes about adultery is important to the therapeutic process.
- The therapist must help bring ongoing affairs out into the open and should not support one member's desire to keep the affair hidden.
- Therapy with couples who have experienced an EMA has two distinct phases, an emergency period and a separate time when key couple issues are faced.
- Getting over an affair, when it can be done, takes months or years. Patience and professional support are required.

Affairs promise so much: an opportunity to pursue dreams that have been dormant, to come alive again, to find someone who truly understands. Their hidden promise is pain.
Brown, 1991, p. 3

A friend purchased an antique oak bed at an auction, and one of its "romantic" features was the well-preserved bullet holes in the headboard just above where someone might have lain. The bed is a good conversation piece but, at the same time, a grim reminder that intimacy can be betrayed and that love can turn to murderous rage. An EMA is emotional dynamite to a relationship; many, if not most, precipitate a divorce (Glass, 2002). It exhilarates the unfaithful partner and can cast the spouse into a living hell. The unfaithful partner feels guilty and happy at the same time, while the spouse feels ugly and used and hates him- or herself for having been so trusting. The couple in crisis stays up late arguing, spends sleepless nights, and often experiences wild mood swings and irrational outbursts. A television series, *Cheaters,* was released that showed private detectives uncovering affairs with the accompanying reactions of the people involved.

When you are going through this roller coaster of emotions, the situation appears hopeless, and the relationship seems to be dead. But as Simone de Beuvoir said, a relationship is not like a chain that is broken; a hundred individual threads connect people. When the tornado of an affair hits a relationship, there are still connections that can form the basis of a new relationship if the therapist can find them. Couples can come back from the brink and forge a new relationship.

The couples therapist must remember that there is hope for the marriage if both people are willing to be patient, if the unfaithful partner is willing to change, if the spouse is willing to forgive, and if the couple is willing to confront the issues that may have given rise to the affair. These are four big "ifs." These "ifs" and the fact that the dynamite can explode at any moment is what makes working with affairs among the most challenging issues in couples therapy (Blow & Hartnett, 2005).

DEFINITIONS

Extramarital sex is the usual definition for an EMA, but this may be a male definition (Glass & Wright, 1992). Emotional involvement is more important in an affair to most women, and many emotional affairs are damaging to relationships even if sex is not involved. Respondents usually don't consider emotional affairs as EMAs, and the line between friendship and an emotional affair is sometimes difficult to draw. Glass and Wright (1985, 1992) were the first to identify three types of affairs: emotional involvement, sexual involvement, and a combined type.

Frank Pittman, who wrote the influential book about men's affairs called *Private Lies* (1989), indicates that the definition of whether an affair has taken place is based on the couple's definition of the contract. A man may not have had a sexual affair, but his time, interest, and intimacy may have been spent on another woman. Such situations must be dealt with as affairs if it breaks the couple's agreements or threatens the primary relationship. In this chapter, we use the term *unfaithful partner* to refer to the member of the relationship who has formed an intimate relationship with the third party (the "lover"). We use the term *spouse* to refer to the member of the couple who is not involved in an EMA. The use of these terms is based on a trend in the literature to refer to the members in this fashion and is not designed to blame.

How Prevalent Are Extramarital Affairs?

A study of marriage and family therapists (see Moultrup, 1990) revealed that nearly half of their clients came to treatment for issues associated with one or both partners having an EMA. There are a variety of estimates about the current percentage of married people having affairs, but most suggest around 60% of men and 45% of women are willing to report that an affair has occurred sometime in their marriage (see Glass & Wright, 1992). Brown (1991, 2001) suggests in her research that about 70% of all marriages experience an affair. The results of these surveys are suspect because people are unlikely to be honest. If this is true, the prevalence of affairs is underreported. It is staggering to presume that at least half of marriages experience an affair and that nearly half of the couples seeking therapy come on the heels of an affair. It is therefore incumbent on all therapists working with couples to be extremely familiar with the course and treatment of the affair.

Are There Types of Affairs?

So far, we have learned that an affair may be sexually based, emotionally based, or both (Glass & Wright, 1992). The way to assess these is to ask unfaithful partners about justifications and look at their thinking patterns. The combined type is the most difficult to disengage from because there is excitement reward and the fantasy of "true love" waiting just around the corner. It is presumed that these affairs normally destroy the primary relationship. Besides these global types, writers and researchers have looked at environmental, life stages, and psychological issues that may lead to an affair. This assumes that besides seeking sex, intimacy, or both, unfaithful partners are reacting to other pressures as well. Brown (1991, 2001) classifies the most common affairs seen in clinical practice in this way:

1. *Conflict avoidance affair.* The issue is frustration and inability for the couple to deal with conflict.
2. *Empty-nest affair.* The couple's relationship is unfulfilling after children leave home.
3. *Out-of-the-door affair.* The unfaithful partner, not wanting to take responsibility for ending the marriage, concocts this type of affair to induce the spouse to end the marriage.
4. *Intimacy-avoidance affair.* After several years of marriage, intimacy becomes overwhelming. An affair puts more comfortable distance in the relationship. Both members of the couple may have an affair.
5. *Sexual addict's affair.* The affair is entered into to make sexual conquests involving an element of daring.

Pittman (1989) classifies affairs in a slightly different way from Brown. Brown tends to see at least three of the four types as couples problems. Pittman does not believe that marital problems or developmental or environmental pressure necessarily precede affairs (Pittman & Wagers, 1995). Some types of affairs are simply caused by one person's willingness to have an affair. His clinical experience led him to define four basic types of affairs:

1. *Accidental infidelity*. These are unplanned trysts that are not based on a love relationship. They occur when alone, when traveling, when there are problems at home, or when the spouse is unavailable because of medical problems, pregnancy, or for some other reason. Some affairs are not necessarily the result of a bad marriage according to Michele Weiner-Davis (1992); they are the result of bad judgment. Some are "one-night stands" accompanied by too much alcohol. Even so, trust is destroyed and the primary relationship can be stretched to the breaking point.

2. *Philandering*. Philandering is a virtual career of EMAs and is something like a hobby. Male philandering according to Pittman is to avoid the control of women. It is a hypermasculine behavior that defines all relationships with women as potentially sexual and all relationships with men as competitive. Women philanderers by contrast are thought to be searching for Mr. Perfect. In both men and women, the philanderer lives with a certain amount of risk, and these "dangerous liaisons" are more exciting because of their illicit nature.

3. *Romantic affairs*. Romantic affairs have to do with falling in love. Pittman claims that "romantics" conduct romantic affairs. Romantics do not fall in love with someone who fulfills their dreams; they fall in love when their real life becomes insipid and they are "not quite ready for suicide" (Pittman & Wagers, p. 304). Very often, one person is involved in the affair romantically, and the other is using it for sexual variety. When two romantics team up, they may abandon their other relationships for their "love." Pittman claims that romantic affairs are often the ones that end with explosions and enough hurt to go around for everyone involved.

4. *Marital arrangements*. This is where both partners have openly or unconsciously agreed to have affairs on the side. It is a way of establishing distance in the relationship while maintaining some of the perquisites of marriage. These are situations like the businessman who has a 20-year relationship with his secretary. They can also include permanent separations. These triangles can work as long as the lover or lovers make no demands that the arrangement be modified. Pittman also identifies other more exotic and volatile "arrangements" such as "revenge affairs," "flirtation/jealousy," and other more bizarre agreements that seem to be made for the purpose of arousing the other partner.

Online Infidelity

Due to increased accessibility to the Internet, online infidelity is emerging as a new issue in couples therapy. Kimberly Young (1999a) defines an Internet affair as a romantic or sexual relationship that initiated via the Internet and is maintained primarily by electronic exchanges such as e-mail, virtual chat rooms, and interactive gaming. Use of the Internet to engage in affairs has become more prevalent because it offers anonymity, convenience, and escape for the user (Young, 1998a). Men and women engage in Internet affairs for much the same reasons that they participate in live ones. Men are apt to look for online sexual partners, while women will engage in emotional affairs (Gonyea, 2004).

It is estimated that 1 billion people used the Internet in 2005 (ET Forecasts.com, 2001). People may not perceive the Internet to be a threat because it is such a commonly used tool. However, its potential to be used as a pathway for infidelity should not be overlooked. Warning signs for an Internet affair look similar to those of a live affair: change of habits, evidence of lying, and a demand for privacy (Young, Griffen-Shelley, Cooper, O'Mara, & Buchanan, 2000). The damaging effects of an online affair can become more pervasive in the marital relationship because the computer (the mechanism to engage in the adulterous activity) can remain in the home and is available at all times (Whitty, 2004). In a study of people who meet in chat rooms, 30% indicated that they have had actual sexual relationships with people they met online (Mileham, 2004). Yet, 83% of people in these chat rooms did not consider online flirting as infidelity. More men than women frequent online chat rooms (Whitty, 2003) Couples counseling can be a successful treatment for online infidelity, just as it is for live infidelity. When treating a couple, discerning if an individual's online infidelity is a relationship issue or is an addiction is important. Some research suggests that addictions can be an impetus to engage in adulterous activities online (Cooper, Delmonico, & Burg, 2000). If addiction to the Internet or a sexual addiction is the core issue in an adulterous relationship, it is important that the addicted partner seek treatment in conjunction with counseling for the infidelity. Both professional counseling and support groups are available for sexual addiction (see www.sexaa.org).

WHY DO PEOPLE HAVE AFFAIRS?

Reasons often given by the unfaithful partner include a feeling of entitlement, that one deserves to be happy, that the marriage has been bad for a long time, or the spouse is no longer attractive. Fisher (1992) speculates that people have affairs to get attention, as a search for autonomy and independence, to feel special, desired, or more masculine or feminine. Still others want to prove they are still young in a "last chance" affair.

The spouse often tries to analyze the reasons for the affair, trying to reason out what went wrong in the marriage and may blame him- or herself or the lover rather than the unfaithful partner. Protection of the spouse and deep introspection into the causes of the affair are usually lacking in the unfaithful partner who is afraid to think, afraid to examine the affair very closely for fear that like a mirage it may evaporate. Our experience is that both spouse and unfaithful partner are protecting themselves from feelings of guilt, low self-esteem, and depression, and until the emergency phase is over, their insights are clouded. The reasons given for the development of the affair will come out as therapy progresses but may not be evident in the first pronouncements.

We present some research that tries to shed light on the reasons and justifications, but all are self-reports and retrospective. Pittman & Wagers (1995) have trouble taking any "justifications" seriously because they usually tend to blame the spouse or the marital relationship. They report a justification by one woman who felt that her husband's unwillingness to dance gave her the right to sleep with anyone who would dance with her.

Buunk's 1980 study of couples in the Netherlands asked unfaithful partners to indicate the reason for involvement in an EMA. Reasons included a need for intimacy, a need for variety in a relationship, emotional independence, sex-role equality for women, a need deprivation in the marriage, spouse approval, and social context reasons. Social context characteristics identified by women influencing their first EMA included peer influences such as knowing someone involved in an EMA and talking to that person (Atwater, 1979).

Various studies have increased the list of reasons given, but not until Glass and Wright's (1992) study of justifications was an attempt made to pull the many threads together. In a study of about 300 middle-class, educated travelers at an airport, they looked at 17 justifications for EMAs reported in the literature, asked their subjects about them, and then factor-analyzed the results. Four factors emerged:

1. A *sexual factor* that included novelty, curiosity, and excitement
2. An *emotional intimacy* that involved understanding, companionship, and enhancement of self-esteem
3. An *extrinsic motivation* that subsumed reasons such as career advancement and getting even with a spouse
4. A *love dimension* that included getting love and affection and "falling in love"

To simplify, there is support for the clinician's rule of thumb that there are sex-centered justifications and love-centered justifications.

Gender Differences

Glass and Wright (1992) found that men were more approving of affairs for sexual reasons whereas women approved more of affairs that had emotional justifications. Their research supports earlier data suggesting that men engage in EMAs more frequently, start earlier in marriage, and have more partners than women. While men are more likely to have an affair, evidence shows that younger women are participating in EMAs at higher rates than their husbands (Lawson, 1990). Women regardless of age are more likely to have extramarital emotional affairs without sex. According to Glass and Wright (1992), women who are satisfied sexually in their marriage are less likely to have an affair, but men cheat despite the quality of marital sex.

Among the most interesting analyses of why men have affairs is the work of Pittman (1989). One of his hypotheses is that philandering men have affairs to escape intimacy that they equate with female domination. Male socialization has imprinted the image of a "real man" as being autonomous, independent, and a "stud." Men must live up to the "Playboy Philosophy" which means having more than one sexual partner. To be faithful, in some ways, is seen as enslavement. In various parts of the United States, men develop activities such as softball, bass fishing, bowling, and poker to provide an escape from the pressure of an intimate relationship and the domestication needed to raise children and preserve societal institutions. It is not simply to enjoy the company of other men because normally these relationships are quite shallow. As we discussed, men usually do not seek intimacy in an affair; they are likely seeking sex and excitement. Having an affair also decreases the pressure that some men feel in the intimacy of the primary relationship. Kell (1992) suggests that many men would prefer two partial relationships to a more intimate, single relationship.

Romance: Threat or Menace?

One main reason given by people for having an affair is that they "fell in love." First, they indicate that they "fell out of love" with their original partner. So these people believe that love or romance is something that one can fall in or out of rather rapidly and uncontrollably. As it is sometimes thought, European courtiers did not dream up romantic love. This notion of romantic love has been with us throughout history and has been discovered in 78% of 168 cultures studied by anthropologists (Jankowiak, & Fisher, 1992).

One term that has been linked to romantic love is *limerence*. In her book *Love and Limerence,* Dorothy Tennov (1979) interviewed 400 men and women and found that the condition of infatuation (love sickness) had specific characteristics. One element is that the beloved takes on a "special meaning" or becomes the center of life. As infatuation progresses, intrusive thoughts of the beloved invade waking consciousness. Everything reminds you of the beloved. Depending on the strength of the obsession, many reported that 85% and more of their thoughts were directed to the love object. In addition, Tennov found that love is not blind. The beloved's faults are known but are considered unique and "part of his/her charm."

But limerence is *love sickness*. Besides the obsessive nature, it is imbued with fear. There is constant fear of loss and fear of appearing less than perfect when meeting with the beloved. Other feelings include fear of rejection, worrying anticipation, and longing for the beloved to reciprocate feelings of affection. In W. Somerset Maugham's great work *Of Human Bondage,* he chronicles the love sickness of a young man who becomes obsessed with a pasty, rejecting woman. Her anemic looks become beauty to him, and he fights against the irrational aspects of these feelings. He lives a life of fear and anticipation as he becomes more and more cut off from other relationships and even comes to hate himself for this delusion that has taken over his life. Some people "wake up" from the romantic dream of the affair because, over time, the pedestal must crack.

A key feature of romance is that it does not remain at the same strength as its first appearance. Shakespeare says in one of his sonnets that love that alters is not love. Romance or limerence is not lasting. It can barely last 2 years before the beloved begins to lose that glow. It can happen suddenly or slowly, but romance fades. Most people who have been married a long time have a perspective on this because they know that romance will reappear at intervals, but the real constant is mature love that we call affection or friendship. They recognize that there is a beautiful madness when romance first flares up, but many such relationships have no lasting fuel and quickly die out.

Societal Factors

Social context reasons, or societal factors, are often given short shrift in the literature (Vaughan, 1989). It is understandable that clinicians are more concerned with helping the anorectic/bulimic client rather than attacking the media's glorification of thinness, even though advertising certainly has an impact on this disorder. But just as svelte models in women's magazines may encourage eating disorders, the decision to have an EMA is influenced by those around us and our social conditioning. We are shaped by television programs such as *Desperate Housewives* and by the exploits of movie stars in *People* magazine. We are also influenced by our family members who have had affairs and by our friends. For example, Sue Shellenberger (2006), writing in the online *New York Times,* quotes the work of Yvonne Aberg who studied coworker affairs in Sweden. The study of over 37,000 individuals revealed a 70% probability of divorce if one's coworkers were unmarried. These data are not surprising to therapists who frequently hear how unmarried coworkers entice their married friends to enter flirting scenarios during "happy hour."

Another aspect of this problem is the glorification of love and romance in the media from magazines, to soap operas, to the sonnets of Shakespeare (Zare, 2001). These glossy portraits of unparalleled sexual excitement and "true happiness" shape our ideas about what we should have in a relationship. *The Bridges of Madison County* was a national best seller that was eventually made into a movie. Despite the fact the book was panned by critics, it enthralled millions who yearn for the excitement, romance, and sexual fulfillment portrayed by the author. *Titanic* and *The English Patient* were two Academy Award–winning movies that followed the same theme. Such fictional works morally justify the behavior of the participants because they are "in love" and perhaps they provide justifications for an audience who wants to identify with star-crossed lovers. Perhaps the more realistic picture is found in an older story. The fall of Camelot and the ruin of three lives and a kingdom are blamed on the revelation of an affair between Guinevere and Lancelot. The tale may have been concocted as a moral lesson, but it has survived through the ages because there is another side of the affair story that needs to be told, that romance/lust can be a Pandora's box and not the panacea touted by fairy-tale endings.

Treating Infidelity in Light of Culture

There is no culture in which adultery is unknown, no cultural device or code that extinguishes philandering.
Fisher, 1992, p. 87

Little has been written on the cultural differences between how European American, African American, and Hispanic American couples think about or deal with EMAs. To say a little about each of these three major cultural groups' attitudes would probably provide more of a stereotype than useful data for the clinician. Good information from interviews and research would be enlightening because the meaning of adultery in each culture is bound to be very different. In addition, culturally acceptable ways of dealing with these kinds of situations and specific family patterns might tell us a lot about the expectations that couples have about divorce and the possibility of reconciliation. At this juncture, each therapist should try and gain a better understanding of the cultural context of the affair from the individuals involved. Especially in bicultural couples, experiences of infidelity may have widely different meanings. Culture is only one part of the background that needs to be assessed. Family history and one's past experiences can dramatically affect the response to an affair. Consider the following case example from a real couple with a similar cultural background but different viewpoints on family roles because of different family histories:

Case Example: Elaina and Jorge

Elaina and Jorge are a Mexican American couple in their early 40s who have been married for 20 years and have three teenage children living at home. The couple is currently attempting to restructure their marriage after Elaina discovered that Jorge was having an affair with a 20-year-old woman. Although they have tried to talk about the affair, they have been unable to do so without becoming extremely verbally abusive. Their therapist begins by asking Elaina and Jorge about their views on marriage and fidelity. Elaina is adamant that the family is more important than an affair and that, regardless of what happens between a couple, they should stay together for the sake of the children. Jorge does not want to discuss the affair because it is over and sees no purpose in continuing to revisit it. He believes that Elaina is simply trying to make him look bad.

In Elaina's family of origin, her parents were often unkind and uncaring toward each other but showed affection for Elaina and her sisters. Elaina later found out that her parents had been forced to marry due to her mother's pregnancy. Elaina was always grateful that her parents had made an effort to provide an adequate home for their family.

Jorge was also raised by two parents and maintains that they were very much in love and his father was the leader of the household. Jorge also remembers times when his mother would become very upset because his father would be caught by neighbors or family members having affairs with various women in the town. Although Jorge remembered his mother being upset about the affairs, he never recalls his mother questioning his father's actions because of his status of head of the household.

Elaina is demanding that Jorge be faithful to her and the family. Jorge is angry that Elaina is questioning his commitment to their family. He thinks that Elaina's doubts are a sign of disrespect to him as head of the household.

The therapist works with the couple to understand the messages about marriage that they received from their families of origin. In Elaina's family, the message was "parents must stay together for the sake of the children." In Jorge's family, the message was "the father is the head of the household, regardless of any decisions that he makes that may hurt other family members." Through more dialogue, the couple and therapist begin to see how these covert family messages have caused role confusion in Elaina and Jorge's marriage.

The therapist continues the session by working with the couple to assess their interactive definition of the problem in their marriage. The couple discusses their individual ideas about marriage and fidelity, as well as the roles that they have maintained over the last 20 years. The couple realizes that they have assumed the function of husband and wife that they saw in their individual families of origin. They have never decided what their roles as husband and wife should be in their couplehood.

At this point, the therapist and couple could discuss a new definition of acceptable roles and expectations within the structure of the marriage. Elaina and Jorge agree that the main issue that brings them to therapy is their conflict over their specific roles within the family. The therapist encourages the couple to continue working on clarifying their roles as a couple. Elaina and Jorge are given the task of going home and creating lists of the different tasks that they perform for the family.

In the next therapy session, the therapist helps Elaina and Jorge to differentiate which tasks are most appropriate for each of them. While attempting to negotiate their new roles in the family, the therapist helps the couple increase their communication skills.

The story of Jorge and Elaina demonstrates a couple of important points. First, although the roots of the problem may lie in the couple's family or cultural background, the therapist must be aware of the fact that insight into the causes of the affair might not be as important as identifying an issue that, if solved, would lead the couple to a more secure and productive relationship. This kind of negotiation usually occurs after the couple has settled down emotionally from the first few weeks or months of turmoil. Solving a long-standing problem can give the couple confidence and serve as a symbol of a new relationship.

HELPING PEOPLE DEAL CONSTRUCTIVELY WITH AFFAIRS: PRACTICAL ISSUES

Is an Affair the End of the Relationship?

Michele Weiner-Davis, in her book *Divorce Busting,* (1992) identifies a number of illusions or irrational beliefs that prevent people from rebuilding their relationships. Illusion 5 is "My Spouse Had An Affair, the Marriage Can't Work." Arnold Lazarus (1985) calls this Myth 3: "Extramarital Affairs Will Destroy a Marriage." Both see the crisis of an affair as an opportunity to reform the relationship. Still, an affair often signals the end of a marriage. From their clinical population, Pittman and Wagers (1995) estimate that 90% of first marriages that broke up involved some form of infidelity. Pittman and Wagers feel that the people involved, including therapists, do not often acknowledge this grim truth. Couples develop elaborate self-protective reasons for divorce that they can explain simply to other people. "Sure I had an affair, but by that time, the marriage was over anyway."

Certainly, affairs can be a method used to exit a relationship while thumbing one's nose at the partner. But the revelation of affair can also be the cause of an irreparable tear in a good relationship, which makes the slope to divorce even slipperier. For whatever reason, the revelation of an affair seems to have different effects on men and women. Pittman and Wagers (1995) suggest that men appear in therapy at this stage and seem to be more emotionally devastated on the average than women whose husbands are having an affair. Regardless of gender, the spouse of an unfaithful partner can experience elevated emotional reactions, such as depression or extreme anger (Gordon, Baucom, & Snyder, 2004). Lawson (1990) found in her research that a woman revealing an affair to her husband is tantamount to ending the marriage. Possibly this is because men see their affairs as based on sex whereas women indicate more often that there is a serious emotional involvement. Thus, when a woman reveals an affair, it is more likely to be a serious relationship. In fact, many marriages weather affairs, but it requires time and emotional pain. Many people find it easier to end a relationship than face the humiliation, death of the dream, and the anger that must surface.

Can We Help People Fall Out of Love?

The most difficult situation that confronts a couples therapist is trying to help a couple with an affair when one member is deep in limerence with a third party. Perhaps we need to help clients face the fact that romance is an everyday phenomenon and not to place so much stock in its power or its unannounced appearance. If we can convey this to someone who has fallen in love and explain it more like a case of mononucleosis, we would have a chance of fighting some of the irrational and obsessive thinking that the unfaithful partner is experiencing. Pittman & Wagers (1995) recommend treating unfaithful partners as if they are "manic." People suffering from manic highs often do not wish to take medication to end their mania. In trying to address the unfaithful partners, we confront the same problem of motivation. Unfaithful partners are having their cake and eating it too: They hold on to the security of the marriage and experience the exhilaration of the affair. This is why unfaithful partners want the affair to remain a secret and tell lies to maintain this position.

Should the Therapist Who Learns About an Affair From One Spouse Keep It a Secret?

A good rule when seeing one member of a couple is to get a written understanding at the initial session that the therapist will not keep important information secret from the spouse. The American Association for Marriage and Family Therapy's (2001) Code of Ethical Principles indicates that without a written release it would be unethical to release information about one family member to another. In the event that the unfaithful partner wants to be counseled alone and confidentially, the therapist should inform the client that individual therapy about the affair is possible but that any couples work would have to be done with a different therapist. The obvious reason for this is that couples therapy is very unproductive when therapist and the unfaithful partner collude to hide something from the spouse. It restricts the ability of the therapist to explore all aspects of the relationship and, because of strong conflicting emotions, erects a barrier between the therapist and the spouse.

If we are working with an individual who wishes to end an affair, we have three goals to accomplish:

1. Help the individual find a way to reveal the affair to the spouse.
2. End the extramarital relationship.
3. Refer the individual to couples therapy.

These three tasks are listed in priority order. Many individuals having affairs do not come to therapists necessarily to end the affair. They are experiencing some guilt and anxiety, which they hope that the therapist can take away, or they may be looking for a place to dump the spouse if the marriage collapses. Sometimes they want to talk to someone about the juicy details and relive the experience. In general, they want to maintain the status quo as long as possible. The therapist, on the other hand, must advocate for change.

When Should Affairs Not Be Revealed?

Most therapists indicate that there are very few situations in which the unfaithful partner should not be instructed to level with the spouse (Brown, 1991, 2001; Pittman & Wagers, 1995). Among these rare situations are the following:

- *When there is potential for physical violence.* The spouse is unstable, has a history of volatile and violent behavior, or has threatened violence
- *When the divorce proceedings are rather far along and the revelation could bring about destructive litigation.* Here, the purpose of revealing the affair is to force the spouse to divorce the unfaithful partner (a manipulation). This is what Brown (1991; 2001) calls an "out-of-the-door" affair.
- *When the affair is ancient history.* This situation requires a judgment call on the part of the therapist. One rule of thumb here is to help the unfaithful partner reveal affairs that explain current marital problems or have an impact on the present relationship. Revealing ancient affairs may be an out-of-the-door strategy. Even if the unfaithful partner wants to reveal a very old affair to relieve guilt, the matter should be carefully considered. It may mean creating months of pain for the spouse so that the unfaithful partner can feel less guilty. Very often, this is a moot point because the unfaithful partner may already have revealed ancient affairs at the time the current affair came to light. An alternate point of view is that the dishonesty involved in previous affairs cannot be addressed and true intimacy cannot be restored until these secrets are brought out (Blanton, 1996).

What if You Are Not Sure That an Affair Is Taking Place?

A common scenario is when a couple comes for couples therapy and the therapist suspects an affair. The spouse may have suggested this, but the suspected unfaithful partner denies it. One alternative is to have an individual session with each member of the couple with the understanding that the essence of these meetings will be shared with the other member of the couple. During the session with the suspected unfaithful partner, the therapist confronts the person in the following way: "I know that you are having an affair. It is affecting the couples therapy session, and we need to find a way to resolve this problem by bringing it to light." Because those having EMAs are unlikely to admit to suspicions, sometimes this tactic helps move the process past the denials. When the unfaithful partner admits to the affair, a plan for a joint session to reveal the affair is made. If the unfaithful partner wishes to do this privately with the spouse, the therapist coaches the unfaithful partner to do this in the least harmful way possible. A follow-up appointment for the couple or the spouse following the revelation should be set up because one or both will need support as the postrevelation crisis develops.

Guidelines for Revealing an Affair

Whether the unfaithful partner reveals the affair privately with the spouse or during a couples session, some directions by the therapist can help the process.

Directions to the Unfaithful partner
- *Be patient; getting past the affair will take at least a year.* There are no exact time limits, and the revelation may in fact cause a problem that can never be repaired or may take years to get over. But not telling the spouse can create long-term difficulties and a worse situation when the spouse finds out on his or her own.
- *Be as honest as you can be with the spouse but try to avoid making comparisons between the lover and the spouse.* The spouse may ask for such comparisons about attractiveness, penis size, and the like. Total honesty can be taken to an extreme. There is no need to compare sexual satisfaction between lover and spouse. One woman told her husband that he was like a comfortable old sweater and her lover was like a new silk shirt. Nobody wants to be an old sweater.
- *Don't blame the spouse for the affair; take responsibility.* It is important for the spouse to hear that the unfaithful partner is taking responsibility for the behavior and that the infidelity was wrong. What the spouse needs to hear is that the unfaithful partner recognizes this as a personal problem, not a justification of the affair.
- *Try to avoid relating the small details.* The unfaithful spouse should divulge the big facts including who, when, and why but not necessarily how and what. Graphic detail of the sexual act and the places where this took place can be damaging. For example, if the spouse is told which motel was used, the issue resurfaces for the spouse every time that he or she drives by. This is an issue of compassion. The unfaithful partner may feel less guilty after purging all the information, but the spouse will be left with haunting images for years. If the spouse wants information that might be hurtful, the unfaithful partner can put off giving this information until the couples therapy session, letting the therapist handle the extent of revelations. Some therapists recommend letting the spouse write down a list of every question that needs to have an answer. Rather than getting all the answers immediately, the list is answered by the end of couples therapy.
- *Don't expect to get trust or forgiveness right away.* The unfaithful partner cannot really imagine how devastating the news of an affair can be. Simply admitting one's wrong will not gain instant forgiveness. Forgiveness must come in its own time, when it is sincere and the crisis is past. You cannot decide to start trusting a person again just because it seems to be the rational thing to do. Trust builds over time, and when it has been breached, it remains fragile. If the spouse displays distrust and suspiciousness, this is a protection against being hurt again.

Guidelines for the Spouse

• *Get support.* A spouse needs a great deal of support from close friends. But bringing family into the picture is a risky matter until divorce proceedings are underway. The reason is that if the marriage stays together, family members may carry resentment years later even after the spouse has forgiven and the marriage has been rebuilt.

• *Watch out for paranoia and becoming a detective.* Because one has been lied to, suspiciousness is a natural consequence. But a spouse should beware of letting the affair take over all of his or her life. Searching for clues of continued infidelity increases the obsessiveness and retards the healing process. For example, some spouses go through the unfaithful partner's pockets, wallets, or purses and follow them. The only way to prevent a husband's or wife's infidelity is to be with them 24 hours each day. Some spouses try to do just that, but it boils down to a simple fact: A spouse cannot prevent an affair if the unfaithful partner wishes to continue it. One choice is to spend the rest of life as a detective. The other is to make sure that you can survive whatever the future brings. This second choice means that the spouse focuses energy on healing the self, not reforming the unfaithful partner. Either the unfaithful partner will change or the marriage will end at some time. It does not work to merely protect oneself from hurt. One must develop a life that can withstand an affair and a divorce.

• *Don't confront the lover.* Little good comes from these encounters, and there is the possibility of violence and the unfaithful spouse's attempts to protect the lover.

• *Don't involve the entire family.* Although the spouse needs support, the more family involved, the more hurdles there will be to get over should the relationship be mended. Affairs are adult issues; children should not be included in the spouse's support system.

• *Take care of yourself.* Besides the suggestion given above, the spouse needs to take good physical care. At times it may be difficult to eat; the mouth may be dry, and only liquid can be taken; a stunned depression may take over. The spouse should be told that eating will be difficult at times and to eat more when hungry. Exercise is important too. Signs of major depression or adjustment disorder with depressed mood should be noted, and referral should be made for medication evaluation if needed (Gordon et al., 2004). In our experience, about 5% of situations require medication or hospitalization of one of the partners following the revelation of an affair.

GUIDELINES FOR THE THERAPIST USING
THE INTEGRATIVE MODEL

We see an EMA as a crisis in the relationship that has two phases: the emergency phase and the counseling phase dealing with longer-term issues associated with reconstructing and reinventing the relationship. The crisis of revelation is often what brings a couple to treatment. The unfaithful partner may offhandedly admit to the spouse's suspicions, creating an unexpected ultimatum or separation. In many cases, spouses discover their mates *in flagrante delicto,* and a violent aftermath brings them to the session. Others discover e-mail, cards, letters, or suspicious phone bills. Another common scenario is when the spouse's suspicions are brought into the session and the unfaithful partner denies the affair but admits to some kind of relationship with the lover. Later, the full extent of the affair is revealed.

Affairs and the Integrative Model: A Case Example

Figure 12.1 shows the integrative model of couples therapy. Once the couple has made it past the emergency stage, brief couples therapy can be implemented according to the model. The goals that the couple set might include the following:

- Engage in more recreational activities together (behavioral) so that we can enjoy our relationship (affective).
- Set times to talk about the affair (behavioral) so that anger and jealousy do not build up (affective).

Because of the intricacies of dealing with an affair and emotional volatility that threatens to derail progress, we present a case study that illustrates recovery from the emergency phase to couples counseling using the integrative model.

Case Example: Clarice and William

Clarice and William are an African American couple, married for 6 years, with a 2-year-old child, who came for therapy when Clarice found out that William was having

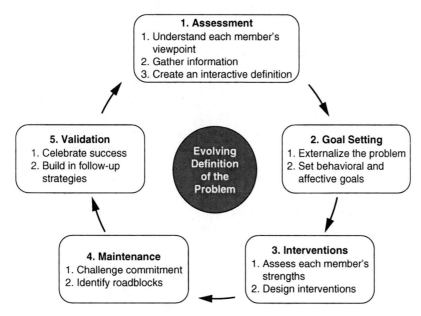

Figure 12.1   Circular model for integrative couples therapy

an affair with a coworker. William is a vice principal at a junior high school, and his lover, Donna, was a single faculty member. According to William, the affair had been going on for about 1 year and had started as they found themselves together at Friday Happy Hours. Their first sexual encounter had occurred as an "accident," but they continued the affair after that. Clarice found greeting cards in William's briefcase from Donna that suggested a personal relationship. Clarice threatened to leave William and divorce him if he didn't break up with Donna immediately. Clarice listened on the extension phone while William relayed his decision to Donna. When the couple came for therapy, the affair had been known for about 5 days.

Emergency Period: Sessions 1 Through 4

In the first few minutes of the session, the therapist took a brief history of the marriage to get some background and to determine if this was the first such incident. It was. William indicated that the affair with Donna was over and that he was relieved and regretted the pain caused to Clarice. He indicated that he wanted the marriage to work and felt that the problems in the marriage caused his decision to have the affair.

Clarice responded that she agreed things had not been going well but pointed out that she did not feel the need to have an affair. In summary, Clarice was openly expressing a great deal of hostility and had threatened to go over and "have it out" with Donna. She appeared agitated at times and tearful at others and indicated that she had not slept in several days. When the affair was revealed, Clarice had slapped William and had thrown her wedding ring at him. During the first session, William was calm, appeared sad, and looked down as he spoke. One of his chief concerns was that Clarice would confront Donna in a public place and the affair would become common knowledge at the school. William also felt guilty about the way that Donna was treated in the situation and wanted an opportunity to talk with her, something that Clarice was decidedly against.

The therapist spent most of the session eliciting the feelings of each member of the couple and providing support to Clarice. By the end of the session, the therapist had obtained a written contract from Clarice and William that indicated that there would be no confrontation of Donna and no violence in the relationship. On William's part, he was to make no personal contact with Donna and was to be truthful. It was agreed that he would send a letter to Donna, indicating his regrets, which Clarice could read. Finally, the therapist worked hard to instill hope in the couple that the relationship could continue, that couples overcome such problems, and that no drastic measures needed to be undertaken at this moment. The therapist told Clarice that William has the power to correct this problem if she will give him the opportunity. Clarice was encouraged to obtain support and take care of her physical health. The couple was to call before the next session if any problems arose.

The second and third sessions of couples therapy were more of the same. The major effort of the therapist was to try and keep the situation from exploding, either by William contacting Donna and lying about it or some kind of physical altercation between Donna and Clarice or Clarice and William. During these sessions, Clarice had been placed on a mild tranquilizer by her family physician whose main effect seemed to be more restful sleep. Clarice indicated that she was willing to work on putting the marriage back on track but that she was still dealing with a lot of anger.

William indicated that he had received an angry reply letter from Donna, who wished to meet him in person. He had declined and shared the letter with Clarice.

During the fourth session, William complained that all of their waking hours were spent taking care of their son or talking about the affair. Clarice worked part time but spent the rest of the time at home with their child. She said that by the time William got home she was "bursting" with fear and suspicion and needed to talk. The therapist encouraged her to tell her two best friends and to call them on alternate days for support. William agreed to this plan. The therapist reassured the couple that things were proceeding well. Then, the couple arranged a daily time, about 30 minutes, to talk about burning issues immediately after William arrives home so that their entire time together is not consumed by the affair.

In the assessment phase, it may be useful to use Brown's or Pittman's typology to characterize the affair. In the case of William and Clarice, Brown would see this as a conflict-avoidance scenario; from Pittman's concepts this would be a romantic affair.

Case Example: Clarice and William (continued)

Stage 1: Assessing and Obtaining an Interactional View of the Problem
Each person's view of the problem   In the fifth session, Clarice and William spent some time indicating what they felt to be the major issues in the relationship apart from the affair. Clarice indicated that the couple spent very little time together and that William found ways to avoid intimacy and contact with her. In a moment of anger and honesty, William complained that Clarice was boring and all she talked about was the baby and what her friends said. He missed the excitement in the marriage and felt that the relationship was "in neutral."

Assessment: Family of origin   When genograms were drawn for the couple, the therapist found that William was the oldest of five children and had always been very responsible. His father had left his mother when the children were in high school and even before that was known as a philanderer. William met Clarice in college while she was recovering from a severe auto accident. She feels that he was responsible for helping her through that difficult period. As time went on, they continued the overfunctioning–underfunctioning relationship. Clarice has only worked part time even before the child was born. William took care of all the finances and made most of the decisions. As William discussed his genogram, he indicated that, as much as he hated to admit it, his father's behavior was coming back to haunt him.

The genogram for Clarice revealed that Clarice's father was an alcoholic and she came from a home with three children of which she was the youngest. She had supportive grandparents though whom she feels were instrumental in her upbringing. Clarice's mother is "very religious," but Clarice does not feel she can go to her mother for support because of their religious differences. There was a great deal of conflict in her home growing up, and she said she was determined not to live in such a situation herself. This, she said, is what is so hard about the present situation. She feels that she is going back on the promise that she made to herself.

Assessment: Interactive definition   The sixth therapy session was spent pulling together the couple's complaints into a joint statement of the problem. In essence, they both felt that the *relationship had lapsed into a set of responsibilities, that they had stopped trying to be attractive to the other person, and that they were more like roommates.* The therapist asked them if this problem had ever occurred before, and the couple admitted that the issue had surfaced about 3 years ago when Clarice was pregnant. At that time, they spent more time together, went on a long weekend to the beach, and started designing their dream home together. They both recalled that period as a good time in the relationship.

Stage 2: Goal Setting

At the seventh session, the couple reported a rocky week. Although they still agreed on the joint definition of the problem, William had become distant and appeared sad, which heightened Clarice's suspicions. In the session, William admitted that he had been thinking about the relationship with Donna but had not contacted her. The therapist confronted William by asking him how much energy he was putting into the marriage compared with thinking about the affair. The therapist then normalized this stage as a transitional state before the marriage gets back on track. The therapist expressed optimism that things would soon improve and that it was necessary for the couple to continue along the present lines until a breakthrough occurred. This kind of reframing through normalizing is especially important when the couple sees little hope in the daily grind of the relationship. By the end of the session, the couple had agreed on a set of joint goals for the marriage. They envisioned a relationship where Clarice was more a partner in the marriage and in which both members of the couple made an effort to confront boredom and sameness in the marriage and to bring it to the attention of the other person rather than avoiding it.

Externalizing the problem   In the eighth session, the couple reported some relief, feeling that they had enjoyed a good week and had spent time together every night after the baby had gone to bed. William said he realized that he didn't really listen to Clarice's opinions when she expressed them. Clarice lashed out, saying that William had better get used to hearing her opinions because from now on the decisions in the family would include her input. The therapist reinforced this breakthrough by indicating that this was the major change that had been expected. The therapist externalized the problem by indicating that the couple had joined together to attack the boredom problem and it had taken both of them working together to allow Clarice's voice to be heard. William would have to listen, and Clarice would have to speak loudly and clearly.

The major accomplishment of the session was that the couple seemed to have changed their perspective from self-centered to couple centered. On the other hand, the therapist realized that Clarice was starting to get in touch with her anger. Although it might be healing for her, it could disrupt the progress in the relationship.

Stage 3: Adopting New Perceptions and Behaviors

The therapist's interventions   The next session started off with the therapist asking the couple about each other's strengths. Could any of these strengths or skills help them overcome the boredom problem and the problem of excluding Clarice from the decision-making processes? The therapist suggested that Clarice talk about William's strengths and that William identify Clarice's. They both agreed that Clarice was a very organized person and liked to check out all of the options before making a decision. William seemed to be the more spontaneous of the two and had the ability to make work fun and to keep them laughing.

The couple was then asked to write down two or three things that they felt were assets or supports in the relationship. William indicated that the relationship's stability was a great support to him. His home life was ordered, predictable, and safe after a stressful day. Clarice indicated that some of the best times in the marriage came when they took on a joint project such as landscaping the back yard. The therapist asked if this decorating task had used the best assets of the individuals and the relationship.

The couple was then asked to turn their strengths on the problem at hand, creating a more exciting relationship and balancing the power in the relationship. Surprisingly, the couple had decided that they were going to plan a monthly getaway for the next 12 months. The therapist considered this a risk (what if the time away was spent fighting?) but attempted to build on this plan and incorporate the couple's goals into the process. Clarice was to make the basic arrangements with regard to scheduling the time and place and making sure finances would allow for the trip. William's job was to add a touch of creativity to each minivacation.

During the session, the therapist noticed that Clarice was rather silent and that William was doing most of the talking. Although Clarice did not appear depressed, the therapist seemed to have assessed a basic communication pattern of the couple related to the problem of Clarice's lack of power in the relationship. The pattern appeared to be that William often expressed strong opinions and Clarice was either silent or went along with William so as not to cause waves. When Clarice was questioned about this pattern, she said, "I think it comes from my family. There was so much fighting; I don't want to live like that." About half of the session was spent in discussing how Clarice might learn to disagree with William without causing an argument.

The couple was given a homework assignment. Clarice was to, at least once per day, tell William how she was feeling using "I" statements. William was to respond with a listening response rather than disagreeing or trying to talk Clarice out of her feeling. This was considered to be a preliminary attempt to change the couple's communication problem, which seemed to be based on Clarice's fear of fighting and William's tendency to not listen to Clarice's opinions.

Stage 4: Maintaining New Perceptions and Behaviors

As therapy progressed, the couple began to see that their individual behaviors had an effect on each other. It was perhaps William who had the first insight when he said, "I think I was trying to avoid arguments by making all the decisions." Their arrangement in which he decided and she suppressed her feelings was coming unraveled. At this point, they were asked to indicate things they could do that would maintain the changes and things they might do that would send them back to their old pattern. They came up with the following list with some help from the therapist:

Things That Will Help Us Change

- Clarice continues to express her opinion to William when a problem comes up, and William listens.
- We finish an argument and come to a decision together.
- We continue to have positive, fun new experiences together.

Things That Will Keep Us From Changing

- Clarice agrees just to avoid a fight, and William lets her by taking over the decision-making process.
- William gets so involved in work and doesn't try when he gets home and Clarice doesn't mention it.
- We stop trying to fight the boredom and let the relationship get back in a rut.

Stage 5: Validating New Perceptions and Behaviors

After two sessions of working on maintenance behaviors and helping the couple antic-ipate the tendency to relapse, the couple was told that they were greatly improved and that the next session could be scheduled in about 3 months. Clarice, especially, seemed nervous about such a long hiatus, but they were assured that they could be seen immediately if something came up.

When the couple came for the follow-up session, they indicated that the changes they had begun were holding. After some discussion, it appeared that there was a change in the communication and decision-making process and that they both felt the relationship was more fun and exciting than it had been in years. The therapist encour-aged them to celebrate this change and to look for ways that they could continue this upward trend by seeing how their teamwork could address future problems. They also felt that their sexual relationship was much better than it ever had been. They attrib-uted this to better communication.

Although the couple was mostly upbeat, they had to admit that the affair was still a problem in the relationship. Donna (William's ex-lover) had sent him a message that Clarice had been driving by her house after school. Clarice admitted that she still had moments of suspicion and jealousy and that she tried to suppress this but she felt she had to talk about it. When she talked to William, the outcome was that he felt guilty and then got angry because he felt helpless to alleviate her unhappiness. It had been 7 months since William announced the affair, and it seemed to them that little progress had been made. The therapist indicated that normally 1 year is needed before the spouse can stop bringing this up in the relationship and get over the hurt and suspi-ciousness. The therapist suggested that Clarice consider 1 year as a time limit when she would cease bringing up the past to William as long as there were no future inci-dents of infidelity. Clarice said that she was ready to stop now but she needed some guarantee from William that she would not be hurt again.

The therapist spent some time suggesting to Clarice and William that there were no guarantees about these things. Instead, the therapist asked Clarice what she would do if she discovered that William was having a new affair. She said that she would leave him immediately, move in with her sister, and file for divorce. The therapist tried to promote the idea that the only way she could absolutely guarantee that it wouldn't happen again was to leave at this point in time. Otherwise, she would have to take a risk and express her doubts and negative feelings to her close circle of friends. Clarice appeared angry at first. She felt that William was getting off too easy. Rather than try to persuade Clarice to stop bringing up the affair, the therapist suggested a strategy. Each time the affair was mentioned by either party, they were to pay the other person one penny. They were also to indicate what situations led to the affair being mentioned. At the next therapy session in 3 months, they were to bring in their proceeds.

CONCLUSION

In this chapter, we addressed one of the thorniest problems in therapy: how to deal with an affair. Most of the writers in this field believe that couples can survive the affair if they are willing to face it and to improve the relationship. But with all this hope, there is the ever-present specter of divorce or separation. The spouse sees the affair as an insult and a rejection. Both members of the couple become defensive and focus on themselves rather than the relationship. It is a difficult task to open people to new hope in a relationship where they have been severely hurt. Many, if not most, couples end their relationships.

Despite the devastating impact of the affair, they are quite common, probably affecting the majority of couples. People engage in affairs for sex, for romance, for intimacy, to avoid intimacy, to advance themselves in jobs, and for a variety of other reasons. American society promotes romantic ideals in the media such as television, films, and books. These irrational ideas and mistaken beliefs about the importance of romance give people justification for affairs and tell them that "the grass is greener" somewhere.

The literature suggests that couples therapists cannot keep information about an affair secret when it is revealed by one member of a couple except under extreme circumstances such as imminent danger. Therapists must help their clients face these secrets and deal with the outcomes. Beginning therapists can easily fall into a trap of agreeing to confidentiality with a client and then finding themselves faced with doing couples therapy with this secret in the background.

Helping the couple dealing with an affair is a delicate business. It involves dealing with a crisis or emergency period before the couple can even begin to think about reconstructing the relationship. It is a period filled with doubt and pain that has to be gone through. Even when the initial crisis is passed, the issue will emerge and retard the therapy process with each member of the couple running for cover. The therapist's job is to help couples who want to stay together cope with the aftermath. The affair must end, and eventually the spouse must stop bringing it up. These are the two major hurdles that are easier said than jumped. The therapist's role as an instiller of hope is never more tested than in dealing with an affair. But couples find that if they can weather the affair, they may address deeper issues in their relationship and build a new and stronger foundation.

THREE

SPECIAL CHALLENGES

13

Counseling Couples
With Alcohol Problems

MARK E. YOUNG AND BRIGID M. NOONAN

KEY CONCEPTS

- Alcohol abuse and dependence affects more relationships than any other drug problem and is a contributing factor in divorce, physical abuse, and lowered marital satisfaction.
- Co-dependency is a term that describes the psychological effects and the role induced by being in a relationship with an alcoholic. Al-Anon is one organization that provides support for co-dependents.
- Sometimes a couple's habitual interactions support the alcoholic's tendency to continue to drink. But the couple's relationship can also help support sobriety, especially if both members get treatment.
- A systems approach to alcoholism treatment sees drinking as a symptom over the entire family system's malfunction. Alcoholics Anonymous (AA), by contrast, sees alcoholism as a disease of the individual.
- Some approaches to treating alcohol problems are based on a family systems approach, but the disease concept of AA is much more prevalent. This means that for the most part, the alcoholic gets treated first and family and couple interventions occur later.
- One of the most difficult issues is getting the alcoholic member of the couple into treatment. In this chapter, the Intervention is described along with the technique of Total Disengagement.
- Couples therapy can help the alcoholic in other ways such as providing an ally when antabuse is prescribed, using a couples group and focusing on the positives in the relationship.
- Behavioral Couples Therapy (BCT) is briefly described in this chapter because it is now being used when one or both members of the couple are alcoholic.

- Relapse prevention is a key component of treatment in the Maintenance stage of the Integrative Model.
- The Integrative Model's approach to dealing with a couple affected by alcohol is described in this chapter and a case example is given.

We chose to look at couples' alcohol problems rather than at substance abuse as a whole because alcohol affects so many relationships. One counselor we know likes to joke that "if it weren't for alcohol, we would be out of a job!" Alcohol is the drug of choice for our society. In 2001, 49% of the U.S. adult population consumed alcohol at least once, and at some point, 90% of adults in the United States will consume alcohol (Doweiko, 2006). It is legal and extolled as beneficial despite the fact that it disables millions. It is touted as a tranquilizer on popular television shows, sold as a sign of maturity in beer commercials, and designated as a mark of sophistication in wine and whiskey ads. A young woman once told us that her wedding reception would be terrible if she was not able to serve alcohol because people "can't have any fun without it." Those who do not drink on a regular basis (teetotalers) are ridiculed. Young people do not have to wait for peer pressure to drink; the whole society is pushing them to use alcohol. Not many can resist this advertising blitz.

ALCOHOL AND THE COUPLE

Alcoholism can be considered one of the most serious health problems in the United States. It affects the physical health of the alcoholic and the mental health of millions of families. In 1998 the costs of alcohol disorders and their social consequences were estimated at $185 billion dollars (National Institute on Alcohol Abuse and Alcoholism [NIAAA], 2000). More than 100,000 Americans die each year from alcohol-related causes, which makes it the third leading cause of death related to lifestyle (nicotine and diet-activity rank first and second, respectively) (NIAAA, 2000).

Additionally, NIAAA (2000) reports that marital relationships suffer when problem drinking is evident even when the relationship is beginning. "Significant associations have been reported between excessive consumption by the husband, perceptions of marital dissatisfaction and belief in alcohol as an excuse for aggression" (NIAAA, 2000, p. 20). The effects of growing up in an alcoholic family can linger into adult life. Despite the efforts to change the view of alcoholism from a weakness to a disease, the public perception is that alcoholics drink to escape their troubles and either don't want to quit or simply cannot control their behavior. Consequently, family members and other affected feel a sense of shame, worthlessness, and helplessness (Fields, 2004). The families contribute to the cycle in a number of ways: Deny that the problem exists; avoid the alcohol abuser and care for oneself only; become a caregiver and work to control and/or support the behavior; cover it up and maintain the family secret (Kinney, 2003). All family members are affected by drinking, and the partner who drinks probably bears the greatest burden.

Alcoholics are just as likely to be married as anyone else is, but they are more likely to be divorced (Halford, Price, Kelly, Bouma, & Young, 2001; Sanchez & Gager, 2000). In fact, couples who present for counseling often are struggling with an alcohol problem, and conversely, those who present for alcohol treatment often are struggling in their marriage (Roberts & McCrady, 2003). Many times, we hear in a counseling session that the partner without the alcohol problem expresses bewilderment that he or she could not identify this problem when dating. What he or she does not realize is that the partner more than likely reduced alcohol intake during that time (Doweiko, 2006).

Marital support is highly conducive to a strong recovery and is predictive of successful treatment (Engel, 2003; O'Farrell & Fals-Stewart, 2000; Walitzer & Dermen, 2004). Alcoholics assigned to couples and family therapy while undergoing alcohol treatment are less likely to drop out of treatment (Epstein & McCrady, 2002; Roberts & McCrady, 2003). In short, alcoholism and the couple's problems can exacerbate each other, and a good relationship can aid recovery.

ASPECTS OF ALCOHOLISM: TERMINOLOGY

Alcoholic

It is traditional for speakers in Alcoholics Anonymous (AA) groups to begin by saying their first name, followed by "and I'm an alcoholic." Therapists and substance abuse–treatment workers consider recognizing one's problem as an essential first step. Anyone who has a problem with drinking needs treatment, whether they wish to call themselves alcoholic or not. Referring to oneself as an alcoholic indicates only that the person has reached the stage where he or she is no longer in denial and is taking responsibility for the problem. We generally use the terms *alcoholic* and *alcoholism* in this chapter—rather than problem drinking, alcohol abuse, or dependence—simply for convenience.

Codependency

The term *codependency* has been in existence since the late 20th century when many people realized that they needed help dealing with alcoholic individuals in their lives. Although there is no standard definition of codependency, Doweiko (2006) identifies the core aspects of codependency as (1) overinvolvement in the other person's drinking, (2) attempts to obsessively control, (3) use of external sources for self-worth, and (4) making personal sacrifices. To assist individuals who have identified some or all of these aspects, support groups designed to help codependents are available. Al-Anon assists the codependent to enter the recovery process, and Adult Children of Alcoholics (ACOA) is another that supports those who grew up with alcoholics in their families. It is important to note that not all codependents grew up with alcoholics in their families and not all family members who grew up in alcoholic homes become codependent.

The term *codependency* has come under attack, perhaps because it has been overapplied and has become synonymous with nonassertiveness and lack of control, thus losing its original reference to someone in an alcoholic relationship. Many clinicians reject the term because it carries with it the language of "disease" inherent in 12-step programs, suggesting that codependents are never cured but are recovering for life, just as the alcoholics are. It has been suggested that although treatment for the partner is also necessary, the term *codependency* need not be used. Couples and family counselors tend to shy away from labeling individuals and instead focus on the family system and its responsibility in supporting the drinking behavior and allowing the drinkers to experience the consequences of their behaviors.

Alcohol Dependence and Alcohol Abuse

The *Diagnostic and Statistical Manual of Mental Disorders* differentiates between alcohol dependence and alcohol abuse (American Psychiatric Association, 2000). Both are mental disorders, but dependence is more severe. A diagnosis of *alcohol dependence* requires at least three of the following symptoms: tolerance, withdrawal, loss of control of drinking once started, unsuccessful attempts to cut down or stop, spending an inordinate amount of time obtaining alcohol and recovering from its effects, and giving up all social, occupational, or recreational activities. Note that alcohol dependence can be diagnosed with or without physical dependence, withdrawal, or tolerance.

One or more of the following symptoms characterize *alcohol abuse* within a 12-month period: continual drinking resulting in the failure to fulfill major roles in work and family life, drinking repeatedly such that there is a potential for harm (drunk driving), recurring legal difficulties, and continued drinking despite social or interpersonal consequences caused by alcohol ingestion. Some clinicians and researchers think that dependence, abuse, nonproblem alcohol use, and abstinence are points on a continuum rather than separate disorders (Doweiko, 2006). Patterns of use and abuse vary, and people move from one point to the next. The important point is that just because someone is not diagnosed as alcohol dependent does not mean that the drinking problem does not need treatment.

Abstinence and Sobriety

Two other important terms are *sobriety* and *abstinence*. Abstinence means completely refraining from drinking. Sobriety, on the other hand, has taken on a positive connotation, meaning a rewarding lifestyle without alcohol.

THE COUPLE RELATIONSHIP THAT SUPPORTS ALCOHOLISM

Referring the Couple for Alcohol Treatment

Alcohol problems are associated with more severe marital distress, financial problems, poor sexual relations, low confidence in resolving marital conflict, nagging, poor communication skills, and domestic violence (Connors, Donovan, & DiClemente, 2001; Kelly, Halford, & Young, 2000). Although alcohol abuse differs among cultures, when couples come for couples therapy, a considerable number come with alcohol in the background of the relationship. Including a cultural assessment in the initial stages of therapy is critical. Proceeding with couples therapy alone may not suffice to deal with this tenacious addiction.

When a therapist determines that one member of the couple needs treatment for alcohol addiction and the therapist has the skills necessary to make an assessment, it can be done at that time. If a referral is necessary for assessment and treatment, then this information is conveyed to the couple. This evaluation will determine the severity of the disease and will constitute whether inpatient or outpatient treatment will work best. Depending on the type of treatment, couples therapy may need to be suspended until such a time is deemed appropriate to begin again. If the partner requires inpatient treatment, decisions regarding child care, communicating with employers (if the individual works outside of the home), and what to tell other family and friends will need to be made.

Couple Patterns That Support Alcoholism

Couples fall into patterns where the alcoholic member's addiction allows the other person to care for the alcoholic, an asymmetrical relationship. This caretaker arrangement does not help the alcoholic gain insight, nor does it help the enabling partner achieve self-actualization because both are centered on their too-significant other. An analysis of genograms of enablers (codependents) shows that they often come from alcoholic families where this kind of behavior is normal. This is not to say that the spouse of an alcoholic wants the spouse to remain addicted. Living with an alcoholic has significant negative consequences, and spouses of alcoholics are more likely than others are to experience physical and psychological problems (Fals-Stewart & Birchler, 2001). Unlike the effects of prescription painkillers or crack cocaine addiction, the deterioration due to alcoholism takes place over years rather than months. The spouses and families habituate and adapt to the alcoholic's behavior.

Besides habituation, another reason alcoholic relationships become stabilized is that they support unspoken agreements. An example is, "I won't make you deal with your drinking, if you won't make me deal with my obesity." The award-winning film *Leaving Las Vegas* depicted this kind of arrangement between a man who decided to drink himself to death and his prostitute girlfriend. He needs company while he kills himself, and she needs someone to nurture who will not make her face the fact that she is despised by society. In this dark movie, the collusion of two individuals that allows them both to destroy themselves is a disturbing look at how one dysfunctional behavior can support another.

Other common patterns include an arrangement where the partners cease to have any interaction with each other and stay together out of convenience, arguing only occasionally about the drinking issue. If money is not a problem, such arrangements can go on for decades. Often, couples share alcohol or other addictions and develop a lifestyle based on their shared drinking. When both partners have alcohol problems (for example, dependence/abuse disorders), the priority shifts from the relationship to the physical health of both. From there work can begin to focus on the relationship and the problems/issues caused by the alcohol use. Aftercare for the couple following treatment often means constructing a completely new relationship when the primary source of interaction is eliminated.

How the Partner Can Help the Alcoholic

Partners of alcoholics can best help by seeking their own treatment because recovery demands changes in both partners. One of the best avenues for this kind of help is Al-Anon, the support group for people who live with alcoholics. In the beginning, most people who go to Al-Anon meetings are searching for ways to change their alcoholic partners, but they soon find out that they need to work on themselves instead. Al-Anon helps the family members, especially husbands and wives, to stop enabling the alcoholic spouse. One woman described to me her life before and after Al-Anon. She told me that when her binge-drinking husband came home drunk, he invariably picked a fight with her and their children, vomited, and passed out on the living room floor. She would get him to bed, clean up the mess, and quiet the kids. The next morning, he would remember nothing, she would be silent, and the children would avoid him. He was bewildered and she was angry. Through Al-Anon, she learned to stop "cleaning up his messes." She developed a plan to take the children to her friend's house when he came home drunk. After the third time he woke up alone amid a mess on the living room floor, he agreed to seek treatment for his problem.

We do not mean to give the impression that the sole goal of Al-Anon or any treatment for concerned significant others (CSOs) is to induce the alcoholic to stop drinking. Spouses of alcoholics very often believe that once alcohol is gone from the marriage, harmony will return. Rather, the goal of Al-Anon and other CSO treatment is to help them detach from the alcoholic as an enabler and allow them (alcoholics) to experience the consequences of their continued drinking (Connors et al., 2001). Developing a healthy lifestyle and focusing on the emotional needs of the CSO is another goal of Al-Anon. It is true that an alcoholic's best chance for recovery is when the partner is not "walking on eggshells" or centering his or her life around the drinker. Nevertheless, it is equally important for CSOs to begin their own process of treatment and self-examination, whether or not their partner starts down the road of recovery.

The Systems Approach Toward Alcoholic Behavior

Systems approaches to family therapy, such as the Bowen theory, have traditionally looked at symptoms such as alcoholism and asthma as signals of underlying dysfunction and stress that serve to maintain the family system. The term *alcoholic system* is often used to refer to families that are in denial and are adjusting to the alcoholic. Normally, the aim of systems theory is to treat the system rather than the symptom bearer—that is, the alcoholic or asthmatic.

Roberts and McCrady (2003, p. 42) point out that the systems approach "focuses on altering couple interactions that might be sustaining the drinking, as well as each partner's views of the meaning of drinking." That the family interactions become organized around the drinking is a central theme in the systems model. Alcoholism can serve either as a signal of underlying dysfunction or as an organizing principle around which the family stabilizes (homeostasis). One difficulty in such systems is that sobriety leads to instability, and so there is pressure to return to the familiar homeostatic state. This finding addresses the question that everyone who works with couples and families always faces: Why does everyone seem to return to unproductive relationships despite their determination to change? Researchers suggest that, besides offering familiarity and stability, alcoholism allows these families to express feelings not allowed during sobriety (Center for Substance Abuse Treatment [CSAT], 2004). Therapy with alcoholic families and couples in recovery, then, would be aimed at enhancing emotional expression and improving relationships among family members, which would support changes and a positive homeostatic level.

The Alcoholics Anonymous Approach and the Systems Approach

AA and Al-Anon tend to focus on each individual's recovery and generally do not favor family or couples therapy as the treatment for alcoholism. Most couples and family therapists today support this approach to some extent. It is certainly true that little progress is made in couples therapy when one member of the couple is actively alcoholic. The difference in the two approaches may not be so much about whether couple or family treatment is needed but *when* it is needed.

AA believes that alcoholism is a chronic disease and that the solution to an alcoholic's problems is found in the simple statement "Don't drink and go to meetings." Although most disease concept–oriented treatment centers are now including spouses and families earlier in treatment, there persists the notion, based on the experience of alcoholics in AA, that focusing too much on one's relationships can distract one from developing a high-quality recovery.

The orthodox family systems approach suggests that the cause of alcoholism is a dysfunctional family system and that marriage or family therapy may be effective in treating the family's problems associated with alcoholism. There is little support for this kind of treatment today, and we are unaware of any therapists who practice couples or family therapy when one member is in crisis or denial. That approach is too risky, creating more discouragement to family members.

What, then, does couples or family therapy have to offer to alcohol treatment? Although many treatment programs do not use couples therapy until recovery is fairly well established, others are beginning couples work immediately after detoxification. Alcohol-focused behavioral couples therapy (ABCT) has been shown to improve marital stability, increase marital satisfaction, decrease domestic violence, and improve drinking outcomes (McCrady, Epstein, & Kahler, 2004). The goals of ABCT are to assist the alcoholic in achieving and maintaining abstinence, teach couples how to support change and cope with drinking situations, and enhance relationship functioning (Epstein & McCrady, 2002).

The Problem Drinker

What if the person is a problem drinker but not an alcoholic? Problem drinkers are those individuals who are nondependent drinkers but still experience adverse consequences because of their drinking. Their problem may or may not be severe enough to warrant an alcohol-abuse diagnosis. Before prescribing a medication, a physician sometimes refers a patient to a specialist, such as a cardiologist, to make sure that the patient's heart is healthy and can tolerate the treatment. By this analogy, couples therapists should be willing to postpone treatment when they suspect alcoholism and first have the necessary assessment taken. Given the prevalence of drinking problems, it would be useful to have some brief screening procedures handy. Brief screening identifies any individuals or family members experiencing alcohol-related problems, identifies those individuals or family members at-risk for developing alcohol-related problems, and determines the need for further assessment and intervention (Roberts & McCrady, 2003). Regardless of whether alcohol treatment is initiated, the screening can get the couple to contemplate the seriousness of the alcohol problem.

In borderline cases where alcoholism cannot be clearly diagnosed, treatment for alcohol problems can still be advised. In such cases, alcohol is probably still a problem in the relationship, and beginning to solve that problem can be insisted on before couples therapy begins. Often the couple disagrees on the importance of the drinking behavior. In the classic scenario, the drinker claims that the partner is exaggerating the drinking, and the partner claims that the drinker is minimizing it. One therapist who we know tells her clients, "If alcohol is not a problem or an addiction for you, I would like to try something. I'd like you to experiment and see if you can eliminate alcohol entirely for 6 weeks. If you can, then you probably don't need treatment. If you can't, then I'd like you to agree to get treatment." Usually, when the couple returns, the problem drinker has failed and has many excuses. This therapist's ploy sometimes works to make both members of the couple aware that the drinking is out of control. In some cases, it helps propel the problem drinker into treatment.

Zweben and Barrett (1993) recommend getting couples to work together to assess the costs and benefits of drinking in their lives. Box 13.1 contains an outline of brief couples treatment. This treatment protocol was used in mental health centers with clients who had low to moderate alcohol problems. The program required that participants have no major psychiatric disorders, have alcohol as a primary concern, have a moderate score on the Michigan Alcohol Screening Test, and have a partner willing to participate in all aspects of the program. As the outline indicates, the program lasts about six sessions.

In the first session, the couple is interviewed, the alcoholic is assessed, and the couple's commitment to therapy is reinforced. A unique aspect of the program is the team conference. Here, the therapist reports the findings of the therapists who have reviewed the couple's situation, presenting the team's suggestions about appropriate goals of treatment. Then an initial treatment goal is established, which may or may not be abstinence, though normally a 3-week period of abstinence is prescribed. The next session is spent on firming up these goals, considering maintenance, and addressing relapse prevention. Follow-up sessions continue this process.

Box 13.1
Outline of Brief Couples Treatment for Alcohol Problems

A. Assessment interview and screening (one session)
1. Preparing the client for change
2. Owning the change process
3. Gathering information (particular assessments are discussed later in this chapter)

B. Team conference (one meeting of professional team)
1. Reviewing assessment and preparing personalized feedback and advice to the couple
2. Formulating drinking goal based on individualized assessment
3. Preparing strategy for use by counselor in feedback session

C. Feedback session (one meeting)
1. Identifying the severity of the alcohol problem and issues associated with alcohol use
2. Establishing a consensus about change
3. Setting drinking goals
4. Requesting a period of abstinence
5. Delaying a commitment to change
6. Enhancing a commitment to change
7. Maintaining a commitment to change

D. Follow-up session 2–4 weeks later (one or two sessions)

E. Emergency session (if necessary)

Source: From "Brief Couple Treatment for Alcohol Problems," by A. Zweben and D. Barrett. In *Treating Alcohol Problems: Marital and Family Interventions,* by T. J. O'Farrell (ed.) p. 356, New York: Guilford Press. Reprinted by permission.

THERAPY TECHNIQUES

The process of recovery for couples struggling with alcoholism is unique, complex, and multifaceted. Using elements from a number of models, CSAT (2004) discusses stages of change for couples and families as

- *Attainment of sobriety.* The couple (family system) is unbalanced, but healthy change is possible.
- *Adjustment to sobriety.* The couple (family) works on developing and stabilizing a new system.
- *Long-term maintenance of sobriety.* The couple (family) must rebalance and stabilize a new and healthier lifestyle.

These three interventions could also be considered phases of recovery for the couple. The first is a treatment phase for the alcoholic, the second is an adjustment phase for the family, and the third is a lifestyle-building phase that promotes sobriety and prevents the alcoholic's relapse into drinking. These distinctions seem to be a good way to organize our thinking as we describe some techniques for working with couples experiencing alcohol problems.

Interventions to Support the Alcoholic's Change

Roberts and McCrady (2003) offer the following brief interventions (when the drinker is present) for therapists seeing an alcoholic or an alcoholic couple. Elements of the brief intervention include

- *Careful assessment* (some assessments are discussed later in this chapter).
- *Feedback.*   Providing feedback helps the drinker recognize inconsistencies that exist between current circumstances and the personal and family goals that he or she may have.
- *Drinker choices.*   After discussing feedback and reactions to the feedback, the therapist introduces the issue of choice. Providing options to the drinker is essential. Total abstinence is always one choice; however, there are times when reduction in drinking serves as an avenue to abstinence. Discussing the advantages and disadvantages of the choices is important for the therapist and couple, to give voice to the consequences of these choices.
- *Emphasis on personal responsibility.*   Clear communication is important about the choices available (to both the drinker and the partner [family]) and that it is ultimately the responsibility of each to decide their course of action.
- *Involvement of the family.*   Many times, additional information is needed to begin the change process. This can include providing additional feedback, how to support the drinker in making these changes, and the time limits that may needed to be implement what will/will not be tolerated.
- *Follow-up.*   Similar to other sessions, follow-up is an essential piece to the therapeutic process. After the brief intervention, the therapist and couple will continue to work together toward the set goals.

Using an adapted motivational interviewing (empathetic, client-centered therapeutic approach), the therapist can assist the couple in enhancing the alcoholic's readiness to address his or her drinking problems, which may result in accepting the need for treatment. Motivational interviewing employs three major principles: express empathy, rolling with resistance, and enhancing and supporting self-efficacy (Miller & Rollnick, 2002).

The Therapist's and the Spouse's Conviction

The scenario with the highest probability of success is a couple who presents as a unit deciding that the couple wants to go in the direction of recovery (Connors et al., 2001). However, this situation is still relatively rare. More often, it is a matter of dealing with a partner who is acutely aware of the problem and the alcoholic who is still in denial.

How do you convince someone to go into treatment? No matter how severe the alcoholic's condition, there is always some measure of ambivalence about the necessity of treatment. Once it is clear to the therapist that treatment is necessary, it is important to convey a clear message to the alcoholic and partner. Individually or during the couple's session, the therapist enlists the partner's aid to maintain pressure on the alcoholic. This might include suspending couple therapy until the alcohol problem has been treated. At some point, the partner begins to realize the personal costs associated with the alcoholic's going into an inpatient treatment, such as "I'll be taking care of the kids myself," "Treatment will be *very* expensive," "Everyone will know," or "I don't want my spouse to suffer in that cold environment." Such thoughts can easily waylay the decision to force the alcoholic into treatment. However, once the partner has decided to do so, the therapist must help the partner remain firm and deliver a strong message to the alcoholic, who is already wavering. The alcoholic should not get the idea that the therapist or spouse is not sure whether treatment is needed or that the treatment can be handled in some other way. The person struggling with an alcohol addiction is looking for a way out. The partner's support is important, but so is the partner's determination not to allow the alcoholic to go untreated.

If inpatient treatment is deemed as inappropriate, whether because of finances or time, outpatient treatment also needs to be considered. Today, outpatient treatment is considered the most common approach for substance-abuse treatment (CSAT, 2004). Roberts and McCrady (2003) suggest that therapists, depending upon the evaluation, can refer their clients to not only inpatient treatment but also residential rehabilitative, intensive outpatient, outpatient, or self-help treatments.

The Intervention Technique

It is often said that people do not stop drinking because it sounds like a good idea; they stop when they hit bottom. The pressure from those around them and their life circumstances cause hitting bottom. The most powerful motivators are hospitalization caused by physical effects of alcohol, threatened loss of job, and threat to the couple relationship. If the partner can communicate that the relationship cannot continue with alcohol in the picture, this provides great leverage for change.

The Johnson intervention, a treatment technique developed in the 1980s, involves bringing family and friends (CSOs) together for confronting an alcoholic about his or her behavior and how it is affecting everyone. Specifically, the people invited to the intervention are those who have witnessed the drinking behavior and its consequences, such as older children, friends, family members, and coworkers. The aim is to get the alcoholic to agree to treatment, but these interventions have high risk. They may propel the drinker to seek treatment, or they may alienate the person from the nonalcoholic support system. Orchestrated by a trained professional, the intervention is a carefully planned and rehearsed process with the CSOs. In the session preceding the actual intervention, all participants are asked to bring forward specific incidents where the alcoholic's behavior affected them (Connors et al., 2001; Doweiko, 2006).

Total Disengagement

One method for putting pressure on the alcoholic to change is to counsel the partner to totally disengage and not react to the alcoholic's behavior. Although the partner is not to become cold and indifferent, efforts should be focused primarily on developing a positive lifestyle with or without the alcohol abuser. The partner agrees to no longer shelter the alcoholic, enabling that person to face the consequences of drinking. Al-Anon does not recommend abandoning the alcoholic but encourages the partner to break long-term patterns to control the drinking of their loved one and establish newer healthier lifestyle patterns.

Partner Involvement With Drug Therapy

Disulfram (Antabuse) and similar drugs are best used with individuals who have repeatedly relapsed following treatment. In this circumstance, a drug that causes nausea, vomiting, and extreme discomfort when alcohol is ingested can support abstinence. In fact, one can actually become dangerously ill when these two substances are combined. Besides disulfram providing a powerful motivator not to drink, lapses are accompanied by immediate punishment, creating a classical conditioning scenario in which alcohol ingestion becomes associated with nausea and pain even when the drug is discontinued.

Compliance with disulfram is a problem. Alcoholics on their own are likely to forget or purposely discontinue use, but both compliance and abstinence are positively affected when the partner administers the drug. In fact, couples can learn to make it a kind of ritual. One couple we know turned it into a part of their contact over breakfast; she would get the disulfram and place it next to his juice or coffee. Both described this action as a sign of caring rather than as nagging.

Interventions to Enhance the Quality of the Relationship Following Treatment

When one member of a couple stops drinking, there is an initial period of disequilibrium and confusion in the relationship. Often the nonalcoholic partner does not trust this "new person" and is reluctant to relinquish control of finances or family responsibilities just because the person is now sober. The CSO feels less important, has to give up "being strong," and always worries about relapse. There may also be residual anger covering hurt and feelings of betrayal. On the other hand, the alcoholic may be struggling with guilt, shame, and anxiety, and the alcoholic's need to focus on his or her own treatment may appear self-centered. Both partners can feel that their efforts are unappreciated.

Together, the partners struggle with a fear of conflict and a tendency to suppress feelings as family tensions build. Before the relationship difficulties can be faced, each person normally needs to work through some personal feelings (Epstein & McCrady, 2002. AA and Al-Anon meetings allow partners to work through these issues on their own, but eventually the two must face each other and deal with present problems; the repressed conflict must eventually emerge.

The therapeutic methods for enhancing relationships are not much different for couples with alcohol problems than for other kinds of couples. Methods include (1) couples therapy focusing on goals that would bring back pleasure and positive experiences for the couple, (2) a "recovering couples" group, and (3) coping and communication skills training groups for alcoholics and their spouses using a psychoeducational format.

"Catch Your Partner Doing Something Nice"

O'Farrell (1993) describes an exercise called "Catch Your Partner Doing Something Nice" that helps improve the caretaking and communication skills of the couple. The couple is initially asked to observe and write down at least one nice thing the other has done each day that shows love and caring to the other. Within the counseling session, the couple is asked to describe to the other these nice acts. Each person is then asked to pick a favorite loving behavior and to role-play. The therapist gives positive feedback and suggestions based on the role play. The individual can replay the role play, incorporating the suggestions given. In addition to building caretaking and communication skills, this exercise helps build appreciation for each other.

The "Recovering Couples" Group

Shields (1989) describes a recovering couples group that can be effective as early as 1 month following sobriety when each member of the couple continues in AA/Al-Anon treatment and is fully committed to the relationship and to recovery. Couples who are engaging in severe emotional or physical abuse or making suicide or homicide threats are screened out. Shields suggests a group size of five to six couples. Group therapy for recovering couples is not much different from other group approaches for couples except that the goals may be more explicit and therapy may be time limited. Shields takes an educational approach to recovering couples groups, and the following are some of the goals that he establishes for the members:

1. Remember that they are a couple and to strive for conflict resolution, expression of feelings, and stress reduction.
2. Understand dysfunction in terms of patterns rather than as random events.
3. Identify realistic and unrealistic expectations of each other.
4. Become comfortable with self-disclosure and the disclosures of others.
5. Develop awareness of the postacute withdrawal (PAW) syndrome—a set of symptoms that includes recurrence of mood disorders, memory loss, and fragmented thinking. Similar to posttraumatic stress disorder, the PAW syndrome is apparently common enough following recovery that couples need to be aware of it as a threat. It can lead to relapse and can disrupt the relationship by causing emotional distance.
6. Identify power and control issues in the relationship and negotiate new agreements.
7. Squarely address the subject of relapse.
8. Identify "markers" for success. Each couple sets up unique goals, which can be observed in group.
9. Develop a "validation process" between partners—that is, to increase the compliments and "positive strokes."

Behavioral Couples/Marital Therapy

Many researchers have identified behavioral couples/marital therapy (BCT/BMT) as an effective therapy technique when working with couples affected by alcohol (Connors et al., 2001; McCrady et al., 2004; O'Farrell & Fals-Stewart, 2003;

Walitzer & Dermen, 2004; Winters, Fals-Stewart, O'Farrell, Birchler, & Kelley, 2002). BCT/BMT is effective when either one or both members are alcoholic. Besides setting goals concerning abstinence, the program addresses (1) increasing positive shared behavioral exchanges and activities and (2) enhancing communication skills. Usually, within the first four to five sessions, the first component is designed to increase positive affect and marital satisfaction. The second goal, taking place in the last five to six sessions, is designed to increase the couple's communication skills, particularly surrounding areas of conflict. For example, the alcoholic may need to improve assertiveness skills to refuse drinks, and the partner may need to learn to communicate his or her need to share household and family responsibilities.

Another approach is to teach these skills to family members and alcoholics separately. Family education programs are available from most alcohol treatment programs and may take place when the couple is receiving aftercare services.

Relapse Prevention

Relapse prevention has become a necessary component when working with alcoholics. Polivy and Herman (2002) note that 90% of individuals treated for alcohol dependence will consume alcohol, at least once, within the first 90 days following discharge. Of those, 45 to 50% will have returned to pretreatment drinking within a year. Witkiewitz and Marlatt (2004) identify seven factors that contribute to an individual's relapse:

1. *Self-efficacy.* How well does the alcoholic cope when in high-risk situations?
2. *Outcome expectancies.* What are the alcoholic's anticipatory expectations regarding any future alcohol use?
3. *Craving.* A poorly understood concept as well as predictor of relapse, craving may be triggered by the cue (alcohol) exposure. This exposure to the drug (whether it is smells, sights, or sounds) can trigger the alcoholic to drink.
4. *Motivation.* Does the alcoholic want to change his or her behavior or continue to drink? Motivation centers around these two principles because it relates to what will happen if he or she stops drinking ("Who will I hang out with, what will happen to all my friends?") and what will happen if he or she continues to drink ("I really want to stop, but I just don't think that I'll be able to pass up an invitation to go out").
5. *Coping.* What are the alcoholic's learned coping resources (cognitive, behavioral, and so on) when under stress and confronted with alcohol cues?
6. *Emotional states.* A strong correlation exists between negative affect and relapse.
7. *Interpersonal support.* Strong social support systems are predictive of continued abstinence.

Relapse prevention focuses on identifying high-risk situations that create urges to drink and on developing assertiveness skills to refuse invitations or fulfill needs in more ways that are positive. Prevention also includes psychoeducation, individualized strategies for dealing with cravings and urges, developing healthy support systems and lifestyle changes, and strategies that prevent slips from mounting into relapse. Couples work can be important in relapse prevention. One way to address this directly is through the use of a "recovery contract" (Stappenbeck, Logsdon, Gorman, & Fals-Stewart, 2004). On a daily basis, each partner engages in maintaining sobriety. For the alcoholic, he or she states the intention not to drink that day; for the CSO, he or she verbally expresses positive support for the partner to remain alcohol free. The couple agrees that between their counseling sessions they will not discuss past drinking or fears of returning to drinking. Some recovery contracts also stipulate attendance at both AA and Al-Anon meetings for the couple.

THE INTEGRATIVE MODEL AND COUPLES WITH ALCOHOL PROBLEMS

Assessment Issues

Before looking at an example of how the integrative model of couples therapy can be applied to alcohol problems, let's spend a little more time on the area of assessment and interactive definitions, the first two steps in the process. Because of the denial and defensiveness of both alcoholics and their partners, these are the trickiest steps.

When couples come for therapy, they may be willing to discuss problems in communication or disagreements over finances, but they have unspoken agreements not to publicly mention certain topics. Anything that would embarrass the other partner and disrupt the fragile agreement to seek therapy is usually avoided until much later in the therapy process. Among the issues avoided are sexual dissatisfactions, extended family problems, and substance abuse. When these areas are assessed in the initial sessions, couples may deny or hedge when asked directly about them. A couple may have to have some confidence in the therapy process and the therapist before getting to these highly charged issues.

Another factor to consider is that a high percentage of alcoholics also suffer from some other psychiatric disorder. Specifically, sobriety uncovers depression and anxiety disorders. Miller (1999) notes that approximately 30 to 50% of alcoholics have major depression and one-third have an anxiety disorder.

Assessing the Alcoholic and the Relationship

Any screening questionnaire or interview should contain questions about alcohol and other substance abuse. Asking such questions in a structured way and as a matter of course takes away some of their sting. When substance abuse is suspected, a medical history should be taken, as well as a review of the immediate stressors in the couple's life and the availability of social support.

The Revised Marital Relationship Scale (RMRS) (Azrin, Naster, & Jones, 1973) can be used to gauge the strength of the cohesiveness in the relationship. As indicated previously, if the partner is to be involved in treating the alcoholic, this bond must be strong. The Coping Questionnaire (Orford et al., 1998), the Significant-Other Behavior Questionnaire (Love, Longabaugh, Clifford, Beattie, & Peaslee (1993), and the Spouse Enabling Inventory (Fisher & Corcoran, 1994) can be used to assess how well the couple is coping with the drinking behavior. Roberts and McCrady (2003, p. 37) point out that it is important to approach these assessments "in a spirit of inquiry by engaging the family in a discussion that reveals their perceptions about positive and negative actions, as well as the subjective feelings about interactions with the drinker."

Further assessment of the alcoholic is available from standardized instruments. Among these are the well-known Michigan Alcohol Screening Test (MAST) (Selzer, 1971), which contains 24 items answered either yes or no. The questions are administered via interview and take very little time. A score of 7 indicates an alcohol-use problem. In addition, therapists might use the CAGE questionnaire (Ewing, 1984), the Alcohol Use Disorders Identification Test (AUDIT) (Saunders, Aasland, Babor, de la Fuente, & Grant, 1993), and the Alcohol Dependence Scale (Skinner & Horn, 1984) to look at current consumption patterns and degree of dependence on alcohol.

The genogram discussed in earlier chapters is a particularly useful assessment tool that can be used in charting family histories of chemical dependency. It can also be a means for confronting a client or couple in denial. Recently, we saw a client's genogram in which 60% of the people depicted were acknowledged to be chemically dependent. Whether one believes this trend is genetic transmission or a family or cultural tradition, one begins to see the pattern that shapes current behavior. Evidence is strong that the closer the contact with an "alcoholic family of origin," the more likely one is to experience alcohol problems (CSAT, 2004).

The genogram, the MAST, CAGE, AUDIT, and other screening devices serve dual functions of heightening client awareness and giving information to the therapist. Another avenue is to require a medical examination in cases where alcohol dependence is suspected because habitual use over time affects the entire system. Other physical signs and concern from a knowledgeable physician can help push a client toward treatment. Alternately, a general practitioner who is not well schooled in substance abuse can strengthen the client's denial process.

Developing the Interactive Definition

Earlier, a three-stage model of alcohol interventions was discussed. At each stage, a different set of problems becomes focal for the couple, and each stage involves couple patterns, not just issues for the alcoholic. The integrative model is appropriate for helping couples identify interactionally defined problems at each of these stages of recovery. Couples who are struggling with alcohol issues may initially decide on an interactive definition such as "We will each seek our own treatment for alcohol and enabling (codependency) issues." A holistic treatment approach will not stop once a couple has been convinced to enter a treatment facility. Later, when the alcoholic is sober, the couple will develop interactive definitions based on issues in their new relationship. Finally, couples therapy can be aimed at helping couples deal with relapse prevention by (1) engaging in wellness behaviors that prevent relationship problems and enhance sobriety and (2) identifying high-risk situations that endanger sobriety and how the partner can deal with these situations. For example, how will the partner react when the alcoholic, recently out of treatment, goes to a favorite bar with coworkers and orders a soft drink? The partner's view of this action as a high-risk behavior could be crucial information for the alcoholic; on the other hand, it might be considered interference. A couple can develop an *interactional definition* of these problems during the recovery process.

In short, the integrative model recommends a start-and-stop approach to couples therapy. The initial issue can require specific inpatient treatment, but couples therapy can be resumed immediately as part of the aftercare plan, first to deal with issues around supporting sobriety and eventually to deal with relationship enhancement and relapse prevention.

Case Example: Ed and Beth

Ed and Beth had been married 4 years when Ed's drinking became a problem. As his drinking increased, he worked less at his municipal job (he was a refuse worker) and spent less time with his wife and two children, ages 1 and 3 years old. Beth asked Ed to leave because of his drinking because he was becoming increasingly belligerent when he came home after a night of drinking. Ed moved in with a coworker, Tomas, who was a drinking buddy of Ed's, and an occasional marijuana user. After 2$\frac{1}{2}$ months, Ed asked Beth if he could return home, telling her he "wasn't drinking as much." Beth found out, after Ed returned, that the return home was also prompted by the fact that his supervisor confronted him about his absences from work, as well as showing up late for work.

While Ed was living with Tomas, Beth had been in individual counseling with her pastor. When Ed returned, Beth insisted that he enter alcohol treatment before discussing the future of their marriage. Ed went to a detoxification/treatment program sponsored by a local alcohol and drug treatment agency. Beth took part in the family education meetings while Ed was in an intensive outpatient facility, but she carried a lot of resentment and made no agreement to stay married once he completed treatment. After being released from the intensive outpatient program, Ed went to live in a halfway house on his release because of Beth's ambivalence. After about 40 days in the halfway house, Beth and Ed had decided that they wanted to reunite and have Ed move back home. Since his return, the couple has been having problems.

Application of the Integrative Model: Alcoholism

Stage 1: Assessing and Developing an Interactive Definition of the Problem

During the initial couples therapy session, a genogram was completed for each member of the couple, and the history of the relationship was discussed. In many ways, the couple had lived together more as roommates. Each kept a separate checking account, they shared the bills equally, and each had a scheduled night out each week with friends. The two were sexually compatible, but both admitted that there was little understanding of their differences. They were also concerned that every discussion turned into a fight. Apparently, the relationship had changed after the birth of their first child and changed further after their second child was born. Ed complained that Beth took less interest in the relationship and their old "party friends." Beth indicated that Ed became involved with drinking to the exclusion of his family. Beth admitted that she withdrew; turning her attention to the children, and Ed grudgingly agreed that he ignored the relationship and children as well. The couple speculated that Ed's drinking gave Beth all the responsibility for decision making and thus reduced conflict. Since he became sober, though, conflict has returned. The therapist reinforced the fact that both members of the couple should continue in aftercare through AA and Al-Anon.

When these two sides of the story had been brought to light, the couple was able, during the first session, to agree that one of the most important issues was dealing with conflict. They felt that if they could communicate and deal with the many problems by negotiating they would be able to improve the relationship and reduce the overall level of stress. The interactive definition of the problem was framed as "We tend to withdraw and retreat when a conflict or crisis occurs."

Stage 2: Goal Setting

During the same session, the therapist explained that, rather than focus on the problems of the past, the couple should identify some specific goals regarding conflict. The therapist was surprised when the couple indicated that they would like to have an open disagreement. They felt that they would have a healthy relationship when they could directly face a particular issue.

Externalizing in this session, the therapist picked up on the couple's goal statement about being able to handle conflict. The therapist continued to refer to the problem as "the conflict phobia." This actually helped the partners see the problem in a less pathological way. They were able to laugh about it when they realized that they were avoiding conflict rather than blaming each other as they had before. The therapist reinforced the fact that the couple was well on their way to conquering the "phobia" by getting together.

Stage 3: Adopting New Perceptions and Behaviors

Before the third session, each partner was instructed to think about the other partner's strengths. They were each to bring a list to the next session. When the couple arrived, neither partner had completed a list, but both said they had thought about it. Rather than chastise the couple, the therapist proceeded to make a list of each person's strengths as identified by the other partner. Beth saw Ed as a hard worker and as determined, humorous, and creative. Ed said that Beth was sensitive to feelings, intelligent, and a good planner. When Ed started to list the downside of each trait, the therapist stopped him and focused him back on the goal of looking at strengths.

Next (externalizing) the therapist asked both partners to indicate how they might use their individual strengths to attack the "conflict phobia." Ed immediately chimed in that Beth was more sensitive to recognizing when the problem was happening and that she could be the one to signal when a discussion was needed. The therapist suggested that Ed's persistence and perseverance would help the couple stay with the argument until a conclusion was reached. By the end of the third session, the couple had indicated that Beth would bring up an issue that they were avoiding during the next week, and both would take turns expressing themselves uninterrupted for 5 minutes. Before beginning again, each member would have to correctly paraphrase the partner's statement. It was Ed's job to make certain that they stick to the argument and not "kitchen sink," or bring in other outside issues. They were to engage in this conflict for no more than 15 minutes, but they were to continue these 15-minute sessions each day until the issue was resolved. If the issue was still not resolved by the next therapy session, the couple would discuss it in session. The therapist indicated that because the two were not used to dealing with conflict, they should keep it to a minimum at first. The therapist went on to indicate that conflict was a normal part of relationships and the key to growth.

The next two sessions of couples therapy were spent in communication and conflict-management training using homework assignments and role playing in the session. It turned out that both members of the couple had difficulty talking about sexual issues, and their first conflict had been over this issue. There had been immediate improvement in the relationship, however, because Beth finally admitted she did not like to have sex late at night when she was tired, something Ed never knew. The two changed their schedules, and both partners felt more satisfied.

Stage 4: Maintaining New Perceptions and Behaviors

By the sixth session, the couple was ready to end couples therapy; however, the therapist believed that communication skills had not been fully learned. The couple seemed to be experiencing less stress and a better sexual relationship, so the therapist agreed to see the couple on a monthly basis for "booster sessions." During the booster sessions, both partners were asked to list those things that they were doing to further the change process. Beth indicated that she was bringing up her concerns more frequently but that Ed seemed to be withdrawing. Ed eventually admitted that he was depressed and was having urges to drink. He said that he did not always feel like dealing with problems when he came home from work. His attendance at AA had dwindled, and he had not engaged a sponsor; Beth had not been attending Al-Anon at all. The therapist focused immediately on this issue and indicated that regular AA and Al-Anon attendance was necessary for couples therapy to continue. The therapist did not see any indication of major depression, but Ed's down moods appeared to be related to a letdown after the rosy period immediately following sobriety. The couple agreed to the stipulation of continued support group attendance.

During the session, the couple identified the fact that not having enough "fun time" was affecting the relationship and that simply dealing with difficulties was turning their interactions into a chore. The couple agreed to build in more time together doing inexpensive things for fun. They indicated that they must now find a balance between not avoiding important issues and spending all of their time hashing things out. The therapist congratulated the couple for addressing one of the obstacles to change that they had encountered and continued to schedule monthly sessions.

Stage 5: Validating New Perceptions and Behaviors

Three months after they had begun couples therapy, Ed's sobriety was of good quality, and the couple was more stable than when therapy first began. Certainly, a number of issues still needed to be dealt with. There were still extreme financial problems, issues about child-care and household responsibilities, and issues about how to spend free time. During these final sessions, the therapist directed the partners to recognize their achievement in learning to deal more effectively with conflict and supporting each other's recovery. The therapist asked both members of the couple to indicate something that each has appreciated in the other during the past 3 months. Ed said, "She never got discouraged and always fought back to make everything work." Beth said, "He felt like drinking but didn't. I hope he was thinking about me and the children."

The therapist asked the two what sort of issues they thought might be the biggest threat to the kinds of changes that had been made. Both agreed that Ed's return to drinking was the biggest issue. The therapist again encouraged attendance at AA and Al-Anon groups, also asking the partners to think about what they had learned in couples therapy or in their support group over the past weeks and how they might apply that learning to upcoming stressors in the future. Ed said, "This time, if we have a fight, I am going to hang in there until we get it resolved. If I am mad, I'll call my sponsor or someone else, but eventually we will get it straightened out." Beth said, "I am not going to hide my feelings when something Ed does disappoints me. But I am not going to make him feel bad, just work it out." The therapist scheduled a follow-up session in 3 months.

CONCLUSION

Alcohol is the cause of many couples problems, and many people drink to cope with problems in their relationships. This chapter addressed the treatment of a couple when alcohol affects one of the partners. We chose not to address other substances of abuse for brevity's sake and because alcohol is the most significant drug problem today.

It is clear that couple patterns such as enabling (codependency) can actually support alcoholism, but it is also the case that the relationship can be the medium for achieving sobriety. The traditional wisdom has been that each member of a couple must be treated separately before the two can work on the issues that confront them jointly. Evidence suggests that interventions aimed at improving the quality of the couple relationship will not embroil the couple in more conflict and may establish a good environment to support sobriety. Couples who improve their communication skills and who develop relapse prevention strategies together can create a higher level of sobriety in the alcoholic partner and eliminate maladaptive patterns in the relationship.

14

Blending Couples

KEY CONCEPTS

- Blending couples and families are distinctly different from first-married couples and biological nuclear families, and they experience unique problems and concerns.
- There are many myths about stepfamilies that can limit growth and positive interactions among family members.
- There are predictable stages through which blending couples and blending families progress.
- Nonresidential parents usually play an important role in a blending family formation.
- The couple is the foundation of a blending family and requires special considerations in therapy.
- Family therapy and group therapy are the preferred methods of treatment for blending families after the couple's relationship is stabilized.

SOCIOLOGICAL CONTEXT

Remarried couples is the fastest growing family form in the United States with more than half of Americans living in a stepfamily situation (Clark, Recher, & Foote, 2004). It is predicted that stepfamilies will be the most common family formation by 2010 (Hetherington, 1999; Visher, Visher, & Pasley, 1997). A *stepfamily* is defined as one in which children live some, most, or all of the time with two married adults, one of whom is not a biological parent (Ganong & Coleman, 2004). Although this family unit is becoming the norm, most of these families are attempting to model their relationships after a biological nuclear family (Kelley, 1992). However, remarried couples and their stepchildren are different from traditional families and often exhibit stress when they attempt to replicate the structure of the nuclear family. Clearly, under these conditions, stepfamilies begin with a great challenge (Gladding, 2002; Satir, 1972).

In blending relationships, traditional couple intimacy is challenged by the formation of the "instant family," whose focus becomes the stepparent–stepchild relationship. Little attention is paid to the needs of couples because the needs of children receive priority. It becomes more complicated by former spouses, who influence new couple relationships through contact with their biological children.

ISSUES FOR BLENDING COUPLES

There is a vast array of complex pairings for remarried couples:

1. Both previously married but have no children.
2. Both previously married and each has children.
3. Both previously married and only one has children.
4. One previously married and has children, and one has not been married before.
5. One has not been previously married but has a biological child, and the other has not been married before.
6. One has never been married and does not have children, and one has been previously married with no children.

Often, in addition to the various pairings, new couples play host to a cast of characters ranging from former spouses, children who were not expected to live with the couple or visit often, former in-laws, old friends, or even old bill collectors (Kaslow & Schwartz, 1987). Unfortunately, the couple does not have time to establish a separate identity before dealing with these other people. Thus, rarely is there time to build a strong foundation to support the remarriage before the couple is involved with the challenges of stepfamily formation (Kaslow & Schwartz, 1987).

Differences Between Blending Families and Biological Nuclear Families

Usually, in a blending family, each member has experienced significant loss. Dreams for the future have been shattered, and even if the dissolution was desired, sorrow and pain accompany the loss of a previous relationship. Newly divorced individuals, who are saddled with their own pain, venture to develop new, exciting relationships. Children may have lost contact with a biological parent, a grandparent, other relatives, friends, or schoolmates (Bobes & Rothman, 2002).

In stepfamilies, each person brings a set of expectations about how to parent, clean house, cook, socialize, or work. These expectations come not only from each partner's family of origin but also former relationships (Magnuson & Shaw, 2003). Often, individual beliefs are in contradiction with other family member's beliefs and become targets for unresolved pain in the family.

Alternatively, a stepfamily created from loss can provide a safe arena for intimacy. A quest for intimacy is reported to be one of the most important aspects of newly formed relationships (Eckstein, Belongia, & Elliott-Applegate, 2000). Intimacy includes caring, affection, closeness, and understanding. Family unity

1. Bride 2. Groom 3. Groom's daughter from first marriage 4. Bride's mother 5. Bride's mother's current lover 6. Bride's sperm donor father 7. & 8. Sperm donor's parents who sued for visitation rights to bride 9. Bride's mother's lover at time of bride's birth 10. Groom's mother 11. Groom's mother's boyfriend 12. Groom's father 13. Groom's stepmother 14. Groom's father's third wife 15. Groom's grandfather 16. Groom's grandfather's lover 17. Groom's first wife

Source: Cartoon by Signe Wilkinson, USA. Reprinted by permission of Cartoonists & Writers Syndicate.

and shared goals and values along with external family and community support are also highly valued (Eckstein et al., 2000). Restoration of the security of companionship, partnership, and creating satisfying sexual relationships are examples of goals for remarried couples (Clapp, 2000). Economic gains and relief from single-parenting responsibilities are also cited as goals to help generate growth and increased stability in the family (Hobart, 1989).

In blending families, the bond between a biological parent and a child proves stronger than a newly created relationship between a stepchild and a stepparent. There may be loyalty conflicts because a biological parent–child relationship has more longevity than a new couple relationship. In some families, a nonresidential parent may continue to be actively involved with a child and, at times, is viewed as interfering in the couple's life. In some cases, one child may be active in going back and forth to both parents' household, while another child may have little contact with the nonresidential parent. These conflicting schedules can create jealousy and logistical challenges for families.

Stepfamilies are also required to accept the lack of a legal relationship between a stepparent and stepchild. This places the stepparent in a position of assuming responsibilities without rights or privileges (Visher & Visher, 1990). Often, this task can be overwhelming for partners who have not yet developed their own style of problem solving and negotiating with each other. The most challenging task, however, is establishing the creditability of the stepparent regarding parental authority in the home (Hetherington, 2002).

The Role of Stepmother

In addition to the complexities involved in stepfamily formation, stepmothers face their own unique challenges. Children often idealize a biological mother, whether she is deceased, absent, or available (Cath & Shopper, 2001). The negative stereotype of the "wicked" stepmother found in several traditional fairy tales continues to have an impact on contemporary imagination (Jones, 2003; Salwen, 1990). In fact, many stepmothers struggle with the internalized negative self-concept related to the connotations of evil, cruelty, jealousy, and selfishness derived from the stories of Hansel and Gretel, Snow White, and Cinderella (Salwen, 1990).

Bettelheim (1977) explains the persistent stereotype as related to the psychological needs that the negative stepparent role meets for stepchildren. The fantasy of the wicked stepmother allows the child who cannot integrate loving and hateful feelings toward a new and highly influential person in his or her life to cope, by focusing anger and rage on the mythical evil person. Thus, the relationship with the biological mother remains intact. Feelings of anger and disappointment that the child may harbor about the biological parent's role in the divorce are unexpressed and instead are directed toward the "new" person in the child's life.

The role of stepmother may be most difficult in traditional family structures where the father is the primary breadwinner and the mother remains in the home, assuming responsibility for the household, the cooking, and child care. Stepmothers most often are thrust into roles of disciplinarians and rule setters more intensely than are traditional stepfathers.

The Role of Stepfather

Because mothers often continue to be the primary custodians of their children after divorce, more stepfamilies address issues related to the integration of a stepfather in the family. The stepfather is often viewed as the financial rescuer or supporter of the new family, but he may be minimally involved with child care. A stepfather may view the mother–child bond as strong and exclusive and may not make attempts to integrate himself in the relationship. Conversely, a stepfather may attempt too early to discipline stepchildren and consequently faces conflict and rejection with the child and his new partner.

Just as negative stereotypical myths pollute the vision of a stepmother, stereotypes of an "abusive" (both physically and sexually) stepfather is perpetuated by the media. These myths serve the same purpose of distancing the stepparent and stepchild, regardless of the gender of the stepparent (Claxton-Oldfield, 1992).

Some stepfathers feel guilty about the lack of time they spent with their biological children, and so they become extremely involved in the lives of their stepchildren. On the other hand, some perceive their roles as the one who should be in control in order to "shape up" the new family. This situation can be particularly destructive if the stepchild is an adolescent girl (Ganong & Coleman, 2004).

The following are concerns often described by stepfathers:

1. Uncertainty over the degree of authority to exert in the new family
2. The amount and type of expression of affection toward stepchildren
3. The discipline of stepchildren and the enforcement of rules
4. Financial conflicts
5. Guilt over leaving children from a previous marriage
6. Loyalty conflicts with the mother–child relationship
7. Sexual conflicts between stepfather and stepchild or sibling conflicts
8. Conflict over surnames

Although these issues may be prevalent to some extent in biological nuclear families, the stigma against stepfamilies continues to exist in our society (Robinson, 1984). In fact, clinical researchers cite evidence showing that some stepparents camouflage their step status or deny that they are in a stepfamily (Claxton-Oldfield, 1992).

HEALTHY STEPFAMILY CHARACTERISTICS

Flexibility and Adaptability

The need for flexibility in stepfamilies is paramount. Holidays, birthdays, vacations, and other family events require the accommodation of two families' schedules. Sometimes, plans and ideas must be changed at a moment's notice (Kelley, 1992).

Patience

Patience is crucial because remarried couples do not have the time to develop cohesiveness before they become an instant family. Attempting to prematurely force the family to become a unit can lead to anger and resentment. Children must adjust respect for their stepparent at their own pace. Love for a stepparent does not come automatically, and it may never occur. Stepparents can demonstrate respect for the stepchildren by being aware of the changes that they are forced to make by the addition of an unfamiliar parent in the home.

Realistic Expectations

There must be a realization that a stepfamily will be different from a biological nuclear family. When family members do not mourn the loss of their previous family structure and continue to idealize the former family, progress is unlikely to be made in the newly created family formation. A stepfamily cannot replicate the biological nuclear family, nor should it try. Roles within the family for each person must be renegotiated, thus establishing a unique relationship among family members.

Cooperation of Separate Households

For healthy stepfamily functioning, it is important for couples to develop a parenting coalition that includes adults from both households who are involved in raising the children. Sometimes there may be stepparents from two families involved in the coalition. In cases where all parents have remarried, six adults could be providing input to raise the children. With several conflicting ideas, needs, and agendas, it is easy to imagine how complicated this task might be (Visher & Visher, 1996).

A Unified Couple

Strong, unified couples create healthy stepfamilies. With a parent–child bond preceding the new couple relationship, stepfamily couples must plan time to nourish each partner and the relationship. Lack of trust of intimate relationships resulting from the divorce and guilt from spending time away from the children can weaken the relationship. The security of a strong, stable, and happy couple is essential for the couple to provide guidance and direction for the stepfamily (Visher & Visher, 1996).

Establishment of Constructive Rituals

Solid relationships grow from positive shared memories, just as feelings of belonging develop from familiar ways of interacting (Gladding, 2002; Visher & Visher, 1996). The establishment of rituals and traditions is important for healthy stepfamilies. When possible, positive former traditions should be retained or at least be combined to form new traditions. For example, one family had always opened gifts on Christmas Eve, whereas the other had opened them on Christmas Day during a large family celebration. The stepfamily decided to open one special gift on Christmas Eve with caroling and a light dinner afterward. On Christmas Day, they would open the remainder of the gifts and celebrate with a family gathering at breakfast because two of the children were leaving to celebrate the holiday with the other parent in the early afternoon. These accommodations include both families yet provide new experiences for the stepfamily.

Formation of Satisfactory Step-Relationships

Step-relations develop over a long period of time and not necessarily at the same time that the couple is achieving a strong bond (Visher & Visher, 1996). Stepparents enter the family with little power. In fact, most experts recommend that stepparents form a friendly relationship with their stepchildren first, rather than an authoritative one, and then gradually assume more of the discipline.

The relationship between the stepparent and the stepchild is also affected both by the messages that the child receives from the biological parent about the stepparent and by the child's view of the stepparent relationship in the home. Couples should balance time spent on themselves and time spent on family needs so that jealousies and resentments do not emerge.

STRENGTHS OF STEPFAMILIES

Although much of the research focuses on problems in stepfamilies, members of such families have the potential for growth from the many positive experiences of living in a stepfamily. Coleman, Ganong, and Gingrich (1985) have identified the following 10 most often mentioned strengths of stepfamilies:

1. Each family member is exposed to a broader range of people and life experiences. Diverse traditions, careers, hobbies, foods, vacations, and family daily life can enrich the lives of all family members.
2. The couple exhibits a positive rather than a negative model of adult intimacy.
3. There are more adults available when children require assistance. A stepparent may compensate for a quality that the biological parent lacks and can serve as a guide for the children.
4. Parents are typically happier and less strained in the stepfamily than in the biological nuclear family.
5. Stepparents can be more objective and can provide a more rational opinion than can the biological parent whose emotional bond is strong.
6. Adults may be more experienced, mature, and motivated to create a successful relationship and family after being embroiled in conflict and disappointment in the former marriage.
7. Parents exhibit more cooperation and sharing because the roles must be flexible and constantly in a state of change. The blending of two disparate family styles provides opportunity for negotiation and problem solving.
8. Stepchildren become more adaptable so that parents can focus on their own relationship and adult needs.
9. Stepfamilies are more stable emotionally and economically than are single-parent families. In fact, research indicates that stability for stepfamilies is very similar to that for biological nuclear families.
10. Sometimes there is a "change" in birth order, so that the oldest child gets a chance to be a middle child or the youngest now has a younger brother or sister. This new view of self in relation to the family can produce new perceptions and expectations of each family member.

In addition to these 10 strengths, Hobart (1989) reports that "if the trend of increasing numbers of remarried families and declining birth rates continues, there is a possibility that remarried families will have more available extended family resources than nuclear families."

STEPFAMILY HURDLES AND CHALLENGES: STRESSORS IN THE FAMILY

It is generally agreed that the most frequent problem area in stepfamilies is the stepparent–stepchild relationship. In many families, the biological parent remains very involved and continues to set limits and provide guidance to the children.

The stepparent's assumption of an immediate parental role is detrimental in these situations. In fact, a significant number of stepparents don't ever choose a parental role with stepchildren. The age of the children and the involvement of the nonresidential parent significantly influence this decision (Mills, 1984). Research indicates that stepfamilies with preadolescents and adolescents have the most difficulty adjusting (Coleman, Marshall, & Ganong, 1986; Visher & Visher, 1988).

Lack of time and energy for the couple to nurture their relationship is also cited as problematic for many remarried couples. Orchestrating many family member's activities and responding to their varied needs leaves many parents drained physically and emotionally, with little time to spare for their partner. Learning how to balance the adult and child needs and to prioritize the marital relationship requires commitment and flexibility from both partners. Other challenges include the establishment of a new hierarchy and more clear boundaries. Many children have had more elevated status in a single-parent home and are required to adjust to a new situation (Gladding, 2002). In addition, economic issues and conflicting loyalties add to the stress of many stepfamilies.

STAGES OF STEPFAMILY DEVELOPMENT

Papernow (1984, 1995) describes seven stages of stepfamily development. In the three early stages, the family remains primarily divided along biological lines. Most styles of nurturing, rules, limit setting, and rituals occur within the biological subsystems. During the middle stages, the family loosens biological boundaries and begins to restructure the family on the basis of the step-relations.

The couple must be the first to begin making these changes, becoming the architects of the stepfamily systems (Mills, 1984). In later stages, the stepfamily structure is in place, and the role of the stepparent emerges. These seven stages typically require between 4 and 12 years to complete.

> *Stage 1: Fantasy.* Stepfamilies embrace many myths and have many unrealistic ideas about blending together. Some of these ideas include rescuing children from the ex-spouse, healing a "broken family," having a stepparent adoring their stepchildren, marrying a nurturing parent, and having someone with whom to share the load.
>
> *Stage 2: Assimilation.* The couple joins in an attempt to carry out the plan of the fantasy of the new family. As one stepmother described it, "I was trying so hard to put the two pieces of the broken plate back together again, but they didn't fit. They came from two different plates" (Papernow, 1984, p. 357). Stepparents who attempt to join the biological unit feel jealous, resentful, confused, and inadequate when they are unsuccessful in their attempt.
>
> *Stage 3: Awareness and Getting Clear.* Increasing clarity of the reality of the difficulties of blending helps the couple understand what is happening. Sometimes resolving the relationship with a previous spouse takes place in this stage. The step-relations open somewhat to the stepparent and

include the stepparent in some decision making or family structuring. There is still much reservation though, because biological parents are low in trust yet do not want to fail in another relationship.

Stage 4: Mobilization and Airing Differences. During this stage, stepfamilies begin to voice opinions about their thoughts, perceptions, and feelings. Arguments may be more prevalent as the stepparent makes more demands on the biological parent's time and parenting style. Dissatisfaction is usually high because the biological parent becomes more distressed.

Stage 5: Action or Going Into Business Together. The energy and expressiveness of the prior stage initiates an "unfreezing " of the old system and marks the beginning of a new phase of building a family unit with some integration of all family members. The couple is the driving force in this stage because the partners actually change the family structure by establishing boundaries such as creating time to be alone together, closing the bedroom door, and consulting each other on childrearing and visitation issues. Decisions are also made about how the nonresidential parent is going to be involved in the stepfamily structure. Celebrations of holidays, rituals, and traditions are reestablished at this stage.

Stage 6: Contact and Intimacy in Step-Relationships. In this stage, the partners previously polarized by stepfamily issues view each other as someone with whom they can express feelings and share issues, including painful or difficult ones. The role of stepparent is more solid, with clearer communication evident between the couple and the children. The couple experiences the relationship as separate from the children and from the stepfamily.

Stage 7: Resolution: Holding On and Letting Go. Step relationships provide some sense of satisfaction as the family settles in a lifestyle more reliable for each person in the family. Members know what to expect from each other, and they communicate their needs more openly. Occasionally, issues about how closely or distantly to interact with stepchildren emerge, although at times a distant relationship is established and maintained throughout the family cycle.

The resolution stage is also a time for grieving. The stepparent realizes that he or she must share the stepchild with the biological and more "entitled" parent. This realization is most acute at visitation and holiday times. The biological parent realizes that there will be interrupted parenting and significant influences on the children from someone outside of the home. Letting go becomes easier because it occurs on a regular basis as children move back and forth between parents. In this stage, however, the stepparent has become the "intimate outsider" and can be a confidante of children when biological parents may be too involved to be objective.

During all these stages, couples must continually evaluate and reevaluate their relationship and provide protective boundaries around the couple unit. Children will attempt to permeate the boundaries, as will such outsiders as former spouses, in-laws, or social institutions that are not sensitive to stepfamily issues.

The Impact of Blending Families at Various Stages of the Life Cycle

Spouses at Different Life-Cycle Stages

In general, the wider the discrepancy in family life-cycle experiences between the new partners, the greater the difficulty of transition and the longer it will take to integrate a functioning stepfamily (McGoldrick & Carter, 1980). A woman with two small children who marries a man with grown children is likely to have more difficulty adjusting than will a man and a woman of similar ages and life stages who both have young children or children who are grown and live on their own.

Children at Various Life Stages

The most complex remarried families are those in which one or both partners have children under the age of 18. There are some indications that preschool children, if they are able to mourn their losses successfully, are the most adaptable to the new stepfamily, while adjustment is most difficult for teenagers (Visher & Visher, 1979). Children of latency age seem to have the most difficulty resolving their feelings of divided loyalties and benefit from contact with both biological parents (Wallerstein & Kelley, 1980). It is clear that children in divorced families adapt best when they have parents who are cooperative and they have continuous contact with both parents (Landis, 1991; Luepnitz, 1986).

Stepfamilies with Adolescents

The nuclear family with adolescents is frequently at a turbulent stage, and the difficulties are usually exacerbated in stepfamilies. Conflict often occurs because the stepfamily is promoting cohesiveness at a time when the adolescent needs to separate from the family and form an independent identity. Boundaries must be renegotiated when adolescents want freedom and fewer restrictions and home responsibilities, even if the stepfamily is in an infant stage.

Blending in Later Life Stages

Remarriage or recoupling in later life requires significant readjustment of relationships throughout both family systems, which may include in-laws or grandchildren (McGoldrick & Carter, 1980). Grown children sometimes complain when family traditions change and family events such as graduations, weddings, or birthdays are rearranged. Sometimes there are conflicts about how much financial assistance to provide for adult children and how legal wills are to be designed. If the families of the new couple, including former spouses, are cooperative and attend family functions together, acceptance of the new marriage and blending of the families is optimum (McGoldrick & Carter, 1980).

ISSUES WITHIN BLENDING COUPLES AND FAMILIES

In addition to issues relevant to couples in general, some common therapeutic themes are particular to blending couples.

Economic Issues

Unresolved issues from prior marriages often haunt stepfamilies. Initially, there may be unfinished economic connections (Kaslow, 1993). Rarely does the economic marriage end at the same time as the legal marriage. Sale of properties in common, child support, and in some cases, permanent alimony are issues in most stepfamilies. Sometimes one partner may feel resentful toward the ex-spouse because there is little money left available after child support payments are made. One stepparent may also feel deprived or may view the other children as deprived if more money is available for only one child because of incoming financial support from a biological, nonresidential parent.

Conflicted Feelings and Behaviors

Conflicted feelings and loyalties about former relationships are often a central theme in blending relationships. In addition, ineffective behaviors and coping styles developed during difficult first marriages may continue into second marriages if issues are not resolved. Couples may be too tired or overwhelmed initially to resolve their own strains when much of the attention is paid to the children and the stepsibling relationships in the new household. Feelings of incompetence and powerlessness negatively affect problem solving at a time when these skills are necessary for a successful transition (Kaslow, 1993).

Movement of Children Between Households

Parents often feel a lack of autonomy over their family life when they must share decision making with the other biological parent. Vacations, holidays, and activities for school and weekends are now subject to the approval of the nonresidential parent. When conflicts cannot be accommodated, hostility may develop between households, and loyalty issues may arise for the children. This often results in the child's placing increased pressure on the stepfamily by refusing to be cooperative or by attempting to reunite the biological parents, thus sabotaging the new couple.

New Roles and Rules

One of the most common tasks in stepfamily development is the negotiation of new roles and rules in the family. The biological parent must adjust to another person in the household who takes on the role of parent, in addition to the role of partner (Bobes & Rothman, 2002; Casado, Young, & Rasmus, 2002; Ganong & Coleman, 2004; Gladding, 2002). Partners need to be flexible and supportive of each other as they "try on" these new roles. Rules that worked in a previous relationship may no longer work because they were based on the prior family structure of the two adults. For example, a husband who had a very active role in nurturing and disciplining the children with his former wife may feel rejected or unimportant if he remains in the background while his new wife sets limits and cares for her children. If the discrepancy is not discussed and a plan made for parenting the children, resentment and hostility may develop.

Treatment Issues

Developmental Versus Clinical

It is important to remember that couples enter into new partnerships with high hopes and much trepidation. Therapists must distinguish between normal step-family issues and clinical issues such as personality disorders, addictions, sexual problems, or clinical depression and other diagnosable disorders. Clinical issues can exacerbate an already tenuous situation in blending families and can make decision making more difficult (Kaslow, 1993).

Normalization and the Development of Love

A basic therapeutic task is to normalize the stepfamily and help all members feel positive about their new family structure. This includes dispelling the notion that they must behave and be organized the same as a biological nuclear family. Ways that therapists can validate the family include focusing on the couple as the primary unit, empathizing with the feelings emerging from the stepfamily situation, and emphasizing the positive attributes and possibilities for stepfamilies (Visher & Visher, 1990).

Therapists can also assist a stepfamily with the formation of realistic expectations about the development of love between stepparents and their stepchildren and the acceptance of a new partner by extended family members. Time and patience are key elements in this process.

Retaining Old Loyalties

Blending couples and families can retain loyalties with former family members and friends without being disloyal to their new relationships. It is healthy and often necessary for new couples to maintain ties with their former partners in order to effectively parent their children. Often, a partner continues to have contact with former in-laws or friends they made while married to their former partner. If these ties are viewed as positive by the couple, it is easier to encourage their children to maintain contact with both families. If children are discouraged from thinking or talking about their other family members, they can repress feelings and become depressed, angry, or withdrawn (Gladding, 2002).

Negotiations

Therapists can facilitate negotiations about how the new couple and family couple will spend their time together and their time apart. Couples decide how much influence that the biological parents of their children and their extended families will have on their decisions and new way of life together. Interventions such as behavioral contracts, task assignments, and other problem-solving techniques can be helpful tools.

Boundary Setting

With overwhelming issues involved in blending two families, couples frequently place their needs last in the hierarchy. Therapists can help couples arrange time for nurturing their relationship and supporting their adult goals. Often, difficulties in

setting appropriate boundaries in prior relationships may have led to their dissolution. Therapists can guide couples in formulating, maintaining, and renegotiating healthy couple boundaries by focusing on specific behaviors that contribute to
the problem and by helping the couple brainstorm about more viable interactions
that can protect their relationship.

Embracing Cultural and Racial Differences

Other blending issues can be complicated when there are cultural or racial differences within the new family structure. Religious or cultural codes rather than
preferences may be issues for negotiation and may have great emotional implications for family members. Sometimes strong influences from the nonresidential
parent can sabotage the customs and cultural traditions of the new partner. In
extreme situations, the nonresidential parent may pursue these issues in court in
an attempt to thwart any new cultural influences over the children. Therapists
can help couples clarify which customs are most important to maintain and
which can be accommodated or changed for the new family. A genogram is useful
in these situations to highlight each family's culture and traditions (Magnuson &
Shaw, 2003).

Differences in Sexual Orientation

Increasing numbers of individuals are identifying themselves as gay or lesbian.
Many have declared their sexual identities after years of living in a heterosexual relationship that produced children (Baptiste, 1987). The challenges of gay and lesbian
stepfamilies are vast, ranging from the belief that homosexuality is psychologically
unhealthy and that it is a choice made, not an inherent characteristic. Choice theory
complicates these issues because the other biological parent may be concerned that
children raised by a gay or lesbian parent will be taught to be gay or lesbian.

Therapists must educate themselves and their clients about these notions and
help couples address these stereotypes. At the same time, they must also deal with
complexities common to stepfamily living (Baptiste, 1987).

Creating Rituals and Tradition

One way of helping stepfamilies create a positive new family structure is through
the use of rituals. Rituals can be developed to help stepfamilies address loss of the
former family structure, determine new family holiday traditions, or create
lifestyle changes that incorporate all family members. These lifestyle changes can
include emerging roles, family rules, ways to spend money, or how to spend leisure
time together (Gladding, 2002).

Treatment Modalities

Couples Counseling

The couple is the relationship that must first be addressed in counseling. Partners
examine their intimate relationship and make decisions on how they will honor
their relationship at a time when their children will also be going through major
changes. They negotiate time together and identify potential issues and challenges

for their families. Together they establish new roles, rules, hierarchy, daily living arrangements, and child care. They must be able to move between the roles of spouse and parent effectively in order to successfully make the transition for the blending process.

Family Therapy

Because there are many players in the drama of blending families, all parties involved must have access to therapy in order to effect change. The therapist can decide which dyads or family members should be at each session. Sometimes the session will include the whole family, and at other times it might include the couple, the stepparent and stepchild, or stepsiblings.

On some occasions, it may be necessary to include nonresidential parents or grandparents, depending on the presenting issues for therapy. Shifts in roles, rules, and loyalties are addressed in a family format.

Group Work

The group process provides a psychoeducational forum for helping members of stepfamilies share their concerns and receive support from others who share similar circumstances. This arena can provide an air of normalcy and can provide information about typical developmental sequences that families may have in common. This may offer a more realistic picture of family life, allowing families to focus on a variety of possibilities rather than on replication of the "old" structure from the original blueprint of the nuclear family.

Individual Therapy

Although individual therapy is not often recommended for blending families, it should not be discounted if one member suffers from a clinical disorder such as anxiety, panic, depression, addiction, or other personality disorders—apart from the reaction to the stepfamily transition. The therapist can then refer the individual to couples, group, or family therapy, depending on the needs of the individual family members.

Case Example: Corey and Corina

Corey and Corina have been married for 6 months. Corey was married previously for 9 years and has two children, ages 7 and 9 years old. Both children currently reside with Corey's former wife, and his contact consists of every Wednesday evening and every other weekend. Corina was married for a brief 3 years and has a daughter, Alana, age 2. She maintains primary residence for her daughter with flexible contact for her former spouse. Because of her child's age, Corina has frequent contact with Alana's father. He is also very active in all decision making regarding the child's welfare.

Corey and Corina expected that they would jointly make parenting decisions for Alana. However, Alana's biological father calls or comes over on a daily basis to see her or to bring her special treats. He maintains that it is his right and that no one else is going to raise his daughter. Recently, Corey has become angry about the time Corina spends talking to her "ex" on the phone and about the frequent intrusions into their family life by his constant visits. When Corey and Corina try to talk about this problem, they argue and Corina cries. Corey slams the door and leaves the house to "cool off." The two spend less time together doing pleasant activities because they are angry and frustrated. Corina feels helpless and cannot disappoint her former spouse because of the guilt she feels for taking his daughter from his home. Corey says that the ex-husband might as well move in with them because he is present so often. Many times, when Corey's children come to visit, they cannot do things as a family because Alana is with her father. Corey's children have little contact with Alana, so when she is at home they ignore her.

The couple comes to marriage therapy with the following concerns:

1. Corina is frustrated with the constant criticism that she hears from Corey and feels very unsupported.
2. Corey wants to limit the time that Alana's father spends with her so that they can be "a family."
3. Corey wants his children to have more contact with Alana.
4. Corey and Corina want to be able to communicate more effectively as a couple.
5. Corey wants more time alone with Corina and would like to hire a babysitter more often.

Application of the Integrative Model: Blending Couples

Stage 1: Assessing and Obtaining an Interactional View of the Problem

Corey and Corina each have an individual concern about the problem. Corina wants Corey to stop criticizing her and to be more supportive; Corey wants to spend more time with Corina and to be more included in the decisions regarding Alana. After some discussion in therapy, the two agree that they need to learn how to set limits with Alana's father and how to implement a more structured schedule of contact. In addition, Corey and Corina express a desire to increase their time together as a couple while decreasing disputes pertaining to Alana.

Stage 2: Goal Setting

The couple agrees to work on the following goals:

1. Create a detailed contact schedule so that they will both know exactly when Alana will be with them and when she will be with her father. This schedule will free them to plan family events and begin to feel more connected as a family.
2. Learn how to negotiate rules for the family and decide how they want to organize their time at home. Each wants to feel more equally included in making family plans.
3. Spend time alone at least once a week in order to feel more intimate with each other.

Stage 3: Adopting New Perceptions and Behaviors

Corey and Corina reflect on times when they were dating and were making specific arrangements to spend time together. Corina says she loves to plan creative activities for them, but she is less energetic about the details involved in implementing the plan. Corey admits that he can be very detailed if he knows exactly when they will have opportunities for time alone and assurance that either her father or a trusted caretaker cares for Alana.

They also discuss the need for both of them to be involved in their dating plans. It is agreed that each week they will alternate in planning and implementing their date. Corina agrees to discuss the plan with her ex-spouse if any variation of the contact schedule is involved.

Stage 4: Maintaining New Perceptions and Behaviors

Corey and Corina agree that they will exercise caution to implement their plan while maintaining specific structure about their time schedule. Corina voices concern that she will have difficulty being assertive with Alana's father. To provide support, they agree that a schedule change will not occur until they have an opportunity as a couple to discuss the deviation and potential change of circumstances. Corina will inform her former spouse that she will consider his request and respond at a designated time. Corey and Corina emphasize their commitment to their dates together and agree to hold each other responsible for continued success.

Stage 5: Validating New Perceptions and Behaviors

Corey and Corina compliment each other on their abilities to problem-solve together and to remain firm in their plan to manage Alana's contact schedule. They report that they each feel more freedom and personal power over their daily lives and feel more supported in their relationship. Both vow to continue communication about these issues and agree to confront the other if either perceives that one of them is returning to "old ways."

Summary of Techniques for Working With Blending Couples

1. Basic communication and listening skills training
2. Problem-solving methods training
3. Role reversal
4. Contracting
5. Time management planning
6. Detriangulating the family (moving the ex-partner from the family while being aware of his or her influence in their lives)
7. Creating couple time and a boundary around the couple dyad
8. Slowly creating a stepparent role that is different from a parent role

SCENARIOS FOR DISCUSSION AND ROLE PLAYING

Following are some sample scenarios that can be used to stimulate discussion and as topics for role playing.

"Who's the Fairest of Them All?"

Jane has been married to Mark for 2 years. Her stepdaughter, Maxi, is openly hostile and refuses to respond to Jane's requests of her. Mark is out of town frequently and does not like to discipline his daughter when he is home. Maxi invites her father to attend her school functions but does not want Jane to attend because "she is not comfortable with the situation yet." Jane expresses to Mark that she does not agree with the idea, yet Mark sides with Maxi and informs Jane that she just needs to be patient.

"The Great Escape"

Malia and Derek have been married 4 years and reside with two of Malia's children from a previous marriage and one child of their own. Both work outside the home and are tired at night. Weekends are typically spent getting the house in order, running errands, and attending parenting events with the children. Derek is unhappy and complains to Malia that they do not seem to have any fun with each other. Malia says she is too tired and hopes that in a few years, when the children are older, she and Derek will have more time together as a couple.

"The 'Brady Bunch'"

Sharla and Todd have been married for 1 year and have five children residing with them. Two are from Sharla's previous marriage, and three are from Todd's first two marriages. The house they live in is too small and requires that two of the male stepsiblings share a room. The teenagers are seeking more autonomy and want to spend less time at home, which requires the use of the family car. Sharla works outside the home but also transports the girls to ballet classes and softball practice on Tuesdays, Thursdays, and Saturdays. She also participates in a carpool for their youngest son's karate lessons. Often these activities conflict, but Todd cannot assist her with the driving because another child has use of his car in the afternoons. There is insufficient money to purchase another automobile, and both parents agree that the activities are important for the children. Sharla and Todd once enjoyed going to the lake for fishing and boating, but they recently realized they had not done so in quite a while.

"'Til Death Do Us Part"

Pam and Paul married 6 months ago and have two children from Pam's prior marriage. Paul does not have any biological children, but he was close to his stepdaughter from his previous marriage. Paul's former wife will not allow any contact between Paul and her daughter because she believes that Pam would be a "bad influence" on her daughter. Paul has no legal recourse, but he misses the child a great deal. He had raised her from the time she was an infant. Paul feels guilty for the divorce and is withdrawn and depressed much of the time. Pam interprets his behavior as being regretful that he left his former wife. Paul resists talking to Pam about his guilt because she reacts angrily.

"The Birds and the Bees Revisited"

Robin and Justin have been married for 3 years, and each has a son and a daughter from previous marriages. Justin's son and Robin's daughter are in the same grade in school and have some of the same friends. Lately, Robin has noticed that her daughter is not dressing properly around the house and enters her stepbrother's room without knocking and when inappropriately dressed. One day Justin came home early from work and found the two stepsiblings in their underclothing on the family room sofa. They seemed embarrassed, but later when Robin confronted her daughter she was told that she was overreacting and being ridiculous.

CONCLUSION

A blending family is a unique family constellation that requires special considerations from therapists. Some of the issues these families face include the usage of joint monies, creating couple time together, parenting with two households, rule setting, grieving the previous family structure, and stepparent–stepchild relationships.

Sometimes, the manner in which these issues are addressed depends on the ages of the children and the life stages of the adults. However, there are predictable stages through which most stepfamilies progress, from the fantasy stage, through assimilation, awareness, airing differences, action, and intimacy to resolution. Stepfamilies need to be made aware that these are normal stages that require time and effort to negotiate successfully.

Once the family members relinquish the myth that they should interact in the same way as a biological nuclear family they can define their roles more realistically and can negotiate rules more appropriate for all family members. Partners must create clear boundaries, and they must establish time for themselves as a couple. In healthy stepfamilies, the development of love between stepparent and stepchild is viewed as a gradual process that may never develop as the parents would like. However, a realistic, consistent relationship can be defined for each parent and child. Blending couples become aware that the challenge of creating a new family structure is a long, complicated one that can be very gratifying for all family members if they can be flexible and patient.

15

Same-Sex Couples

KEY CONCEPTS

- Although there are similarities between the types of issues same-sex couples and heterosexual couples face, a number of differences must be addressed in therapy.
- Role models for same-sex couples have been limited. For this reason, couples may attempt to fit their relationships into traditional marriage models.
- Same-sex relationships have many of the same stressors as heterosexual relationships, but they are also unique. Same-sex couples have special difficulties dealing with their families, work situations, and a legal system that does not recognize their relationship.
- Same-sex couples are as likely as other couples to experience domestic violence.
- Therapists must examine their personal values and beliefs about same-sex couples before they can be effective as clinicians.

SOCIOLOGICAL CONTEXT

Gay and lesbian couples experience many of the same issues as heterosexual couples. They struggle with finances, division of household duties, career-related stress, intimate relations, and extended family relationships. In addition, there are issues that are unique to same-sex couples, which we describe in this chapter. As larger numbers of Americans identify themselves as gay or lesbian, we are more aware of gay and lesbian couples as members of our families, friends, coworkers, or as public figures featured in the media. However, homophobia continues to be an issue for many individuals and social institutions (Nichols, 2000). It is manifested by discrimination within families with gay or lesbian members, in the workplace, in schools, in the church or synagogue, and in society at large. Most recently, there has been much public attention regarding gay leaders in traditional churches and gay and lesbian marriages in some states. Civil unions have been explored as an option for some states that do not want to recognize same-sex marriages.

There is still confusion over appropriate terms to use to define same-sex relationships. Terms such as *husband* and *wife* assume that the husband is a man and the wife is a woman. *Lover, partner, significant other, roommate, friend,* or other vague descriptors do not adequately express the committed relationship that many same-sex couples experience. These terms appear to omit same-sex couples who are in a committed relationship (Bepko & Johnson, 2000), although "partner" is probably the most widely used term. It does not, however, adequately express the love and intimate attachment of an intimate relationship. For example, in business, we use the word partner to signify an associate or close affiliate, not someone we love and care about deeply (Long et al., 2006)

Homosexual bias is also evident in the professional literature. In fact, it was not until 1980 that the American Psychiatric Association removed homosexuality from the list of mental disorders in the *Diagnostic and Statistical Manual*. However, the picture is not as bleak as it may appear. There has been a proliferation of research and literature on same-sex therapy issues as society continues to address the nature or nurture debate (Ellis & Mitchell, 2000).

There is also debate over the terminology for homosexuality; most prefer the term *gay* for male homosexuals and *lesbian* for female homosexuals. Gay men are identified as those who view themselves as interested in sexual and love relationships with other men, and lesbians are interested in love and sexual relationships with women. It must be noted, however, that some might identify themselves as gay or lesbian without ever having a sexual relationship, either by choice or by circumstance. In fact, one lesbian client reports that "it is safer to be nonsexual and 'pass' in a straight society."

There are many faulty assumptions about being gay or lesbian in a heterosexual society. For example, it is not true that in a gay relationship one man must be the "effeminate" one, while the other is more traditionally identified as the "macho male." Nor is it accurate to project an image of a lesbian couple as one where one woman bears masculine traits, while the other is more passive and "feminine." It is also inappropriate to assume that all lesbian women exhibit masculine physical characteristics. Some lesbian women appear very feminine by society's standard (Degges-White, Rice, & Myers, 2000; Fukuyma & Ferguson, 2000). It has also been said that gay men are afraid of women. There is no evidence of misogyny or fear of women as a major characteristic of gay men. Neither must lesbians be "manhaters."

THE GAY OR LESBIAN LIFESTYLE'S EFFECTS ON THE COUPLE

Heterosexual couples have a variety of traditional role models, including families, friends, fictional couples, and famous couples in history. The incongruity between these role models and role models that exist for same-sex couples is vast (Bepko & Johnson, 2000; Bernstein, 2000; Degges-White et al., 2000). Consequently, applying models of couple development to gay and lesbian couples is likely to be a bad fit.

Stage Model of Relationship Development for Same-Sex Couples

Degges-White and colleagues (2000, p. 318) describe Cass's (1979) six-stage model as one in which "individuals progress through each stage or remain at a particular stage which prevents forward movement in the homosexual identity formation process." The model identifies cognitive, behavioral, and affective components of lesbian/gay identity issues:

Stage 1: Identity confusion. Feelings of internal stress and alienation are characteristic of this stage. One realizes that feelings or behaviors could be associated as homosexual.

Stage 2: Identity comparison. There is a tentative commitment to a gay or lesbian self. Issues of alienation are addressed.

Stage 3: Identity tolerance. There is a development of a support system with other gay or lesbian individuals.

Stage 4: Identity acceptance. There is selective identity disclosure as the gay or lesbian lifestyle is viewed more positively.

Stage 5: Identity pride. There is an immersion into the gay and lesbian culture and more acceptance of one's sexual identity.

Stage 6: Identity synthesis. The view of gay or lesbian becomes but one part of a person's self. Lifestyle with family and friends become more important.

Coleman (1982) describes a similar stage model that includes precoming out, coming out, exploration, relationships, and integration. Coleman suggests that it will take at least 10 to 14 years to progress through the stages.

SOURCES OF CONFLICT IN THE GAY OR LESBIAN LIFESTYLE

As with other couples, relationship stressors for same-sex couples can come from both external and internal sources.

External Factors

Legal System
An important issue facing same-sex couples is the absence of legal privileges granted to heterosexuals. Marriage has not been recognized until recently for gay men and lesbians in the United States. Massachusetts became the first state to legalize marriage between same-sex partners in 2004. The Massachusetts Supreme Judicial court found that denying same-sex couples the right to marry violated the state's constitution. Since this ruling, "more than 35 states have introduced legislation to preserve the definition of marriage as a union between a man and a woman" (Peterson, 2004, p. 1). Thirty-nine states prohibit gay and lesbian couples from marriage based on the Defense of Marriage Act passed by the U.S. Congress in 1996. Vermont created civil unions in 2000 in order to provide same-sex couples with the same state rights to benefits. A civil union addresses the business aspects of relationship but stops short of defining partners as loving and committed couples (Long et al., 2006; Peterson, 2004).

These legal decisions have implications for automatic inheritance under probate, paid bereavement for family illness or death, the ability to file joint tax returns, reduced family insurance rates, immediate access to each other in an emergency, decision making for an incompetent partner, the right to claim the partner's body after death, or shared parental rights. Parental issues can be extremely problematic. The possibility for adoption for same-sex couples is rare and in some states is illegal. A major deterrent for same-sex couples to present themselves together is the problems they face in custody battles. If a gay or lesbian parent had children in a previous heterosexual marriage, his or her ability to gain custody may be in jeopardy if judged "unfit" because of sexual orientation.

Family of Origin

Frequently, there is a lack of emotional and economic support from families when gays and lesbians "come out" or make their sexual orientation known to their families. The emotional stress is often quite painful for one who is already feeling different and isolated from society (Long et al., 2006). LaSala (2000) supports the notion that gays and lesbians should come out to their families. Bepko and Johnson (2000) assert that couple relationships suffer if there is a hidden or secretive part of each partner's life that is unknown to their families. They also caution that the family's response is likely to be a long process, much like their own coming out and identity acceptance.

Often, family members who are opposed to the lifestyle cut off or deny that their relative is gay or lesbian. There can be legal consequences for couples when family members omit them from their wills so that "someone outside the family will not inherit family money."

Social Pressure

Same-sex couples have many social pressures that heterosexual couples do not experience (Ussher, 1991). Prejudice is apparent in most social settings, including schools, courts, businesses, housing, medical settings, and churches and synagogues.

Gender socialization issues also affect same-sex couples. Our culture has promoted the notion that males are predators in their pursuit of women. Women, on the other hand, are thought to be more passive and dependent on men for survival. Society views gay couples as consisting of two predators and views lesbian couples as consisting of two passive, dependent individuals.

Career

The choice of a suitable career has important considerations for gay and lesbian couples. A lesbian may realize at an early age that she will not ever depend on a man's salary (Pope & Barret, 2002) and may therefore choose a traditionally male-dominated profession in order to maximize her earning potential. Because women are still not widely accepted in male-dominated fields, lesbians who choose these occupations may be discriminated against. Similarly, gay men may choose careers that are not traditionally male in order to escape discrimination. Many gay men express the belief that heterosexual women are more supportive of their lifestyles than are heterosexual males.

Both gay men and lesbians must decide whether to work in a setting where sexual orientation must be hidden or to self-disclose and risk discrimination. For example, many gay men and lesbians remain "closeted" in such fields as teaching, child care, and child psychology because of the widespread belief that they recruit children to the same-sex lifestyle or that they are more prone to molest children (Browning, Reynolds, & Dworkin, 1991).

Same-sex couples face the same dual-career issues that heterosexual couples do, but because their relationship is not validated by society, they do not receive the support or assistance they require. Many same-sex couples choose to live in large metropolitan areas because of a wider variety of career opportunities and the ability to contact other same-sex couples for support.

Race, Ethnicity, and Socioeconomic Factors

For men and women in some cultures and social strata, gay and lesbian lifestyles violate the culture's role expectations (Drescher, 1998; Fukuyama & Ferguson, 2000). For example, a lesbian raised in an upper-income family may choose a predominantly male-dominated career in order to maximize her earning potential. Her family may consider her chosen career inappropriate, and she may feel denigrated by family members.

Same-sex, biracial couples who live within a gay or lesbian community report widespread racism (Greene & Boyd-Franklin, 1996). Because coming out to families within some racial or ethnic communities often means rejection and loss of support, survival in a racist culture becomes more difficult. Larger urban areas may be more suitable for same-sex couples because of the availability of a wider variety of racial and ethnic gay and lesbian organizations (Browning et al., 1991).

Internal Factors

Identity Development

By coming out, one is adopting a nontraditional identity that involves restructuring one's self-concept, reorganizing one's personal sense of history, and altering one's relations with others and with society (Bernstein, 2000). Three phases of self-definition have been identified for lesbians that may apply to gay men in reverse order: (1) critical evaluation of dominant social norms, (2) encounters with stigma and internalized homophobia, and (3) sexual experiences.

Because gay and lesbian couples see themselves as violating social norms, they may come to view themselves in a negative light. Internalized homophobia is the conscious or nonconscious self-hatred that results from growing up with this conflict. The devaluing of the gay or lesbian self may also be influenced by the attitudes of family members and early caregivers.

It is certain that antihomosexual expressions by society adversely affect the self-perceptions of gay and lesbian people (Bepko & Johnson, 2000). Among the consequences of unconscious homophobia include a feeling that one is not entitled to give and receive love. Internalized homophobia is organized around feelings of shame, guilt, anger, and anxiety (Friedman, 1991). These feelings may be manifested in the couple's sexual experiences as lack of commitment to one partner, lack of trust, fear of intimacy, and problems of sexual expression.

Identity Management

Identity management is an ongoing, ever-changing process through which one defines and redefines what it means to be gay or lesbian (Cass, 1979). It has been suggested that increased contact with the gay and lesbian community, as well as a broadening definition of the meaning of *gay* and *lesbian,* creates opportunity for a positive identity even within a homophobic culture (Browning et al., 1991).

Coming out to friends and family is an important step toward claiming an integrated identity and is important for self-acceptance and self-esteem (Degges-White et al., 2000). Gay men and lesbians may come out with family and friends in order to decrease feelings of isolation and to maintain a sense of personal integrity (LaSala, 2000). Keeping secrets can be detrimental to a person's self-image and can create feelings of shame and worthlessness. Families often do not respond favorably to admissions of being gay or lesbian. Many parents may believe their own identity is threatened if they accept that they have a gay or lesbian child. Parents may believe that they contributed to the homosexuality and berate themselves as having failed. Nongay friends may have less difficulty accepting a friend's disclosure than family members do because they have less at stake in the person's identity and less involvement in his or her future life.

Age-Related Factors

The notion that same-sex couples can be happy and grow old together is a new concept in our society (Lee, 1991). One widely recognized difficulty for an aging same-sex couple is the lack of social and legal support. The later life stage of development is typically described as one of trust and security. However, gay and lesbian couples must continue to advocate and challenge issues ranging from legal constraints to health and medical concerns. Older same-sex couples fear they will not receive adequate care in institutions and senior-services centers because of discrimination (Browning et al., 1991). Older gay men and lesbians may have come out during an era when they were viewed as sick or sinful. Often, they have abandoned their religious values because of discrimination and may be fearful of death and the afterlife. Many gay men and lesbians do not feel welcome today in mainstream churches.

Fusion or Distance Under Stress

Krestan and Bepko (1980) found that a major gender issue for lesbians that is different from gay men is their style of relating, which they call "lesbian fusion." This concept refers to women's socialization process that makes them more homebound, erodes boundaries between them, and fuses them in a dysfunctional way under stress. It has also been described as a "two against the world" posture. Men, on the other hand, tend to distance themselves when under stress, staying away from home, involving themselves in other activities, and experimenting with extra-relationship sexual activity (Carl, 1990).

This difference is not surprising given that traditionally women have been the ones to hold the family together and keep the home intact. In addition, women have been the main source of emotional support for the family. Men still work outside the home and avail themselves of a larger world experience more frequently than women do (Carl, 1990). Lesbians report that they must work outside the home because it takes two women's salaries to support the household.

Coparenting Issues

Many gay and lesbian couples desire to have and raise children. They are primarily forming new families through previous heterosexual relationships, adoption, artificial insemination, foster care, and surrogacy. Options vary from state to state (Long et al., 2006). Twenty-one states offer second-parent adoption and recognize parenting qualities of gay and lesbian couples. Two states, however, Florida and New Hampshire, have legislation that prevents gays and lesbians from adopting children (Perrin, 2002).

If same-sex couples choose to have children, they often do not have adequate support services and resources. There are many choices about how to become parents. Some of the options raise legal concerns. Disclosure related to the nature of conception is an important issue. Also, legal documents about coparenting structure in the event of a breakup are necessary. This is of particular concern in a lesbian relationship where one parent has conceived the child and carried the child throughout pregnancy. A counselor and an attorney help couples sift through these complicated decisions.

THERAPY ISSUES FOR SAME-SEX COUPLES

The most common therapy issues for same-sex couples are feelings of anxiety and stress. They also report significant levels of anger, depression, and a sense of alienation from society and family. This sense of aloneness is evident by the lack of support from religious groups and heterosexual friends. A constant theme for many gay men and lesbians is that of grief and loss. Suicidal ideation is cited frequently, especially among adolescents. Family problems, however, are the most traumatic. Many same-sex couples do not seek therapy because of the fear and implications of disclosure of their sexual identity (Savin-Williams, 1994).

There are differences in the presenting issues reported by gay men and lesbians when they seek therapy. Roth (1985) identified the following five issues most often presented by lesbians at the beginning of therapy:

1. Problems of distance and boundary maintenance
2. Problems of sexual expression
3. Problems related to unequal access to resources
4. Problems about ending the relationship, even when one or both have decided to do so
5. Problems arising from stage differences in coming out and in the development and management of each partner's lesbian identity

Couples Issues

George and Behrendt (1987) offer four possibilities for *relationship conflict* in addition to the individual challenges faced by gay men and lesbians:

- Stereotypic male roles
- Stereotypic sexual roles
- Homophobia
- Sexual dysfunctions

Table 15.1   Types of Problems for Which Professional Help Would Be Sought by Gay and Lesbian Couples, in Rank Order

Problem	Number	Percentage
Communication	30	26
Sexual	22	19
Unspecified	17	15
Impending separation	11	10
Alcohol or drug	7	6
Uncertain	6	5
Problems with children	5	4
Nonmonogamy	5	4
Financial	4	4
Spiritual	3	3
Pressure	2	2
AIDS	1	1
Boredom	1	1

Source: From "Lesbian and Gay Couples: Where They Turn When Help Is Needed," by M. Modcrin and N. Wyers, *Journal of Gay and Lesbian Psychotherapy*, 1, p. 99. Copyright 1990 by Haworth Press, Inc. Reprinted by permission.

The array of problems identified is substantial. Overall, communication, sexual problems, and problems associated with possible separation were most often identified as the reasons same-sex couples seek help (Modcrin & Wyers, 1990). Table 15.1 lists a number of presenting problems, in rank order.

Specific presenting issues addressed in therapy with these couples focus on relationship interactions and issues surrounding coming out, the lack of appropriate couple rituals, the lack of avenues for meeting partners in nonbar and nonalcoholic atmospheres, legal issues, relationships with children, stepfamily issues, alcohol and substance abuse, AIDS, domestic violence, sexual problems, sexual abuse, and spirituality.

Relationship Interactions

Many of the difficulties experienced in same-sex relationships are centered on role definitions for each partner. Because of the lack of understanding of roles and the associated stress, there is often an imbalance between intimacy and autonomy that can result in either emotional distance or enmeshment (Browning et al., 1991). Sometimes couples find themselves merged when they perceive a threat to their relationship or to one member of the couple; societal homophobia forces them to define and affirm relational boundaries (Browning et al., 1991). For example, during a family anniversary, the parents of a gay male might ask their son to come home to celebrate the event. They may ignore his partner and refuse to invite him, thereby arousing anger in the son, who must choose between his family and his significant other.

Coming out can create the greatest amount of stress on couples, depending on how each partner has addressed the issue with friends, family, and coworkers. For example, Jane may be "out" to her family and friends but at work. Susan, her partner, is "out" to her friends and her coworkers but cannot find the courage to tell her parents. Jane cannot take Susan with her to work-related social functions, and so she leaves Susan alone quite often. Susan, on the other hand, does not take Jane with her when she goes home for all major holidays, leaving Jane to celebrate without her significant other.

Couple Rituals

Rituals are important markers of life experiences and for resolving major life events (Imber-Black, 1989). Unfortunately, there are no legal rituals equivalent to marriage for same-sex couples. Weddings can be arranged, but they take place without legal sanctions. Also, depending on "who is out to whom," many family celebrations may be stressful for same-sex couples and may exclude some family members. Rituals provide a sense of social support so that if there is a negative response from others, it treats the relationship as nonexistent (Ossana, 2000). Counselors help couples memorialize their relationship and personalize it to reflect their relationship. Other rituals can be designed to celebrate children, career success, anniversaries, or special holidays much like those of heterosexual couples (Long et al., 2006).

Legal Issues

In addition to the issue of marriage, the legal rights of survivorship, and decisions on illness and death, an important legal issue is the effect of gay and lesbian identity on legal rights over children. Some people marry and have children long before they accept their homosexuality. Decisions about how open one can be is also influenced by fear of losing children in court decisions. Attempting to retain custody, fighting for joint custody, and fighting for alimony are legal issues that gay and lesbian parents must face. An increasing number of gay fathers are seeking, at a minimum, joint custody. These options will continue to bring gay and lesbian issues to the forefront in the legal system, but in doing so they will engender feelings of anger, depression, and resentment for those who find that legal decisions seemingly are made on the basis of sexual orientation.

Child Custody

When children are already present in a gay or lesbian relationship, the role of the nonbiological parent must be considered as well as the role of the biological parent who may have an influence the child's development. Most children in same-sex households were conceived in the context of a heterosexual relationship. Today, many lesbian women are choosing to have children either within a relationship or as a single parent (Clunis & Green, 1988). Studies have not found any deleterious effects on children raised by lesbian mothers (Falk, 1989). Raising children in same-sex families requires that parents clearly define their parenting roles and identify their support systems outside their families. Lack of role models is frequently cited as problematic for these families (Browning et al., 1991).

Alcohol and Substance Abuse

Research indicates that the rates of alcohol abuse are higher for lesbians than for heterosexual women and that lesbians are more apt to be children of alcoholic parents (Barret & Logan, 2002; Glaus, 1989). Internalized homophobia is thought to influence the use of drugs and alcohol, which may be an attempt to numb oneself to emotions and to avoid accepting being gay or lesbian (Browning et al., 1991). Thus, chemically dependent gay men and lesbians may be reacting with denial to a hostile environment (Glaus, 1989). Twelve-step programs such as Alcoholics Anonymous (AA) and similar support groups can be helpful, but, again, the issue of coming out will influence the decision to participate in the groups. Fortunately, AA has many established gay and lesbian support groups.

AIDS

Although AIDS is prevalent in many communities, it has popularly been associated with gay men. If a gay man or lesbian tests HIV-positive, they are not only devastated by knowledge of the disease but also feel the need for renewed secrecy in the workplace or with extended family members. An initial response of depression, fear, and anger permeate the relationship. Fear that the other partner will contract the disease is also a factor. Although gay men may be limiting the number of partners with whom they have sex for fear of contracting the AIDS virus, previous relationships may resurface as topics of conversation between the members of the couple. It is noteworthy that lesbians are currently one of the lowest-risk groups.

Domestic Violence

Same-sex couples may not receive the same attention from support groups when domestic violence is reported, but it is clear that violence transcends all socioeconomic classes, all ages, all ethnic groups, and all sexual orientations (Crooks & Baur, 2002). There is a myth that lesbians, because of their socialization as women, do not perpetrate or encounter domestic violence. Gay men and lesbians have attitudes similar to those of their heterosexual counterparts. These include the belief that people exist for the abuser's well-being, feelings of possessiveness, and the need to dominate. Abuse of alcohol and drugs can also be a factor (Crooks & Baur, 2002). Unfortunately, in the legal system, abuse of same-sex partners is not always considered to be domestic violence.

Sexual Abuse

A survey by Loulan (1987) found that 38% of lesbians had experienced sexual abuse from a family member or stranger before the age of 18 (Browning et al., 1991). Statistics for gay males remain unclear. The high proportion of women who have experienced abuse suggests that one or both partners of a couple may be survivors of abuse. They may be at different stages of awareness or recovery and may have different needs (Hall, 2001).

Flashbacks can produce anger, frustration, or fear of sexual experiences. Some people believe that their own gay or lesbian identity is a result of the abuse. The abuse, if not addressed as a couple, can create relationship and individual stress similar to the stress that affects heterosexual couples in similar circumstances. However, support groups for gay men and lesbians may be limited in number, and support groups for partners of survivors are almost nonexistent.

Sexual Problems

Differences in and absence of sexual desire are the most frequently reported problems of lesbians (Nichols, 2000; Ossana, 2000). Lack of desire is related to lack of time, lack of energy, and lack of understanding of one's partner. Absence of desire may be related to mixed messages that women receive in our culture about female sexuality, added to the negative messages about lesbian sexuality. As the negative messages are internalized, they can be evidenced by shame, anxiety, guilt, or avoidance of sex. Also the process of recovery influences lesbian sexuality, including recovery from drug or alcohol abuse, illness, eating disorders, or from sexual abuse (Browning et al., 1991).

Monogamy has been a controversial issue in gay couples (Berger, 1990). Until recently, many gay men began relationships with the expectation of sexual exclusivity but later moved to a more open relationship sexually. With the fear of AIDS in the forefront, there has been a move to monogamous relationships. In the early stage of the relationship, gay men report a high frequency of sexual activity with high sexual exclusivity. Any interruption in sexual rapport, such as a late night at work or phone call from a former lover, can be experienced as a threat to the relationship and can create jealousy, anxiety, and hurt. As more gay couples continue to be sexually exclusive, there will be more emphasis on working at loving relationships.

Spirituality

Spirituality concerns one's direct relationship with some higher power; religion, on the other hand, refers to institutions and organizations. There has been much interest in spirituality in the gay and lesbian community. Because of the discrimination still prevalent in many organized religions, gay men and lesbians have left the church in vast numbers and have attempted to express their spirituality through alternative communities and support groups. Extended family members can be critical of their relative who has left the church and no longer embraces family tradition at family events. In addition, as same-sex couples age or become physically ill, there are questions about death and dying that they wish to discuss. If communication is open, partners can explore their spirituality with each other and identify a deeper, more personal meaning of life.

Working with Same-Sex Couples

As gay and lesbian couples are more visible, they are more willing to seek therapy to address stress in their relationship and to strengthen it (Long et al., 2006). Starting with the initial session, clinicians must form conceptual models that focus on the uniqueness of the same-sex couple. Counselors must first examine their own attitudes and bias about gay and lesbian relationships. Same-sex couples deserve the right to expect that their relationship will be validated when they seek therapy (Bepko & Johnson, 2000). They have a right to be treated with respect and to have a well-trained counselor who understands the gay and lesbian culture. Bernstein (2000) suggests that the best way for counselors to become knowledgeable is to develop friends and professional colleagues from the gay and lesbian community. Reading and viewing films are also sources of information.

Many same-sex couples come to therapy with issues of loss and grief. Therapists should be aware of stages-of-grief models and be willing to help the couple express the grief. If the therapist is uncomfortable with same-sex couples, it is the responsibility of the therapist to refer the couple to someone who is accepting and understanding. The couple has spent years learning to read prejudice and will not be fooled by a therapist who is uneasy about the sexual orientations of clients.

Key areas for clinical evaluation of the couple include the following:

1. Determine the extent of self-disclosure to parents and to others.
2. Focus on decisions about secrecy and disclosure to parents.
3. Provide support to each partner when one partner desires to come out to parents or others.
4. Help the couple grieve over the loss of "heterosexual privilege" in the family of origin.
5. Encourage the couple to challenge the ways that they tolerate or perpetuate parental homophobia.
6. Help the couple affirm their couple boundaries with parents, coworkers, and friends.
7. Recognize the need for couples to build and validate their friendship networks.
8. Affirm the couple's past history and hopes for the future.
9. Help the couple address issues related to children.
10. Help the couple learn to affirm themselves and each other and form a bond of friendship.

With these principles in mind, it is possible to assist same-sex couples as they adjust to a world where they have been ridiculed and oppressed and create a community where they can live in peace.

THE INTEGRATIVE MODEL AND SAME-SEX COUPLES

Case Example: Barbara and Melissa

Barbara and Melissa have been in a committed relationship for 3 years. They have been having conflict because Melissa believes that Barbara does not really love her. This issue has come to a head recently because Barbara is unwilling to take Melissa back to her hometown to attend Barbara's parents' 25th wedding anniversary. Melissa's parents have known she is a lesbian for many years, and they accept their daughter and her partner, Barbara. The couple frequently visits Melissa's parents and spends some holidays there.

Barbara has not come out to her family although she thinks her sister may know. Melissa says that if Barbara does not tell her parents soon, she will leave the relationship because she is unwilling to spend one more Christmas or Thanksgiving alone. Barbara is angry and accuses Melissa of pressuring her and not understanding her situation. Barbara is from a small town in Georgia, and her father is mayor of the town. Barbara believes that such a disclosure would devastate her parents and perhaps jeopardize her father's career. On the other hand, she loves Melissa and does not want to lose her.

Application of the Integrative Model: Same-Sex Couple

Stage 1: Assessing and Obtaining an Interactional View of the Problem
Barbara and Melissa each have different perspectives of the problem. Melissa feels unloved and interprets Barbara's lack of self-disclosure as a lack of commitment. Barbara feels pressured and does not feel supported by her partner. Because Barbara perceives her family as rejecting and rigid, she believes that they will be critical and rejecting if they learn that she is a lesbian. Melissa has not had the same experience with her parents and does not believe Barbara's parents will reject her. A shared view of the problem on which they can both agree is that they have difficulty with their relationship boundaries and need to find a way to create their own holidays, even if they are independent from their families.

Stage 2: Goal Setting
Together Barbara and Melissa agree they will (1) plan to create their own traditions for the upcoming holidays of Thanksgiving and Christmas that will promote intimacy, (2) spend time together doing couple activities so that they feel connected and appreciated, and (3) talk about how they can handle Barbara's parents in a way that they can both feel support. The couple agrees to take control of their relationship and "act like a couple" and conquer fears of being rejected by each other and by parents.

Stage 3: Adopting New Perceptions and Behaviors
The couple explores how they have handled celebrations in the past and point out that they both are very creative in their jobs. They determine to use that creativity to adopt new possibilities for shared time together. They also agree to begin a weekly meeting at their favorite restaurant to discuss some couple issues but will spend only 1 hour of the time together discussing problems. Finally, they decide to enact a weekly date to do some of the fun things they used to do when they were first dating.

Stage 4: Maintaining New Perceptions and Behaviors
The couple agrees that they will need to have a plan when Barbara's mother tries to use guilt to induce her to come home every holiday. They agree that Barbara will not make any concrete plans with her family until she has discussed them with Melissa. They also agree that it will be easy to get off track with their couple play time, so they will spend time at the beginning of each week with their calendars to discuss a time for togetherness.

Stage 5: Validating New Perceptions and Behaviors
Each compliments the other on the willingness to work on these issues and the commitment to the relationship. As a result, Melissa feels more loved, and Barbara feels

more supported. They also have more confidence in their problem-solving skills and are anxious to try the same approach on another issue they have been fearful of addressing—the possibility of buying a home together.

At the completion of therapy, the couple that had arrived with a problem leaves with a solution appropriate to the couple's unique situation.

Intervention Strategies Useful for Same-Sex Couple Therapy

Although many of the strategies may be appropriate for many populations and situations, we discuss a ritual of a committed relationship, a genogram of the family of creation, a role-reversal strategy, and a narrative storytelling.

Rituals of Commitment

Because same-sex relationships are not legally sanctioned, a ceremony of commitment is one way to memorialize their joining. The ceremony can be planned by the couple and may include spoken vows, traditional toasts, and good wishes, surrounded by friends and family (if appropriate). The affair can be quite lavish or simple depending on the couple's wishes.

Genogram of Family of Creation

This genogram is very similar to the traditional genogram but differs in the definitions of *family* and the chronology of significant love relationships, rather than legal or biological unions. To accomplish this task, it is necessary to create appropriate symbols for the genogram and determine what information is useful to obtain for examining family messages, patterns, and behaviors.

Role Reversals

The purpose of this intervention is to bring about change by helping each partner be more empathic of the other's position in the relationship. The technique also reduces blame because it fosters support for both perspectives. Using our previous case example, the therapist asks each member of the couple to "reverse roles" and then asks questions of each person, who responds as the partner might. For example, Melissa might play the role of Barbara and discuss how difficult it is to think of the possibility of losing her parents. In so doing, Melissa may be able to empathize with Barbara's dilemma. Barbara might then play the role of Melissa, experiencing some of Melissa's fear that the relationship is just "pretend" because Barbara does not want to make it public. Later, when both assume their own roles, Barbara may be able to understand how desperate Melissa must feel when they cannot share and create holiday memories together.

Narrative Storytelling

Narrative interventions are designed to help their lives and create a history, present, and future that focuses on their sexual identity, coming-out process, and family and social relationships. The narratives provide alternatives to the internalized negativity and shame-based messages that gays and lesbians may have received. Couples can retell the story of their family in a healthy and integrated manner and include their sexual orientation and stages of relationships as they experienced them rather than adapting them to heterosexual models. They can also incorporate the "new self" into the larger community (Addelston, 2000).

SCENARIOS FOR DISCUSSION AND ROLE PLAYING

Following are some sample scenarios that can be used to stimulate discussion and as topics for role playing.

"Guess Who's Coming to Dinner?"

Angelina and her partner, Josie, are going to her parents' home for dinner with the intent to tell them that they are a couple and want to purchase a home together. Angelina is anxious, but Josie insists they must confront the situation together because they are a couple. As they are about to leave to go to dinner, an argument ensues and Angelina goes alone.

"The Great Wall"

Jim has been attending graduate classes at a local university and has become quite friendly with several of the students. One night, a student saw Jim and his partner, Alan, at a local theater sitting close together and obviously involved in intimate conversation. Two weeks later, Jim discovered that several students had been at a party on the weekend to which Jim was not invited. The students also did not ask him to work with them on a class project due the following week. Jim arrives home and tells Alan he has "blown it" and that they cannot be seen in public together.

"The Wicked Stepmother"

Nathetta and Tanella have been together for 3 years. Nathetta's daughter, Leticia, resides with them and has recently found out that her mother is a lesbian. Leticia is embarrassed and blames her mother's sexual identity on Tanella. Leticia has become hostile toward Tanella and refuses to eat meals or be seen in public with the two of them.

"Who's That Knocking at the Door—Oh! It Must Be Our Imagination"

Bob recently came out to his family and coworkers because he didn't want to live with secrecy anymore. Although most of his friends said they were comfortable with the admission, they have not contacted Bob since that time. Bob's attempts to get the old group together have been unsuccessful. Bob tries to talk to his partner, Sam, about his feeling of isolation, but Sam tells him that all they need is each other.

"Peggy and Sue Get Married"

Peggy and Sue have been in a relationship for 2 years and have decided to have a commitment ceremony in the fall. They are concerned about whom to invite because one family is aware of their lesbian identities, and one is not. Also, some of their friends and coworkers are aware, and others are not. As the date draws near, both Peggy and Sue become anxious and consider canceling the idea. Peggy is resentful, however, and blames Sue for not wanting to tell the world about her love for Peggy.

"A Day in Court"

Frank and Carlos are in court attempting to get visitation rights to see Frank's son on a weekly basis. Frank's former wife is opposed to the idea because she is concerned that her son might become gay by associating with his father. Carlos has offered to leave the home that he and Frank share in hopes that it will give Frank the opportunity to retain visits with his son. Frank is angry and refuses to consider the possibility.

"Is This All There Is?"

Ana and Jean have been experiencing sexual difficulty since Jean began attending therapy to work on her issues of childhood sexual abuse. Jean does not appear to have much desire for a physical relationship with Ana. Ana interprets Jean's behavior as rejection of her and begins to make comments about Jean having someone else. Jean accuses her of being jealous and claims she does not trust her.

"'I Do,' 'We Do,' 'Do We?'"

Sims wants to be in an exclusive relationship with Mike, but Mike has met someone at work to whom he is attracted. Sims is fearful of disease and also fearful that Mike will leave him altogether. Mike feels restricted and would like to continue the relationship with Sims but does not want to limit his opportunities. After many arguments, Sims threatens Mike that he will not have any involvement with him if he is not faithful. Mike refuses to be controlled but does not want to lose the relationship with Sims.

CONCLUSION

Same-sex couples experience some problems similar to those of heterosexual couples and many unique problems as they attempt to live harmoniously in a society that continues to reject and discriminate against them. Same-sex couples follow predictable stages and experience sources of conflict over communication, finances, recreational time, and problem solving. Compared to heterosexual couples, same-sex couples may have other, more complicated issues regarding role identification, children, family of origin, legal concerns, and self-identity.

Same-sex couples also come to therapy to address coming out, lack of appropriate rituals, legal dilemmas, blending family concerns, substance abuse, sexual abuse, domestic violence, and spiritual concerns. Often these issues are misunderstood in society, so same-sex couples feel alienated and unsupported by social institutions. The therapist's attitudes of acceptance and knowledge about the gay and lesbian lifestyle are important if the therapist wishes to work with these couples.

REFERENCES

ACTION WISCONSIN. (2005). Retrieved June 21, 2005, from http://www.actionwisconsin.org/civilmarriage/whymarriage.html

ADAMS, J. S. (1965). Inequity in social exchange. In L. Berkowitz (Ed.), *Advances in experimental social psychology* (Vol. 2) (pp. 267–299). New York: Academic Press.

ADDLESTON, J. (2000). *The use of narrative therapy with families of gay, lesbian, bisexual and transgendered people.* Unpublished manuscript.

AINSCOUGH, C., & TOON, K. (2000). *Surviving childhood sexual abuse.* Tucson, AZ: Fisher Books.

ALBEE, E. (1991). *Who's Afraid of Virginia Woolf?* In E. Albee, *Edward Albee: The plays.* New York: Macmillan. (Originally published in 1962)

ALTERNATIVES TO MARRIAGE PROJECT. (2005). Retrieved September 12, 2005 from http://www.unmarried.org

ALTHOF, S. E. (2000). Erectile dysfunctions: Psychotherapy with men and couples. In S. R. Leiblum & R. C. Rosen (Eds.), *Principles and practice of sex therapy* (3rd ed.) (pp. 242–304). New York: Guilford Press.

AMBROZIAK, J., & LEVY, J. A. (1999). Epidemiology, natural history, and pathogenesis of HIV infection. In K. K. Holmes, P. F. Sparling, P. Mardh, S. M. Lemon, W. E. Stamm, P. Piot, & J. N. Wasserheit (Eds.), *Sexually transmitted diseases* (3rd ed.) (pp. 251–258). New York: McGraw-Hill.

AMERICAN ASSOCIATION FOR MARRIAGE AND FAMILY THERAPY. (2001). *AAMFT code of ethical principles for marriage and family therapists.* Washington, DC: Author.

AMERICAN PSYCHIATRIC ASSOCIATION. (2000). *Diagnostic and Statistical Manual of Mental Disorders* (4th ed.), text revision. Washington, DC: American Psychiatric Association.

ANDERSEN, M. L. (2003). *Thinking about women: Sociological perspectives on sex and gender* (6th ed.). Boston: Allyn & Bacon.

ANDERSON, C. M., & MALLOY, E. S. (1976). Family photographs. *Family Process, 6,* 313–321.

ANDERSON, W. T. (1990). *Reality isn't what it used to be.* San Francisco: Harper.

APONTE, H. J., & DICESARE, E. (2000). Structural therapy. In F. Dattilio & L. Bevilacqua (Eds.), *Comparative treatments for relationship dysfunction* (pp. 45–57). New York: Springer.

ARGYLE, M., & FURNAM, A. (1983). Sources of satisfaction and conflict in long-term relationships. *Journal of Marriage and the Family, 9,* 481–492.

ARREDONDO, P., & ARCINIEGA, G. M. (2001). Strategies and techniques for counselor training based on the multicultural counseling competencies. *Journal of Multicultural Counseling and Development, 29,* 263–273.

ATWATER, L. (1979). Getting involved: Women's transition to first extramarital sex. *Alternative Lifestyles, 1,* 33–68.

ATWOOD, J., & DERSHOWITZ, S. (1992). Constructing a sex and marital therapy frame: Ways to help couples deconstruct sexual problems. *Journal of Sex and Marital Therapy, 18,* 196–218.

ATWOOD, J., & WEINSTEIN, E. (1989). The couple relationship as the focus of sex therapy. *Journal of Family Therapy,* *10,* 161–168.

AYLMER, R. C. (1986). Bowen family systems marital therapy. In N. S. Jacobson & A. S. Gurman (Eds.), *Clinical handbook of marital therapy* (pp. 107–148). New York: Guilford Press.

AZRIN, N. H., NASTER, B. J., & JONES, R. (1973). Reciprocity counseling: A rapid learning based procedure for marital counseling. *Behavior Research and Therapy, 11,* 365–382.

BAGAROZZI, D. A., & ANDERSON, S. A. (1989). *Personal, marital and family myths: Theoretical formulations and clinical strategies.* New York: Norton.

BALL, F. L. J., COWAN, P., & COWAN, C. P. (1995). Who's got the power? Gender differences in partner's perception of influence during marital problem-solving discussions. *Family Process, 34,* 303–321.

BANDURA, A. (1969). *Principles of behavior modification.* New York: Holt, Rinehart & Winston.

BAPTISTE, D. (1987). Psychotherapy with gay/lesbian couples and their children in "stepfamilies": A challenge for marriage and family therapists. *Journal of Homosexuality, 14,* 223–238.

BARBACH, L. (2001). *For each other: Sharing sexual intimacy.* New York: Signet.

BARNETT, J. K., & YOUNGBERG, C. (2004). Forgiveness as a ritual in couples therapy. *Family Journal, 12*(1), 14–20.

BARRET, B., & LOGAN, C. (2002). *Counseling gay men and lesbians.* Pacific Grove, CA: Brooks/Cole.

BARUTH, L. G., & MANNING, M. L. (2003). *Multicultural counseling and psychotherapy: A lifespan perspective* (3rd ed.). Upper Saddle River, NJ: Merrill/Prentice Hall.

BATESON, G., JACKSON, D. D., HALEY, J., & WEAKLAND, J. H. (1956). Toward a theory of schizophrenia. *Behavioral Science, 1,* 251–264.

BAUCOM, D. H., & ADAMS, A. N. (1987). Assessing communication in marital interaction. In K. D. O'Leary (Ed.), *Assessment of marital discord: An integra-* *tion for research and clinical practice* (pp.139–181). Hillsdale, NJ: Erlbaum.

BAUCOM, D. H., & EPSTEIN, N. (1990). Attributions in marriage: Review and critique. *Psychological Bulletin, 107,* 3–33.

BAUGH, C. W., AVERY, A. W., & SHEETS-HAWORTH, K. L. (1982). Marital Problem-Solving Scale: A measure to assess relationship conflict negotiation ability. *Family Therapy, 9,* 43–51.

BAYER, R., & THOMPSON, K. (2000). Counselor response to clients' metaphors: An evaluation and refinement of Strong's model. *Counseling Psychology Quarterly, 13*(1), 37–49.

BEAVERS, W. R. (1985). *Successful marriage: A family systems approach to couples therapy.* New York: Norton.

BEAVERS, W. R., & HAMPSON, R. B. (1990). *Successful families assessment and intervention.* New York: Norton.

BECK, A. T. (1988). *Love is never enough.* New York: Harper & Row.

BECVAR, D. S., & BECVAR, R. J. (1988). *Family therapy: A systemic integration.* Boston: Allyn & Bacon.

BECVAR, D., & BECVAR, R. (2000). *Family therapy* (4th ed.). Needham Heights, MA: Allyn & Bacon.

BEPKO, C., & JOHNSON, T. (2000). Gay and lesbian couples in therapy: Perspective for the contemporary family therapist. *Journal of Marital and Family Therapy, 26*(4), 409–419.

BERGER, R. (1990). Men together: Understanding the gay couple. *Journal of Homosexuality, 19,* 31–47.

BERNAL, M., & CASTRO, F. (1994). Are clinical psychologists prepared for service and research with ethnic minorities? *American Psychologist, 49*(9), 794–805.

BERNE, E. (1961). *Transactional analysis in psychotherapy.* New York: Grove Press.

BERNE, E. (1964). *Games people play.* New York: Grove Press.

BERNE, E. (1970). *Sex in human loving.* New York: Simon & Schuster.

BERNSTEIN, A. (2000). Straight therapists working with lesbians and gays in family therapy. *Journal of Marital and Family Therapy, 26*(4), 443–454.

BETTELHEIM, B. (1977). *The uses of enchantment: The meaning and importance of fairy tales.* New York: Vintage Books.

BIRCHLER, G. R., WEISS, R. L., & VINCENT, J. P. (1975). A multimethod analysis of social reinforcement exchange between maritally distressed and nondistressed spouse and stranger dyads. *Journal of Personality and Social Psychology, 31,* 349–360.

BLANTON, B. (1996). *Radical honesty.* New York: Dell.

BLOW, A. J., & HARTNETT, K. (2005). Infidelity in committed relationships. *Journal of Marital and Family Therapy, 28,* 423–434.

BOBES, T., & BOBES, N. S. (2005). *The couple is telling you what you need to know: Couple-directed therapy in a multicultural context.* New York: Norton.

BOBES, T., & ROTHMAN, B. (2002). *Doing couple therapy.* New York: Norton.

BOEN, D. L. (1988). A practitioner looks at assessment in marital counseling. *Journal of Counseling and Development, 66,* 484–486.

BOHANNON, P. (1973). The six stages of divorce. In M. E. Lasswell & T. E. Lasswell (Eds.), *Love, marriage and family: A developmental approach* (pp. 475–489). Glenview, IL: Scott Foresman.

BORNSTEIN, P. H., & BORNSTEIN, M. T. (1986). *Marital therapy: A behavioral-communications approach.* New York: Pergamon Press.

BOSZORMENYI-NAGY, I, & ULRICH, D. N. (1981). Contextual family therapy. In A. S. Gurman & D. P. Kniskern (Eds.), *Handbook of family therapy* (pp. 159–225). New York: Brunner/Mazel.

BOURNE, E. J. (2000). *The anxiety and phobia workbook* (Rev. 3rd ed.). Oakland, CA: New Harbinger.

BOWEN, M. (1978). *Family therapy in clinical practice.* New York: Aronson.

BOWLBY, J. (1973). *Separation.* New York: Basic Books.

BOWLBY, J. (1988). *A secure base.* New York: Basic Books.

BRATTER, T. (1974). Dynamics of role reversal. In I. A. Greenberg (Ed.), *Psychodrama, theory and therapy* (pp. 101–109). New York: Behavioral Publications.

BRIGGS, K., & MYERS, I. (1977). *Myers-Briggs Type Indicator, form G.* Palo Alto, CA: Consulting Psychologists Press.

BRIGGS-MYERS, I., & MCCAULEY, M. (1985). *Manual: A guide to the development and use of the Myers-Briggs Type Indicator.* Palo Alto, CA: Consulting Psychologists Press.

BROWN, E. M. (1991). *Patterns of infidelity and their treatment.* New York: Brunner/Mazel.

BROWN, E. M. (2001). *Patterns of infidelity and their treatment* (2nd ed.). Philadelphia: Brunner/Routledge.

BROWN, J. H., & CHRISTENSEN, D. N. (1986). *Family therapy: Theory and practice.* Pacific Grove, CA: Brooks/Cole.

BROWN, J., & HANNA, S. M. (2004). *The practice of family therapy* (3rd ed.). Belmont, CA: Brooks/Cole.

BROWN, S. L. (2004). Family structure and child well-being: The significance of parental cohabitation. *Journal of Marriage and the Family, 66,* 351–367.

BROWNING, C., REYNOLDS, A., & DWORKIN, S. (1991). Affirmative psychotherapy for lesbian women. *Counseling Psychologist, 19,* 177–196.

BRUNNER, A. (1986). Self-understanding through movement-experiential dimensions of education. *Dissertation Abstracts International,* 46 (9A).

BUBENZER, D. L., & WEST, J. D. *Counselling couples.* London: Sage.

BUDMAN, S. H. (1992). *The first session in brief therapy.* New York: Guilford Press.

BUMPASS, L., & LU, H. (2000). Trends in cohabitation and implications for children's family contexts in the U.S. *Population Studies, 54,* 29–41.

BUUNK, B. (1980). Extramarital sex in the Netherlands: Motivation in social and marital context. *Alternative Lifestyles, 3,* 11–39.

BYRNE, D., & OSLAND, J. A., (2000). Sexual fantasy and erotica/pornography: Internal and external imagery. In

L. Szuchman & F. Muscarella (Eds.), *Psychological perspectives on human sexuality* (pp.283–308). New York: Wiley.

CADE, B., & O'HANLON, W. H. (1993). *A brief guide to brief therapy.* New York: Norton.

CAHN, D. (1992). *Conflict in intimate relationships.* New York: Guilford Press.

CAMPBELL, J., ELDER, J., GALLAGHER, D., SIMON, J., & TAYLOR, A. (1999). Crafting the "tap on the shoulder": A compliment template for solution-focused therapy. *American Journal of Family Therapy, 27,* 35–47.

CARL, D. (1990). *Therapy with same sex couples.* New York: Norton.

CARLSON, J., & ELLIS, C. M. (2004). Treatment agreement and relapse prevention strategies in couple and family therapy. *Family Journal, 12,* 352–358.

CARNS, A. W., & CARNS, M. R. (1994). Making behavioral contract successful. *School Counselor, 42*(2), 155–160.

CARRERE, S., & GOTTMAN, J. M. (1999). Predicting divorce among newlyweds from the first three minutes of a marital conflict discussion. *Family Process, 38,* 293–301.

CARTER, E., & MCGOLDRICK, M. (1980). *The family life cycle: A framework for family therapy.* New York: Gardner.

CASADO, M., YOUNG, M., & RASMUS, S. (2002). *Exercise in family therapy.* Upper Saddle River, NJ: Pearson Education.

CASS, V. C. (1979). Homosexuality identity formation: A theoretical model. *Journal of Homosexuality, 4,* 219–235.

CATH, S., & SHOPPER, M. (2001). *Step parenting.* Mahwah, NJ: Analytic Press.

CENTER FOR SUBSTANCE ABUSE TREATMENT. (2004). *Substance abuse treatment and family therapy.* Treatment Improvement Protocol (TIP) Series, No. 39 (DHHS Publication No. [SMA] 05-4006). Rockville, MD: Substance Abuse and Mental Health Services Administration.

CHRISTENSEN, A., & JACOBSON, N. (2000). *Reconcilable differences.* New York: Guilford Press.

CLAPP, G. (2000). *Divorce and new beginnings* (2nd ed.). New York: Wiley.

CLARK, L., RECHER, N., & FOOTE, R. A. (2004). Blending families: Newsletter addresses stepfamily issues. *Journal of Family and Consumer Sciences, 96*(2), 62.

CLAXTON-OLDFIELD, S. C. (1992). Perceptions of stepfathers: Disciplinary and affectionate behaviors. *Journal of Family Issues, 13,* 378–389.

CLUNIS, D. M., & GREEN, G. D. (1988). *Lesbian couples.* Seattle: Seal Press.

Coalition for Marriage and Family and Couples Education. (2000). *The marriage movement: A statement of principles.* Washington, DC: Author.

COAN, J., GOTTMAN, J. M., BABCOCK, J., & JACOBSON, N. S. (1997). Battering and the male rejection of influence from women. *Aggressive Behavior, 23,* 375–388.

COLAPINTO, J. (1991). Structural family therapy. In A. M. Horne & J. L. Passmore (Eds.), *Family counseling and therapy* (pp. 77–106). Itasca, IL: Peacock.

COLEMAN, E. (1982). Developmental stages of the coming out process. *Journal of Homosexuality, 7*(2/3), 31–43.

COLEMAN, E. (1988). *Chemical dependency and intimacy dysfunction.* New York: Haworth Press.

COLEMAN, M., GANONG, L., & GRINGICH, R. (1985). Stepfamily strengths: A review of popular literature. *Family Relations, 34,* 583–589.

COLEMAN, M., MARSHALL, S., & GANONG, L. (1986). Beyond Cinderella: Relevant reading for young adolescents about stepfamilies. *Adolescence, 11,* 553–560.

COMER, R. J. (1998). *Abnormal psychology* (3rd ed.). New York: Freeman.

CONNORS, G. J., DONOVAN, D. M., & DICLEMENTE, C. C. (2001). *Substance abuse treatment and the stages of change: Selecting and planning interventions.* New York: Guilford Press.

COOPER, A., DELMONICO, D. L., & BURG, R. (2000). Cybersex users, abusers and compulsives: New findings and implications. *Sexual Addiction & Compulsivity, 7*, 5–29.

COOPER-HILBERT, B. (1998). *Infertility and involuntary childlessness: Helping couples cope*. New York: Norton.

COREY, G. (2004). *Theory and practice of counseling and psychotherapy* (7th ed.). Pacific Grove, CA: Brooks/Cole.

COREY, G., COREY, M. S., & CALLANAN, P. (2003). *Issues and ethics in the helping professions* (6th ed.). Pacific Grove, CA: Brooks/Cole.

CORMIER, W. H., & CORMIER, L. S. (1991). *Interviewing strategies for helpers: Fundamental skills and cognitive behavior interventions* (3rd ed.). Pacific Grove, CA: Brooks/Cole.

CORSO, K. (1993). *Testing options for use in family therapy*. Unpublished manuscript.

COSER, L. A. (1956). *The functions of social conflict*. New York: Free Press.

COTTRIL, J. (2004, April 30). Is divorce the right choice for you? *Divorce Magazine, 6*.

CROMWELL, R. E., & PETERSON, G. W. (1983). Multisystem-multimethod family assessment in clinical contexts. *Family Process, 22* 147–164.

CROOKS, R., & BAUR, K. (2002). *Our sexuality* (8th ed.). Belmont, CA: Wadsworth.

CROSBY, J. F. (1991). Cybernetics of cybernetics in assessment of marital quality. *Contemporary Family Therapy, 13*, 3–15.

CROSBY, J. F., GAGE, B. A., & RAYMOND, M. C. (1983). The grief resolution process in divorce. *Journal of Divorce, 7*, 3–18.

CROWE, M., & RIDLEY, J. (1990). *Therapy with couples: A behavioural-systems approach to marital and sexual problems*. Oxford, UK: Blackwell Scientific.

CUNNINGHAM. P. B., & HENGGELER, S. (1999). Engaging multiproblem families in treatment: Lessons learned throughout the development of multisystemic therapy. *Family Process, 38*(3), 265–281.

CUPACH, W. R., & COMSTOCK, J. (1990). Satisfaction with sexual communication in marriage: Links to sexual satisfaction and dyadic adjustment. *Journal of Social and Personal Relationships, 7*, 179–186.

DARNLEY-SMITH, R., & PATEY, H. M. (2003). *Music therapy*. London: Sage.

DATTILIO, F. M., & PADESKY, C. A. (1990). *Cognitive therapy with couples*. Sarasota, FL: Professional Resources Exchange.

DEGGES-WHITE, S., RICE, B., & MYERS, J. (2000). Revisiting Cass' theory of sexual identity formation: A study of lesbian development. *Journal of Mental Health Counseling, 22*(4), 318–333.

DEJONG, P., & BERG, I. K. (1998). *Interviewing for solutions*. Pacific Grove, CA: Brooks/Cole.

DEJONG P., & BERG, I. K. (2002). *Interviewing for solutions* (2nd ed.). Pacific Grove: Brooks/Cole.

DEMARIA, R., HANNAH, M. T., & GORDON, L. (Eds.). (2003). *Building intimate relationships: Clinical applications of the PAIRS program*. New York: Brunner/Routledge.

DENTON, W. H. (1991). The role of affect in marital therapy. *Journal of Marital and Family Therapy, 17*, 257–261.

DEROGATIS, L. R., LOPEZ, M. C., & ZINZELETTA, E. M. (1988). Clinical applications of the DSFI in the assessment of sexual dysfunctions. In R. Brown & E. Roberts (Eds.), *Advances in the understanding and treatment of sexual disorders* (pp. 167–186). New York: PNA Publishing.

DEROGATIS, L. R., & MELLISARATOS, N. (1979). The DSFI: A multidimensional measure of sexual functioning. *Journal of Sex & Marital Therapy, 5*, 244–281.

DE SHAZER, S. (1984). The death of resistance. *Family Process, 23*, 79–93.

DE SHAZER, S. (1985). *Keys to solution in brief therapy*. New York: Guilford Press.

DE SHAZER, S. (1988). *Clues: Investigating solutions in brief therapy*. New York: Norton.

DE SHAZER, S. (1991). *Putting difference to work*. New York: Norton.

DE SHAZER, S., BERG, I., & NUNNALLY, E., et al. (1986). Brief therapy: Focused solution development. *Family Process, 25*, 207–221.

DEUTSCH, M. (1973). *The resolution of conflict: Constructive and destructive processes.* New Haven, CT: Yale University Press.

DIAMOND, R., KEZUR, D., MEYERS, M., SCHARF, C. N., & WEINSHEL, M. (1999). *Couple therapy for infertility.* New York: Guilford Press.

DICKS, H. V. (1967). *Marital tensions.* New York: Basic Books.

DIMIDJIAN, S., MARTELL, C.R., & CHRISTENSEN, A. (2002). In A. S. Gurman & N. S. Jacobson (Eds.), *Clinical handbook of couple therapy* (3rd ed.) (pp. 251–277). New York: Guilford Press.

DOVE, N., & WIEDERMAN, M. (2000). Cognitive distraction and women's sexual functioning. *Journal of Sex and Marital Therapy, 26,* 67–78.

DOWEIKO, H. E. (2006). *Concepts of chemical dependency.* Belmont, CA: Brooks/Cole.

DRESCHER, J. (1998). I'm your handyman: A history of reparative therapies. *Journal of Homosexuality, 36,* 19–42.

DRUMMOND, R. J. (2000). *Appraisal procedures for counselors and helping professionals* (4th ed.). Upper Saddle River, NJ: Merrill/Prentice Hall.

DUHL, B., & DUHL, F. (1981). Integrative family therapy. In A. Gurman and D. Kniskern (Eds.), *Handbook of family therapy.* New York: Brunner/Mazel.

DYM, B. (1995). *Readiness and change in couple therapy.* New York: Basic Books.

DYM, B., & GLENN, M. (1993). *Exploring and understanding the cycles of intimate relationships.* New York: HarperCollins.

DZELME, K., & JONES, R. A. (2001). Male cross-dressers in therapy: A solution-focused perspective for marriage and family therapists. *American Journal of Family Therapy, 29,* 293–305.

ECKSTEIN, D. (2001). A F.A.M.I.L.Y. approach to self-care: Creating a healthy balance. *Family Journal: Counseling and Therapy for Couples and Families, 9*(3), 327–336.

ECKSTEIN, D., BELONGIA, M., & ELLIOT-APPLEGATE, G. (2000). The four directions of encouragement within families. *Family Journal, 8*(4), 406–415.

ECKSTEIN, D., & GOLDMAN, A. (2001). The Couple's Gender-based Communication Questionnaire (CGCQ). *Family Journal, 9,* 62–74.

ECKSTEIN, D., JUNKINS, E., & MCBRIEN, R. (2003). Ha, ha, ha: Improving couple and family healthy humor (healthy humor quotient). *Family Journal: Counseling and Therapy for Couples and Families, 11*(3), 301–305.

EDWARDS, D. (2004). *Art therapy.* London: Sage.

EHRENSAFT, M., & VIVIAN, D. (1996). Spouses' reasons for not reporting existing physical aggression as a marital problem. *Journal of Family Psychology, 10,* 443–453.

ELLIS, A. (1977). The nature of disturbed marital interactions. In A. Ellis & R. Greiger (Eds.), *Handbook of rational-emotive therapy* (pp. 170–276). New York: Springer.

ELLIS, A. (1985). Jealousy: Its etiology and treatment. In D. C. Goldberg (Ed.), *Contemporary marriage* (pp.420–428). Homewood, IL: Dorsey Press.

ELLIS, A., & MITCHELL, R. (2000). Sexual orientation. In L. Szuchman & F. Muscarella (Eds.), *Psychological perspectives on human sexuality* (pp. 196–208). New York: Wiley.

ENGEL, B. (2003, June). Relationship healing for couples: When one or both are in recovery. *Counselor, 43–47.*

EPPERLY, T. D., & MOORE, K. E. (2000). Health issues in men: Part I. Common genitourinary disorders. *American Family Physician, 61*(12) 3657–3664.

EPSTEIN, E. E., & MCCRADY, B. S. (2002). Couple therapy in the treatment of alcohol problems. In A. S. Gurman & N. S. Jacobsen (Eds.), *Clinical handbook of couple therapy* (3rd ed.) (pp. 597–628). New York: Guilford Press.

EPSTEIN, N. (1986). Cognitive marital therapy: A multilevel assessment and intervention. *Journal of Rational Emotive Therapy, 4,* 68–81.

EPSTEIN, R. (2002). M words. *Psychology Today, 35*(1), 1.

ERIKSON, E. H. (1950). *Childhood and society.* New York: Norton.

ETCHISON, M., & KLEIST, D. M. (2000). Review of narrative therapy: Research and utility. *Family Journal: Counseling and Therapy for Couples and Families, 8*(1), 61–66.

ET FORECASTS.COM (2001, February 6). Internet users will surpass 1 billion in 2005. Buffalo Grove, IL: Author. Retrieved March 7, 2005, from http://www.etforecasts.com.pr/pr201.htm

EVANS, P. (1992). *The verbally abusive relationship.* Holbrook, MA: Bob Adams.

EWING, J. A. (1984). Detecting alcoholism: The CAGE questionnaire. *Journal of the American Medical Association, 252,* 1905–1907.

FAIRBAIRN, W. R. D. (1952). *An object-relations theory of the personality.* New York: Basic Books.

FALK, P. (1989). Lesbian mothers: Psychosocial assumptions in family law. *American Psychologist, 44,* 941–947.

FALS-STEWART, W., & BIRCHLER, G. R. (2001). A national survey of the use of couples therapy in substance abuse treatment. *Journal of Substance Abuse Treatment, 20,* 277–283.

FENNELL, D. L. (1993). Characteristics of long-term first marriages. *Journal of Mental Health Counseling, 15,* 446–460.

FENNELL, D. L., & WEINHOLD, B. K. (2003). *Counseling families: An introduction to marriage and family therapy* (3rd ed.). Denver: Love.

FIELDS, R. (2004). *Drugs in perspective: A personalized look at substance use and abuse* (5th ed.). New York: McGraw-Hill.

FINCHAM, F., BEACH, R. H., & DAVILA, J. (2004). Forgiveness and conflict resolution in marriage. *Journal of Family Psychology, 18*(1) 72–81.

FINKELSTEIN, L. (1987). Toward an object-relations approach in psychoanalytic marital therapy. *Journal of Marital and Family Therapy, 13,* 287–298.

FISCHER, R. (2004). Assessing client change in individual and family counseling. *Research on Social Work Practice, 14*(2), 102–111.

FISH, L. S., & PIERCY, F. P. (1987). The theory and practice of structural and strategic family therapies: A Delphi study. *Journal of Marital and Family Therapy, 13,* 113–125.

FISHER, H. (1992). *Anatomy of love: The mysteries of mating, marriage and why we stray.* New York: Fawcett Columbine.

FISHER, J., & CORCORAN, K. (1994). Spouse Sobriety Influence Inventory. In J. Fisher & K. Corcoran (Eds.), *Measures for clinical practice: A sourcebook* (Vol. 1) (2nd ed.) (pp. 183–189). New York: Free Press.

FITZPATRICK, M. A. (1988). Approaches to marital interaction. In P. Noller & M. A. Fitzpatrick (Eds.), *Perspectives on marital interaction* (pp. 98–120). Clevedon, UK: Multilingual Matters.

FLOYD, F. J., MARKMAN, H. J., KELLY, S., BLUMBERG, S. L., & STANLEY, S. M. (1995). Preventive intervention and relationship enhancement. In N. S. Jacobson & A. S. Gurman (Eds.), *Clinical handbook of couple therapy* (2nd ed.) (pp. 212–226). New York: Guilford Press.

FOW, N. R. (1998). Partner-focused reversal in couple therapy. *Psychotherapy: Theory, Research, Practice, Training, 35*(2), 231–237.

FRAMO, J. L. (1970). Symptoms from a family transactional viewpoint. In N.W. Ackerman (Ed.), *Family therapy in transition* (pp. 125–171). Boston: Little, Brown.

FRAMO, J. L. (1976). Family of origin as a therapeutic resource for adults in marital and family therapy: You can and should go home again. *Family Process, 15,* 193–201.

FRAMO, J. L. (1990). Integrating families of origin into couple therapy. In R. Chasin, H. Grunebaum & M. Herzig (Eds.), *One couple, four realities: Multiple perspectives on couple therapy* (pp. 49–82). New York: Guilford Press

FRAMO, J. L. (1992). *Family of origin therapy: An intergenerational approach.* New York: Brunner/Mazel.

FRAMO, J. L. (1993). *Demonstrations with couples in counseling: Dealing with family of origin problems* [Videotape]. (Available from American Counseling Association, 5999 Stevenson Ave., Alexandria, VA 22304.)

FRANK, J. D., & FRANK, J. P. (1991). *Persuasion and healing: A comparative study of psychotherapy.* Baltimore: Johns Hopkins University Press.

FREDMAN, N., & SHERMAN, R. (1987). *Handbook of measurements for marriage and family therapy.* New York: Brunner/Mazel.

FREEDMAN, J., & COMBS, G. (1996). *Narrative therapy: The social construction of preferred realities.* New York: Norton.

FREUD, S. (1963). *Introductory lectures on psychoanalysis, Part 3* (Standard ed.) (Vol. 16). London: Hogarth. (Originally published in 1917)

FRIEDMAN, E. H. (1990). *Friedman's fables.* New York: Guilford Press.

FRIEDMAN, M. (2004). The so-called high-conflict couple: A closer look. *American Journal of Family Therapy, 32,* 101–117.

FRIEDMAN, R. (1991). Couple therapy with gay couples. *Psychiatric Annals, 21,* 485–490.

FRIEDMAN, S. (1992). Constructing solutions (stories in brief family therapy). In S. H. Budman (Ed.), *The first session in brief therapy* (pp. 282–305). New York: Guilford Press.

FRIESEN, J. D. (1985). *Structural–strategic marriage and family therapy.* New York: Gardner.

FUKUYAMA, M., & FERGUSON, A. (2000). Lesbian, gay, and bisexual people of color: Understanding cultural complexity and managing multiple oppression. In R. Perez, K. DeBord, & K. Bieschke (Eds.), *Handbook of counseling and psychotherapy with gay, lesbian, and bisexual clients* (pp. 81–106). Washington, DC: American Psychological Association.

FURSTENBERG, F. (2005). Can marriage be saved? *Dissent, 52,* 76–80

GANONG, L., & COLEMAN, M. (2004). *Stepfamily relationships.* New York: Kluwer.

GEORGE, K., & BEHRENDT, A. (1987). Therapy for male couples experiencing relationship problems and sexual problems. *Journal of Homosexuality, 14,* 77–88.

GIGY, L., & KELLY, J. B. (1992). Reasons for divorce: Perspectives of divorcing men and women. *Journal of Divorce and Remarriage, 18,* 169--187.

GILBERT, L. A., & SCHER, M. (1999). *Gender and sex in counseling and psychotherapy.* Needham Heights, MA: Allyn & Bacon.

GILBERT, R. M. (1992). *Extraordinary relationships: A new way of thinking about human interactions.* Minneapolis: Chronomed Publishing.

GILLIGAN, C. (1982). *In a different voice: Psychological theory and women's development.* Cambridge, MA: Harvard University Press.

GLADDING, S. (1998). *Counseling as an art: The creative arts in counseling* (2nd ed.). Alexandria, VA: American Counseling Association.

GLADDING, S. (2002). *Family therapy* (3rd ed.). Upper Saddle River, NJ: : Merrill/Prentice Hall.

GLADDING, S. (2005). *Counseling as an art: The creative arts in counseling* (3rd ed.). Alexandria, VA: American Counseling Association.

GLASS, S. P. (2002). *Not "just friends": Protect your relationship from infidelity and heal the trauma of betrayal.* New York: Free Press.

GLASS, S, P., & WRIGHT, T. L. (1992). Justifications for extramarital relationships: The association between attitudes, behaviors, and gender. *Journal of Sex Research, 29,* 361–387.

GLASSER, W. (1999). *Reality therapy in action.* New York: HarperCollins.

GLASSER, W. (2004). *Family Journal: Counseling and Therapy for Couples and Families, 12*(4), 339–341.

GLAUS, K. O. (1989). Alcoholism, chemical dependency, and the lesbian client. *Women and Therapy, 8,* 131–144.

GOLDBERG, A. N. (1999). The schemagram: Mapping your client's thought processes. *Journal of Humanistic Counseling, Education and Development, 38*(1), 19–28.

GOLDENBERG, I., & GOLDENBERG, H. (2002). *Family therapy: An overview* (4th ed.). Pacific Grove, CA: Brooks/Cole.

GOLDENBERG, I., & GOLDENBERG, H. (2000). *Family therapy: An overview* (5th ed.). Pacific Grove, CA: Brooks/Cole.

GOLDENBERG, I., & GOLDENBERG, H. (2004). *Family therapy: An overview* (6th ed.). Pacific Grove, CA: Brooks/Cole.

GOLOMBOK, S., RUST, J., & PICKARD, C. (1984). Sexual problems encountered in general practice. *British Journal of Sexual Medicine, 11,* 65–72.

GONYEA, J. L. J. (2004). Internet sexuality: Clinical implications for couples. *American Journal of Family Therapy, 32,* 375–390.

GORDON, D. (1978). *Therapeutic metaphors.* Cupertino, CA: Meta Publications.

GORDON, K. C., BAUCOM, D. H., & SNYDER, D. K. (2004). An integrative intervention for promoting recovery from extramarital affairs. *Journal of Marital and Family Therapy, 30*(2), 213–231.

GORDON, L. (1990). *Love knots.* New York: Bantam Books.

GORDON, L. H. (1986). Assessment as an option in divorce mediation. In J. C. Hansen (Ed.), *Divorce and family mediation* (pp. 66–70). Washington, DC: American Bar Association.

GOTTMAN, J. M. (1991). Predicting the longitudinal course of marriages. *Journal of Marital and Family Therapy, 17,* 3–7.

GOTTMAN, J. M. (1994). *Why marriages succeed or fail . . . and how you can make yours last.* New York: Simon & Schuster.

GOTTMAN, J. M. (1998). Psychology and the study of marital processes. *Annual Review of Psychology, 49,* 169–197.

GOTTMAN, J. M. (1999). *The marriage clinic: A scientifically based marital therapy.* New York: Norton.

GOTTMAN, J. M. (2002). A multidimensional approach to couples. In F. W. Kaslow & T. Peterson (Eds.), *Comprehensive handbook of psychotherapy: Cognitive-behavioral approaches* (Vol. 2) (pp. 355–372). New York: Wiley.

GOTTMAN, J. M., COAN, J., CARRERE, S., & SWANSON, C. (1998). Predicting marital happiness and stability from newlywed interactions. *Journal of Marriage and the Family, 60,* 5–22.

GOTTMAN, J. M., DRIVER, J., & TABARES, A. (2002). Building the sound marital house: An empirically derived couple therapy. In A. S. Gurman & N. S. Jacobson (Eds.), *Clinical handbook of couple therapy* (3rd ed.) (pp. 373–399). New York: Guilford Press.

GOTTMAN, J. M., & KROKOFF, L. J. (1989). Marital interaction and satisfaction: A longitudinal view. *Journal of Consulting and Clinical Psychology, 57,* 47–52.

GOTTMAN, J. M., & LEVENSON, R. W. (1988). The social psychophysiology of marriage. In P. Noller & M. A. Fitzpatrick (Eds.), *Perspectives on marital interaction* (pp.182–200). Clevedon, UK: Multilingual Matters.

GOTTMAN, J. M., NOTARIUS, C. I., GONSO, J., & MARKMAN, H. J. (1976). *A couple's guide to communication.* Champaign, IL: Research Press.

GRAY, J. (1993). *Men are from Mars, women are from Venus.* New York: Bantam Books.

GREENBERG, S. M., & JOHNSON, L. S. (1994). *The heart of the matter: Perspectives on emotion in marital therapy.* New York: Brunner/Mazel.

GREENE, B., & BOYD-FRANKLIN, N. (1996). African American lesbian couples: Ethnic cultural considerations in psychotherapy. *Women and Therapy, 19*(3), 49–60.

GROTEVANT, H. D., & CARLSON, C. I. (1989). *Family assessment: A guide to methods and measures.* New York: Guilford Press.

GUANIPA, C., & WOOLLEY, S. R. (2000). Gender biases and therapists' conceptualization of couple difficulties. *American Journal of Family Therapy, 28,* 181–192.

GUERIN, P., FAY, L., BURDEN, S., & KAUTTO, J. (1987). *The evaluation and treatment of marital conflict.* New York: Basic Books.

GUERNEY, B., JR., BROCK, G., & COUFAL, J. (1986). Integrating marital therapy and enrichment: The relationship enhancement approach. In N. S. Jacobson & A. S. Gurman (Eds.), *Clinical handbook of marital therapy* (pp. 151–172). New York: Guilford Press.

GURMAN, A. S. (2003). Marital therapies. In A. S. Gurman & S. B. Messer (Eds.), *Essential psychotherapies: Theory and practice* (pp. 463–514). New York: Guilford Press.

GURMAN, A. S., & FRAENKEL, P. (2002). The history of couple therapy: A millennial review. *Family Process, 41,* 199–260.

GURMAN, A. S., & JACOBSON, N. S. (2002). *Clinical handbook of couple therapy* (3rd ed.) New York: Guilford Press.

HACKNEY, H. (1992). *Differentiating between counseling theory and process.* Ann Arbor, MI: ERIC Clearinghouse on Counseling and Personnel Services. (ERIC Document Reproduction Service No. ED347485)

HACKNEY, H., & CORMIER, S. (2001). *The professional counselor: A process guide to helping* (4th ed.). Boston: Allyn & Bacon.

HALEY, J. (1963a). Marriage therapy. *Archives of General Psychiatry, 8,* 213–234.

HALEY, J. (1963b). *Strategies of psychotherapy.* New York: Grune & Stratton.

HALEY, J. (1976). *Problem-solving therapy.* Harper Colophon Books.

HALEY, J. (1989, May). *Strategic family therapy.* Symposium presented at Stetson University, DeLand, FL.

HALFORD, W. K., & MOORE, E. N. (2002). Relationship education and the prevention of couple relationship problems. In A. S. Gurman & N. S. Jacobson (Eds.), *Clinical handbook of couple therapy* (3rd ed.) (pp. 400–419). New York: Guilford Press.

HALFORD, W. K., PRICE, J., KELLY, A. B., BOUMA, R., & YOUNG, R. M. (2001). Helping the female partners of men abusing alcohol: A comparison of three treatments. *Addiction, 96,* 1497–1508.

HALL, M. (2001). Beyond forever after: Narrative therapy with lesbian couples. In P. Kleinplatz (Ed.), *New directions in sex therapy* (pp. 279–301). Philadelphia: Brunner/Routledge.

HAMAMCI, Z. (2002). The effect of integrating psychodrama and cognitive behavioral therapy on reducing cognitive distortions in interpersonal relationships. *Journal of Group Psychotherapy, Psychodrama, and Sociometry, 55*(1), 3–14.

HAMBERGER, L. K., & PHELAN, M. B. (2004). *Domestic violence screening and intervention in medical and mental healthcare settings.* New York: Springer.

HARRIS, S., & DERSCH, C. (2001). "I'm just not like that": Investigating the intergenerational cycle of violence. *Family Journal: Counseling and Therapy for Couples and Families, 9*(3), 250–258.

HARVEY, J. (1995). *Odyssey of the heart: The search for closeness, intimacy, and love.* New York: Freeman.

HAWLEY, D. R. (1995). Using self-report assessment in couples counseling. *Family Journal: Counseling and Therapy for Couples and Families, 3*(1), 27–36.

HEIMAN, J., LOPICCOLO, L., & LOPICCOLO, J. (1976). *Becoming orgasmic: A sexual growth program for women.* Englewood Cliffs, NJ: Prentice Hall.

HELLER, P. E., & WOOD, B. L. (1998). Process of intimacy: Similarity, understanding, and gender. *Journal of Marital and Family Therapy, 24*(3), 273–288.

HENDERSON, S. (1999). The use of animal imagery in counseling. *American Journal of Art Therapy, 38*(1), 20–29.

HENDRICK, C. A., & HENDRICK, S. S. (2000). *Close relationships: A sourcebook.* Thousand Oaks, CA: Sage.

HENDRICK, S. (1988). A generic measure of relationship satisfaction. *Journal of Marriage and the Family, 50,* 93–98.

HETHERINGTON, E. M. (1999). Should we stay together for the sake of the children? In E. M. Hetherington (Ed.), *Coping with divorce, single parenting, and remarriage: A risk and resiliency perspective* (pp. 93–116). Mahwah, NJ: Erlbaum.

HETHERINGTON, E. M. (2002, April 8). Marriage and divorce American style. Retrieved April 17, 2006, from www. prospect.org/print/V13/7/hetherington-e. html

HILLIER, S., & HOLMES, K. K. (1999). Bacterial vaginosis. In K. K. Holmes, P. F. Sparling, P. Mardh, S. M. Lemon, W. E. Stamm, P. Piot, & J. N. Wasserheit (Eds.), *Sexually transmitted diseases* (3rd ed.) (pp. 563–586). New York: McGraw-Hill.

HO, D. (1995). Internalized culture, cultural-centrism, and transcendence. *Counseling Psychology, 23*(1), 4–24.

HOBART, C. (1989). Experiences of remarried families. *Journal of Divorce, 13,* 121–144.

HOF, L., & BERMAN, E. (1986). The sexual genogram. *Journal of Marital and Family Therapy, 12,* 39–47.

HOFFMAN. L. (2002). *Family therapy: An intimate history.* New York: Norton.

HOLTZWORTH-MUNROE, A., MEEHAN, J. C., REHMAN, U., & MARSHALL, A. D. (2002). Intimate partner violence: An introduction for couples therapists. In A. S. Gurman & N. S. Jacobson (Eds.), *Clinical handbook of couple therapy* (pp. 441–465). New York: Guilford Press.

HOOK, E. W., & HANDSFIELD, H. H. (1999). Gonococcal infections in the adult. In K. K. Holmes, P. F. Sparling, P. Mardh, S. M. Lemon, W. E. Stamm, P. Piot, & J. N. Wasserheit (Eds.), *Sexually transmitted diseases* (3rd ed.) (pp. 451–466). New York: McGraw-Hill.

HORNE, A. M. (1991). Social learning family therapy. In A. M. Horne & J. L. Passmore (Eds.), *Family counseling and therapy* (pp.464–496). Itasca, IL: Peacock.

HORNE, A. M., & PASSMORE, J. L. (Eds.). (1991). *Family counseling and therapy.* Itasca, IL: Peacock.

HOVESTADT, A., ANDERSON, W., PIERCY, F., COCHRAN, S., & FINE, M. (1985). A family of origin scale. *Journal of Marriage and Family Therapy, 11,* 287–298.

HOYT, M. F. (2002). Solution-focused couple therapy. In A. S. Gurman & N. S. Jacobson (Eds.), *Clinical handbook of couple therapy* (3rd ed.) (pp. 335–369). New York: Guilford Press.

HOYT, M. F., ROSENBAUM, R., & TALMON, M. (1992). Planned single session psychotherapy. In S. H. Budman (Ed.), *The first session in brief therapy* (pp. 59–86). New York: Guilford Press.

HUNT, R., HOF, L., & DEMARIA, R. (1998). *Marriage enrichment: Preparation, mentoring, and outreach.* Philadelphia: Brunner/Mazel.

IBSEN, H. (1911). *Ghosts and other plays* (R. F. Sharp, Trans.). London: Dent.

IMBER-BLACK, E. (1989). Rituals of stabilization and change in women's lives. In M. McGoldrick, C. M. Andersen, & F. Walsh (Eds.), *Women in families: A framework for family therapy* (pp. 451–469). New York: Norton.

IMBER-BLACK, E. (2002). Family rituals—from research to the consulting room and back again: Comment on the special section. *Journal of Family Psychology, 4,* 445–446.

INKSON, K., & AMUNDSON, N. (2002). Career metaphors and their application in theory and counseling practice. *Journal of Employment Counseling 39,* 98–108.

INSTITUTE FOR PERSONALITY AND ABILITY TESTING. (1967). *The Cattell 16-PF manual.* Champaign, IL: Author.

IRVING, L. M., CHEAVENS, J., SYNDER, C. R., GRAVEL, L., HANKE, J., HILBERG, P., & NELSON, N. (2004). The relationships between hope and outcomes at the pretreatment, beginning, and later phases of psychotherapy. *Journal of Psychotherapy Integration, 14*(4), 419–443.

IVEY, A. E., & MATHEWS, J. W. (1986). A metamodel for structuring the clinical interview. In W. P. Anderson (Ed.), *Innovative counseling: A handbook of readings* (pp. 77–83). Alexandria, VA: American Association for Counseling and Development.

JACOBSON, N. S., & CHRISTENSEN, A. (1996). Studying the effectiveness of psychotherapy: How well can clinical trials do the job? *American Psychologist, 51,* 1030–1039.

JACOBSON, N. S., & HOLTZWORTH-MUNROE, A. (1986). Marital therapy: A social learning–cognitive perspective. In N. S. Jacobson & A. S. Gurman (Eds.), *Clinical handbook of marital therapy* (pp. 29–70). New York: Guilford Press.

JACOBSON, N. S., & MARGOLIN, G. (1979). *Marital therapy: Strategies based on social learning and behavior exchange principles.* New York: Brunner/Mazel.

JACOBSON, N. S., WALDRON, H., & MOORE, D. (1980). Toward a behavioral profile of marital distress. *Journal of Consulting and Clinical Psychology, 49,* 269–277.

JACQUET, S., & SURRA, C. A. (2001). Parental divorce and premarital couples: Commitment and other relationship characteristics. *Journal of Marriage and Family, 63*(3) 627.

JANKOWIAK, W. R., & FISHER, E. F. (1992). A cross-cultural perspective on romantic love. *Ethnology, 31,* 149–155.

JOHNSON, S. M., & DENTON, W. (2002). Emotionally focused couple therapy: Creating secure connections. In A. S. Gurman & N. S. Jacobson (Eds.), *Clinical handbook of couple therapy* (3rd ed.) (pp. 221–250). New York: Guilford Press.

JOHNSON, S. M., & GREENBERG, L. S. (1994). *The heart of the matter: Perspectives on emotion in marital therapy.* New York: Brunner/Mazel.

JOHNSON, S. M., & GREENBERG, L. S. (2002). Emotionally focused couple therapy: Creating secure connections. In A. S. Gurman & N. S. Jacobson (Eds.), *Clinical handbook of couple therapy*

(3rd ed.) (pp. 221–250). New York: Guilford Press.

JOHNSON, S. M., HUNSLEY, J. L., GREENBERG, L., & SCHLINDER, D. (1999). Emotionally focused couples therapy: Status and challenges. *Journal of Clinical Psychology: Science and Practice, 6,* 67–79.

JOHNSTON, J., & CAMPBELL, L. (1988). *Impasses of divorce.* New York: Free Press.

JONES, A. (2003). Reconstructing the stepfamily: Old myths, new stories. *Social Work. 48*(2), 228–236.

JORDAN, K. (2001). Family art therapy: The joint family holiday drawing. *Family Journal, 9*(1), 52–54.

JORDAN, K., & QUINN, W. H. (1994). Session two outcome of the formula first session task in problem and solution-focused approaches. *American Journal of Family Therapy, 22,* 3–6.

JOURARD, S. M. (1964). *The transparent self: Self-disclosure and well-being.* Princeton, NJ: Van Nostrand.

KAPLAN, H. (1979). *Disorders of sexual desire.* New York: Brunner/Mazel.

KAPLAN, H. S. (1983). *The evaluation of sexual disorders: Psychological and medical aspects.* New York: Brunner/Mazel.

KARPEL, M. A. (1993, October). *Wounded hearts: Restoring trust in couples therapy.* Workshop presented at the 51st Annual Conference of the American Association for Marriage and Family Therapy, Anaheim, CA.

KASLOW, F. W. (1984). Divorce: An evolutionary process of change in the family system. *Journal of Divorce, 7,* 21–39.

KASLOW, F. W. (1993). Understanding and treating the remarriage family. *Directions in Marriage and Family Therapy, 1*(3), 1–16.

KASLOW, F. W. (1996). *Handbook of relational diagnoses and dysfunctional family patterns.* New York: Wiley.

KASLOW, F. W., & FRIEDMAN, J. (1977). Utilization of family photos in family therapy. *Journal of Marriage and Family Counseling, 3,* 19–25.

KASLOW, F. W., & SCHWARTZ, L. (1987). *Dynamics of divorce: A life cycle perspective.* New York: Brunner/Mazel.

KAZDIM, A. E. (2000). *Encyclopedia of psychology* (Vol. 5). New York: Oxford University Press.

KEENEY, B. P. (1983). *The aesthetics of change.* New York: Guilford Press.

KEENEY, B. P. (1985). *Mind in therapy.* New York: Basic Books.

KEIM, J., & LAPPIN, J. (2002). Structural–strategic marital therapy. In A. S. Gurman & N. S. Jacobson (Eds.), *Clinical handbook of couple therapy* (3rd ed.) (pp. 86–117). New York: Guilford Press.

KELL, C. (1992). The internal dynamics of the extramarital relationship: A counselling perspective. *Sexual and Marital Therapy, 7,* 157–172.

KELLEY, G. (2004). *Sexuality today: The human perspective* (7th ed.) New York: McGraw-Hill.

KELLEY, P. (1992). Healthy stepfamily functioning. *Families in Society: The Journal of Contemporary Human Services, 73,* 579–587.

KELLY, A. B., HALFORD, W. K., & YOUNG, R. M. (2000). Maritally distressed women with alcohol problems: The impact of a short-term alcohol-focused intervention on drinking behaviour and marital satisfaction. *Addiction, 95*(10), 1537–1549.

KILPATRICK, A., & HOLLAND, T. (2003). *Working with families: An integrative model by level of need* (3rd ed.). Boston: Allyn & Bacon.

KILPATRICK, A. C., & KILPATRICK, E. G., JR. (1991). Object relations family therapy. In A. M. Horne & J. L. Passmore (Eds.), *Family counseling and therapy* (pp. 207–234). Itasca, IL: Peacock.

KINNEY, J. (2003). *Loosening the grip: A handbook of alcohol information.* New York: McGraw-Hill.

KIPPER, D. (1996). The emergence of role playing as a form of psychotherapy. *Journal of Group Psychotherapy, Psychodrama & Sociometry, 49*(3), 99–119.

KOSCH, S. (1982). Sexual dysfunction. In E. Medley (Ed.), *Common health problems in medical practice.* Baltimore: Williams & Wilkins.

KOTTLER, J. (1994). *Beyond blame.* New York: Jossey-Bass.

KRESTAN, J., & BEPKO, C. (1980). The problem of fusion in the lesbian relationship. *Family Process, 19,* 277–289.

L'ABATE, L. (1999). Taking the bull by the horns. Beyond talk in psychological interventions. *Family Journal: Counseling and Therapy for Couples and Family, 7*(3), 206–230.

L'ABATE, L., & BAGAROZZI, D. A. (1993). *Sourcebook of marriage and family evaluation* (pp. 77–94). New York: Brunner/Mazel.

L'ABATE, L., & TALMADGE, W. C. (1987). Love, intimacy, and sex. In G. R. Weeks & L. Hof (Eds.), *Integrating sex and marital therapy: A clinical guide* (pp. 23–34). New York: Brunner/Mazel.

L'ABATE, L., & WEINSTEIN, S. E. (1997). *Structured enrichment programs for couples and families.* New York: Brunner/Mazel.

LAIRD, W., & HARTMEN, A. (1988). *Women, rituals, and family therapy.* New York: Haworth Press.

LAMANNA, M. A., & RIEDMANN, A. (1991). *Marriages and families: Making choices and facing change.* Pacific Grove, CA: Brooks/Cole.

LANDIS, L. (1991). *Interparental conflict and postdivorce adjustment.* Unpublished doctoral dissertation.

LANDIS, L., & YOUNG, M. (1994). The reflecting team in counselor education. *Journal of Counselor Education and Supervision, 23,* 112–118.

LANGER, E., & RODIN, J. (1976). The effects of choice and enhanced personal responsibility for the aged: A field experiment in an institutional setting. *Journal of Personality and Social Psychology, 33,* 563–573.

LASALA, M. (2000). Lesbians, gay men, and their parents: Family therapy for the coming-out crisis. *Family Process, 39,* 67–81.

LAURENCEAU, J. P., BARRETT, L. F., & ROVINE, M. J. (2005). The interpersonal process model of intimacy in marriage: A daily-diary and multilevel modeling approach. *Journal of Family Psychology, 19,* 314–323.

LAWSON, A. (1990). *Adultery.* Oxford, UK: Oxford University Press.

LAZARUS, A. A. (1985). *Marital myths.* San Luis Obispo, CA: Impact.

LEE, J. (1991). Can we talk? Can we really talk? Communication as a key factor in the maturing homosexual couple. *Journal of Homosexuality, 14,* 143–168.

LEFRANCOIS, G. (1993). *All about sex therapy.* New York: Plenum.

LEIBLUM, S., & PERVIN, L. (1980). Introduction: The development of sex therapy from a sociocultural perspective. In S. Leiblum & L. Pervin (Eds.), *Principles and practices of sex therapy.* New York: Guilford Press.

LEIBLUM, S., & ROSEN, R. (1984). *Alcohol and human sexual response.* New York: Haworth Press.

LEIBLUM, S., & ROSEN, R. (1989). *Principles and practice of sex therapy: Update for the 1990s.* New York: Guilford Press.

LEIBLUM, S. R., & ROSEN, R. C. (Eds.). (2000). *Principles and practice of sex therapy* (3rd ed.). New York: Guilford Press.

LERNER, H. G. (1985a). *The dance of anger: A woman's guide to changing patterns in intimate relationships.* New York: Harper & Row.

LERNER, H. G. (1985b). *The dance of intimacy: A woman's guide to courageous acts of change in key relationships.* New York: Harper & Row.

LEVINGER, G., & SENN, D. J. (1967). Disclosure of feelings in marriage. *Merrill-Palmer Quarterly, 13,* 237–249.

LEVI-STRAUS, C. (1969). *The elementary structures of kinship.* Boston: Beacon Press.

LEW, A. & BETTNER, B. L. (1999). Establishing a family goal. *Journal of Individual Psychology, 55,* 105–108.

LEWIS, T. F., & OSBORN, C. J. (2004). Solution-focused counseling and motivational interviewing: A consideration of confluence. *Journal of Counseling and Development, 82,* 38–48.

LIDDLE, H. A. (1983). Diagnosis and assessment in family therapy: A comparative study of six schools of thought. In J. C. Hansen & B. P. Keeney (Eds.), *Diagnosis and assessment in family therapy.* Rockville, MD: Aspen.

LIPCHIK, E. (1994). The rush to be brief. *Networker, 14,* 35–39.

LIPCHIK, E. (2002). *Beyond technique in solution focused therapy.* New York: Guilford Press.

LOCKE, H. J., & WALLACE, K. M. (1959). Short marital adjustment and prediction tests: Their reliability and validity. *Marriage and Family Living, 2,* 251–255.

LOFTUS, E. (2003). Make-believe memories. *American Psychologist, 58,* 11.

LONG, E. C. J. (1993). Perspective-taking differences between high and low-adjustment marriages: Implications for those in intervention. *American Journal of Family Therapy, 21,* 248–259.

LONG, L., BURNETT, J., & THOMAS, V. (2006). *Sexuality counseling.* Upper Saddle River, NJ: Pearson Education.

LOPICCOLO, J. (1985). Diagnosis and treatment of male sexual dysfunction. *Journal of Sex and Marital Therapy, 11,* 215–233.

LOPICCOLO, J., & LOPICCOLO, L. (1978). *Handbook of sex therapy.* New York: Plenum.

LOPICCOLO, J., & STEGER, J. C. (1974). The Sexual Interaction Inventory: A new instrument for assessment of sexual dysfunction. *Archives of Sexual Behavior, 3,* 585–595.

LOULAN, J. (1987). *Lesbian passion: Loving ourselves and each other.* San Francisco: Spinster/Aunt Lute.

LOVE, C. T., LONGABAUGH, R., CLIFFORD, P. R., BEATTIE, M., & PEASLEE, C. F. (1993). The Significant-Other Behavior Questionnaire (SBQ):

An instrument for measuring the behavior of significant others towards a person's drinking and abstinence. *Addiction, 88,* 1267–1279.

LUEPNITZ, D. (1986). A comparison of maternal, paternal, and joint custody: Understanding the varieties in post-divorce life. *Journal of Divorce, 9,* 1–13.

LUKAS, S. (1993). *Where to start and what to ask.* New York: Norton.

LYDDON, W., CLAY, A., & SPARKS, C. (2001). Metaphor and change in counseling. *Journal of Counseling and Development, 79*(3), 269–274.

MAGNUSON, S., & SHAW, H. (2003). Adaptations of the multifaceted genogram in counseling, training, and supervision. *Family Journal, 11*(1), 45–54.

MAHONEY, M. (1991). *Human change processes.* New York: Basic Books.

MALTZ, W. (2001). *The sexual healing journey: A guide for survivors of sexual abuse.* New York: HarperCollins.

MARINO, T. (1994). O. J. aftermath: The battering of American women. *Guidepost, 27,* 12, 23.

MARKMAN, H. H., STANLEY, S., & BLUMBERG, S. L. (1994). *Fighting for your marriage: Positive steps for preventing divorce and preserving a lasting love.* San Francisco: Jossey-Bass.

MARKMAN, H. H., STANLEY, S., JENKINS, S. H., BLUMBERG, S. L., & WHITELEY, C. (2004). *12 hours to a great marriage: A step by step guide for making love last.* New York: Wiley.

MARKMAN, H. J., RENICK, M. J., FLOYD, F. J., STANLEY, S. M., & CLEMENTS, M. (1993). Preventing marital distress through communication and conflict management training: A 4- and 5-year follow-up. *Journal of Consulting and Clinical Psychology, 61,* 70–77.

MARR, L. (1998). *Sexually transmitted diseases.* Baltimore: Johns Hopkins University Press.

MARTIN, P. A., & BIRD, H. W. (1959). The "love sick wife" and the "cold sick" husband. *Psychiatry, 22,* 246.

MASH, E. J., & FOSTER, S. L. (2001). Exporting analogue behavioral observation from research to clinical practice: Useful or cost-defective? *Psychological Assessment, 13,* 86–98.

MASTERS, W. H., & JOHNSON, V. E. (1970). *Human sexual inadequacy.* London: Churchill.

MAYER, J. E. (1989). Strategies and techniques for the initial clinical interview. *Clinical Supervisor, 7,* 89–99.

MCCABE, R., & PRIEBE, S. (2004). The therapeutic relationship in the treatment of severe mental illness: A review of methods and findings. *Journal of Social Psychiatry, 50*(2), 115–128.

MCCARTHY, J., & HOLLIDAY, E. L. (2004). Help-seeking and counseling within a traditional male gender role: An examination from a multicultural perspective. *Journal of Counseling and Development, 82,* 25–30.

MCCRADY, B. S., EPSTEIN, E. E., & KAHLER, C. W. (2004). Alcoholics Anonymous and relapse prevention as maintenance strategies after conjoint behavioral alcohol treatment for men: 18-month outcomes. *Journal of Consulting and Clinical Psychology, 72*(5), 870–878.

MCGOLDRICK, M., & CARTER, E. (Eds.). (1980). *The family life cycle.* New York: Gardner Press.

MCGOLDRICK, M., GERSON, R., & SHELLENBERGER, S. (1999). *Genograms: Assessment and intervention* (2nd ed.). New York: Norton.

MCKAY, M., FANNING, P., & PALEG, K. (1994). *Couple skills: Making your relationship work.* Oakland, CA: New Harbinger.

MECCA, W., RIVERA, A., & ESPOSITO, A. (2000). Instituting and outcomes assessment effort: Lessons from the field. *Journal of Contemporary Human Services, 81*(1), 85–89.

MEHRABIAN, A. (1972). *Nonverbal communication.* Chicago: Aldine.

MILEHAM, B. A. (2004). Cheating by chatting. *Hispanic, 17*(3), 28–30.

MILES, E. (1997). *Tune your brain.* New York: Berkley.

MILLER, G. A. (1999). *Learning the language of addiction counseling.* Boston: Allyn & Bacon.

MILLER, S., WACKMAN, D. B., & NUNNALLY, E. W. (1983). Couple communication: Equipping couples to be their own best problem solvers. *Counseling Psychologist, 11,* 73–77.

MILLER, W. R., & ROLLNICK, S. (2002). *Motivational interviewing: Preparing people for change* (2nd ed.). New York: Guilford Press.

MILLS, D. (1984). A model for stepfamily development. *Family Relations, 33,* 365–372.

MINUCHIN, S. (1974). *Families and family therapy.* Cambridge MA: Harvard University Press.

MINUCHIN, S. (1984). *Family kaleidoscope.* Cambridge, MA: Harvard University Press.

MINUCHIN, S., & NICHOLS, M. P. (1993). *Family healing: Tales of hope and renewal from family therapy.* New York: Free Press.

MODCRIN, M., & WYERS, N. (1990). Lesbians and gay couples: Where they turn when help is needed. *Journal of Gay and Lesbian Psychotherapy, 1,* 89–104.

MOLNAR, A., & DE SHAZER, S. (1987). Solution-focused therapy: Toward the identification of therapeutic tasks. *Journal of Marriage and Family Therapy, 13,* 349–358.

MONES, A. G. (2001). Exploring themes of sibling experience to help resolve couples conflict. *Family Journal: Counseling and Therapy for Couples and Families, 9*(4), 455–460.

MOULTRUP, D. J. (1990). *Husbands, wives and lovers.* New York: Guilford Press.

MURRAY, C. E., & MURRAY, T. L., JR. (2004). Solution-focused premarital counseling: Helping couples build a vision for their marriage. *Journal of Marital and Family Therapy, 30,* 349–358.

MURRAY, P. E., & ROTTER, J. C. (2002). Creative counseling techniques for family therapists. *Family Journal: Counseling and Therapy for Couples and Families, 10*(2), 203–206.

MURSTEIN, B., WADLIN, R., & BOND, C., JR. (1987). The revised exchange-orientation scale. *Small Group Behavior, 18,* 212–223.

MYERHOFF, B. (1983, November). *Rites of passage.* Symposium presented by the National Association of Social Workers, Washington, DC.

MYERS, J., SWEENEY, T., & WITMER, M. (2000). The Wheel of Wellness counseling for wellness: A holistic model for treatment planning. *Journal of Counseling and Development, 78* (3).

NATIONAL MARRIAGE PROJECT. (2005). Retrieved September 12, 2005, from http://marriage.rutgers.edu/Publications/swlt2.pdf

NAVRAN, L. (1967). Communication and adjustment in marriage. *Family Process, 6,* 173–184.

NEGY, C., SNYDER, D. K., & DIAZ-LOVING, R. (2004). A cross-national comparison of Mexican and Mexican American couples using the Marital Satisfaction Inventory—Revised (Spanish). *Assessment, 11*(1), 49–56.

NELSON, T. S., & KELLEY, L. (2003). Solution-focused couples groups. *Journal of Systemic Therapies, 20,* 47–66.

NIAAA (National Institute on Alcohol Abuse and Alcoholism). (2000, October). *The National Institute on Alcohol Abuse and Alcoholism Strategic Plan 2001–2005.* Bethesda, MD: U.S. Department of Health and Human Services.

NICHOLS, M. (2000). Therapy with sexual minorities. In S. R. Leiblum & R. C. Rosen (Eds.), *Principles and practice of sex therapy* (3rd ed.) (pp. 335–365). New York: Guilford Press.

NICHOLS, M. P., & SCHWARTZ, R. C. (2006). *Family therapy: Concepts and methods* (7th ed.). Boston: Allyn & Bacon.

NOLLER, P., & VERNARDOS, C. (1986). Communication awareness in married couples. *Journal of Social and Personal Relationships, 3,* 31–42.

NORCROSS, J. C., & GOLDFRIED, M. R. (2003). *Handbook of psychotherapy integration* (2nd ed.). New York: Oxford University Press.

NORCROSS, J. C., & NEWMAN, C. F. (1992). Psychotherapy integration: Setting the context. In J. C. Norcross & M. R. Goldfried (Eds.), *Handbook of psychotherapy integration* (pp. 3–45). New York: Basic Books.

NOTARIUS, C. I., & VANZETTI, N. A. (1983) The marital agendas protocol. In E. E. Filsinger (Ed.), *Marriage and family assessment: A sourcebook for family therapy* (pp. 209–227). Beverly Hills, CA: Sage.

O'FARRELL, T. J. (1993). A behavioral marital therapy couples group program for alcoholics and their spouses. In T. J. O'Farrell (Ed.), *Treating alcohol problems: Marital and family interventions* (pp. 170–209). New York: Guilford Press.

O'FARRELL, T. J., & FALS-STEWART, W. (2000). Behavioral couples therapy for alcoholism and drug abuse. *Journal of Substance Abuse Treatment, 18*, 51–54.

O'FARRELL, T. J., & FALS-STEWART, W. (2003). Alcohol abuse. *Journal of Marital and Family Therapy, 29*(1), 121–146.

O'HANLON, W. (1999). *Do one thing different: Ten simple ways to change your life.* New York: Morrow.

O'HANLON, W., & WEINER-DAVIS, M. (1989). *In search of solutions.* New York: Norton.

O'LEARY, K. D., & TURKEWITZ, H. (1978). The treatment of marital disorders from a behavioral perspective. In T. J. Paolino & B. S. McCrady (Eds.), *Marriage and marital therapy: Psychoanalytic, behavioral and systems theory perspectives.* New York: Brunner/Mazel.

OLSHANSKY, E. (2000). Integrated women's health: Holistic approaches for comprehensive care. Gaithersburg, MD: Aspen.

OLSON, D. H. (1977). Insiders and outsiders view of relationships. In G. Levinger & H. Rausch (Eds.), *Close relationships: Perspectives on the meaning of intimacy* (pp. 115–135). Amherst: University of Massachusetts Press.

OLSON, D. H. (2002). *PREPARE/ENRICH counselor's manual.* Minneapolis: Life Innovations.

OLSON, D. H., DYER, P., & DYER, G. (1997). *Growing together: Leaders manual. A group program for couples.* Minneapolis: Life Innovations.

OLSON, D. H., FOURNIER, D. G., & DRUCKMAN, J. M. (1986). *PREPARE/ ENRICH counselor's manual.* Minneapolis: PREPARE/ENRICH.

OLSON, D. H., & OLSON, A. K. (1997) PREPARE/ENRICH program: Version 2000. *Journal of Family Ministry, 11*, 28–53.

OLSON, D. H., & OLSON, A. K. (2000). *Empowering couples: Building on your strengths* (2nd ed.). Minneapolis: Life Innovations.

ORFORD, J., NATERA, G., DAVIES, J., NAVA, A., MORA, J., RIGBY, K., et al. (1998). Tolerate, engage, or withdraw: A study of the structure of families coping with alcohol and drug problems in south west England and Mexico. *Addiction, 93*, 1799–1813.

OSSANA, S. (2000). Relationships and couples counseling. In R. Perez, K. DeBord, & K. Bieschke (Eds.), *Handbook of counseling and psychotherapy with lesbians, gay, and bisexual clients* (pp. 375–202). Washington, DC: American Psychological Association.

PAGE, L., & ECKSTEIN, D. (2003). The Full Resource Partnering Questionnaire (FRPQ). *Family Journal: Counseling and Therapy for Couples and Families, 11*(4), 413–419.

PALAZZOLI-SELVINI, M., BOSCOLO, L., CECCHIN, G., & PRATA, G. (1980). Hypothesizing-circularity-neutrality: Three guidelines for the conductor of the session. *Family Process, 19*, 3–12.

PALMER, N. (1993, May). *Notes on mediation.* Symposium presented at Stetson University, DeLand, FL.

PALMER, N., & LANDIS, L. (1989). Child custody arrangements: Application of the "best interest" standard. *Florida Family Law Reporter, 4*(9), 283–923.

PAOLINO, T., & MCGRADY, B. (Eds.). (1978). *Marriage and marital therapy.* New York: Brunner/Mazel.

PAPERNOW, P. (1984). The stepfamily cycle: An experimental model of stepfamily development. *Family Relations, 33,* 355–363.

PAPP, P. (1983). *The process of change.* New York: Guilford Press.

PARRY, R. H. (2004). Communication during goal-setting in physiotherapy treatment sessions. *Clinical Rehabilitation, 18,* 668–682.

PASSLEY, K., RHODEN, L., VISHER, E. B., & VISHER, J. S. (1996). Successful stepfamily therapy: Client's perspective. *Journal of Marital and Family Therapy, 22*(3), 343–357.

PATTERSON, G. R., HOPS, H., & WEISS, R. L. (1975). Interpersonal skills training for couples in early stages of conflict. *Journal of Marriage and the Family, 37,* 295–302.

PAUL, P. (2003). *The starter marriage and the future of matrimony.* New York: Villard Books.

PENN, P. (1982). Circular questioning. *Family Process, 21,* 267–280.

PENNEBAKER, J. W. (1990). *Opening up: The healing power of confiding in others.* New York: Morrow.

PERRIN, E. (February, 2002). Technical report: Co-parent or second-parent adoption by same sex parents. Retrieved June 3, 2004, from http://pediatrics.aa.publication.org/cgi/content/full/109/2/341

PETERS, D. P. (1987). The impact of naturally occurring stress on children's memory. In S. J. Ceci, M. P. Toglia, & D. F. Ross (Eds.), *Children's eyewitness memory* (pp. 122–141). New York: Springer-Verlag.

PETERS, J. S. (1987). *Music therapy: An introduction.* Springfield, IL: Thomas.

PETERSON, K. (July, 2004). 50-state rundown on gay marriage laws. Retrieved July 12, 2004, from http://www.stateline.org

PETERSON, K. S. (2004, February 17). "Marriage movement" could face division over gay unions. *USA Today.*

PICHOT, T., & DOLAN Y. M. (2003). Solution-focused brief therapy: Its effective use in agency settings. Binghamton, NY: Haworth Press.

PITTMAN, F. S. (1989). *Private lies: Infidelity and the betrayal of intimacy.* New York: Norton.

PITTMAN, F. S. (2004). A buyer's guide to psychotherapy. *Psychology Today, 27,* 50–54.

PITTMAN, F. S., & WAGERS, T. P. (1995). Crises of infidelity. In N. Jacobson & A. Gurman (Eds.), *Clinical handbook of couple therapy* (2nd ed.) (pp. 295–316). New York: Guilford Press.

POLIVY, J., & HERMAN, C. P. (2002). If at first you don't succeed. *American Psychologist, 57,* 677–689.

POLONSKY, D. C. (2000). Premature ejaculation. In S. R. Leiblum & R. C. Rosen (Eds.), *Principles and practice of sex therapy* (3rd ed.) (pp. 305–332). New York: Guilford Press.

POPE, M., & BARRET, B. (2002). Counseling gay men toward an integrated sexuality. In L. Burlew & D. Capuzzi (Eds.), *Sexuality counseling* (pp. 149–175). New York: Nova Science.

POPENOE, D., & WHITEHEAD, B. (2002). *Should we live together? What young adults need to know about cohabitation before marriage—a comprehensive review of recent research* (2nd ed.). New Brunswick, NJ: National Marriage Project, Rutgers University.

PRIDAL, C. G., & LOPICCOLO, J. (2000). Multielement treatment of desire disorders: Integration of cognitive, behavioral, and systemic treatment. In S. R. Leiblum & R. C. Rosen (Eds.), *Principles and practice of sex therapy* (3rd ed.) (pp. 57–81). New York: Guilford Press.

PROCHASKA, J. O., NORCROSS, J. C., & DICLEMENTE, C. C. (1994). *Changing for good.* New York: Morrow.

PROSKY, P. (1991). Marital life. *Family Therapy, 18,* 129–143.

PROVOST, J. A. (1990). *Work, play and type: Achieving balance in your life.* Palo Alto, CA: Consulting Psychologists Press.

PROVOST, J. A. (1993). *Applications of the Myers-Briggs Type Indicator in counseling: A casebook.* Gainesville, FL: Center for Application of Psychological Type.

QUICK, E. (1998). Doing what works in brief and intermittent therapy. *Journal of Mental Health, 7*(5), 527–533.

REIG-FERRER, A., CEPEDA-BENITO, A., & SNYDER, D. K. (2004). Utility of the Spanish translation of the Marital Satisfaction Inventory—Revised in Spain. *Assessment, 11*(1), 17–26.

REISER, P. (1994). *Couplehood.* New York: Bantam Books.

RENCKEN, R. (2000). *Brief and extended interventions in sexual abuse.* Alexandria, VA: American Counseling Association.

RIGAZIO-DIGILIO, S. A. (1999). Ethics and family therapy: Working within a co-constructive, eco-systemic paradigm. *Guidance & Counseling, 14*(2), 22–28.

RIPLEY, J. S., & WORTHINGTON, E. L. (2002) Hope-focused and forgiveness-based group interventions to promote marital enrichment. *Journal of Counseling & Development, 80,* 452–464.

ROBERTS, L. J., & MCCRADY, B. S. (2003). *Alcohol problems in intimate relationships: Identification and intervention. A guide for marriage and family therapists* (NIH Publication No. 03-5284). Bethesda, MD: National Institute on Alcohol Abuse and Alcoholism.

ROBERTS, S. (2004, June 27). Till death do us part, or whatever. *New York Times,* p. 4014.

ROBINSON, B. (1984). The contemporary American stepfather. *Family Relations, 33,* 381–388.

ROLAND, C. (2002). Counseling adult survivors of childhood sexual abuse. In L. Burlew & D. Capuzzi (Eds.), *Sexuality counseling* (pp. 285–306). New York: Nova Science.

ROSENBAUM, A., & O'LEARY, K. D. (1986). The treatment of marital violence. In N. S. Jacobson & A. S. Gurman (Eds.), *Clinical handbook of marital therapy* (pp. 385–405). New York: Guilford Press.

ROSENBAUM, J. (1992). *The use of metaphor.* Unpublished manuscript. Available from Counseling Department, Stetson University, DeLand, FL.

ROSSI, E. (1980a). *Collected papers of Milton Erickson on hypnosis* (Vol. 1). New York: Irvington.

ROSSI, E. (1980b). *Collected papers of Milton Erickson on hypnosis* (Vol. 2). New York, Irvington.

ROTH, A. (1985). Psychotherapy with lesbian couples: Individual issues, female socialization, and the social context. *Journal of Marital and Family Therapy, 121,* 273–286.

ROUGHAN, P., & JENKINS, A. (1990). A systems-developmental approach to counselling couples with sexual problems. *A.N.Z. Journal of Family Therapy, 2,* 129–139.

RUBIN, J., & BROWN, B. (1975). *The social psychology of bargaining and negotiation.* New York: Academic Press.

RUST, J., BENNUN, I., CROWE, M., & GOLOMBOK, S. (1988). *The Golombok Rust Inventory of Marital State (GRIMS) (test and handbook).* Windsor, Ontario, Canada: NFER-Nelson.

SAGER, C. (1976). *Marriage contracts and couple therapy.* New York: Brunner/Mazel.

SALWEN, L. (1990). *The myth of the wicked stepmother.* Binghamton, NY: Haworth Press.

SANCHEZ, L., & GAGER, C. T. (2000). Hard living, entitlement to a great marriage, and marital dissolution. *Journal of Marriage and Family, 62,* 708–722.

SARNOFF, D. P., & SARNOFF, P. (2005). Assessing interactive creativity in couples. *Family Journal: Counseling and Therapy for Couples and Families, 13*(1), 83–86.

SATIR, V. (1964). *Conjoint family therapy.* Palo Alto, CA: Science and Behavioral Books.

SATIR, V. (1972). *Peoplemaking.* Palo Alto, CA: Science and Behavioral Books.

SATIR, V., BANMEN, J., GERBER, J., & GOMORI, M. (1991). *The Satir model:*

Family therapy and beyond. Palo Alto, CA: Science and Behavior Books.

SAUNDERS, J. B., AASLAND, O. G., BABOR, T. F., DE LA FUENTE, J. R., & GRANT, M. (1993). Development of the alcohol use disorders identification test (AUDIT): WHO collaboratives project on early detection of persons with harmful alcohol consumption–II. *Addiction, 88,* 791–804.

SAVIN-WILLIAMS, R. C. (1994). Verbal and physical abuse as stressors in the lives of lesbian, gay male, and bisexual youths: Associations with school problems, running away, substance abuse, prostitution, and suicide. *Journal of Consulting and Clinical Psychology, 62,* 266–267.

SCANZONI, J. (1978). *Sex roles, women's work, and marital conflict: A study of family change.* Lexington, MA: Heath/ Lexington Books.

SCANZONI, J., & POLONKO, K. (1981). A conceptual approach to explicit marital negotiation. *Journal of Marriage and the Family, 42,* 31–44.

SCHAEFER, M. T., & OLSON, D. H. (1981). Diagnosing intimacy: The PAIR inventory. *Journal of Marital and Family Therapy, 7,* 47–60.

SCHARFF, D. E., & SCHARFF, J. S. (1991). *Object relations couple therapy.* Northvale, NJ: Aronson.

SCHILSON, E. A. (1991). Strategic therapy. In A. M. Horne & J. L. Passmore (Eds.), *Family counseling and therapy* (pp.142–178). Itasca, IL: Peacock.

SCHULZ, W. (1976). The individual and the others. *Praxis-der-Psychotherapie, 21,* 149–157.

SCHUNK, D. H. (2001). Self-regulation through goal setting. Retrieved April 17, 2006, from http://www.ericdigests.org/ 2002-4/goal.html

SEGAL, L. (1991). Brief family therapy. In A. M. Horne & J. L. Passmore (Eds.), *Family counseling and therapy* (pp. 180– 205). Itasca, IL: Peacock.

SEINFELD, J. (1993). *Interpreting and holding: The maternal and paternal functions of the psychotherapist.* Northvale, NJ: Aronson.

SELZER, M. (1971). The Michigan Alcoholism Screening Test: The quest for a new diagnostic instrument. *American Journal of Psychiatry, 127,* 1653–1658.

SHELLENBERGER, S. (2006). How co-workers can wreck your marriage. Retrieved April 14, 2006, from http:// www.careerjournal.com/columnists/ workfamily/20031114-workfamily.html

SHERMAN, R. (2000). The intimacy genogram. In R. E. Watts & J. Carlson (Eds.), *Techniques in marriage and family counseling* (Vol. 1) (pp. 81–84). Alexandria, VA: American Counseling Association.

SHERMAN, R., & FREDMAN, N. (1986). *Handbook of structured techniques in marriage and family therapy.* New York: Brunner/Mazel.

SHERMAN, R., ORESKY, P., & ROUNTREE, Y. (1991). *Solving problems in couples and family therapy.* New York: Brunner/Mazel.

SHIELDS, P. (1989). The recovering couples group: A viable treatment alternative. *Alcoholism Treatment Quarterly, 6,* 135–149.

SHOHAM, V., & ROHRBAUGH, M. J. (2002). Brief strategic couple therapy. In A. S. Gurman & N. S. Jacobson (Eds.), *Clinical handbook of couple therapy* (3rd ed.) (pp. 5–25), New York: Guilford Press.

SHULMAN, P. (2004). Great Expectations. *Psychology Today, 37*(1), 32.

SIEGEL, J. (1991). Analysis of projective identification: An object relations approach to marital treatment. *Clinical Social Work Journal, 19,* 71–81.

SIMMEL, G. (1950). Fundamental problems in sociology. In *The sociology of George Simmel* (K. Wolff, Trans.) (pp. 3– 84). New York: Free Press.

SKINNER, H.A., & HORN, J. L. (1984). *Alcohol Dependence Scale (ADS). User's guide.* Toronto, Ontario, Canada: Addiction Research Foundation.

SLIPP, S. (1991). *The technique and practice of object relations family therapy.* Northvale, NJ: Aronson.

SMOCK, P. J. (2000). Cohabitation in the United States. *Annual Review of Sociology, 26,* 34–37.

SNYDER, D. K. (1997). *Manual for the Marital Satisfaction Inventory–Revised (MSI-R)*. Los Angeles: Western Psychological Services.

SNYDER, D. K., HEYMAN, R. E., & HAYNES, S. N. (2005). Evidence based approaches to assessing couple distress. *Psychological Assessment, 17*(3), 288–307.

SNYDER, M. (2002). Applications of Carl Rogers' theory and practice to couple and family therapy: A response to Harlene Anderson and David Bott. *Journal of Family Therapy, 24* (3), 317–325.

SOBAL, B., & WILLIAMS, K. (2001). Systemic Approaches. In J. A. Rubin (Ed.), *Approaches to art therapy* (pp. 257–280). London: Brunner/Routledge.

SPANIER, G. B. (1976). Measuring dyadic adjustment: New scales for assessing the quality of marriage and similar dyads. *Journal of Marriage and the Family, 38,* 15–28.

SPANIER, G. B., & FILSINGER, E. (1983). The Dyadic Adjustment Scale. In E. Filsinger (Ed.), *Marriage and family assessment.* Beverly Hills, CA: Sage.

SPANIER, G. B., & LEWIS, R. A. (1980). Marital quality: A review of the seventies. *Journal of Marriage and the Family, 42,* 825–839.

SPECTOR, I., & CAREY, M. (1990). Incidence and prevalence of the sexual dysfunctions: A critical review of the empirical literature. *Archives of Sexual Behavior, 19,* 389–403.

SPEROFF, L., GLASS, R. H., & KASE, N. G. (1994). *Clinical gynecologic endocrinology and infertility* (5th ed). Baltimore: Williams & Wilkins.

SPERRY, L., & CARLSON, J. (1991). *Marital therapy: Integrating theory and technique.* Denver: Love.

SPERRY, L., CARLSON, J., & PELUSO, P. (2005). *Marital therapy: Integrating theory and technique* (2nd ed.). Denver: Love.

SPIEGLER, M. D., & GUEVREMONT, D. C. (1993). *Contemporary behavior therapy.* Pacific Grove, CA: Brooks/Cole.

SPRECHER, S., & MCKINNEY, K. (1993). *Sexuality.* Thousand Oaks, CA: Sage.

SPRENKLE, D. H., & STORM, C. L. (1983). Divorce therapy and outcome research: A substantive and methodological review. *Journal of Marriage and the Family, 9,* 239–258.

SPREY, J. (1971). On the management of conflict in families. *Journal of Marriage and the Family, 33,* 722–731.

ST. CLAIR, M. (2003). *Object relations and self-psychology: An introduction* (4th ed.). Pacific Grove, CA: Brooks/Cole.

STANTON, M. D. (1980). Marital therapy from a structural/strategic viewpoint. In P. Sholevar (Ed.), *Marriage is a family affair.* New York: Spectrum Press.

STANTON, M. D., TODD, T. C., & ASSOCIATES. (1982). *The family therapy of drug abuse and addiction.* New York: Guilford Press.

STAPPENBECK, C. A., LOGSDON, T., GORMAN, C., & FALS-STEWART, W. (2004, February). When kids won't (or can't) come for help: Treating substance abusing parents to help their children. *Counselor, 24*–29.

STEVENS, P. (2000). Practicing within our competence: New techniques create new dilemmas. *Family Journal: Counseling and Therapy for Couples and Families, 8*(3), 278–280.

STONE, J. D. (1987). Marital and sexual counseling of elderly couples. In G. R. Weeks & L. Hof (Eds.), *Integrating sex and marital therapy: A clinical guide* (pp. 221–244). New York: Brunner/ Mazel.

STRAUS, M. A. (1979). Measuring intrafamily conflict and violence: The conflict tactics (CT) scale. *Journal of Marriage and the Family, 41,* 75–88.

STRAUS, M. A., HAMBY, S. L., BONEY-MCCOY, S., & SUGARMAN, D. B. (1996). The Revised Conflict Tactics Scales (CTS2): Development and preliminary psychometric data. *Journal of Family Issues, 17,* 283–316.

STRAUS, M. A., HAMBY, S. L., & WARREN, W. L. (2003). *The Conflict Tactics Scales handbook.* Los Angeles: Western Psychological Services.

STREAN, H. S. (1985). *Resolving marital conflicts: A psychodynamic perspective.* New York: Wiley.

STRONG, B., DEVAULT, C., SAYAD, B. W., & YARBER, W. L. (2005). *Human sexuality: Diversity in contemporary America* (5th ed.). New York: McGraw-Hill.

STRONG, S., & CLAIBORN, C. (1982). *Change through interaction: Social psychological process of counseling and psychotherapy.* New York: Wiley.

STRUPP, H. H., & BINDER, J. L. (1984). *Psychotherapy in a new key.* New York: Basic Books.

STUART, R. B. (1969). Operant-interpersonal treatment for marital discord. *Journal of Consulting and Clinical Psychology, 33,* 675–682.

SUE, S., & ZANE, N. (1987). The role of culture and cultural techniques in psychotherapy: A critique and reformulation. *American Psychologist, 42,* 37–45.

SUGG, N. K., & INUI, T. (1992). Primary care physicians' response to domestic violence: Opening Pandora's box. *Journal of the American Medical Association, 267,* 3157–3160.

SULLAWAY, M., & CHRISTENSEN, A. (1983). Assessment of dysfunctional interaction patterns in couples. *Journal of Marriage and the Family, 45,* 653–659

SWEEN, E. (2003). Accessing the rest-of-the-story in couples therapy. *Family Journal: Counseling and Therapy for Couples and Families, 11*(1), 61–67.

SWENSON, C. H., & FIORE, A. (1982). A scale of marriage problems. In P. A. Keller & L. G. Ritt (Eds.), *Innovations in clinical practice: A source book* (pp. 240–256). Sarasota, FL: Professional Resource Exchange.

TANNEN, D. (1986). *That's not what I meant: How conversational style makes or breaks relationships.* New York: Ballantine Books

TANNEN, D. (1994). *Gender and discourse.* Oxford, UK: Oxford University Press.

TANNEN, D. (2001). *You just don't understand: Women and men in conversation.* New York: Quill.

TAYLOR, R. (2002). Why marriage? The tie that binds need not be legal. *Free Inquiry Magazine, 23*(3), 3–5.

TEACHMAN, J. (2003). Premarital sex, premarital cohabitation, and the risk of subsequent marital disruption among women. *Journal of Marriage and the Family 65,* 444–455.

TENNOV, D. (1979). *Love and limerence: The experience of being in love.* New York: Stein & Day.

THIBAUT, J. W., & KELLEY, H. H. (1959). *The social psychology of groups.* New York: Wiley.

THOMAS, F. (1999). Competency-based relationship counseling: The necessity of goal setting and counselor flexibility in efficient and effective couples counseling. *Journal of Pastoral Care, 53*(1), 87–99.

THOMPSON, R. A. (1996). *Counseling techniques.* Washington, DC: Taylor & Francis.

TODD, T. C. (1984). Strategic approaches to marital stuckness. *Journal of Marriage and Family Therapy, 10,* 373–379.

TODD, T. C. (1986). Structural strategic marital therapy. In N. S. Jacobson & A. S. Gurman (Eds.), *Clinical handbook of marital therapy* (pp. 71–106). New York: Guilford Press.

TOMM, K. (1984a). One perspective on the Milan systemic approach: Part I. Overview of development, theory, and practice. *Journal of Marital and Family Therapy, 10,* 113–123.

TOMM, K. (1984b). One perspective of the Milan systemic approach: Part II. Description of session format, interviewing style, and interventions. *Journal of Marital and Family Therapy, 10,* 253–271.

TOMM, K. (1987a). Interventive interviewing: Part I. Strategizing as a fourth guideline for the therapist. *Family Process, 26,* 3–13.

TOMM, K. (1987b). Interventive interviewing: Part II. Reflexive questioning as a means to enable self-healing. *Family Process, 26,* 167–183.

TOMM, K. (1991, October). *Therapeutic conversation.* Presentation at Marriage and Family Therapy Fall Conference, Stetson University, DeLand, FL.

TRZEPACZ, P. T., & BAKER, R. W. (1993). *The psychiatric mental status examination.* Oxford, UK: Oxford University Press.

TURNER, R. H. (1970). *Family Interaction.* New York: Wiley.

UNIVERSITY OF LOUISVILLE. (2005). *Music therapy.* Retrieved June 4, 2005, from http://www.louisville.edu/music/therapy/

USSHER, J. (1991). Couples therapy with gay clients: Issues facing counselors. *Consulting Psychologist Quarterly, 3,* 109–116.

VAUGHAN, P. (1989). *The monogamy myth.* London: Grafton.

VIERE, G. M. (2001). Examining family rituals. *Family Journal, 9*(3), 285–288.

VILLARD, K., & WHIPPLE, L. (1976). *Beginnings in relational communication.* New York: Wiley.

VINCENT, J. P., & CARTER, A. S. (1987). Family assessment: Practical and methodological considerations. In K. D. O'Leary (Ed.), *Assessment of marital discord.* Hillsdale, NJ: Erlbaum.

VISHER, E. B., & VISHER, J. S. (1979). *Stepfamilies: A guide to working with stepparents and stepchildren.* New York: Brunner/Mazel.

VISHER, E., & VISHER, J. (1988). *Old loyalties, new ties: Therapeutic strategies with stepfamilies.* New York: Brunner/Mazel.

VISHER, E. B., & VISHER, J. S. (1996). *Therapy with stepfamilies.* Philadelphia: Brunner/Routledge.

VISHER, E., VISHER, J., & PASLEY, K. (1997). Stepfamily therapy from the client's perspective. *Marriage and Family Review, 26*(1–2), 191.

VISHER, J., & VISHER, E. (1990). Therapy with stepfamily couples. *Psychiatric Annals, 21,* 462–465.

VUCHINICH, S. (1984). Sequencing and social structure in family conflict. *Social Psychology Quarterly, 47,* 217–234.

WALITZER, K. S., & DERMEN, K. H. (2004). Alcohol-focused spouse involvement and behavioral couples therapy: Evaluation of enhancements to drinking reduction treatment for male problem drinkers. *Journal of Consulting and Clinical Psychology, 72*(6), 944–955.

WALKER, L. (1994). *Abused women and survivor therapy.* Washington, DC: American Psychological Association.

WALLERSTEIN, J. (1993, October). *The psychological tasks of marriage.* Paper presented at Harvard Medical School Couples Workshop, Boston.

WALLERSTEIN, J., & KELLY, J. (1980). *Surviving the breakup: How children and parents cope with divorce.* New York: Basic Books.

WALTON, M. S. (2004). *Generating buy-in: Mastering the language of leadership.* New York: AMACOM.

WARING, E. (1980). Marital intimacy, psychosomatic symptoms, and cognitive therapy. *Psychosomatics, 21,* 595–601.

WARING, E. M. (1988). *Enhancing marital intimacy through facilitating cognitive self-disclosure.* New York: Brunner/Mazel.

WATERS, D., & LAWRENCE, E. (1993, November/December). Creating a therapeutic vision. *Networker,* 53–58.

WATZLAWICK, P., WEAKLAND, J., & FISCH, R. (1974). *Change: Problem formation and problem resolution.* New York: Norton.

WEEKS, G., & TREAT, S. (1992). *Couples in treatment.* New York: Brunner/Mazel.

WEEKS, G., & TREAT, S. (2001). *Couples in treatment: Techniques and approaches for effective practice* (2nd ed.). Philadelphia: Brunner/Routledge.

WEINER-DAVIS, M. (1992). *Divorce busting.* New York: Summit Books.

WEINER-DAVIS, M. (2001). *The divorce remedy, the proven 7-step program for saving your marriage.* New York: Simon & Schuster.

WEINSTEIN, E., & ROSEN, R. (1988). Sexuality and aging. In E. Weinstein & R. Rosen (Eds.), *Sexuality counseling: Issues and implications* (pp. 81–100). Pacific Grove, CA: Brooks/Cole.

WEISS, R. L. (1975). Contracts cognition and change: A behavioral approach to marital therapy. *Counseling Psychologist, 5,* 15–26.

WEISS, R. L., & BIRCHLER, G. R. (1975). *Areas of change questionnaire.* Unpublished manuscript, University of Oregon.

WEISS, R. L., & CERRETO, M. (1980). The Marital Status Inventory: Development of a measure of dissolution potential. *American Journal of Family Therapy, 8,* 80–85.

WEISS, R. L., HOPS, H., & PATTERSON, G. R. (1973). A framework for conceptualizing marital conflict: A technology for altering it, some data for evaluating it. In L. A. Hammerlynck, L. C. Handy, & E. J. Marsh (Eds.), *Behavior change: Methodology, concepts and practice* (pp. 309–342). Champaign, IL: Research Press.

WHITAKER, C. A., & BUMBERRY, W. M. (1988). *Dancing with the family: A symbolic-experiential approach.* New York: Brunner/Mazel.

WHITE, M. (1989). *The externalizing of the problem and the re-authoring of lives and relationships.* Adelaide, Australia: Dulwich Centre Publishers.

WHITE, M., & EPSTON, D. (1990). *Narrative means to therapeutic ends.* New York: Norton.

WHITE, V. (2002). Developing counseling objectives and empowering clients: A strength-based intervention. *Journal of Mental Health Counseling, 24*(3), 270–280.

WHITTY, M. T. (2003). Pushing the wrong buttons: Men's and women's attitudes toward online and offline infidelity. *CyberPsychology &Behavior, 6*(6), 569–571.

WHITTY, M. (2004). Cybercheating. *Counseling & Psychotherapy Journal, 15*(8), 38–40.

WIENER, D. J. (1999). *Beyond talk therapy: Using movement and expressive techniques in clinical practice.* Washington, DC: American Psychological Association.

WILE, D. (1993). *Couples therapy: A non-traditional approach.* New York: Wiley.

WILLBACH, D. (1989). Ethics and family therapy: The case management of family violence. *Journal of Marital and Family Therapy, 15,* 43–52.

WILLI, J. (1982). *Couples in collusion.* New York: Aronson.

WILLIAMS, L., & TAPPAN, T. (1995). The utility of the Myers-Briggs perspective in couples counseling: A clinical framework. *American Journal of Family Therapy, 23*(4), 367–371.

WILLS, T. A., WEISS, R. L., & PATTERSON, G. R. (1974). A behavioral analysis of the determinants of marital satisfaction. *Journal of Consulting and Clinical Psychology, 42,* 802–811.

WILSON, K., & JAMES, A. (1992). Child sexual abuse and couples therapy. *Journal of Sexual and Marital Therapy, 7,* 197–212.

WINCZE, J. P., & CAREY, M. P. (2001). *Sexual dysfunction: A guide for assessment and treatment* (2nd ed.). New York: Guilford Press.

WINEK, J. L., & CRAVEN, P. A. (2003). Healing rituals for couples recovering from adultery. *Contemporary Family Therapy, 25*(3), 249–266.

WINTERS, J., FALS-STEWART, W., O'FARRELL, T. J., BIRCHLER, G . R., & KELLEY, M. L. (2002). Behavioral couples therapy for female substance-abusing patients: Effects on substance use and relationship adjustment. *Journal of Consulting and Clinical Psychology, 70*(2), 344–355.

WITKIEWITZ, K., & MARLATT, G. A. (2004). Relapse prevention for alcohol and drug problems: That was Zen, this is Tao. *American Psychologist, 59*(4), 224–235.

WOOD, B., & HELLER, P. E. (2000). The influence of religious/ethnic intramarriage vs. intermarriage on intimacy. *Journal of Marital and Family Therapy, 26,* 241–52.

YALOM, I. (1995). *The theory and practice of group psychotherapy.* New York: Basic Books.

YOUNG, K. S. (1998). Internet addiction: The emergence of a new clinical disorder. *CyberPsychology & Behavior, 3*(1), 237–244

YOUNG, K. S. (1999). The evaluation and treatment of Internet addiction. In

L. Van deCreek & T. Jackson (Eds.) *Innovations in clinical practice: A source book* (Vol. 17) (pp. 19–31). Sarasota, FL: Professional Resource Press.

YOUNG, K. (2005). An interview with Eve Lipchik: Expanding solution-focused thinking. *Journal of Systemic Therapies,* 24(1), 67–74.

YOUNG, K. S., GRIFFEN-SHELLEY, E., COOPER, A., O'MARA, J., & BUCHANAN, J. (2000). Online infidelity: A new dimension in couple relationships and implication for evaluation and treatment. *Sexual Addiction & Compulsivity, 7,* 59–74.

YOUNG, M. A. (2004). Healthy relationships: Where's the research? *Family Journal, 12,* 159–162.

YOUNG, M. E. (1992). *Counseling methods and techniques: An eclectic approach.* New York: Macmillan.

YOUNG, M. E. (2001). *Learning the art of helping: Building blocks and techniques* (2nd ed.). Upper Saddle River, NJ: Prentice Hall.

YOUNG, M. E. (2005). *Learning the art of helping: Building blocks and techniques* (3rd ed.). Upper Saddle River, NJ: Prentice Hall.

YOUNG, M. E., & BEMAK, F. (1996). The role of emotional arousal and expression in mental health counseling. *Journal of Mental Health Counseling, 18,* 316–332.

YOUNG, M. E., & LONG, L. L. (1998). *Counseling and therapy for couples.* Pacific Grove, CA: Brooks/Cole.

ZARE, B. (2001). "Sentimentalized adultery": The film industry's next step in consumerism? *Journal of Popular Culture, 35*(3), 29–41.

ZETIK, D., & STUHLMACHER, A. F. (2002). Goal setting and negotiation performance: A meta-analysis. *Group Process & Intergroup Relations, 5*(1), 35–52.

ZIMMER, D. (1987). Does marital therapy enhance the effectiveness of treatment of sexual dysfunction? *Journal of Sex and Marital Therapy, 12,* 193–207.

ZIMMERMAN, B. J. (2000). Attaining self-regulation: A social cognitive perspective. In M. Boekaerts, P. R. Pintrich, & M. Zeidner (Eds.), *Handbook of self-regulation* (pp. 13–39). San Diego: Academic Press.

ZWEBEN, A., & BARRETT, D. (1993). Brief couple treatment for alcohol problems. In T. J. O'Farrell (Ed.), *Treating alcohol problems: Marital and family interventions* (pp. 353–380). New York: Guilford Press.

NAME INDEX

SUBJECT INDEX

CPSIA information can be obtained
at www.ICGtesting.com
Printed in the USA
FFOW02n0931070114
3004FF